SPECIAL EDUCATIONAL NEEDS
(SEN)

SPECIAL EDUCATIONAL NEEDS (SEN)

Strategies, Guidelines and Initiatives

Dolly Singh

KANISHKA PUBLISHERS, DISTRIBUTORS
NEW DELHI-110 002

KANISHKA PUBLISHERS, DISTRIBUTORS
4697/5-21A, Ansari Road, Daryaganj
New Delhi-110 002
Phones : 2327 0497, 2328 8285
Fax : 011-2328 8285
e-mail: kanishka_publishing@yahoo.co.in

First Published 2010

ISBN 978-81-8457-240-7

PRINTED IN INDIA

Published by Madan Sachdeva for Kanishka Publishers, Distributors, 4697/5-21A, Ansari Road, Daryaganj, New Delhi-110 002; Typeset by Manas Enterprises, Delhi, and Printed at Rajdhani Printers, Delhi.

Preface

This book entitled "Special Educational Needs (SEN): Strategies, Guidelines and Initiatives" is a kind of reference book on this subject. The books works towards creating a global understanding of special educational needs (SEN) and disability of various types. SEN is defined and described in detail. The focus lies on understanding the relationship between disability and SEN. The issues which have been highlighted include the SEN data sources, quality standards for SEN support and outreach services. Besides illustrating about the inclusion development programme, this book also presents readers with guidance on the education of children and young people with behavioural, emotional and social difficulties. Both developmental and learning disabilities have been discussed in detail, so has been the shifting models of disability. An overview of the process of assessment of SEN and poor school performance has been presented. Case studies of East Sussex, India, etc. have been discussed. Major causes for poor school performance of physically and mentally challenged students have been identified following the multidisciplinary approach. The emotional and behavioural problems involved in such situations, besides the kinds of medications required have been covered. The issues like support strategies help, and partnership with parents, have been discussed.

Model guidelines and provisions existing in developed countries regarding the education of children with behavioural, emotional and social difficulties have been provided with focus on meaning, prevention, identification, intervention, curriculum development, monitoring, evaluation, training, development, use of force to control or restrain, and improvement in attendance etc. The usefulness of guidance on exclusion from schools and pupil referral units has been described. This book also outlines the guidelines framed towards tackling bullying of children with SEN and various kinds of disabilities. Both actions required for responding to bullying and the possible effects afterwards have been covered in terms of legal duties and guidance. A western perspective on required initiatives towards aiming high for disabled children in terms of access, empowerment, responsive services and timely support has been outlined herein. This book also deals with SEN support, outreach services and related quality standards. SEN related laws in England, Scotland and Wales have been described in depth, so has been the guidelines for parents to appeal before the Tribunal. An elaborate legal perspective has been provided on this subject, highlighting aspects, such as, disability discrimination and tribunal hearing process. Finally, this book also provides an insight into various SEN strategies, progression guidance and NASEN. A glossary of SEN related terms, annotated bibliography and summary of useful websites/links have been given so as to make this publication more user-friendly.

Dolly Singh

Contents

Preface v

1. **Special Educational Needs (SEN) and Disability: Towards a Global Understanding** 1
   - Understanding Learners with Special Educational Needs
   - Definition of Special Educational Needs
   - Definition of Disability
   - Special Educational Needs and Disability
   - Listing the SEN Data Sources
   - Towards Quality Standards for SEN Support and Outreach Services
   - Inclusion Development Programme
   - Guidance on the Education of Children and Young People with Behavioural, Emotional and Social Difficulties
   - Revisiting Disability
   - Developmental Disability
   - Learning Disability and It's Classification
   - Towards Understanding the Shifting Models of Disability

2. **Assessment of Special Educational Needs and Poor School Performance: An Overview** 37
   - Assessment of Special Educational Needs: A Case Study
   - Major Causes for Poor School Performance of Physically and Mentally Challenged Students
   - A Multidisciplinary Approach for Diagnosing Poor School Performance: A Case Study
   - Towards Listing Emotional and Behaviour Problems in Children with Poor School-Performance
   - Kinds of Medications Required to Help Children with Poor School Performance
   - Help and Support for Children with Poor School Performance
   - Required Support Strategies for Children having Emotional and Behaviour Problems
   - Partnership with Parents for Improving Poor School Performance

3. **Education of Children with Behavioural, Emotional and Social Difficulties: Model Guidelines** 65
   - Introduction

- Meaning
- Prevention, Identification and Intervention
- Curriculum for Children and Young People with BESD
- Towards Developing a Range of Provision for Children and Young People with BESD
- Monitoring and Evaluation
- Training and Development
- Use of Force to Control or Restrain
- Guidance w.r.t. Improving Behaviour and Attendance, Exclusion from Schools and Pupil Referral Units

4. Developing Guidelines Towards Tackling Bullying of Children with SEN and Disabilities 93

- Introduction
- Legal Duties and Guidance Relating to Learners with SEN and Disabilities
- Prevention
- Responding to Bullying—Actions and Afterwards
- Legal Duties and Guidance for Schools

5. Initiatives Towards Aiming High for Disabled Children: A Western Perspective 141

- Introduction
- Aiming High for Disabled Children
- Access and Empowerment
- Responsive Services and Timely Support

6. SEN Support, Outreach Services and Related Quality Standards: A UK Perspective 188

- SEN Support and Outreach Services
- SEN Support and Quality Standards

7. SEN Related Laws in England, Scotland and Wales: Guidelines for Appeal Before the Tribunal 200

- SEN Related Laws in England and Wales
- Education (Additional Support for Learning) (Scotland) Act
- Related to SEN Oriented Tribunals and Inquiries in England and Wales
- SEN: A Scottish Legal Perspective
- SEN Related Aspects of Disability Discrimination Act
- Guidelines for Parents for Appealing a SEN Decision: A Case Study
- First-Tier Tribunal (Special Educational Needs and Disability) in England and Wales
- Tribunal Hearing

Glossary of SEN Related Terms 294
Bibliography 298
Web Links 304
Index 307

1

Special Educational Needs (SEN) and Disability: Towards a Global Understanding

UNDERSTANDING LEARNERS WITH SPECIAL EDUCATIONAL NEEDS

In India a learner with SEN is defined variously in different documents. For example, a child with SEN in a District Primary Education Programme (DPEP) document is defined as a child with disability, namely, visual, hearing, locomotor, and intellectual (DPEP, 2001). However, the country report in the NCERT-UNESCO regional workshop report titled Assessment of needs for Inclusive Education: Report of the First Regional Workshop for SAARC Countries (2000) states that SEN goes beyond physical disability. It also refers to, ...

> the large proportion of children—in the school age—belonging to the groups of child labour are, street children, victims of natural catastrophes and social conflicts, and those in extreme social and economic deprivation. These children constitute the bulk of dropouts from the school system (p. 58).

The SSA Framework for Implementation covers children with Special Needs (SN) under the section on Special Focus Groups. While separating children with disabilities from other groups like girls, Scheduled Castes (SC), Scheduled Tribes (ST), and urban deprived children, it makes provisions for these children under the section on SEN. The Department of Education of Groups with SN in the NCERT itself, initiates programmes for meeting the learning needs of the disabled and the socially disadvantaged and marginalised, such as the SCs, STs, and minorities.

According to the International Standard Classification of Education (ISCED-97) (UNESCO, 1997), the term Special Needs Education (SNE) means educational intervention and support designed to address SEN. The term "SNE" has come into use as a replacement for the term "Special Education". The earlier term was mainly understood to refer to the education of children with disabilities that takes place in special schools or institutions distinct from, and outside of, the institutions of the regular school and university system. In many countries today a large proportion of disabled children are in fact educated in institutions under the regular system. Moreover, the concept of children with SEN extends beyond those who may be included in handicapped categories to cover those who are failing in school, for a wide variety of reasons that are known to be likely impediments to a child's optimal progress. Whether or not this more broadly defined group of children is in need of additional support, depends on the extent to which schools need to adapt their curriculum, teaching, and organisation and/or to provide additional human or material resources so as to stimulate efficient and effective learning for these pupils.

However, only in a few instances and documents, across the various States of the country, has SEN been accepted in its broad perspective. On the whole, the focus has remained on learners with specific disabilities. This view is supported by the fact that the draft Inclusive Education Scheme (MHRD, 2003), available on the website of the Ministry of Human Resources Development (MHRD), www.education.nic.in/html web/iedc_sch_draft.htm (accessed on February 15, 2001), which addresses the needs of learners with disabilities, focuses on the following categories of disability: visual disabilities (blind and low vision), speech and hearing disabilities, locomotor disabilities, and neuromusculoskeltal and neuro-developmental disorders, including cerebral palsy, autism, mental retardation, multiple disability, and learning disabilities. Keeping this reality in mind the main focus of this position paper is on learners with such disabilities.

The Gender Issue

There is ample evidence that women with disabilities experience major psycho-social problems, including depression, stress, lowered self-esteem, and social isolation, which remain largely neglected (Nosek and Hughes, 2003). Evidence also suggests that women tend to be restricted to home-based activities, while men are likely to be supported in more public and outward-looking avenues. Stereotypes are artefacts of culture that can only be understood by exploring their relations to each other in the cultural system. Gender stereotypes interact with disability stereotypes to constitute a deep matrix of gendered disability in every culture, developed within specific historical contexts, and affecting those contexts over time. While language is the most analysed site for the examination of both gender (Connell, 2002) and disability (Corker and French, 1999), they interact in many other cultural locations—cinema, television, fiction, clothing, and body language. Thus, cultures sustain the social relations of gendered disability in constant reiterations of stereotypes and expectations (Meekosha). In the education scene, discrimination on account of gender has been reported in many studies. However, girls with disabilities have remained invisible both from the writings on gender and on disability. Therefore, the needs of girls with disabilities may be more special than needs of any other group and have to be addressed in all spheres of education.

DEFINITION OF SPECIAL EDUCATIONAL NEEDS

The US Education Act 1996 says that '*a child has special educational needs if he or she has a learning difficulty which calls for special educational provision to be made for him or her.*' It also says that '*a disability, which prevents or hinders them from making use of education facilities'*, amounts to a learning difficulty if it calls for special educational provision to be made. Special educational provision is provision that is additional to or otherwise different from that normally available in the area to children of the same age. The definition includes more children than those who have 'learning difficulties' in the commonly accepted sense. This is because the definition of learning difficulties in the legislation includes children who have a disability and who need something additional or different to be provided for them. So, for example, a child with a visual impairment who needs materials to be provided in an enlarged font is defined in the legislation as having a learning difficulty even if they are not behind in their learning.

DEFINITION OF DISABILITY

Duties are owed to all pupils who are defined by the Disability and Discrimination Act (DDA) as being disabled and under the planning duties schools and local authorities have a general duty to improve the accessibility of schools for disabled pupils. The DDA definition is broad and includes a wide range of impairments including learning disabilities, dyslexia, diabetes or epilepsy where the effect of the impairment on the pupil's ability to carry out normal day-to-day activity is adverse, substantial and long-term. The Disability Discrimination Act 1995 (DDA) defines a disabled person as someone who has:

> *'a physical or mental impairment which has a substantial and long-term adverse effect on his or her ability to carry out normal day-to-day activities.'*

A common perception is that the definition of a disability applies to a small group of people, commonly thought to be only those with a physical or sensory impairment. In practice it applies to a much larger group of people. A report from the Cabinet Office (2005) *Improving the Life Chances of Disabled People,* draws on estimates that suggest that about 11 million adults and 772000 children in the UK are disabled, equivalent to 24 per cent of the adult population and seven per cent of all children.

Appendix 1 of the Disability Rights Commission's Code of Practice for Schools: Disability Discrimination Act 1995: Part 4 provides a more detailed account of the definition of disability. Other guidance has been produced by individual organisations representing disabilities covered by the DDA 2005.

SPECIAL EDUCATIONAL NEEDS AND DISABILITY

It is the ambition of the special educational needs (SEN) and disability division that every child with special educational needs reaches their full potential in school, and can make a successful transition to adulthood and the world of further and higher education, training or work.

To promote the welfare and interests of disabled children, and to improve the support they receive, this area of the site provides a wide range of SEN and disability advice and materials for teachers, parents and others working with children with SEN in England.

LISTING THE SEN DATA SOURCES

The Department is planning to publish an annual guide to special educational need (SEN) data for the first time in 2009 which will have data relevant to SEN provision which includes local authority level information about attainment of pupils with SEN and additional local authority level information about the characteristics of pupils with SEN. In the meantime data on the characteristics of children with SEN and services provided for them are available at the following sources.

TOWARDS QUALITY STANDARDS FOR SEN SUPPORT AND OUTREACH SERVICES

These standards are intended to be used by all those offering SEN support and outreach services, including local authorities, school clusters and special schools, early–years settings and other provision. The standards were commissioned by the DCSF and produced jointly by the South East and South West Regional Partnerships. These generic standards are not in any way intended to be mandatory, but rather to offer some common markers against which service providers might assess and evaluate provision either delivered directly, or commissioned, to help improve consistency.

The standards are designed to help lead to improved outcomes for children and young people with SEN and disabilities, against the backdrop of the five Every Child Matters outcomes, and the core offer standards set out as part of the Government's Aiming High for Disabled Children's programme.

INCLUSION DEVELOPMENT PROGRAMME

The National Strategies is responsible for taking forward the commitment made in Removing Barriers to Achievement by providing a four–year programme of continuing professional development (CPD). This is designed to increase the confidence and expertise of mainstream practitioners in meeting high incidence of SEN in mainstream settings and schools.

The aim of the programme is to support schools and Early Years settings through web–based materials, which will include:

- teaching and learning resources
- training materials
- guidance on effective classroom strategies
- models of good practice for multi-disciplinary teams
- information about sources of more specialist advice.

In 2008, the IDP will focus on dyslexia and speech, language and communication needs (SLCN). In 2009, the focus will be on autistic spectrum disorders (ASD), and after that, on behavioural, emotional and social difficulties (BESD).

GUIDANCE ON THE EDUCATION OF CHILDREN AND YOUNG PEOPLE WITH BEHAVIOURAL, EMOTIONAL AND SOCIAL DIFFICULTIES

In May 2008, the DCSF issued revised guidance on the education of children and young people with BESD. A link to an electronic version of this guidance can be found below.

You will also find a link to the Department's 2001 guidance on promoting mental health in schools and early years settings. This explains how teachers and others, working alongside other agencies as appropriate, can promote children and young people's mental health and can intervene effectively with those experiencing problems. It provides case studies of children and young people whose behaviour, social and/or emotional development is causing concern and suggests strategies to address both the presenting behaviour and the underlying causes.

Some schools' provision for children with BESD includes nurture groups.

REVISITING DISABILITY

Disability is defined by the Americans with Disabilities Act of 1990 as "a physical or mental impairment that substantially limits one or more major life activities." An individual may also qualify as disabled if he/she has had an impairment in the past or is seen as disabled based on a personal or group standard or norm. Such impairments may include physical, sensory, and cognitive or intellectual impairments. Mental disorders (also known as psychiatric or psychosocial disability) and various types of chronic disease may also be considered qualifying disabilities.

A disability may occur during a person's lifetime or may be present from birth.

Current Issues

Current issues and debates surrounding disability include social and political rights, social inclusion and citizenship. In developed countries, the debate has moved beyond a concern about the perceived cost of maintaining dependent people with disabilities to an effort of finding effective ways to ensure that people with disabilities can participate in and contribute to society in all spheres of life.

Many are concerned, however, that the greatest need is in developing nations—where the vast bulk of the estimated 650 million people with disabilities reside. A great deal of work is needed to address concerns ranging from accessibility and education to self-empowerment and self-supporting employment and beyond.

In the past few years, disability rights activists have also focused on obtaining full citizenship for the disabled.

However obstacles reside in some countries in getting full employment, also public perception of disabled people may vary in areas.

Disability Rights Movement

The disability rights movement, led by individuals with disabilities, began in the 1970s. This self-advocacy is often seen as largely responsible for the shift toward independent living and accessibility. The term "Independent Living" was taken from 1959 California legislation which enabled people who had acquired a disability due to polio to leave hospital wards and move back into the community with the help of cash benefits for the purchase of personal assistance with the activities of daily living.

With its origins in the U.S. civil rights and consumer movements of the late 1960s, the movement and its philosophy have since spread to other continents influencing self-perception, organization and social policy.

Definitions and Models

The International Classification of Functioning, Disability and Health (ICF), produced by the World Health Organization, distinguishes between body functions (physiological or psychological, e.g. vision) and body structures (anatomical parts, e.g. the eye and related structures). Impairment in bodily structure or function is defined as involving an anomaly, defect, loss or other significant deviation from certain generally accepted population standards, which may fluctuate over time. Activity is defined as the execution of a task or action. The ICF lists 9 broad domains of functioning which can be affected:

- Learning and applying knowledge
- General tasks and demands
- Communication
- Mobility
- Self-care
- Domestic life
- Interpersonal interactions and relationships
- Major life areas
- Community, social and civic life.

In concert with disability scholars, the introduction to the ICF states that a variety of conceptual models has been proposed to understand and explain disability and functioning, which it seeks to integrate. These models include the following:

The Medical Model

The medical model is presented as viewing disability as a problem of the person, directly caused by disease, trauma, or other health condition which therefore requires sustained medical care provided in the form of individual treatment by professionals. In the medical model, management of the disability is aimed at a "cure," or the individual's adjustment and behavioural change that would lead to an "almost-cure" or effective cure. In the medical model, medical care is viewed as the main issue, and at the political level, the principal response is that of modifying or reforming healthcare policy.

The Social Model

The social model of disability sees the issue of "disability" as a socially created problem and a matter of the full integration of individuals into society [see Inclusion (disability rights)]. In this model, disability is not an attribute of an individual, but rather a complex collection of conditions, many of which are created by the social environment. Hence, the management of the problem requires social action and is the collective responsibility of society at large to make the environmental modifications necessary for the full participation of people with disabilities in all areas of social life. The issue is both cultural and ideological, requiring individual, community, and large-scale social change. From this perspective, equal access for someone with an impairment/disability is a human rights issue of major concern.

The Market Model

The market model of disability is a new model that builds on the social model in recognizing people with disabilities and their Stakeholders represent a large group of consumers, employees and voters. This model looks to personal identity to define disability and empowers people to chart their own destiny in everyday life, with a particular focus on economic empowerment. This model makes no judgements about ability, focusing on tangible and measurable results. Its mantra is 'results, at all levels, create value'. By this model, based on US Census data, there are 1.2 billion people in the world who consider themselves to have a disability. An additional two billion people are considered Stakeholders in disability (family/friends/employers), and when combined to the number of people without disabilities, represents 53 per cent of the population. This model states that, due to the size of the demographic, companies and governments will serve the desires, pushed by demand as the message becomes prevalent in the cultural mainstream.

Other Modells

- The **spectrum model** refers to the range of visibility, audibility and sensibility under which mankind functions. The model asserts that disability does not necessarily mean reduced spectrum of operations. Instead, it could also include distorted/shifted spectrum. For instance, a blind person may be extra sensitive to infrared or ultraviolet waves. See also ESP.
- The **moral model** (Bowe, 1978) refers to the attitude that people are *morally responsible* for their own disability. For example, the disability may be seen as a result of bad actions of parents if congenital, or as a result of practicing witchcraft if not. This attitude may also be viewed as a religious fundamentalist offshoot of the original animal roots of human beings when humans killed any baby that could not survive on its own in the wild.
- The **expert/professional model** has provided a traditional response to disability issues and can be seen as an offshoot of the Medical Model. Within its framework, professionals follow a process of identifying the impairment

and its limitations (using the Medical Model), and taking the necessary action to improve the position of the disabled person. This has tended to produce a system in which an authoritarian, over-active service provider prescribes and acts for a passive client.

- The **tragedy/charity model** depicts disabled people as victims of circumstance who are deserving of pity. This, along with the Medical Model, are the models most used by non-disabled people to define and explain disability.
- The **legitimacy model** views disability as a value-based determination about which explanations for the atypical are legitimate for membership in the disability category. This viewpoint allows for multiple explanations and models to be considered as purposive and viable (DePoy & Gilson, 2004) (Elizabeth DePoy & Stephen Gilson).
- The **social adapted model** states although a person's disability poses some limitations in an able-bodied society, often times the surrounding society and environment are more limiting than the disability itself.
- Economic Model.
- The **empowering model** allows for the person with a disability and his/her family to decide the course of their treatment and what services they wish to benefit from. This, in turn, turns the professional into a service provider whose role is to offer guidance and carry out the client's decisions. In other words, this model "empowers" the individual to pursue his/her own goals.

Terminology

People First Language

The American Psychological Association style guide states that, when identifying a person with an impairment, the person's name or pronoun should come first, and descriptions of the impairment/disability should be used so that the impairment is identified, but is not modifying the person. Improper examples are "a borderline," "a blind person," or "an autistic boy;" more acceptable terminology includes "a woman with Down syndrome" or "a man who has schizophrenia." It also states that a person's adaptive equipment should be described functionally as something that assists a person, not as something that limits a person, e.g. "a woman who uses a wheelchair" rather than "a woman in/confined to a wheelchair."

A similar kind of "people first" terminology is also used in the UK, but more often in the form 'people with impairments' (e.g. "people with visual impairments"). However, in the UK, the term "disabled people" is generally preferred to "people with disabilities." It is argued under the social model that while someone's impairment (e.g. having a spinal cord injury) is an individual property, "disability" is something created by external societal factors such as a lack of wheelchair access to their workplace. This distinction between the individual property of impairment and the social property of disability is central to the social model. The term "disabled people" as a political construction is also widely used by international organisations of disabled people, such as Disabled Peoples' International (DPI).

Literature

Many books on disability and disability rights point out that 'disabled' is an identity that one is not necessarily born with, as disabilities are more often acquired than congenital. Some disability rights activists use an acronym TAB, "Temporarily Able-Bodied", as a reminder that many people will develop disabilities at some point in their lives due to accidents, illness (physical, mental or emotional), or late-emerging effects of genetics.

Masculinity

According to author Daniel J. Wilson, the characteristics of masculinity include strength, activeness, speed, endurance, and courage. These characteristics are often challenged when faced with a disability and the boy or man must reshape what it means to be masculine. For example, rather than define "being a man" through what one can physically do, one must re-define it by how one faces the world with a disability and all the obstacles and stereotypes that come with the disability.

In Leonard Kriegel's book, *Flying Solo,* he describes his fight with poliomyelitis and the process of accepting his disability in a world that values able-bodiedness. He writes, "I had to learn to be my own hero, my own role model—which is another way of saying that I had to learn to live with neither heroes nor role models" (p. 40).

Femininity

Women who are disabled face what is called a "double handicap," meaning they must not only deal with the stereotypes and challenges posed by femininity, but they must also deal with those posed by being disabled. Just as men are expected to be strong and courageous, women are expected to fill the social roles of mother and housewives. Culture also tends to view women as fragile and weaker than men, stereotypes which are only heightened when the woman has a disability.

According to the "Survey of Income and Programme Participation," as described in the book *"Gendering Disability,"* 74 per cent of women participants and 90 per cent of men participants without disabilities were employed. In comparison, of those with a form of disability, 41 per cent of women and 51 per cent of men were employed. Furthermore, the non-disabled women participants were paid approximately $4.00 less per hour than the non-disabled men participants. With a disability, women were paid approximately $1.00 less than the non-disabled women participants and the men were paid approximately $2.00 less than the non-disabled men participants. As these results suggest, women without disabilities face societal hardships against men, but then add disability to the equation and the hardships increase.

Government Policies and Support

United Nations

On December 13, 2006, the United Nations formally agreed on the Convention on the Rights of Persons with Disabilities, the first human rights treaty of the 21st century, to protect and enhance the rights and opportunities of the world's estimated 650 million disabled people. Countries that sign up to the convention will be required to adopt national laws, and remove old ones, so that persons with disabilities would, for example, have equal rights to education, employment, and cultural life; the right to own and inherit property; not be discriminated against in marriage, children, etc; not be unwilling subjects in medical experiments.

In 1976, the United Nations launched its International Year for Disabled Persons (1981), later re-named the International Year of Disabled Persons. The UN Decade of Disabled Persons (1983-93) featured a World Programme of Action Concerning Disabled Persons. In 1979, Frank Bowe was the only person with a disability representing any country in the planning of IYDP-1981. Today, many countries have named representatives who are themselves individuals with disabilities. The decade was closed in an address before the General Assembly by Robert Davila. Both Bowe and Davila are deaf. In 1984, UNESCO accepted sign language for use in education of deaf children and youth.

Costa Rica

Under the *Ley de Igualdad de Oportunidades* (Law of Equal Opportunities), no person can be discriminated by their disabilities if they are equally capable as another person. This law also promotes that public places and transport should have facilities that enable people with disabilities to access them.

May 28th is the *Día Nacional de la Persona con Discapacidad* (National Disabled People Day) to promote respect for these population.

Currently the political party *Partido de Acceso Sin Exclusión* (Access Without Exclusion Party) fights for the rights of handicapped persons, and one congressman, Oscar López, who is blind.

United Kingdom

Under the Disability Discrimination Act (DDA) (1995, extended in 2005), it is unlawful for organisations to discriminate (treat a disabled person less favourably, for reasons related to the person's disability, without justification) in employment; access to goods, facilities, services; managing, buying or renting land or property; education. Businesses must make "reasonable adjustments" to their policies or practices, or physical aspects of their premises, to avoid indirect discrimination.

A number of financial and care support services are available, including Incapacity Benefit and Disability Living Allowance.

Employment

The Employers' Forum on Disability (EFD) is a membership organisation of UK businesses. Following the introduction of the DDA the membership of EFD recognised the need for a tool with which they could measure their performance on disability year on year.

In 2005 80 organisations took part in the Disability Standard benchmark providing the first statistics highlighting the UK's performance as a nation of employers.

Following the success of the first benchmark Disability Standard 2007 saw the introduction of the Chief Executives' Diamond Awards for outstanding performance and 116 organisations taking the opportunity to compare trends across a large group of UK employers and monitor the progress they had made on disability.

2009 will see the third benchmark, Disability Standard 2009. EFD have promised that for the first time they will publish a list of the top ten performers who will be honoured at an award ceremony in December 2009.

United States

Discrimination in Employment

The US Rehabilitation Act of 1973 requires all organizations that receive government funding to provide accessibility programmes and services. A more recent law, the Americans with Disabilities Act of 1990 (ADA), which came into effect in 1992, prohibits private employers, state and local governments, employment agencies and labour unions from discriminating against qualified individuals with disabilities in job application procedures, hiring, firing, advancement, compensation, job training, or in the terms, conditions and privileges of employment. This includes organizations like retail businesses, movie theatres, and restaurants. They must make "reasonable accommodation" to people with different needs. Protection is extended to anyone with (A) a physical or mental impairment that substantially limits one or more of the major life activities of an individual, (B) a record of such an impairment, or (C) being regarded as having such an impairment. The second and third critiera are seen as ensuring protection from unjust discrimination based on a perception of risk, just because someone has a record of impairment or appears to have a disability or illness (e.g. features which may be erroneously taken as signs of an illness).

African Americans and Disability

According to the 2000 U.S. Census, the African American community has the highest rate of disability at 20.8 per cent, slightly higher than the overall disability rate of 19.4 per cent. Although people have come to better understand and accept different types of disability, there still remains a stigma attached to the disabled community. African Americans with a disability are subject to not only this stigma but also to the additional forces of race discrimination. African American women who have a disability face tremendous discrimination due to their condition, race, and gender. Doctor Eddie Glenn of Howard University describes this situation as the "triple jeopardy" syndrome.

Social Administration

The US Social Security Administration defines disability in terms of inability to perform substantial gainful activity (SGA), by which it means "work paying minimum wage or better". The agency pairs SGA with a "listing" of medical conditions that qualify individuals for benefits.

Education

Under the Individuals with Disabilities Education Act, special educational support is limited to children and youth falling into one of a dozen disability categories (e.g., specific learning disability) and adds that, to be eligible, students may require both special education (modified instruction) and related services (supports such as speech and language pathology).

Insurance

It is illegal for California insurers to refuse to provide car insurance to properly licensed drivers solely because they have a disability. It is also illegal for them to refuse to provide car insurance "on the basis that the owner of the motor vehicle to be insured is blind," but they are allowed to exclude coverage for injuries and damages incurred while a blind unlicensed owner is actually operating the vehicle (the law is apparently structured to allow blind people to buy and insure cars which their friends, family, and caretakers can drive for them).

Demographics

Difficulties in Measuring

The demography of disability is difficult. Counting persons with disabilities is challenging. That is because disability is not just a status condition, entirely contained within the individual. Rather, it is an interaction between medical status (say, having low vision or being blind) and the environment.

Estimates Worldwide

Estimates of worldwide and country-wide numbers of individuals with disabilities are problematic. The varying approaches taken to defining disability notwithstanding, demographers agree that the world population of individuals with disabilities is very large. For example, in 2004, the World Health Organization estimated a world population of 6.5 billion people, of those nearly 100 million people were estimated to be moderately or severely disabled. In the United States, Americans with disabilities constitute the third–largest minority (after persons of Hispanic origin and African Americans); all three of those minority groups number in the 30-some millions in America. According to the U.S. Bureau of the Census, as of 2004, there were some 32 million disabled adults (aged 18 or over) in the United States, plus another 5 million children and youth (under age 18). If one were to add impairments—or limitations that fall short of being disabilities—Census estimates put the figure at 51 million.

There is also widespread agreement among experts in the field that disability is more common in developing than in developed nations.

Disability Insurance—Nationalized and Private

Disability benefit, or disability pension, is a major kind of disability insurance, and is provided by government agencies to people who are temporarily or permanently unable to work due to a disability. In the U.S., disability benefit is provided within the category of Supplemental Security Income, and in Canada, within the Canada Pension Plan. In other countries, disability benefit may be provided under Social security systems.

Costs of disability pensions are steadily growing in Western countries, mainly European and the United States. It was reported that in the UK, expenditure on disability pensions accounted for 0.9 per cent of Gross Domestic Product (GDP) in 1980, but two decades later had reached 2.6 per cent of GDP. Several studies have reported a link between increased absence from work due to sickness and elevated risk of future disability pension.

A study by researchers in Denmark suggests that information on self-reported days of absence due to sickness can be used to effectively identify future potential groups for disability pension. These studies may provide useful information for policy makers, case managing authorities, employers, and physicians.

Private, for–profit disability insurance plays a role in providing incomes to disabled people, but the nationalized programmes are the safety net that catch most claimants.

Adaptations

Assistive Technology

Assistive Technology (AT) is a generic term for devices and modifications (for a person or within a society) that help overcome or remove a disability. The first recorded example of the use of a prosthesis dates to at least 1800 BC.

A more recent notable example is the wheelchair, dating from the 17th century. The curb cut is a related structural innovation. Other modern examples are standing frames, text telephones, accessible keyboards, large print, Braille, and speech recognition computer software. People with disabilities often develop personal or community adaptations, such as strategies to suppress tics in public (for example in Tourette's syndrome), or sign language in deaf communities. Assistive technology or interventions are sometimes controversial or rejected, for example in the controversy over cochlear implants for children.

A number of symbols are in use to indicate whether certain accessibility adaptations have been made.

Adapted Sports

The Paralympic Games (meaning 'alongside the Olympics') are now held after the (Summer and Winter) Olympics. The Paralympic Games include athletes who have a wide range of disabilities. In many countries, organizations exist to organize competition in the Paralympic sports on levels ranging from recreational to elite (for example, BlazeSports America in the United States).

In 2006, the Extremity Games was formed for people with physical disabilities, specifically limb loss or limb difference, to be able to compete in extreme sports. The College Park Industries, a manufacturer of prosthetic feet, organized this event to give disabled athletes a venue to compete in this increasingly popular sports genre also referred to as action sports. This annual event held in the summer in Orlando, FL includes competitions in skateboarding, wakeboarding, rock climbing, mountain biking, surfing, moto-x and kayaking. Non-profit organizations have created programmes to advance adaptive sports for regular recreation and sport opportunities.

Accessible Computing

As the personal computer has become more ubiquitous, various organizations have formed to develop software and hardware to make computers more accessible for people with disabilities. Some software and hardware, such as SmartboxAT's *The Grid*, and Freedom Scientific's *JAWS* has been specifically designed for people with disabilities; other pieces of software and hardware, such as Nuance's Dragon NaturallySpeaking, were not developed specifically for people with disabilities, but can be used to increase accessibility.

Furthermore, organizations, such as AbilityNet and U Can Do IT, provide assessment services that determine which assistive technologies will best assist an individual client. These organizations also train people with disabilities in how to use computer–based assistive technology.

The LOMAK keyboard was designed in New Zealand specifically for persons with disabilities.

The Internet is also used by disability activists and charities to network and further their goals.

DEVELOPMENTAL DISABILITY

Developmental disability is a term used to describe life-long, disabilities attributable to mental and/or physical or combination of mental and physical impairments, manifested prior to age 18. The term is used most commonly in the United States to refer to disabilities affecting daily functioning in three or more of the following areas:

- capacity for independent living
- economic self-sufficiency
- learning
- mobility
- receptive and expressive language
- self-care
- self-direction

The term first appeared in U.S. law in 1970, when Congress used the term to describe the population of individuals who had historically been placed in state institutions, in its effort to improve conditions in these dehumanizing facilities (P.L. 91-517, "The Developmental Disabilities Services and Facilities Construction Act of 1970"). The law has since been amended many times, and now calls for the full community inclusion and self-determination of people with developmental disabilities (P.L. 106-402).

Frequently, people with mental retardation, cerebral palsy, autism spectrum disorder, various genetic and chromosomal disorders such as Down syndrome and Fragile X syndrome, and Fetal Alcohol Spectrum Disorder are described as having developmental disabilities. This use of the term is synonymous with the use of the term learning disability in the United Kingdom, and intellectual disability in Australia, Europe, Canada and elsewhere. Cognitive disability is also used synonymously in some jurisdictions.

Developmental disabilities are usually classified as severe, profound, moderate or mild, as assessed by the individual's need for supports, which may be lifelong.

Causes of Developmental Disabilities

There are many social, environmental and physical causes of developmental disabilities, although for some a definitive cause may never be determined. Common factors causing developmental disabilities include:

- Brain injury or infection before, during or after birth
- Growth or nutrition problems
- Abnormalities of chromosomes and genes
- Babies born long before the expected birth date—also called extreme prematurity
- Poor diet and health care
- Drug misuse during pregnancy, including alcohol intake and smoking
- Child abuse can also have a severe effect on the development of a child, specifically the socio-emotional development
- Diagnosis of an autism spectrum disorder.

Developmental disabilities affect between 1 and 2 per cent of the population in most western countries, although many government sources acknowledge that statistics are flawed in this area. The worldwide proportion of people with developmental disabilities is believed to be approximately 1.4 per cent. It is twice as common in males as in females, and some researchers have found that the prevalence of mild developmental disabilities is likely to be higher in areas of poverty and deprivation, and among people of certain ethnicities.

Associated Issues

Physical Health Issues

There are many physical health factors associated with developmental disabilities. For some specific syndromes and diagnoses, these are inherent (such as poor heart function in people with Down's syndrome); however lack of access to health services and lack of understanding by medical professionals is also a major contributing factor. People with severe communication difficulties find it difficult to articulate their health needs, and without adequate support and education might not recognise ill health. Epilepsy, sensory problems (such as poor vision and hearing), obesity and poor dental health are over-represented in this population. Life expectancy among people with developmental disabilities as a group is estimated at 20 years below average, although this is improving with advancements in adaptive and medical technologies, and as people are leading healthier, more fulfilling lives, and some specific diagnoses (such as Freeman-Sheldon syndrome) do not impact on life expectancy.

Mental Health Issues (Dual Diagnoses)

Mental health issues, and psychiatric illnesses, are more likely to occur in people with developmental disabilities than in the general population. A number of factors are attributed to the high incidence rate of dual diagnoses:

- the high likelihood of encountering traumatic events throughout their lifetime (such as abandonment by loved ones, abuse, bullying and harassment)
- the social restrictions placed upon people with developmental disabilities (such as lack of education, poverty, limited employment opportunities, limited opportunities for fulfilling relationships, boredom)
- biological factors (such as brain injury, epilepsy, illicit and prescribed drug and alcohol misuse)
- developmental factors (such as lack of understanding of social norms and appropriate behaviour, inability of those around to allow/understand expressions of grief and other human emotions)
- External monitoring factor: all people with developmental disabilities that are in a Federal or State funded residence require the residence to have some form of behavioural monitoring for each person with developmental disability at the residence. With this information psychological diagnosis are more easily given than with the general population that has less consistent monitoring.
- Access to health care providers: in the USA, all people with developmental disabilities that are in a Federal or State funded residence require the residence to have annual visits to various health care providers (nurse, physician, psychologist, psychiatrist, etc.) With consistent visits to health care providers more people with developmental disabilities are likely to receive appropriate treatment than the general population that is not required to visit various health care providers.

These problems are exacerbated by difficulties in diagnosis of mental health issues, and in appropriate treatment and medication, as for physical health issues.

Abuse and Vulnerability

Abuse is a significant issue for people with developmental disabilities, and as a group they are regarded as vulnerable people in most jurisdictions. Common types of abuse include:

- Physical abuse (withholding food, hitting, punching, pushing, etc.)
- Neglect (withholding help when required, e.g., assistance with personal hygiene)
- Sexual abuse
- Psychological or emotional abuse (verbal abuse, shaming and belittling)
- Constraint and restrictive practices (turning off an electric wheelchair so a person cannot move)

- Financial abuse (charging unnecessary fees, holding onto pensions, wages, etc.)
- Legal or civil abuse (restricted access to services)
- Systemic abuse (denied access to an appropriate service due to perceived support needs)
- Passive neglect (a caregiver's failure to provide adequate food, shelter)

Lack of education, lack of self-esteem and self-advocacy skills, lack of understanding of social norms and appropriate behaviour and communication difficulties are strong contributing factors to the high incidence of abuse among this population.

In addition to abuse from people in positions of power, peer abuse is recognised as a significant, if misunderstood, problem. Rates of criminal offending among people with developmental disabilities are also disproportionately high, and it is widely acknowledged that criminal justice systems throughout the world are ill–equipped for the needs of people with developmental disabilities (as both perpetrators and victims of crime).

Challenging Behaviour

Some people with developmental disabilities exhibit challenging behaviour, defined as "culturally abnormal behaviour(s) of such intensity, frequency or duration that the physical safety of the person or others is placed in serious jeopardy, or behaviour which is likely to seriously limit or deny access to the use of ordinary community facilities". Common types of challenging behaviour include self-injurious behaviour (such as hitting, headbutting, biting), aggressive behaviour (such as hitting others, screaming, spitting, kicking), inappropriate sexualised behaviour (such as public masturbation or groping), behaviour directed at property (such as throwing objects and stealing) and stereotyped behaviours (such as repetitive rocking, echolalia or elective incontinence).

Challenging behaviour in people with developmental disabilities may be caused by a number of factors, including biological (pain, medication, the need for sensory stimulation), social (boredom, seeking social interaction, the need for an element of control, lack of knowledge of community norms, insensitivity of staff and services to the person's wishes and needs), environmental (physical aspects such as noise and lighting, or gaining access to preferred objects or activities), psychological (feeling excluded, lonely, devalued, labelled, disempowered, living up to people's negative expectations) or simply a means of communication. A lot of the time, challenging behaviour is learned and brings rewards and it is very often possible to teach people new behaviours to achieve the same aims.

Experience and research suggests that what professionals call 'challenging behaviour' is often a reaction to the challenging environments that those providing services create around people with developmental disabilities. 'Challenging behaviour' in this context is a method of communicating dissatisfaction with the failure of those providing services to focus on what kind of life makes most sense to the person, and is often the only recourse a developmentally disabled person has against unsatisfactory services or treatment and the lack of opportunities made available to the person. This is especially the case where the services deliver lifestyles and ways of working that are centred on what suits the service provider and its staff, rather than what best suits the person.

Societal Attitudes Towards Developmental Disabilities

Throughout history, people with developmental disabilities have been viewed as incapable and incompetent in their capacity for decision-making and development. Until the Enlightenment in Europe, care and asylum was provided by families and the church (in monasteries and other religious communities), focusing on the provision of basic physical needs such as food, shelter and clothing. Stereotypes such as the dimwitted yokel, and potentially harmful characterisations (such as demonic possession for people with epilepsy) were prominent in social attitudes of the time.

The movement towards individualism in the 18th and 19th centuries, and the opportunities afforded by the Industrial Revolution, led to housing and care using the asylum model. People were placed by, or removed from, their families (usually in infancy) and housed in large institutions (of up to 3,000 people, although some institutions were home to many more, such as the Philadelphia State Hospital in Pennsylvania which housed 7,000 people through the 1960s), many of which were self-sufficient through the labour of the residents. Some of these institutions provided a very basic level of education (such as differentiation between colours and basic word recognition and numeracy), but most continued to focus solely on the provision of basic needs. Conditions in such institutions varied widely, but the support provided was generally non-individualised, with aberrant behaviour and low levels of economic productivity regarded as a burden to society. Heavy tranquilisation and assembly line methods of support (such as 'birdfeeding' and cattle herding) were the norm, and the medical model of disability prevailed. Services were provided based on the relative ease to the provider, not based on the human needs of the individual.

Ignoring the prevailing attitude, Civitans adopted service to the developmentally disabled as a major organizational emphasis in 1952. Their earliest efforts included workshops for special education teachers and daycamps for disabled children, all at a time when such training and programmes were almost non-existent. The segregation of people with developmental disabilities wasn't widely questioned by academics or policy-makers until the 1969 publication of Wolf Wolfensberger's seminal work "The Origin and Nature of Our Institutional Models", drawing on some of the ideas proposed by SG Howe a hundred years earlier. This book posited that society characterises people with disabilities as deviant, sub-human and burdens of charity, resulting in the adoption of that 'deviant' role. Wolfensberger argued that this dehumanisation, and the segregated institutions that result from it, ignored the potential productive contributions that all people can make to society. He pushed for a shift in policy and practice that recognised the human needs of "retardates" and provided the same basic human rights as for the rest of the population.

The publication of this book may be regarded as the first move towards the widespread adoption of the social model of disability in regard to these types of disabilities, and was the impetus for the development of government strategies for desegregation. Successful lawsuits against governments and an increasing awareness of human rights and self–advocacy also contributed to this process, resulting in the passing in the US of the *Civil Rights of Institutionalized Persons Act* in 1980.

From the 1960s to the present, most states have moved towards the elimination of segregated institutions. Along with the work Wolfensberger and others including Gunnar and Rosemary Dybwad, a number of scandalous revelations around the horrific conditions within state institutions created public outrage led to change to a more community-based method of providing services. By the mid-1970s, most governments had committed to de-institutionalisation, and had started preparing for the wholesale movement of people into the general community, in line with the principles of normalization. In most countries, this was essentially complete by the late 1990s, although the debate over whether or not to close institutions persists in some states, including Massachusetts.

It could be argued that we still have a very long way to go before people with such disabilities are seen as full citizens of society. Person Centred Planning and Person Centred Approaches are seen as methods of addressing the continued labelling and exclusion of socially devalued people, such as people with a developmental disability label, encouraging a focus on the person as someone with capacities and gifts, as well as support needs.

Services and Support

Today, support services are provided by government agencies, non-governmental organizations and by private sector providers. Support services address most aspects of life for people with developmental disabilities, and are usually theoretically based in community inclusion, using concepts such as social role valorization and increased self-determination (using models such as Person Centred Planning). Support services are funded through government block funding (paid directly to service providers by the government), through individualised funding packages (paid directly to the individual by the government, specifically for the purchase of services) or privately by the individual (although they may receive certain subsidies or discounts, paid by the government).

Education and Training

Education and training opportunities for people with developmental disabilities have expanded greatly in recent times, with many governments mandating universal access to educational facilities, and more students moving out of special schools and into mainstream classrooms with support.

Post-secondary education and vocational training is also increasing for people with these types of disabilities, although many programmes offer only segregated "access" courses in areas such as literacy, numeracy and other basic skills. Legislation (such as the UK's Disability Discrimination Act 1995) requires educational institutions and training providers to make 'reasonable adjustments' to curriculum and teaching methods in order to accommodate the learning needs of students with disabilities, wherever possible. There are also some vocational training centers that cater specifically to people with disabilities, providing the skills necessary to work in integrated settings, one of the largest being Dale Rogers Training Center in Oklahoma City.

At-Home and Community Support

Many people with developmental disabilities live in the general community, either with family members, or in their own homes (that they rent or own, living alone or with flatmates). At-home and community supports range from one-to-one assistance from a support worker with identified aspects of daily living (such as budgeting, shopping or paying bills) to full 24-hour support (including assistance with household tasks, such as cooking and cleaning, and personal care such as showering, dressing and the administration of medication). The need for full 24-hour support is usually associated with difficulties recognising safety issues (such as responding to a fire or using a telephone) or for people with potentially dangerous medical conditions (such as asthma or diabetes) who are unable to manage their conditions without assistance.

In the United States a support worker is known as a Direct Support Professional (DSP). The DSP works in assisting the individual with their ADLs and also acts as an advocate for the individual with a developmental disability, in communicating their needs, self expression and goals.

Supports of this type also include assistance to identify and undertake new hobbies or to access community services (such as education), learning appropriate behaviour or recognition of community norms, or with relationships and expanding circles of friends. Most programmes offering at-home and community support are designed with the goal of increasing the individual's independence, although it is recognised that people with more severe disabilities may never be able to achieve full independence in some areas of daily life.

Residential Accommodation

Some people with developmental disabilities live in residential accommodation (also known as group homes) with other people with similar assessed needs. These homes are usually staffed around the clock, and usually house between 3 and 15 residents. The prevalence of this type of support is gradually decreasing, however, as residential accommodation is replaced by at-home and community support, which can offer increased choice and self–determination for individuals. Some U.S. states still provide institutional care, such as the Texas State Schools.

Employment Support

Employment support usually consists of two types of support:

- Support to access or participate in integrated employment, in a workplace in the general community. This may include specific programmes to increase the skills needed for successful employment (work preparation), one-to-one or small group support for on-the-job training, or one-to-one or small group support after a transition period (such as advocacy when dealing with an employer or a bullying colleague, or assistance to complete an application for a promotion).

- The provision of specific employment opportunities within segregated business services. Although these are designed as 'transitional' services (teaching work skills needed to move into integrated employment), many people remain in such services for the duration of their working life. The types of work performed in business services include mailing and packaging services, cleaning, gardening and landscaping, timberwork, metal fabrication, farming and sewing.

Workers with developmental disabilities have historically been paid less for their labour than those in the general workforce, although this is gradually changing with government initiatives, the enforcement of anti-discrimination legislation and changes in perceptions of capability in the general community.

Day Services

Non-vocational day services are usually known as day centres, and are traditionally segregated services offering training in life skills (such as meal preparation and basic literacy), centre-based activities (such as craft, games and music classes) and external activities (such as day trips). Some more progressive day centres also support people to access vocational training opportunities (such as college courses), and offer individualised outreach services (planning and undertaking activities with the individual, with support offered one–to–one or in small groups).

Traditional day centres were based on the principles of occupational therapy, and were created as respite for family members caring for their loved ones with disabilities. This is slowly changing, however, as programmes offered become more skills-based and focused on increasing independence.

Advocacy

Advocacy is a burgeoning support field for people with developmental disabilities. Advocacy groups now exist in most jurisdictions, working collaboratively with people with disabilities for systemic change (such as changes in policy and legislation) and for changes for individuals (such as claiming welfare benefits or when responding to abuse). Most advocacy groups also work to support people, throughout the world, to increase their capacity for self-advocacy, teaching the skills necessary for people to advocate for their own needs.

Other Types of Supportm

Other types of support for people with developmental disabilities may include:

- therapeutic services, such as speech therapy, massage, aromatherapy, or drama or music therapy
- supported holidays
- short-stay respite services (for people who live with family members or other unpaid carers)

- transport services, such as dial-a-ride or free bus passes
- specialist behaviour support services, such as high-security services for people with high-level, high-risk challenging behaviours
- specialist relationships and sex education services.

LEARNiNG DISABILITY AND IT'S CLASSIFICATION

Learning disability (sometimes called a learning disorder or learning difficulty), is a disorder in which a person has a difficulty to learn effectively, caused by an unknown factor or factors. The unknown factor is the disorder that affects the brain's ability to receive and process information. This disorder can make it problematic for a person to learn as quickly as someone who isn't affected by a learning disability. Learning disability is not indicative of intelligence level. Rather, people with a learning disability have trouble performing specific types of skills or completing tasks if left to figure things out by themselves or if taught in conventional ways.

A learning disability cannot be cured or fixed; it is a lifelong issue. With the right support and intervention, however, people with learning disabilities can succeed in school and go on to successful, often distinguished careers later in life.

Overview

The National Joint Committee on Learning Disabilities (NJCLD) defines the term learning disability as:

> a heterogeneous group of disorders manifested by significant difficulties in the acquisition and use of listening, speaking, reading, writing, reasoning or mathematical abilities. These disorders are intrinsic to the individual and presumed to be due to Central Nervous System Dysfunction. Even though a learning disability may occur concomitantly with other handicapping conditions (e.g. sensory impairment, mental retardation, social and emotional disturbance) or environmental influences (e.g. cultural differences, insufficient/ inappropriate instruction, psychogenic factors) it is not the direct result of those conditions or influences.

The NJCLD used the term to indicate a discrepancy between a child's apparent capacity to learn and his or her level of achievement.

Types of Learning Disabilities

Learning disabilities can be categorized either by the type of information processing that is affected or by the specific difficulties caused by a processing deficit.

Information Processing Deficits

Learning disabilities fall into broad categories based on the four stages of information processing used in learning: input, integration, storage, and output.

- *Input:* This is the information perceived through the senses, such as visual and auditory perception. Difficulties with visual perception can cause problems with recognizing the shape, position and size of items seen. There can be problems with sequencing, which can relate to deficits with processing time intervals or temporal perception. Difficulties with auditory perception can make it difficult to screen out competing sounds in order to focus on one of them, such as the sound of the teacher's voice. Some children appear to be unable to process tactile input. For example, they may seem insensitive to pain or dislike being touched.
- *Integration:* This is the stage during which perceived input is interpreted, categorized, placed in a sequence, or related to previous learning. Students with problems in these areas may be unable to tell a story in the correct sequence, unable to memorize sequences of information such as the days of the week, able to understand a new concept but be unable to generalize it to other areas of learning, or able to learn facts but be unable to put the facts together to see the "big picture." A poor vocabulary may contribute to problems with comprehension.
- *Storage*: Problems with memory can occur with short–term or working memory, or with long–term memory. Most memory difficulties occur in the area of short-term memory, which can make it difficult to learn new material without many more repetitions than is usual. Difficulties with visual memory can impede learning to spell.
- *Output:* Information comes out of the brain either through words, that is, language output, or through muscle activity, such as gesturing, writing or drawing. Difficulties with language output can create problems with spoken language, for example, answering a question on demand, in which one must retrieve information from storage, organize our thoughts, and put the thoughts into words before we speak. It can also cause trouble with written language for the same reasons. Difficulties with motor abilities can cause problems with gross and fine motor skills. People with gross motor difficulties may be clumsy, that is, they may be prone to stumbling, falling, or bumping into things. They may also have trouble running, climbing, or learning to ride a bicycle. People with fine motor difficulties may have trouble buttoning shirts, tying shoelaces, or with handwriting.

Specific Learning Disabilities

Deficits in any area of information processing can manifest in a variety of specific learning disabilities. It is possible for an individual to have more than one of these difficulties. This is referred to as comorbidity or co-occurrence of learning disabilities. In the UK, the term *dual diagnosis* is often used to refer to co-occurrence of learning difficulties.

- *Reading disability* (*ICD-10 and DSM-IV codes: F81.0/315.00*): The most common learning disability. Of all students with specific learning disabilities, 70 per cent

80 per cent have deficits in reading. The term "dyslexia" is often used as a synonym for reading disability; however, many researchers assert that there are different types of reading disabilities, of which dyslexia is one. A reading disability can affect any part of the reading process, including difficulty with accurate and/or fluent word recognition, word decoding, reading rate, prosody (oral reading with expression), and reading comprehension. Before the term "dyslexia" came to prominence, this learning disability used to be known as "word blindness."

Common indicators of reading disability include difficulty with phonemic awareness—the ability to break up words into their component sounds, and difficulty with matching letter combinations to specific sounds (sound-symbol correspondence).

- *Writing disability (ICD-10 and DSM-IV codes F81.1/315.2):* Speech and language disorders can also be called Dysphasia/Aphasia (coded F80.0-F80.2/315.31 in ICD-10 and DSM-IV).

  Impaired written language ability may include impairments in handwriting, spelling, organization of ideas, and composition. The term "dysgraphia" is often used as an overarching term for all disorders of written expression. Others, such as the International Dyslexia Association, use the term "dysgraphia" exclusively to refer to difficulties with handwriting.
- *Math disability (ICD-10 and DSM-IV codes F81.2-3/315.1)*: Sometimes called dyscalculia, a math disability can cause such difficulties as learning math concepts (such as quantity, place value, and time), difficulty memorizing math facts, difficulty organizing numbers, and understanding how problems are organized on the page. Dyscalculics are often referred to as having poor "number sense".
- *Non-verbal learning disability [this disorder is not listed in the ICD-10]:* Non-verbal learning disabilities often manifest in motor clumsiness, poor visual-spatial skills, problematic social relationships, difficulty with math, and poor organizational skills. These individuals often have specific strengths in the verbal domains, including early speech, large vocabulary, early reading and spelling skills, excellent rote-memory and auditory retention, and eloquent self-expression.
- *Dyspraxia:* Sometimes called motor planning, dyspraxia refers to a variety of difficulties with motor skills. Dyspraxia can cause difficulty with single step tasks such as combing hair or waving goodbye, multi-step tasks like brushing teeth or getting dressed, or with establishing spatial relationships such as being able to accurately position one object in relation to another.
- *Disorders of speaking and listening:* Difficulties that often co-occur with learning disabilities include difficulty with memory, social skills and executive functions (such as organizational skills and time management).
- *Auditory processing disorder:* Difficulties processing auditory information include difficulty comprehending more than one task at a time and a relatively stronger ability to learn visually.

Diagnosis

IQ-Achievement Discrepancy

The presence of a learning disability is sometimes suspected by a child's parents long before problems are seen at school. However, the issues typically become visible when a child begins having difficulty at school. Difficulty learning to read is often one of the first signs that a learning disability is present.

Learning disabilities are often identified by school psychologists, clinical psychologists, and neuropsychologists through a combination of intelligence testing, academic achievement testing, classroom performance, and social interaction and aptitude. Other areas of assessment may include perception, cognition, memory, attention, and language abilities. The resulting information is used to determine whether a child's academic performance is commensurate with his or her cognitive ability. If a child's cognitive ability is much higher than his or her academic performance, the student is often diagnosed with a learning disability. The DSM–IV and many school systems and government programmes diagnose learning disabilities in this way.

Although the discrepancy model has dominated the school system for many years, there has been substantial criticism of this approach among researchers. Recent research has provided little evidence that a discrepancy between formally–measured IQ and achievement is a clear indicator of LD. Furthermore, diagnosing on the basis of a discrepancy does not predict the effectiveness of treatment. Low academic achievers who do not have a discrepancy with IQ (i.e. their IQ scores are also low) appear to benefit from treatment just as much as low academic achievers who do have a discrepancy with IQ (i.e. their IQ scores are higher).

Response To Intervention (RTI)

Much current research has focused on a treatment-oriented diagnostic process known as response to intervention (RTI). Researcher recommendations for implementing such a model include early screening for all students, placing those students who are having difficulty into research-based early intervention programmes, rather than waiting until they meet diagnostic criterion. Their performance can be closely monitored to determine whether increasingly intense intervention results in adequate progress. Those who respond will not require further intervention. Those who do not respond adequately to regular classroom instruction (often called "Tier 1 instruction") and a more intensive intervention (often called "Tier 2" intervention) are considered "nonresponders." These students can then be referred for further assistance through special education, in which case they are often identified with a learning disability. Some models of RTI include a third tier of intervention before a child is identified as having a learning disability.

A primary benefit of such a model is that it would not be necessary to wait for a child to be sufficiently far behind to qualify for assistance. This may enable more children to receive assistance before experiencing significant failure, which may in turn result in fewer children who need intensive and expensive special education services. In the United States, the 2004 reauthorization of the Individuals with Disabilities Education Act permitted states and school districts to use RTI as a method of identifying students with learning disabilities. RTI is now the primary means of identification of learning disabilities in Florida.

There are multiple concerns about the use of RTI. The process does not take into account children's individual neuropsychological factors such as phonological awareness and memory, that can help design instruction [Fletcher—Janzen, Reynolds. (2008). Neuropsychological Perspectives on Learning Disabilities in the Era of RTI: Recommendations for Diagnosis and Intervention]. Second, RTI by design takes considerably longer than established techniques, often many months to find an appropriate tier of intervention. Third, it requires a strong intervention programme before students can be identified with a learning disability. If students' receive poor quality interventions, they can be judged non-responsive and thus as having a learning disability when the cause is really only poor instruction. Lastly, RTI is considered a regular education initiative and is not driven by psychologists, reading specialists, or special educators.

Assessment

Many normed assessments can be used in evaluating skills in the primary academic domains: reading, not including word recognition, fluency, and comprehension; mathematics, including computation and problem solving; and written expression, including handwriting, spelling and composition.

The most commonly used comprehensive achievement tests include the Woodcock–Johnson III (WJ III), Weschler Individual Achievement Test II (WIAT II), the Wide Range Achievement Test III (WRAT III), and the Stanford Achievement Test–10th edition. These tests include measures of many academic domains that are reliable in identifying areas of difficulty.

In the reading domain, there are also specialized tests that can be used to obtain details about specific reading deficits. Assessments that measure multiple domains of reading include Gray's Diagnostic Reading Tests–2nd edition (GDRT II) and the Stanford Diagnostic Reading Assessment. Assessments that measure reading subskills include the Gray Oral Reading Test IV—Fourth Edition (GORT IV), Gray Silent Reading Test, Comprehensive Test of Phonological Processing (CTOPP), Tests of Oral Reading and Comprehension Skills (TORCS), Test of Reading Comprehension 3 (TORC–3), Test of Word Reading Efficiency (TOWRE), and the Test of Reading Fluency. A more comprehensive list of reading assessments may be obtained from the Southwest Educational Development Laboratory.

Of course, assessment of learning disabilities requires the consideration of more than test scores. The purpose of assessment is to determine what is needed for intervention, which also requires consideration of contextual variables and whether there are comorbid disorders that must also be identified and treated, such as behavioural issues or language delays.

Treatment and Intervention

Poor academic achievement can be addressed with a variety of interventions. Although the underlying processing difficulty is usually considered to be a lifelong disorder, academic skills themselves can be improved with targeted interventions. Some (adjustments, equipment and assistants) are designed to accommodate or help compensate for the disabilities while others (specialized instruction) are intended to make improvements in the weak areas. Practice is a particularly important component in developing competence, regardless of the starting point. Children who start out with a weakness in a basic skill, such as reading, may miss out on the necessary practice because of the need to catch up with their chronological age peers. Thus a small weakness can snowball into a larger problem.
Interventions include:

- Mastery model:
    - Learners work at their own level of mastery
    - Practice
    - Gain fundamental skills before moving onto the next level
        - Note: this approach is most likely to be used with adult learners or outside the mainstream school system.
- Direct Instruction:
    - Highly structured, intensive instruction
    - Emphasizes carefully planned lessons for small learning increments
    - Scripted lesson plans
    - Rapid-paced interaction between teacher and students
    - Correcting mistakes immediately
    - Achievement-based grouping
    - Frequent progress assessments
- Classroom adjustments:
    - Special seating assignments
    - Alternative or modified assignments
    - Modified testing procedures
    - quiet environment
- Special equipment:
    - Electronic spellers and dictionaries
    - Word processors
    - Talking calculators
    - Books on tape
    - computer
    - dictation programmes
- Classroom assistants:
    - Note-takers
    - Readers
    - Proofreaders
    - scribes

- Special Education:
  - Prescribed hours in a special class
  - Placement in a special class
  - Enrollment in a special school for learning disabled students
  - individual education plan (IEP)

Sternberg has argued that early remediation can greatly reduce the number of children meeting diagnostic criteria for learning disabilities. He has also suggested that the focus on learning disabilities and the provision of accommodations in school fails to acknowledge that people have a range of strengths and weaknesses, and places undue emphasis on academic success by insisting that people should receive additional support in this arena but not in music or sports.

Treatment: Specific Instruction Included in the curriculum should be instruction in: Visual Perception, Visual Memory, Auditory Perception and Auditory Memory.

Cusimano's findings indicate that emphasis should be placed on the development of specific learning skills along with study and basic skills. These learning skills include visual perception, visual memory, auditory perception and auditory memory. Since research indicates that eighty per cent of all learning in school takes place by means of the visual mode, emphasis on the teaching of visual memory skills, and in particular, visual memory of words, is an essential element in the treatment of learning disabilities. In addition, most learning disabled students have extremely weak auditory memory skill development (attention, listening and recall). Instruction for the development of auditory memory for both listening for information presented in isolation such as a series of numbers, letters, and words, as well as specific instruction for the listening of information presented in context is essential in the process of helping these children to learn with ease.

Causes and Risk Factors

The causes for learning disabilities are not well understood, and sometimes there is no apparent cause for a learning disability. However, some causes of neurological impairments include:

- Heredity—Learning disabilities often run in the family.
- Problems during pregnancy and birth—Learning disabilities can result from anomalies in the developing brain, illness or injury, fetal exposure to alcohol or drugs, low birth weight, oxygen deprivation, or by premature or prolonged labour.
- Accidents after birth—Learning disabilities can also be caused by head injuries, malnutrition, or by toxic exposure (such as heavy metals or pesticides).
- Behavioural Factors.
- Social environment factors.
- Cognitive Factors.

Impact on Affected Individuals

Learning disabilities affect interpersonal relationships in a variety of complex ways Neuropsychological differences can impact the accurate perception of social cues with peers and can impact family systems in predictable ways during activities such as homework.

Furthermore, individuals with a learning disability may isolate themselves from society as they may feel:

- Ashamed of the types of difficulties they struggle with, such as poor literacy skills, attention or memory difficulties
- Fear of failure, criticism, ridicule or rejection
- Fear of discrimination
- Fear that others may think that they are stupid or incapable or Mentally disabled
- Ashamed that they are unable to read or that they have poor handwriting
- Left out of everyday discussions due to lack of understanding
- Depressed
- Alone
- "Learned helplessness"

Societal Factors

Society both impacts upon, and is impacted by, individuals with learning disabilities. Significant factors in this relationship include poverty (with its concomitant reliance on welfare/public assistance), gender, and crime/imprisonment.

Welfare/Public Assistance Relating to Educational Development

- A 36 month study conducted by Taylor and Barusch included 284 welfare recipients, who were frequently interviewed, called, and visited with in their homes. In this study the average age was 34 and 97 per cent of the participants were female. Of the welfare participants 22.9 per cent were learning disabled and 32 per cent had no high school diploma or GED. Findings from this study imply that long-term learning disabled welfare recipients will not be able to support their family through employment.
- A study similar to the one stated above, conducted by Margai and Henry found that the laws of identifying special education children have been revised within the past years. Learning disabled children in public schools now make up 6 per cent of all kids.
- High risk neighbourhoods and poor living conditions add to the factor of being more vulnerable to having a learning disability. A study was conducted exploring the areas of pollution and socio-economic factors related to having a higher risk of a learning disability. Margai and Henry used primary data and analyzed clusters of people in a distinct part of a community near a toxic waste place, living in poor neighbourhoods and living in poverty). The

results confirmed that a majority of the people with a learning disability came from some socio-economic indicator such as poverty, sub-divided housing, and lower adult educational attainment. Individuals with a learning disability will rely more heavily on public assistance/welfare than individuals who do not because of their lack of knowledge.

Gender Issues

- Researchers believe that there are more boys in special education programmes compared to girls. Coutinho and Oswald found that data was collected from the U.S. office of Civil Rights to view the underrepresentation of females in special education. Oswald found that 73 per cent of learning disabled individuals in special education programmes were boys.
- Although, in contrast to the statement above if learning disabled students are identified by research criteria as opposed to teachers, the ratio of boys to girls (having a learning disability) is equal. In dealing with learning disabilities no significant gender differences were found in a study of more than 400 children. Bandian found that if identified by research criteria there were no differences in gender, but if learning disabilities were identified by general education teachers and/or special education teachers, there was twice as many boys identified compared to girls. Alongside that, there was another statement said by Bandian that supported the claim stated above "boys were twice as like[ly] to be identified by teachers as in need of a learning disability programmes [sic] [compared to girls]."s
- In a study 266 youths between the ages of 12–18 were voluntarily interviewed with 74 structured questions in a small classroom, question structure was based on "special education, juvenile justice, and child and adolescent development literature," and then categorized into three parts: personal, home, and school. Based on the information the individuals provided to the interviewers the juvenile delinquents were put into a category, special education, or non–special education. Zabel and Nigro stated that "girls are less often viewed as disruptive and disturbing behaviour patterns that often lead to special education." In contrast to that Zabel and Nigro also found that the "gender pattern was reversed for LD classification, with nearly 78.6 per cent of females who had been in special education." This study relates directly to the information provided in the welfare section because females are being identified with in the schools and are in turn receiving help from welfare programmes. Although, this information provided in this section is in contrast to the gender differences section stating that boys are more identified for learning disabled programmes compared to girls, this section supports the welfare section.

Crime and Prison Population

- Individuals in a detention facility are more likely to have a learning disability, receive poor grades, and repeat a grade. Zabel and Nigro conducted a study with 266 youths (currently in a detention facility), with the youths ages ranging from 12–18. The individuals were voluntarily interviewed with 74 structured questions. Based on the information provided from the individuals, the individuals were categorized into two groups, special education or non–special education. Zabel and Nigro stated "a majority of participants had received failing grades, and many had repeated at least one grade." The researchers also found that 88.6 per cent of the youth had been suspended, and those in the SpEd group were more likely than those in the non–SpEd group to report their first instance of trouble in elementary school. This information provided relates to the factor of when most learning disabled individuals are identified is in elementary school thus proving that it would make sense that the individuals in the SpEd group had their first instance of trouble in elementary school and it is hard for LD individuals to complete the education system, thus resulting in having to rely on welfare and public assistance.

- Another statistic (calculated from the study stated above) found by Zabel and Nigro was that 37.1 per cent had been involved with special education, and classified having EBD and/or LD. Zabel also found that those individuals with a learning disability were at a higher risk that those with no special education experience (in the violent inmates, 17 of 30 were LD, and in the nonviolent, 13 of 30 were LD).
- Individuals in detention facilities may have a learning disability and more specifically have dyslexia (severe difficulty in recognizing and understanding written language, leading to spelling and writing problems). Gretchell, Pabreja, Neeld, and Carrio conducted a study that compared the difference of children with dyslexia and without. Twenty six individuals were dyslexic and 23 individuals were not. Individuals were tested with the Test of Gross Motor Development and Movement Assessment Battery for Children. Individuals with dyslexia performed significantly lower than the control group (individuals who aren't dyslexic). Thus, proving the similarities of how it will be hard for someone who has LD to complete the education system.
- Youth in a detention facility are more likely to have a special education problem, such as a learning disability, than not. Zabel and Nigro found in their study that "about one half of SpEd participants and nearly 20 per cent of the total sample reported their classification as learning disabilities." LD individuals make up a large portion of individuals in a detention facility which may have been a result from the LD individual not learning at a significant pace in the education system and also potentially not completing the education system. Zabel and Nigro's study was made up of 266 youth between the ages of 12–18 who were currently in a detention facility.

Contrast with Other Conditions

People with an IQ lower than 70 are usually characterized as having mental retardation (MR), mental deficiency, or cognitive impairment and are not included under most definitions of learning disabilities, because their learning difficulties are related directly to their low IQ scores.

Attention–deficit hyperactivity disorder (ADHD) is often studied in connection with learning disabilities, but it is not actually included in the standard definitions of learning disabilities. An individual with ADHD may struggle with learning, but he or she can often learn adequately once successfully treated for the ADHD. A person can have ADHD but not learning disabilities or have learning disabilities without having ADHD. The conditions can co–occur (see Comorbidity). In order to understand the difference, imagine that someone with a learning disability is affected in only one or a few areas. However, people with ADHD are often affected in all areas.

Some research is beginning to make a case for ADHD being included in the definition of LDs, since it is being shown to have a strong impact on "executive functions" required for learning (planning, organization, etc.). This has not as yet affected any official definitions.

Criticism of the Concept of Learning Disabilities

Some critics of the concept of learning disabilities and of special education take the position that every child has a different learning style and pace and that each child is unique, not only capable of learning but also capable of succeeding. These critics assert that applying the medical model of problem-solving to individual children who are pupils in the school system, and labeling these children as disabled, systematically prevents the improvement of the current educational system.

Describing current instructional methods as homogenization and lockstep standardization, alternative approaches are proposed, such as the Sudbury model of democratic education schools, an alternative approach in which children, by enjoying personal freedom thus encouraged to exercise personal responsibility for their actions, learn at their own pace rather than following a chronologically-based curriculum. Proponents of unschooling have also claimed that children raised in this method do not suffer from learning disabilities.

Gerald Coles asserts that there are partisan agendas behind the educational policy-makers and that the scientific research that they use to support their arguments regarding the teaching of literacy are flawed. These include the idea that there are neurological explanations for learning disabilities.

Marva Collins' Experience

Marva Collins started a low cost private school in inner city Chicago specifically for the purpose of teaching low-income black children whom the public school system had wrongly labeled as being "learning disabled." She once wrote, "I have discovered few learning disabled students in my three decades of teaching. I have, however, discovered many, many victims of teaching inabilities."

One article about Marva Collins' school stated, "Working with students having the worst of backgrounds, those who were working far below grade level, and even those who had been labeled as 'unteachable,' Marva was able to overcome the obstacles.

News of third grade students reading at ninth grade level, four-year-olds learning to read in only a few months, outstanding test scores, disappearance of behavioural problems, second-graders studying Shakespeare, and other incredible reports, astounded the public."

Learning Disabilities and US Law

Disability Discrimination

Disability discrimination has been common throughout the world. People with learning disability may receive offending/negative remarks, harassing, bullying, etc. as a result of a difference in their neurological wiring when compared to the norm. In response to this, countries such as the United States have enacted programmes to help learning disabled people.

Section 504 of the Rehabilitation Act of 1973

The Section 504 of the Rehabilitation Act was first widely recognized as the "first civil–rights statue for persons with disabilities." Taken in effect in May 1977, this American legislation guarantees certain rights to people with disabilities, especially in the cases of education and work, such being in schools, colleges and university settings.

Individuals with Disabilities Education Act

The Individuals with Disabilities Education Act, formerly known as the Education for All Handicapped Children Act, is a United States federal law that governs how states and public agencies provide early intervention, special education and related services to children with disabilities. It addresses the educational needs of children with disabilities from birth to the age of 21. Considered as a civil rights law, states are not required to participate.

United States and Canada

In the United States and Canada, the terms learning disability and learning disorder (LD) refer to a group of disorders that affect a broad range of academic and functional skills including the ability to speak, listen, read, write, spell, reason, organize information, and do math.

United Kingdom

In the UK, terms such as specific learning difficulty (SpLD), dyslexia, dyspraxia and dyscalculia are referred as learning difficulties, rather than learning disabilities. In the UK, the term "learning disability" refers to a range of conditions that are almost invariably associated with more severe cognitive impairments.

TOWARDS UNDERSTANDING THE SHIFTING MODELS OF DISABILITY

The shifting approaches to disability have translated into very diverse policies and practices. The various models of disability impose differing responsibilities on the States, in terms of action to be taken, and they suggest significant changes in the way disability is understood. Law, policy, programmes, and rights instruments reflect two primary approaches or discourses: disability as an individual pathology and as a social pathology.

Within these two overriding paradigms, the four major identifiable formulations of disability are: the charity model, the bio-centric model, the functional model, and the human rights model.

The Charity Model

The charity approach gave birth to a model of custodial care, causing extreme isolation and the marginalisation of people with disabilities. Unfortunately, in some contemporary practices the reflection of this model can still be traced. For instance, the findings of an investigative project undertaken by the National Human Rights Commission of India between 1997–99 confirmed that a large number of mental health institutions today are still being managed and administered on the custodial model of care—characterised by prison-like structures with high walls, watchtowers, fenced wards, and locked cells. These institutions functioned like detention centres, where persons with mental illness were kept chained, resulting in tragedies like the one at "Erwadi" in Tamil Nadu, in which more than 27 inmates of such a centre lost their lives.

The Bio-Centric Model

The contemporary bio-centric model of disability regards disability as a medical or genetic condition. The implication remains that disabled persons and their families should strive for "normalisation", through medical cures and miracles. Although, biology is no longer the only lens through which disability is viewed in law and policy, it continues to play a prominent role in determining programme eligibility, entitlement to benefits, and it also influences access to rights and full social participation (Mohit, 2003).

A critical analysis of the development of the charity and bio–centric models suggests that they have grown out of the "vested interests" of professionals and the elite to keep the disabled "not educable" or declare them mentally retarded (MR) children and keep them out of the mainstream school system, thus using the special schools as a "safety valve" for mainstream schools (Tomlinson, 1982). Inclusive education offers an opportunity to restructure the entire school system, with particular reference to the curriculum, pedagogy, assessment, and above all the meaning of education (Jha, 2002).

The Functional Model

In the functional model, entitlement to rights is differentiated according to judgments of individual incapacity and the extent to which a person is perceived as being independent to exercise his/her rights. For example, a child's right to education is dependent on whether or not the child can access the school and participate in the classroom, rather than the obligation being on the school system becoming accessible to children with disabilities.

The Human Rights Model

The human rights model positions disability as an important dimension of human culture, and it affirms that all human beings are born with certain inalienable rights. The relevant concepts in this model are:

Diversity

The Greek philosopher, Aristotle, once said that "things that are alike should be treated alike, whereas things that are unalike should be treated unalike in proportion to their un–alikeness." The principle of respect for difference and acceptance of disability as part of human diversity and humanity is important, as disability is a universal feature of the human condition.

Breaking Down Barriers

Policies that are ideologically based on the human rights model start by identifying barriers that restrict disabled persons' participation in society. This has shifted the focus in the way environments are arranged. In education, for example, where individuals were formerly labelled as not educable, the human rights model examines the accessibility of schools in terms of both physical access (i.e., ramps, etc.) and pedagogical strategies.

Equality and Non-Discrimination

In international human rights law, equality is founded upon two complementary principles: non-discrimination and reasonable differentiation. The doctrine of differentiation is of particular importance to persons with disabilities, some of who may require specialised services or support in order to be placed on a basis of equality with others. Differences of treatment between individuals are not discriminatory if they are based on "reasonable and objective justification". Moreover, equality not only implies preventing discrimination (for example, the protection of individuals against unfavourable treatment by introducing anti–discrimination laws), but goes far beyond, in remedying discrimination. In concrete terms, it means embracing the notion of positive rights, affirmative action, and reasonable accommodation.

Reasonable Accommodation

It is important to recognise that reasonable accommodation is a means by which conditions for equal participation can be achieved, and it requires the burden of accommodation to be in proportion to the capacity of the entity. In the draft *Comprehensive and Integral and International Convention on Protection and Promotion of the Rights and Dignity of Persons with Disabilities,* "reasonable accommodation" has been defined as the "introduction of necessary and appropriate measures to enable a person with a disability fully to enjoy fundamental rights and freedoms and to have access without prejudice to all structures, processes, public services, goods, information, and other systems."

Accessibility

The United Nations Economic and Special Commission for Asia and the Pacific (UNESCAP) has defined "accessibility" as "the measure or condition of things and services that can readily be reached or used (at the physical, visual, auditory and/or cognitive levels) by people including those with disabilities"(Rioux and Mohit, 2005).

Equal Participation and Inclusion

By focussing on the inherent dignity of the human being, the human rights model places the individual at centre stage, in all decisions affecting him/her. Thus, the human rights model, respects the autonomy and freedom of choice of the disabled, and also ensures that they, themselves, prioritise the criteria for support programmes.

It requires that people with disabilities, and other individuals and institutions fundamental to society, are enabled to gain the capacity for the free interaction and participation vital to an inclusive society.

Private and Public Freedoms

The human rights approach to disability on the one hand requires that the States play an active role in enhancing the level of access to public freedoms, and on the other requires that the enjoyment of rights by persons with disabilities is not hampered by third-party actors in the private sphere. Educational institutions and industry, both in the public and private sectors, should ensure equitable treatment to persons with disabilities.

2

Assessment of Special Educational Needs and Poor School Performance: An Overview

ASSESSMENT OF SPECIAL EDUCATIONAL NEEDS: A CASE STUDY

For a few children the support provided by Action and Action Plus may not be enough to meet their more complex and long-term learning needs. If your child needs more support the school will meet with you and any support services already involved with your child, to discuss whether a statutory assessment should be carried out.

Statutory Assessment

It is a detailed investigation by the Children's Services Authority to find out exactly what your child's needs are and what special help would benefit your child.

A statutory assessment can be requested by:

- your child's school
- a special educational needs professional working with your child, for example an educational psychologist
- you, if you feel your child is not making sufficient progress. You will need to request the assessment from the special educational needs (SEN) team.

Elements of Statutory Assessment

Firstly, detailed consideration is given to whether an assessment is needed. We will tell you within six weeks of receiving the application whether we are going to carry out a statutory assessment.

If we decide to carry out an assessment we have a further 10 weeks to complete it. In this time we collect together detailed information about your child in order to get a clear picture of your child's needs. We will ask you for additional information and we will contact a number of professionals including:

- your child's school
- an educational psychologist
- a doctor
- children's services.

We will also include anyone else whose views you consider would be helpful.

You will be contacted if any assessments or examinations are arranged for your child. You have the right to be present at any medical, test or interview. However, in certain circumstances it is helpful for your child to be seen without you-for example where classroom observation is being carried out.

Once we have received all the information about your child's needs we will consider whether to issue a statement of special educational needs. We will normally write and tell you whether we are going to issue a statement within 12 weeks of starting the assessment.

Forms

All statutory assessment forms can be downloaded from czone, the website for Children's Services professionals in East Sussex.

Follow-up

If we have decided to issue a statement we will send you a 'proposed statement'. This is a draft of the statement and you will be able to comment on it if you wish.

We will usually send you the final statement, which will name the school in Part 4, within eight weeks of issuing the 'proposed statement'. The statement comes into force on the day that it is issued. It is reviewed annually.

If we have decided not to issue a statement we will write to you and explain the reasons for this decision and we will tell you how we think your child's needs can be met in school. We will ask the school to arrange a meeting with you, key school staff and an educational psychologist to discuss the future programme of support for your child. We will also give you information about who you can contact if you disagree with our decision and we will tell you about your right of appeal to the Special Educational Needs and Disability Tribunal.

Statement of Special Educational Needs

The statement describes your child's educational needs and the help they need in order to make progress at school. The statement is in six parts:

Part 1 gives your own and your child's name and address together with other personal details.

Part 2 gives details of all your child's special educational needs which were identified during the assessment.

Part 3 sets out the special educational provision. It describes:

- the special help your child should get to meet the needs listed in part 2
- the long-term educational aims for your child
- the arrangements for setting short-term goals, reviewing your child's progress towards those goals and how your child's progress is to be monitored.

Part 4 tells you about the school your child will attend to get the help set out in **part** 3 or any other arrangements for education other than in school.

Part 5 describes any relevant non-educational needs your child has such as medical needs.

Part 6 gives details of how your child will get the help outlined in part 5.

You will be sent copies of all the reports that we obtain as part of the assessment process.

The final statement will be issued within eight weeks of sending the 'proposed statement'. It will be reviewed annually.

MAJOR CAUSES FOR POOR SCHOOL PERFORMANCE OF PHYSICALLY AND MENTALLY CHALLENGED STUDENTS

A teacher puts in the best of her efforts to help every child achieve optimal academic performance. In spite of this, not all children rise up to the expectations of the teachers or parents. These underachievers are 'Scholastically Backward'. The reasons or causes for this Scholastic Backwardness are several; the objective of this opening chapter is to spell out those various causes:

(1) Some of these children are actually bright, but cannot get marks in spite of effort,
(2) Some others have behaviour problems and may not be keen to make an effort to get good marks;
(3) Some children cannot make adequate effort because of their physical or neurological handicaps.

Whatever be the underlying cause, all of them score 'Poor Marks'.

'Poor Marks' as a Symptom—Basis of 'the Diagnostic Approach'

A cough is a physical symptom due to an underlying cause. When a patient seeks treatment for cough, the doctor uses a 'Logical Approach' to arrive at the diagnosis of the cause for the cough. This Diagnostic Approach is deductionistic and sequential; it follows an 'Algorithm'—a 'Flow Chart'.

In the case of cough, the doctor arrives at a diagnosis by carefully ruling out one cause after the other and decides whether the cough results from Pharyngitis, Pneumonia, Tuberculosis or Cancer. Because this approach is simple and logical, the same 'Diagnostic-Approach' is followed to determine the specific cause for 'Poor Marks' in an underachieving child.

The 'Flow Chart' for Diagnosis

If poor performance in a child is present from the beginning of education, the causes may be one set of Learning problems. If the child's academic performance declines later (e.g., in 8th or 9th Std), the causes may be another set of problems. In a young child, the *causes* for poor marks may lie *in the child* himself. In an older child, the *causes* may be in the *environment.*

All such causes of poor marks in a child are sequentially listed in the Flow Chart given below.

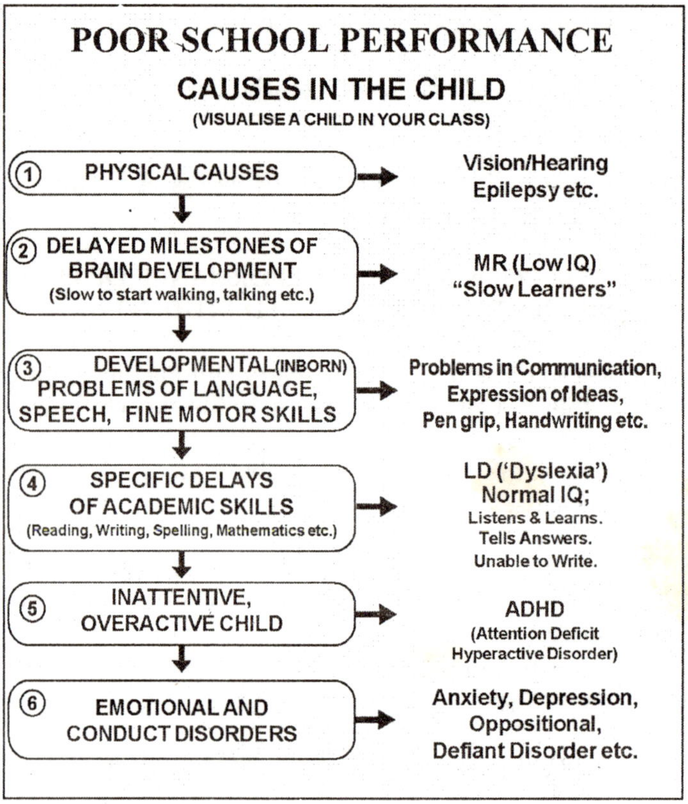

'Poor Marks' as a 'Symptom'—How to Use a 'Flow Chart' for Diagnosis

If a child gets poor marks, we brand him 'lazy' or 'stupid'. No child, we should realise, wants to be lazy or careless. Every child, on the contrary, loves to stand up and be counted. If he gets poor marks, it is only because he suffers from a Learning problem. Therefore, in a young child, Poor School Performance should be seen as a 'symptom' reflecting a larger underlying Disorder.

We should scientifically analyse this symptom, discover its underlying cause and find a remedy to help the child score better marks. This is the 'Diagnostic Approach'—to diagnose the cause of the symptom (of poor marks) and to treat the cause.

Based on the 'Flow Chart', these causes are examined one after the other.

1. Causes in the Child for Poor School Performance (*Based on the Flow Chart*)

Causes in the child may be Physical problems, Intelligence Deficits, or Behavioural Disorders.

(*a*) *Physical Problems: Maya, a 3rd standard student, started faring poorly in class. Her teacher complained that the girl fails to copy what is written on the blackboard and does not complete her notes. By a stroke of luck one day, Maya's mother discovered that the little one could not clearly read the letters on the TV screen. The eye specialist whom they consulted prescribed glasses for her short-sight, and Maya bounced back to excellent academic performance in a few months.*

Like Maya, some children have partial deficits in vision or hearing, which in turn cause poor performance.

(*b*) *Poor Intelligence:* All children are not created equal. Some of them are slow to start standing, walking or talking. Such children with delayed 'milestones of development' may have inadequate global brain development. Therefore, they may have only below average Intelligence. Such children are Mentally Retarded and obviously score poor marks.

It is possible for Clinical or Educational Psychologists to assess Intelligence. Intelligence (IQ) tests tell us whether the child is Mentally Retarded ('Slow Learner'), leading to 'Poor Marks'.

(*c*) *Learning Disorders ('Dyslexia'):* Some young children doing poorly at school are actually Intelligent. Their overall global brain growth is normal, but miniscule brain areas concerned with the Academic skills of Reading, Writing, Spelling, Mathematics or Language have not developed adequately. This is called Specific Delay in Development (in contrast to the global delay in development in the case of Mental Retardation).

The result is that this Intelligent child understands what he is taught, he is able to answer orally, but is not able to express the same in writing; that explains how an LD child gets poor marks.

(*d*) *Other Neurological Disorders Causing Learning Problems: 'Manu is a bright six year old. He is quick on the uptake, quick to respond. But he is a problem child in school: persistently restless, walking around the class, nudging the next child in the assembly or breaking something all the time. He is impulsive and unable to sit still in the chair'.*

Manu is an underachiever, because he has Attention Deficit Hyperactivity Disorder (ADHD). If he cannot hold his attention, he cannot concentrate and therefore he cannot learn.

(*e*) *Emotional Disorders:* We know that many children with Emotional or Conduct problems score low marks, even though they may be intelligent. Some children may have an inherent fear of going to school. Some of them may be emotionally unstable due to reasons like Anxiety, while some others turn out to be Defiant or Disobedient. However, all of them get poor marks due to such 'Emotional Disorders'.

2. *Causes in the Environment for Poor School Performance*

No child can do well in a deprived or discordant environment at home or in school. Causes like poor discipline at home or school, broken homes or fighting parents, frightening friends or punitive teachers, frequent change of school or medium of instruction etc. can lead to poor school performance.

Caveat

It is important to note that in a single child, more than one of the above causes may be affecting the child's scholastic performance at the same time (e.g., a child with Learning Disorder can also have Attention Deficit Disorder).

Unless a teacher or parent is keenly aware of these causes, many children may get wrongly branded as 'Lazy', 'Stupid' or 'Careless'. Such children can end up receiving no educational support or remedies at all.

When you are confronted with a child performing poorly in class, think of the above causes listed above one after the other, before blaming or punishing him—look at the 'Flow Chart' once again.

More than six general causes in the child have been listed in the Flow Chart for Poor School Performance (PSP). The most common, yet the most underdiagnosed, are Learning Disorders (Dyslexia) described in the next chapter.

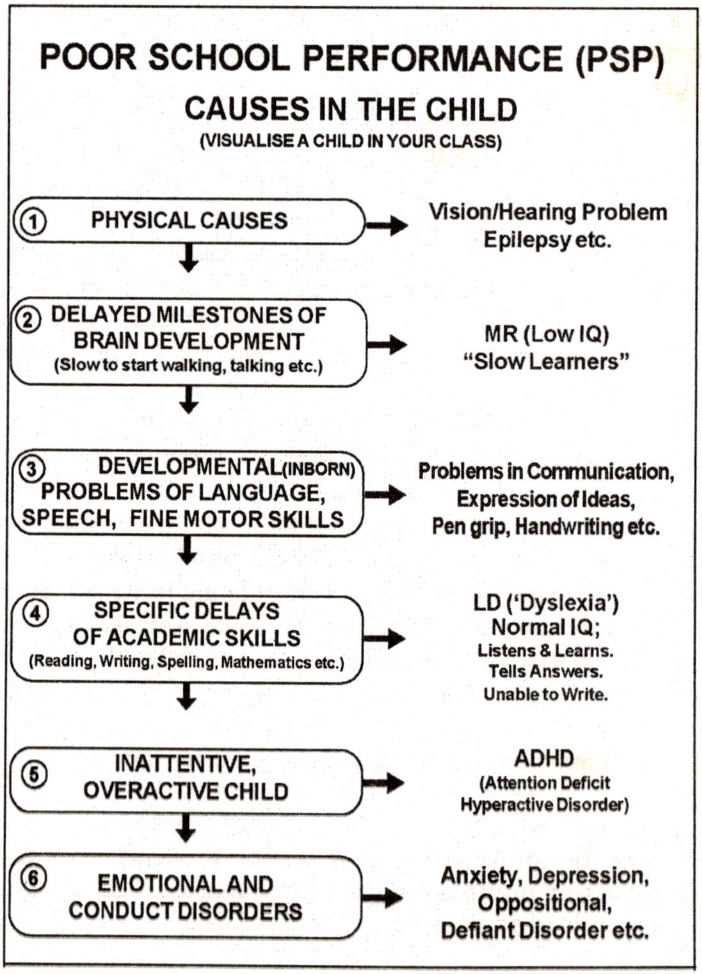

A MULTIDISCIPLINARY APPROACH FOR DIAGNOSING POOR SCHOOL PERFORMANCE: A CASE STUDY

Specific causes for Poor School Performance can be detected by anyone using the Flow Chart (Ch. 1). Children suspected to have Learning Disorders (LD) can be identified by the Teacher in the classroom by using the Flow Chart (Ch. 1) and specific Pointers for Identification (Ch. 3). But a firm diagnosis may need several Specialists.

In Children with *Learning Disorders* (LD), different Academic Skills like Reading, Writing, Spelling, Arithmetic etc. are affected. There may be associated *Developmental Motor Co-ordination* or *Speech* and *Language* Disorders too. *Emotional and Behaviour* Disorders also may co–exist. Every such possible cause for Poor School Performance must be looked for, and diagnosed.

Any child who is referred for a detailed Assessment and Diagnosis of Poor School Performance has to be carefully evaluated from all the above angles. Therefore, it necessitates evaluation by a Multidisciplinary Team ideally consisting of a Special Educator/Teacher, Psychologist, Speech and Language Pathologist, Social Worker and where necessary a Psychiatrist and Pediatrician.

The consent and participation of the parents is mandatory for this stage of Diagnosis. The assessment aims to identify the various Skill Deficits in the particular child, as well as his current level of functioning in various Academic Skills. The assessment also aims to identify the Strengths of each child. The evaluation thus generates adequate information on each child to give the requisite guidelines for Remediation.

The assessment usually proceeds according to a stepwise protocol:

1. Intake Interview

The following details are obtained in the Intake Interview:

The child's Current problems, Developmental history, Home Environment and Inputs, Recent Life events. Educational history, Past Academic progress, Positive attributes, Hobbies etc. A detailed report on the child from the Teacher is an important ingredient at this stage of assessment. The information gathered at this stage determines which other Specialist/Specialists need to examine this child.

2. Examination and Testing of the Child

A physical/neurological examination and tests, if necessary, of hearing and vision. Where indicated, a meticulous examination of the child's central nervous system including soft neurological signs is mandatory.

3. Academic Skills Assessment

The basic assessments are the following:

(*i*) Tests to measure Intelligence (IQ) (Clinical Psychologist) (*ii*) Tests of Academic skills (Reading, Spelling, Writing, Mathematics) (Special Educator)

(*iii*) Tests for Speech and Language (Receptive and Expressive Language ability, Speech clarity etc.) (Speech and Language Pathologist)

(*iv*) Test of Special abilities.

4. Assessment of Co-Morbid Disorders

Specialists may need to examine the child to rule out disorders such as Attention Deficit Hyperactivity Disorder (ADHD), Emotional disorders, Speech and Language disorders and Co-ordination disorders.

Assessment of Learning Disorders

A range of Tests is administered to the child to find out the factors hindering progress at school.

(*i*) *General Intelligence Test:* The most common IQ test for assessing Intelligence is Weschler Intelligence Scale for Children (WISC), originally developed in the US and modified to suit Indian children. This test is suited for children with reading and spelling difficulties as it does not involve reading and writing.
A normal child scores equally well or equally badly on all scales. On the other hand, the child with a Learning Disorder does well in one set of tests and badly in others.

(*ii*) *Assessment of Reading Skills:* To assess the Reading age and Reading Disorders of the child, there are a number of standardized tests. An informal Grade Based Reading Assessment can also be done and more valuable, individualised information can be obtained about Reading (Word attack skills) and Reading Comprehension. Specific Reading Disorders are recorded by analysing the reading performance.

(*iii*) *Assessment of Spelling:* The ability to spell is recognized as a complex and multifaceted process. Besides general Intelligence, the following factors affect the ability to spell words:

(*a*) The ability to spell words that are phonetic

(*b*) The ability to spell words that involve roots, prefixes, suffixes and rules for combining

(*c*) The ability to look at a word and reproduce it later.

An efficient Assessment procedure can clearly outline the relevant skills a child has or has not mastered, pin point patterns of errors and provide directions for systematic remedial instruction.

(*iv*) *Assessment of Maths Skills:* Many Disabled Learners have difficulty Learning Mathematics, experiencing problems at all age levels. Skills in basic computations like Addition, Subtraction, Multiplication and Division and ability to solve statement problems are examined. There are a number of (commercial) Maths assessment kits; however, they yield little usable teaching information. On the other hand, Informal Assessment which consists of Observation, Oral interviews and Error analysis can provide us with enough information regarding the nature of the child's Disabilities.

(*v*) *Other Assessments:* Other areas assessed include Handwriting, Comprehension and Attention. These tests are used for children above six years of age. Children below six years are assessed for Pre-Academic Skills. These include Visual discrimination, Auditory discrimination, Fine Motor Skills, Verbal Fluency, Memory, Attention and Handedness. Brigance Diagnostic Inventory of Basic Skills, Aston Index and Mann Suiter Test are some of the popular tests used to assess the 'Learning Readiness' of the preschool child.

Conclusion

The objective of this detailed Assessment and documentation is to bring out the level at which the particular child functions in each Academic Skill. It also examines the nature of the difficulties that the child exhibits. Based on the report, an Individualised Education Programme (IEP) is drawn up for the child in reference. The Remedial Strategies for each child assessed are worked out by the teachers based on such an IEP.

The concerned laws in the USA and UK make it a legal obligation for each school to undertake this assessment. According to the 1993 Education Act in the UK, each school should maintain a Special Educational Need (SEN) register as per the Legal Code of Practice. Class teachers identify the Special Educational Needs (Learning Disorders) and along with the SEN co-ordinator and the child's parents, help the child undergo a Multidisciplinary Assessment for Diagnosis as well as for Intervention. This procedure emphasises the significance of a Multidisciplinary Team.

TOWARDS LISTING EMOTIONAL AND BEHAVIOUR PROBLEMS IN CHILDREN WITH POOR SCHOOL-PERFORMANCE

'Gaurav, a student of Std V sometimes can disrupt the entire class. Some children get bullied by him and others do not like to sit next to him. He may distract them or even nudge them. He too gets easily distracted by everything that goes on around him. Teachers know that he is smart and quick on the uptake. But he is very inattentive, and hardly sits in his seat. He may blurt out answers in the class out of turn, and is not bothered if he is right or wrong. His parents find his behaviour embarrassing at social gatherings, where he constantly moves around and even opens the food packets before being served'.

Each one of you as teachers may be able to recall some of your pupils in the lower classes who are similar to Gaurav. Gaurav is a child with Attention Deficit Hyperactivity Disorder (ADHD) which is distinct and different from Learning Disorders. But it is extremely common to find the same child suffering from ADHD as well as Learning Disorders. This is called co-morbidity—one disorder co-existing with another in the same child.

There are several such disorders which appear in the child along with Learning

Disorders (LD). These may be called Co-morbid Disorders. Some Co-morbid Disorders, like LD, are Developmental in origin and may be present from birth. Some other Co-morbid disorders like School Phobia or Anxiety may arise in the child *because* of the Learning problems that the child suffers from.

It is essential to identify and differentially diagnose each of these disorders because the management strategies need to involve remediation for all disorders in the child. Correction of one disorder, while leaving another unattended, will not help to improve the child's performance.

Co-Morbid Childhood Disorders (Co-Existing with LD)

There are three broad categories of these disorders—Category (1) Developmental Disorders, Category (2) Disruptive Behaviour Disorders, and Category (3) Emotional Disorders.

Category (1): Developmental Disorders

As has been made clear, Learning Disorders are Developmental disorders. Our experience at Cochin has shown that children with LD almost always have other co-morbid Developmental Deficits. Difficulties in Motor Co-ordination (fine-tuning of movements affecting pencil grip, hand-writing, shoe-lacing, buttoning etc.) are called Developmental Co–ordination Disorders (DCD). A large number of children with LD have problems with Speech and use of Language. This is called Communication Disorder (CD).

It is, therefore, incumbent on us to look for DCD or CD symptoms in every child with LD.

Category (2): Disruptive Behaviour Disorders [(A) ADHD, (B) Conduct Disorders]

(A) ***Attention Deficit Hyperactivity Disorder*** **(*ADHD*)**

Gaurav, whose case is described at the outset, is a child with this disruptive behaviour disorder which has a developmental basis. ADHD is attributed to a delay in the maturation of the brain cells which control Attention and Activity.

The core features of ADHD fall under three headings (*a*) Inattention (*b*) Hyperactivity and (*c*) Impulsivity. These symptoms of the child can disrupt any environment.

(*a*) *Inattention:*

This child –

(*i*) Often fails to give close attention to details, or makes careless mistakes in school work or other activities
(*ii*) Often has difficulty sustaining attention in tasks or play-activities
(*iii*) Often does not seem to listen when spoken to directly
(*iv*) Often does not follow through on instructions, and fails to finish schoolwork, chores, or duties (not due to oppositional behaviour or failure to understand instruction)

(*v*) Often has difficulty organising tasks and activities
(*vi*) Often avoids, dislikes, or is reluctant to engage in tasks that require sustained mental effort (such as schoolwork or homework)
(*vii*) Often loses things necessary for tasks or activities (e.g., toys, school assignments, pencils, books or tools)
(*viii*) Is often easily distracted by extraneous stimuli
(*ix*) Is often forgetful in daily activities

(*b*) *Hyperactivity*

(*i*) Often fidgets with hands or feet, or squirms in seat
(*ii*) Often leaves seat in classroom or in other situations in which remaining seated is expected
(*iii*) Often runs about or climbs excessively in situations in which it is inappropriate (in adolescents or adults, may be limited to subjective feelings of restlessness)
(*iv*) Often has difficulty playing or engaging in leisure activities quietly
(*v*) Is often 'on the go' or often acts as if "driven by a motor"
(*vi*) Often talks excessively

(*c*) *Impulsivity*

(*i*) Often blurts out answers before questions have been completed
(*ii*) Often has difficulty awaiting turn
(*iii*) Often interrupts or intrudes on others (e.g., butts into conversations or games)

ADHD children generally have normal or above normal intelligence. They are usually quick on the uptake and may "speak like elders". Most of them go through tasks with speed and hurry.

A few of the above symptoms do not constitute a disorder; to call it a disorder, there must be evidence of clinically significant impairment in social and academic functioning. The presence of a few of the above pointers would not confirm a diagnosis; absence of some of them may not rule out a diagnosis. Presence of symptoms of Anxiety, Oppositional/ Defiant and reckless behaviour may sometimes complicate the diagnosis.

Classroom observation yields valuable information on children with ADHD. Observation for too brief a period may not show obvious indicators of the problem. Teacher's observation helps in communicating to parents, and aids in drawing up a plan for classroom management.

If a child has ADHD, he has the probability of having LD too. It is seen that ADHD co-exists with LD to a greater degree than all the other co-morbid disorders. Both are brain-Developmental Disorders which significantly affect a child's academic and social functioning.

Children with ADHD can neither control their hyperactivity, nor sustain attention to a task for an adequate period of time, *howsoever deliberately they may try*. This inability explains why children with ADHD do not respond fully to disciplining, and may need judicious medication.

(B) ***Conduct Disorders***

Conduct Disorders are characterised by a repetitive and persistent pattern of dissocial, aggressive or defiant conduct, more severe than ordinary childhood mischief or rebelliousness. Unlike in ADHD, these children may have no brain damage. Some children who perform poorly in school are prone to 'acting out', which results in behaviour that is socially unacceptable. In its milder form, these manifestations may be called Oppositional, Defiant Disorder (ODD).

They may show severe disobedience, defiant and provocative behaviour, frequent and severe temper tantrums, labile mood swings etc. Some of them have a tendency to truant from school, or run away from home. Many of them have the habit of lying or stealing. Frequent fights and bullying make them terrors at school. In truth, these children have abysmally low self–esteem and enormous frustration. They *externalize* these as Conduct Disorders. Effective management of their behaviour problems centres on identifying and openly nurturing their positive qualities.

Often it turns out that these children perform very poorly in class. Remedial help in their academic work and subsequent better performance usually resolves their behaviour problems.

Category (3): Emotional Disorders

Children with these disorders *internalize* their pangs and pains which then manifest as Anxiety or Depression. Most Emotional Disorders are stress related. The children with LD are obviously under chronic stress—stress to perform.

Anxiety Disorders constitute the major category in this group of disorders.

The stress of performance in class can give rise to fear of school and the refusal to start out in the morning. These children develop repeated physical symptoms of Anxiety, like nausea, vomiting, stomachache, headache etc. Younger children may express their distress as screaming and wailing or temper tantrums. If a child shows persistent school refusal, it is worthwhile to check if he has Learning Disorder.

Children with learning problems may experience persistent Anxiety. This affects their performance and sets up a vicious cycle. Although Anxiety is a Psychological disturbance, it produces a great number of corresponding Physical symptoms. The Psychological component is a constant feeling of apprehension — a feeling of weight on the chest. But Children mostly manifest only the physical symptoms which are distressing and therefore easily recognizable. These physical symptoms may be grouped under three headings:

1. Muscle Tension Increase

(*a*) Trembling, Feeling shaky
(*b*) Aches and pains (Headache, backache, chestpain etc.)
(*c*) Fidgettiness, Restlessness
(*d*) Easy fatiguability

2. *Symptoms of Internal Organ Dysfunction*

(*a*) Palpitations (Heart beating fast and hard)
(*b*) Breathlessness/sighing/choking sensation in the chest
(*c*) Dry mouth
(*d*) Blurring of vision
(*e*) Increased sweating esp. palms/soles
(*f*) Dizziness
(*g*) Sense of 'lump in the throat'.
(*h*) Nausea, 'Butterflies in the stomach', 'Gas' problems
(*i*) Frequent urination
(*j*) Tingling/numbness/burning sensation of hands and legs etc.

3. *Symptoms of Vigilance*

(*a*) Feeling keyed up, listless, wound up
(*b*) Loss of concentration
(*c*) Mind 'going blank' due to anxiety (e.g: in exams)
(*d*) Irritability
(*e*) Problems of sleep etc.

Phobia is a type of Anxiety Disorder, but specific to an activity or situation like the examination. Children when faced with that activity or situation can suffer from a frightening panic attack which may produce all physical symptoms of anxiety described above. Social phobia which is a fear of facing social situations such as the class or the assembly is very common among LD children. When these children have an inherent problem to read, asking them to read aloud in the class can be petrifying. Phobia for examination generates severe anxiety in the children, once the exam time table is announced.

These children need to be handled with understanding and 'desensitized' gradually to enable them to comfortably face the phobic situations.

Anxiety is the commonest human emotion. It is abnormal only when it interferes with the child's day-to-day functioning. The Psychological symptoms of Anxiety and Phobia need to be managed through Counseling and Reassurance. The Physical symptoms, when necessary, can be effectively blocked off by the discriminate use of behaviour therapy and medications.

Depression is a mood disorder which many children especially those with learning problems, suffer from. It may be periodic, or often continuous. Children with depression are usually withdrawn and do not undertake pleasurable activities. Games and play are inhibited. They have poor attention and concentration and may seem to be brooding or day-dreaming. They do get recurrent thoughts of unworthiness and pessimism. Some of them are led to tears easily. Sleep may be disturbed, and many of them may appear drowsy in class. Depressed children eat poorly and fatigue very easily. Lack of self-confidence, feelings of guilt and some times suicidal thoughts are characteristic of depression. Irritability and tantrums may often be symptoms of depression in children.

Obsessive Disorders have in our experience a special significance in children with Learning Disorders. Children with Obsessive Disorders have a need for perfectionism. They may need to arrange and rearrange their tables, check and recheck their answers, or clean and wash again and again. These children may be stubborn and excessively fussy about neatness, orderliness and sameness. If some one disturbs their stack of books, they may get into a rage. Obsessive children may not allow others to handle or share or touch their belongings. They may be perfectly–behaved children outside their homes, but inside they may express unbelievable rage when frustrated.

They are meticulous and mostly hardworking. Driven by their obsessive need for perfection, they prepare for examinations well in advance. Unfortunately, this group of children also has the risk of giving up too soon when faced with stress. If, for instance, the revision schedule for the oncoming examination has not been completed perfectly, some of the obsessives panic the night before, and quickly give up.

Another group of obsessive children is afflicted by a slowness which is morbid. To get them started off to school in the morning is a major task for the mother, having to push them from one morning–chore to another. Some of them are obsessive procrastinators, deferring a duty from one day to another.

The past years of working with LD children have clearly shown that a great number of them have disturbing obsessive behaviour. These children tend to be defensive and secretive. It is therefore worthwhile to deliberately look for these symptoms in the perfectionisitic LD children. It is important to identify Obsessive Disorders early, because it is eminently treatable with combinations of medications and behaviour therapy.

Some LD children suffer from **Tic Disorders.** These disorders in children manifest as involuntary, rapid tics, Muscular or Vocal. The common tics are eye-blinking, neck-jerking, shoulder-shrugging or facial grimacing. If worse, child may hit himself, or poke his neighbour impulsively. The vocal tics are throat clearing, grunting, snorting, sniffing, hissing etc. These tics are the result of certain brain disturbances and are treatable with medications.

Self esteem is one of the strongest pre-requisites for successful performance. LD children who fail repeatedly obviously lose their self-esteem. This gives rise to secondary Emotional and Behaviour problems.

Children with low self-esteem are extremely sensitive about discussions on their studies and tend to get angry or start crying. Slowly they develop an aversion to studies, causing distress in the teachers and parents. In view of the importance of self-esteem in Human Excellence, this is discussed in detail in another chapter.

Conclusion

A broad awareness of the existence of these Emotional and Behaviour disorders in children enables the Teacher to identify the symptoms early enough. Giving these disorders a name facilitates Early Intervention. In severe cases, parents need to be notified to convince them about the need for a detailed Multidisciplinary evaluation and further management. Management of these disorders by informed, unbiased teachers, parents and professionals invariably enhances academic performance.

KINDS OF MEDICATIONS REQUIRED TO HELP CHILDREN WITH POOR SCHOOL PERFORMANCE

When we go back to the Flow Chart on the causes of Poor School Performance, it is possible to find a list of Neurological and Neuropsychological Disorders including Attention Deficit Hyperactivity Disorders (ADHD) which are amenable to the use of time tested medications.

In the West, Attention Deficit Hyperactivity Disorder (ADHD) is a condition for which cerebral stimulants have been used with very high rates of success. In children who have ADHD and Learning Disorders, the treatment of ADHD dramatically improves Educational Performance. Children who have spells of altered consciousness lasting for a few seconds, but occurring tens of times during the day ('Absence Attacks') are usually blamed by Teachers for 'daydreaming'. This is a common type of Seizure Disorder in children which responds completely to treatment.

We are familiar with children who have Multiple (Muscle) Tics like eyeblinking, winking, twitching of lips, face etc. as well as vocal tics like sniffing, grunting or even howling noises. Neither teachers nor parents recognize this as a Neurological Disorder which can be easily treated with medications. Unfortunately these poor children go on to become the butt of many jokes in their class with various nicknames.

Children with or without Learning Disorders who have fear of going to school manifest Anxiety with various bodily symptoms. When a child complains of headache or legpain, stomachache or vomiting, he is not pretending to be sick; he genuinely suffers from an Anxiety induced symptom. We often ridicule the child without recognizing this, little realizing that Medications and Counseling together can stop these symptoms.

Other Emotional Disorders including Obsessive symptoms, Anxiety or Depression need a Multidisciplinary management. For some of these, medicines used judiciously become a handy tool.

What You Need to Know About Medications

We lean heavily on two books to apprise readers about the use of medications. Both are books written by Special Educators on poorly-performing children—by Elaine K. Mc Evan and Sandra F. Rief. They are both strong advocates for the sensible use of medications.

Medication is only one of the interventions for improving a child's ability to function and succeed in school. However, medications can make a significant difference in the lives of children with treatable disorders. To quote Sandra F. Rief, "Over years of working with children with ADHD, I have witnessed children improve dramatically once their physician prescribed and regulated the proper medication and dosage". Elaine Mc Evan writes, "The medicine has worked wonderfully. There is a night and day difference with Rachael. She likes school again this year...."

Whether to use medications or not in children on long-term may be one of the most difficult decisions facing parents as well as concerned doctors.

It should be left to the parents and physicians whether the child receives medical treatment. While parents would not refuse insulin for a diabetic child, they may feel differently about medications for Poor School Performance, whatever be the cause. Parents often feel fearful and guilty for administering medication on long-term for children.

However, scientific knowledge today enables the safe use of medications. The popular resistance to medications is often based on myths and old wives' tales. The best advice to give the parents is to ask them to become informed based on scientific material, before a decision is made on medications. Once that decision is made, personal judgements about the 'rights' or 'wrongs' of medications should not become an issue. The child taking medications may need the support of the teacher and the school. Without the right kind of support and optimal changes in the child's school and home environment, these medications don't work either.

Misconceptions that medications prescribed for these purposes are sleeping pills, and may make children sleep, or that they may turn children into zombies or stunt their growth etc. may affect decision making. This kind of stigma can be removed only with knowledge, and parents therefore need to discuss the issue of medications with the child's informed physician.

Children who are on medications need regular periodic follow–up with their doctor. The doctor needs to be in touch with the Team members supporting the child with Remedial Teaching. Teachers also need to provide the physician with appropriate inputs and observations about the child and voice any concerns that they might have about medications. The physician may choose the type and dosage of medications based on these observations of the child's actual functioning.

Conclusion

Medications do not 'control' the child. Medications are not a 'cure'. They help to filter out distractions allowing the child to concentrate. Medicines diminish impulsivity and inhibit overactivity, helping the child to sit down and perform better.

Though medications are best suited for ADHD, this option is also available for Tics, Obsessive Disorders, Anxiety, Phobia, Depression, various bodily symptoms produced through anxiety etc.

Medications are effective when chosen correctly and combined with Educational Strategies specific to the child. Behavioural Modification techniques, Parental Awareness, Remedial Training and Counselling for the child, and Management of the child's environment should be resorted to. Pharmacological support, when required, is only one of the multiple strategies that are put in place for a child with learning problems.

HELP AND SUPPORT FOR CHILDREN WITH POOR SCHOOL PERFORMANCE

Once a child starts struggling with his studies, the school environment turns 'hostile' to him. Teachers scold or punish him, and peers joke about him. The young child is clueless as to why he cannot score like his classmates, in spite of effort. He reacts to all this the way children do-either turn defiant and fight back, or swallow the insults and give up.

A sensitive Teacher, sensitised to the various causes of poor school performance can turn out to be his saviour and guardian angel. She can identify the cause of this particular child's failure and institute an appropriate remedial strategy.

Early identification and remediation of Learning Disorders can prevent accumulation of problems ending in failure and frustration. A child who is told of his academic problems in simple terms by a sensitised teacher can then stop cursing himself for the failures. Identifying a 'guardian angel' in a teacher who understands his problems helps him to keep trying, even if he totters and trips.

A child with Learning problems cannot function successfully in school without adequate support from his teachers, parents and peers. The sheer force of numbers of children doing poorly in school—one fourth of any school—persuades us that help must reach these children in a General Classroom itself.

This Inclusive Classroom environment must be non-threatening and non-ridiculing ("Do no harm") for the LD child with Special Educational Needs. A supportive atmosphere enables the child to 'believe in himself'. This enhances his self-esteem.

Enhancing Self-Esteem

It is Self-esteem that drives any child for endeavour, even if the path of duty does not lead to glory. The will to struggle on this path of *'incessant, desireless action'* gives the child the confidence and courage even to fail.

Self-esteem helps us to seek and find our strengths, talents and potential. Every child struggling with his academic work has other strengths, talents and potential. Only a sensitive teacher can help him to discover them so that he can set realistic academic and life-goals, to help him grow into a self-confident and self-reliant adult.

Therefore, it is realised today that the most important support that an LD child can receive at school is enhancement of Self-esteem. Hence the inclusion of this (non-technical) chapter in this handbook.

The deficits in Academic skills impose limitations on the LD child's performance. The problem is further compounded in these children who may also suffer from Social Skill Deficits. Children compare themselves to their peers form an early age. LD children soon realise that they face hurdles that other children obviously do not. However, children receiving support at school devise successful mechanisms for maintaining their self-esteem despite their difficulties by using their other talents and strengths. Self-esteem is crucial for their survival against odds.

Learning Difficulties
↓
Diagnosed and Remediated
↓
Improved Academic Performance
↓
Taste of Success
↓
Resolution of Emotional Problems
↓
Resolution of Rejection and Frustration
↓
'Belief in Himeself'
↓
Enhanced Self-esteem

If children have faith in themselves, they relentlessly pursue the activities that they have to carry out. If not they give up, eroding their self-esteem. Low self-esteem takes away the motivation to study. This leads to further failure, causing the vicious cycle of failure. Children caught in this vicious cycle try to evade failure by avoiding challenges.

The response of avoiding or facing challenges has important implications for the LD children's future. Children with good self-esteem cope successfully with life, even if their Academic skills are poor.

Role of Teachers

It is pivotal to start by accepting the child as he is, with all his skill deficits. The concern and respect for him as a person should not be contingent upon his achievement. Emphasise a little more on the child's positive attitudes, even on his quality to smile. Give him plenty of praise openly for his efforts and endeavour, instead of performance. Of course, make it clear what he is being praised for—for instance, "You've made a good attempt at reading".

Encourage the child to set realistic goals so that he can taste a bit of success. It is equally important to help the child evaluate his achievement without being too critical of himself. If the child is about to attempt a task too difficult for him, guide him tactfully to a more suitable activity.

The child needs to be taught to praise himself. If he makes some achievement, do ask him, "How do you think you fared?" or "Are you pleased with the spelling of these words now?". He must also be taught to praise others for their good work. Only a Teacher who is pleasant and positive can teach this, seeing "the glass as half-full".

Spend 'quality time' with the child when you can. Give the child attention in a way that he too feels special, in a way that will add to his self-esteem. This can be done even as you pass him on the corridor.

Little things to improve his confidence must come naturally to teachers. Help him make a little choice—like the book to be taken from the library. Admire his choices. Praise his attempts at self-sufficiency. Create opportunities for him to learn self-reliance—in projects he can lead or execute, in monitoring the class for sometime etc.

LD Child in the General Classroom

Supporting an LD child in the classroom depends on the nature and severity of his skill deficits. A lot of general help is, however, always possible.

- Seat the LD children at the front of the class to enable some personal teaching in proximity. These children learn better under your nose.
- Make the child listen to the lesson being read out as an effective strategy for comprehension and retention.
- Give positive feedback and constant encouragement, without drawing undue attention on the pupil.
- Help the pupil to develop effective study skills and personalised learning strategies with one-to-one teaching.

- Unobtrusively check if note-taking and copying have been done efficiently.
- Encourage 'peer support'. An efficient, helping friend can do some 'peer tutoring' which will help both. This also makes the class environment supportive and positive.
- An informal and innovative Teacher can devise many other means of helping a child with Special Educational Needs.

Nevertheless, some of these children may require extra help from a Special Teacher in the Resource Room (RR).

The Resource Room (RR)

It is a special room where the child with Special Educational Needs (enrolled in the regular mainstream class) goes only for special instruction. A Specialist Teacher—Special Educator is available there to help the child during the short periods away from his regular class.

A Resource Room with its trained personnel and infrastructure is not only desirable but essential in every regular school.

- Unlike the popular notion, it is inexpensive to set up and maintain. A properly trained teacher can start the ball rolling.
- Even if 10 per cent of the school population has Special Educational Needs, the number of children that may require special help is enormous.
- Problems are varied and the syllabus too heavy, making it difficult for the class teacher to cater to all these children in the regular classrooms.
- Curriculum-based Remediation is most beneficial in our educational system, and is best provided in the Inclusive schools.
- The class teacher knows the child the best; She must keep herself informed about special support strategies that can benefit every LD child in her class.

There must be co-operation and co-ordination among the Class Teacher, Subject Teachers and the Special Teacher. The regular classroom teachers should be clearly informed about the status of the children attending the Resource Room (RR). Skills that are taught in the RR should be informed to the regular teachers. Learning Strategies which can be used in the regular classroom must be communicated to the subject teachers from time-to-time, so that continuity in the remedial programmes is maintained. A full-time Co-ordinator who may be a trained person needs to be in charge of this function. The same Co-ordinator can also liaison with the child's parents, School Counsellor, outside Professionals and Doctors, the School administration and the Education Board, as and when necessary.

The School Counsellor also may need to know every child in the school with Special Educational Needs, and must function in tandem with the Specialist Teacher and Co-ordinator.

In order to avoid any stigma about the Resource Room and its environment, it is advisable that the Specialist Teachers and Co-ordinator also function as mainstream subject teachers in regular classrooms. This helps better integration of the children with Special Educational Needs.

Other regular teachers should never look at the Resource Room as a 'dumping ground' for poor performers. We have heard stories of children with LD being told in the open class, "If you don't perform better in the next test, I will have you sent to the Resource Room!" On the contrary, the subject teachers need to see the Resource Room as an essential and proud extension of the regular classroom—from which children who use and even those who do not use it regularly can benefit. Even the teachers can benefit by picking up effective teaching strategies.

Working of a Resource Room

A regular classroom with the essential teaching materials like a blackboard, books, cupboards, bulletin boards etc. will suffice. Specially created Worksheets, Flashcards, Educational games, Graded Readers, writing material and Teaching Aids to suit the needs of each type of learning difficulties need to be stored.

Parental consent, individual files and careful documentation about each child attending the resource room are pre-requisites.

Scheduling of the Resource Room

The Specialist Teacher and the Class teachers need to co-ordinate the hours when the child receives help in the resource room. Care must be given not to pull the child out of activities that give him fulfillment and self-esteem, like sports or music in which he is doing well. Teachers should objectively demarcate the subjects and areas that the child must receive inputs in the RR. For instance, if a child of the III grade is functioning at I grade in Maths in the RR evaluation of skill deficits, he receives his Maths instruction in the Resource Room.

Individual Education Programme (IEP)

For effective remediation, every child receiving help in the Resource Room should have a detailed plan which describes the skill deficit areas, the strengths of the child, and the areas to be worked on. IEP refers to instruction that enables the student to work on appropriate tasks or content over time, under conditions that motivate. It outlines the 'plan' (outcomes, curriculum, teacher, responsibility, schedule and settings) that facilitate instruction. It does not imply that each student should receive one-to-one instruction. It means that students receive instruction tailored according to each one's needs. Various instructional arrangements can be opted; small groups, peer teaching, large groups etc.

Components of Integrated Education Programme

Levels of performance: What grade does the child function at, with respect to the Academic skills of Reading, Writing, Spelling, Maths etc. What skill does the child possess, what are his deficits, and what are his strengths.

Short-term goals: They must be described in specific measurable terms as goals to be achieved for a shorter duration. Achievement of short-term goals will lead to successful achievement of the annual goals.

Annual goals: These are what the child should achieve for the particular academic year, comprising the entire spectrum of short-term objectives in each specified area.

Professional Support

Children with Learning Disorders require professional support in terms of Assessment, Diagnostic and Guidance services. Assessment and Guidance services give the child and parents the necessary guidance to cope with the Learning Disorders. This needs the involvement of a Multidisciplinary team doing this type of work.

Provisions

The various Educational Boards, with pioneering efforts from the CBSE, have given several provisions to compensate for the specific handicaps of children with SEN in their examinations. Teachers have to familiarize themselves with these special provisions which can benefit seriously-handicapped children with Special Educational Needs.

Conclusion

It is evident that children with Special Needs require extra effort to optimize their performance. This support needs to be both Educational and Emotional. It is only the Teacher who can facilitate this Emotional component to make the environment encouraging and friendly. Children with Special Needs will yearn to flourish in the warmth of that environment, instead of feeling repelled.

The objective of this chapter is to highlight this aspect in the background of the Comprehensive Support that these children need at School—to ensure 'Education for All'.

REQUIRED SUPPORT STRATEGIES FOR CHILDREN HAVING EMOTIONAL AND BEHAVIOUR PROBLEMS

Emotional and Behaviour problems as enumerated in the previous chapter are common in children with Learning Disorders. Most often, the behavioural disorders in such children may be more distressing than the Learning Disorders. In such cases, the management of disorders co-existing with the Learning Disorder becomes the priority. Children are observed to cope better with Academic skills when the Emotional and Behaviour disorders are resolved appropriately.

Handling such children is a challenge for the Teacher. Co-existence of Emotional Disorders with Learning Disorders significantly affects the child's Behaviour, Social skills, Self-esteem as well as Learning. This means that various facets of the child's life are affected. Therefore, a Multidisciplinary Approach that includes: (*a*) Emotional, (*b*) Behavioural, (*c*) Academic, (*d*) Family, and (*e*) Pharmacological Strategies is called for to manage these Disorders.

Teacher Observation and Diagnosis

In order to arrive at a comprehensive management plan, a precise diagnosis is necessary. An observant teacher is an important facilitator in the diagnostic process, providing information.

The teacher would be able to identify children with suspected problems like ADHD, Anxiety or Tics (refer to symptoms in the previous chapter), once she has made such observations.

She may discuss her observations with her colleagues and also ask for their observations. Wherever a School Counsellor trained in Developmental Disorders is accessible, she can also contribute. Once the teacher has enough information to suspect that the child may be having a Disorder, a discussion must be held with the parents to get additional information from them. This also gives the teacher an opportunity to apprise the parents about a possible problem.

In many cases, the Teacher can attempt intervention in the classroom. If it *proves to be successful,* the intervention may be continued and the progress reviewed periodically. If a Specialist evaluation is necessary, the child must be directed after consulting his parents.

If the intervention in the classroom by the teacher *does not prove successful,* the parents need to be apprised of the need for a Comprehensive assessment. A detailed evaluation by the Specialists makes it possible to co-ordinate with the parents and concerned teachers, and to institute appropriate management strategies for each individual child.

Management Strategies

Understanding the disorders, and the willingness to make thorough changes in the approach to them are keys to the successful handling of children with Emotional disorders. A comprehensive management plan includes the simultaneous use of all strategies described below.

The Management Strategies discussed here are those used for handling children with Attention Deficit Hyperactivity Disorder as a prototype. This can be applied to children with the other disorders too.

(*a*) *Emotional Support Strategies:* A child with emotional and behaviour disorders is often rejected by peers or blamed as 'unmanageable' for no fault of his. His Self-esteem gets significantly eroded and this further affects his behaviour and learning.

Accept the child with his limitations. Avoid gatherings where the child is bound to get into trouble. Never lose an opportunity to give the child some positive strokes. Ignoring his negative behaviour, enable him to thrive on positive reinforcement. Work on the child's self-esteem as the major strategy by praising him for his effort.

(*b*) *Behaviour Support Strategies:* Behavioural problems appear to be more when children are undirected. Well organized and carefully planned behaviour support strategies can help children with Attention Deficit Disorders to cope better with the problem.

'Limit setting' to curb disruptive behaviour is the master plan to manage behaviour problems of a child with Attention Deficit Disorders.

Clarity of expectations is a critical factor in preventing disruptive behaviour. The child needs to be verbally told as to what is acceptable and what is not acceptable (e.g: "You are to remain in the classroom till the bell rings. Your are not to leave the class before the bell rings"). He needs to have a *structure* provided for him through *clear communication, expectations, rules, consequences and follow-up for every activity.* This applies both to the classroom and home situation. (Teach your expectations for materials that are required in the classroom—sharpened pencils, erasers, note books, paper etc. If the student comes to the class unprepared, give him a strong negative stroke. This will show the seriousness of expectations).

Rules need to be taught for the classroom and home situations. Rules should be clear, comprehensive and stated in a positive fashion. (e.g: 'walk on the corridor', rather than 'Do not run on the corridor'). Rules and their rationale need to be reviewed; consequences of infringement should be explained. Consistent firmness is the key.

Positive reinforcement is the best behaviour strategy that builds self-esteem and respect. There is no substitute for positive reinforcement. Spot the student who does what you expect to be done. Reward the student by praising specific instances (e.g: "I like the way Vishnu remembers to raise his hands and wait for his turn"), giving privileges (e.g: classroom jobs and responsibilities), and providing tangible rewards (e.g: stickers, sweets).

'Time-outs' and 'Time-aways' are very effective disciplinary methods which may be necessary for children with Attention Deficit Disorders. This refers to the removal of the child for a specific and relatively short period from a situation that is enjoyable for him and full of positive reinforcement, to a much less pleasant situation. 'Time-out' is a wonderful alternative to scolding or spanking a young child. Asking the child to stand in a corner of a classroom for his negative behaviour during an enjoyable session teaches him self-control. Time-outs should not be overused. The child has to be clearly told about the behaviour that caused him to receive the Time-out.

A child with ADHD and LD cannot handle all of the stimulation in the classroom continuously. He may become worked up and lose control over himself. Time-away from the group may be needed to calm him down and help him regain self-control. It is an excellent way to remove a child from a potentially explosive situation. A child who becomes disruptive in the classroom may be sent, for e.g. to the staff-room to work on a short assignment.

Use of the above methods discriminately is seen to be very effective to introduce firmness and discipline in dealing with children with Disruptive Behaviour Disorders. However, indiscriminate use of these in the cases of emotional disorders like Anxiety or Depression (Internalizing Disorders) may become counter productive.

Proximity control is found to be essential for the child with ADHD. Staying close to the child with attention or behaviour problems is useful. He should be seated close to the teacher or between children with good attention, avoiding a seat near doors, windows or other distractions.

It is important to discuss the specific behaviour problems of the child calmly and across the table, emphasising on his positive qualities. Concerns about the child must also be discussed with his parents in the same vein.

It is crucial for all teachers and the same teacher to apply *consistency* in the behavioural strategies towards the child in question. Being punitive for a disruptive behaviour on one occasion and condescending about the same at another, can only confuse the child.

(*c*) *Academic Support Strategies:* The most important pre-requisite for improving academic skills in children ADD/ADHD include working on (*i*) Attention Enhancement and (*ii*) Organisational skills.

(*i*) *Attention Enhancement:* It is important to rule out Learning Disorder (LD). Presence of LD may require use of additional management strategies. A child with Attention Deficit Disorder needs help to focus and maintain Attention. For instance, this may require a technique of signalling to the child. The teacher may raise one hand to signal the young child to raise hands; she may make a loud command followed by a short silence before proceeding in a normal tone to give directions. The child with Attention Deficits needs training to maintain eye-contact while speaking, especially when instructions are given. Use of short and simple sentences is easier for the child to listen to. Insist on an immediate feedback from the child in order to know how much he has understood.

Use of Multisensory Teaching methods is of great use. A child learns best through auditory, visual, tactile and kinesthetic modalities; combinations of these methods are found to be more useful to sustain attention.

Use of visual aids, or a picture on the board or the overhead projector may hold attention better. Use of colours to highlight on the chalkboard or in the written work can help. Every innovative method to enhance attention improves the child's academic skills and performance.

(*ii*) *Organizational skills:* A vital skill area for optimal academic performance is that of organisational and study skills. Unfortunately, this is an aspect which is overlooked by most educators. It is important to realise that deficits in these areas produce significant problems in the child's performance. Therefore, it is imperative to formally impart assistance and training in organisational and study skills to the child in need.

Time management is a major hurdle for these children. This skill needs to be specifically taught. Practical training to prioritize the daily work, manage the daily class and home assignments, finish the written exam within the given time etc. needs to be imparted.

The child can be taught to record assignments with the use of assignment calendars and diaries. Teacher can check to see if the assignment calendars are complete. The child may be helped to write a 'things-to-do' list for every assignment. Such 'things-to-do'/'things to take' lists serve as an effective organizer. The tasks which are covered or completed can be crossed off. Markers/stickers or book marks to locate pages are always helpful.

The disorganized child must be taught to 'avoid clutter' on desks. He should be guided to keep as little as possible on the desktops. Time must be set aside to sort and clean out the desks and note books. A child with severe problems in organization may need an adult or peer to help him sort and dump unnecessary papers periodically. Organising study material and notes and arranging them in different files help remove a lot of chaos. Finding what he needs quickly is a major pre-requisite to starting his work.

Help the child to split major projects into small segments. Discuss about time frames and sequences for each segment.

Constant assistance and supervision, checking and rechecking and teaching these children to do the same, builds organisational skills by practice.

(*d*) *Family Support Strategies:* Coping with a hard-to-manage child is difficult, be it in the classroom or home. Unless intervention in the classroom extends harmoniously into the home, the child may even get worse. It is therefore, important to be in constant communication with the parents.

Parents are likely to deny the child's problems initially. Some parents may be punitive and may even abuse the child. Over-involvement, sometimes amounting to interference with the classroom strategies, is a response from certain parents. Parental undercutting, leading to one parent being critical and the other condescending, can be a major problem. This one-up-manship leads to serious inconsistency in the child's disciplining.

Saying 'no' to the child's demand in the morning and 'changing it to 'yes' by afternoon following his tantrum is a pattern that many parents in this generation follow. Children of such parents develop very poor frustration tolerance and they aggressively demand instant gratification of their pleasure needs.

Support for the child with an educational problem, therefore, also calls for correcting these parenting patterns with firmness and perseverance.

Extending support for the child into his home also involves adequate information and guidance being given to the parents about the child's skill deficits and remediation. Parents need to be realistic about the slow pace of progress, failing which they are likely to get frustrated. Patience is a great virtue to be cultivated by parents and teachers of children with Special Needs.

(*e*) *Pharmacological (Medical) Support Strategies:* This is a strategy which needs serious consideration in many cases. It is now recognized that many children with various Developmental Disorders have problems which cannot be managed only by the strategies described above. Such cases may benefit a great deal by the discerning use of medications by informed physicians. However, this is an intervention which parents of the child alone can decide on. It is to be understood that this is a modality which is not the anchor of management, but only an adjunct in the comprehensive management plan for the child.

Conclusion

The objective of this chapter is to convey the concept of a Comprehensive management for poor school performance. Dealing only with the academic and educational skill deficits of the child does not consider the issue of *'Human Excellence'*. The child as a human being cannot deal with his academic problems compartmentally. Addressing and resolving his Emotional and Behavioural problems are decisive for his overall well-being and consequent school performance.

PARTNERSHIP WITH PARENTS FOR IMPROVING POOR SCHOOL PERFORMANCE

Learning Disorder is permanent and cannot be prevented or cured; once an LD, always an LD. Consequently these children need long-term support, which can be frustrating and taxing for parents. Beyond school, nevertheless, these children can become successful performers in life provided the school and parents together can discover their talents and nurture them.

Parents play a crucial role in the education of the child with Special Needs. The parent is the child's first and best tutor, if there is emotional commitment. Studies show that children of parents who display interest in their school work and academic success show much greater progress than whose parents are less involved.

It is in this background that parents need to be roped in as partners to work with the school to help the child face his educational difficulties. It is initially difficult for the parents to accept the child's deficits. It then becomes the responsibility of the school to provide parents enough information on the disorders so that they can identify the child's problems and accept him as he is, with his strengths and weaknesses. It is the non-judgemental, unconditional respect and love from the parents that helps the child to evolve into a self-reliant personality.

It is the duty of the sensitized teacher to incorporate the help of the parents to work with the child with Special Needs. The inputs at school and at home should be uniform and complementary. Two areas that are important are:

(*a*) *Self-esteem:* The Self-esteem that the school deliberately generates in the child should not be wiped out by the reprimanding parent at home. The encouragement of independence, self-reliance and responsibility given at school leading to better self-esteem should be continued at home too. It should not be marred by comparisons with siblings or cousins at home. With appropriate participatory inputs from school, the home environment also can become supportive and positive.

(*b*) *Organisation:* Schedules and routines of the child at school and home should be a continuum. The day-to-day activities and study schedule can be worked out at school with the involvement of the parents.
Checklists of things to be taken to school, daily homework, projects, messages etc. can also be worked out with parental participation. A daily diary of this sort generates accountability in the parents. Organizing lessons, simplifying their content, organizing his study materials etc. should have parental participation at home. Proximity control is an essential ingredient of assistance in Learning Strategies even at home. The parents must make sure that the LD child is provided a distraction free environment and a clutter free space for his work at home.

Attributes of Participatory Parents

Working Together

Informed parents maintain a good relationship with school and the teachers who come in contact with the child. Some parents can suggest to the school, ways in which their child can be helped in school. Reading out the question paper during exams or relaxing the ordeal of copying notes are provisions that the parents may request for. Pragmatic parents remember that there is little gain in confronting the teacher if they feel frustrated about an apparent lack of progress. The best way forward for an LD child is through an effective 'Home—School Partnership'.

Patience and Perservance

A child with Developmental Disorders may be slow or clumsy and may need help. He may take longer to learn to do things. Parents need to be taught to show patience and never to give up. They will need to repeat the processes of teaching the child without losing temper, and without being negative.

Awareness and Advocacy

If the parents are not on the child's side, who else will be ? The best that a parent can do for the child with Special Needs is to become informed and aware about the child's condition. The parents should also become aware of their child's particular difficulties. This may need a great amount of communication with the teachers. Awareness also stops the parents from making comparisons with others in the family or at school. It helps them to build on his strengths and skills. Awareness encourages them to praise his little successes and perseverence. Advocacy helps them to talk to parents of similar children and create support groups. The right of children with Special Needs can be secured only through advocacy. It can stop others from teasing or bullying their children with handicaps.

Support for Themselves

Caring for a child with LD can be frustrating because of poor progress despite hardwork. A teacher who has an empathic relationship with the parents can keep them going. The school can share with them experiences of other parents and encourage them by talking to them about their child's accomplishments at school. Teachers can also share with the parents Specialised Teaching Strategies, Books, Reading Materials etc. In this process of partnership, it is the child with the Special Needs who benefits.

Conclusion

The school's partnership with parents ultimately brings benefit to any child by making the school-years a pleasant experience. Parents of children with Special Needs have a greater role to play by being active participants rather than passive consultants. This role for the parents is possible only if the school is pro-active.

3

Education of Children with Behavioural, Emotional and Social Difficulties: Model Guidelines

INTRODUCTION

This guidance is not a definitive interpretation of the law. Interpreting the law is a matter for the courts alone. This guidance is not statutory: it explains some legal duties and powers and it gives good practice advice. However, some of the guidance it quotes (e.g. the SEN Code of Practice) is statutory guidance, to which schools, early years settings and local authorities must have regard.

This guidance on the education of children and young people with behavioural, emotional and social difficulties (BESD) as a special educational need updates and replaces DfEE Circular 9/94 and DH Circular LAC (94) *The Education of Children with Emotional and Behavioural Difficulties,* with the exception of paragraphs 73-76 and 78-101. These paragraphs provide guidance on the use of residential provision and need to be read in the context of the current statutory framework.

The purpose of this guidance is to bring together existing advice on improving achievement, health and emotional well-being for those children and young people whose behavioural, emotional and social difficulties are persistent and provide an obstacle to their learning. The guidance also advises schools and early years settings on how to avoid discrimination against disabled children and young people.

This guidance has been prepared in the context of legislation including the Education Act 1996 (as amended), the Disability Discrimination Act 1995 (DDA) and the Disability Discrimination Act 2005, the Childcare Act 2006, the Special Educational Needs (SEN) Code of Practice and other guidance from the Department.

Children and young people with BESD can miss out on opportunities that others take for granted because they do not always get the support they need. The Children Act 2004 provides a statutory framework for cooperation between local authorities (LAs) and partner agencies to improve the five *Every Child Matters* outcomes for all children and young people in their area—including those with BESD as a special educational need:

- be healthy
- stay safe
- enjoy and achieve
- make a positive contribution
- achieve economic well-being

This guidance is intended to help schools, early years settings and local authorities consider what support and provision are most likely to help remove barriers to achievement, health and emotional well-being for those whose behavioural, emotional and social difficulties are persistent. This guidance does not provide advice on behaviour within the range of what might be generally expected for a particular age, nor does it focus on the needs of children and young people with serious mental health problems or those whose behaviour is so disturbing or dangerous that a secure setting is likely to be indicated.

This guidance has been produced in response to the first recommendation in the *Learning Behaviour* report (2005) of the Practitioners' Group on School Behaviour and Discipline chaired by Sir Alan Steer—which said that the Department "should look separately at how to improve the quality of provision for those with behavioural, emotional and social difficulties (BESD), in particular the recruitment and retention of high quality staff and minimising bureaucracy".

This guidance also draws on the Department's guidance *Promoting Children's Mental Health within Early Years and School Settings*. This provides a useful tool for local authorities, schools and others striving to ensure that the mental health needs of children are met, and that all children enjoy a positive school experience.

MEANING

The Education Act 1996 says that a child has special educational needs if he or she has a learning difficulty which calls for special educational provision to be made for him or her. Special educational provision is provision that is additional to or otherwise different from that normally available in the area to children of the same age.

The Special Educational Needs (SEN) Code of Practice (2001) provides guidance on the SEN duties, guidance to which schools, local authorities and others working with them must have regard. The Code sets out four areas of SEN:

- Cognition and Learning
- Behavioural, Emotional and Social Development
- Communication and Interaction
- Sensory and/or Physical Needs

The SEN Code of Practice, at paragraph 7:60 describes BESD as a learning difficulty where children and young people demonstrate features of emotional and behavioural difficulties such as: being withdrawn or isolated, disruptive and disturbing; being hyperactive and lacking concentration; having immature social skills; or presenting challenging behaviours arising from other complex special needs. Learning difficulties can arise for children and young people with BESD because their difficulties can affect their ability to cope with school routines and relationships.

The Department's guidance, *Promoting Children's Mental Health within Early Years and School Settings*, explains how teachers and others, working alongside other agencies as appropriate, can promote children and young people's mental health and can intervene effectively with those experiencing problems. It provides case studies of children and young people whose behaviour, social and/or emotional development is causing concern and suggests strategies to address both the presenting behaviour and the underlying causes.

Many children and young people with BESD are also covered by the Disability Discrimination Act 1995 (DDA). There is a broad definition of disability in the DDA: someone has a disability if they have *'a mental or physical impairment that has a long-term and substantial adverse effect on their ability to carry out normal day-to-day activities'*. The terms 'long-term' and 'substantial' provide a relatively low threshold and therefore include a significant group of children within the definition. Day-to-day activities are defined in terms of a number of capacities. These include 'memory or ability to concentrate, learn or understand.' The Disability Rights Commission (DRC) Code of Practice for Schools and the then DfES and DRC guidance materials, *Implementing the Disability Discrimination Act in Schools and Early Years settings*, provide guidance on the definition and how it relates to pupils with behavioural, emotional and social difficulties.

Special Educational Needs

Duties in the Education Act 1996 require governing bodies to use their best endeavours to ensure that the necessary provision is made for any pupil who has special educational needs. Paragraph 1:21 in the SEN Code of Practice summarises the statutory duties on governing bodies and the subsequent paragraphs summarise the duties on schools and early years settings.

The Code recognises that each child and young person is unique. Children and young people will have needs and requirements which may fall into one or more of the four areas of SEN and the impact of combinations of needs on their ability to function, learn and succeed should be taken into account.

The term behavioural, emotional and social difficulties (BESD) covers a wide range of SEN. It includes children and young people with emotional disorders, conduct disorders and hyperkinetic disorders (including attention deficit disorder or attention deficit hyperactivity disorder (ADD/ADHD)) and children and young people whose behavioural difficulties may be less obvious, for example, those with anxiety, who self-harm, have school phobia or depression, and those whose behaviour or emotional well-being are seen to be deteriorating.

Whether a child or young person is considered to have BESD depends on a range of factors, including the nature, frequency, persistence, severity and abnormality of the difficulties and their cumulative effect on the child or young person's behaviour and/or emotional well-being compared with what might generally be expected for a particular age.

Initial observation, identification and intervention will often be made by classroom teachers as part of *Quality First* teaching. Special educational needs co-ordinators (SENCOs), local authority advisory and support staff, outreach advisers from special schools, educational psychologists and other specialists such as lead behaviour professionals or behaviour coordinators within schools may all be involved in identifying and supporting children and young people whose needs include BESD.

Pupils with BESD cover the full range of ability. However their difficulties are likely to be a barrier to learning and persist despite the implementation of an effective school behaviour policy and personal and social curriculum. Learning difficulties and behaviour difficulties are often in a two-way relationship with each other. For some pupils, behaviour difficulties may frustrate access to the curriculum, for example if aggressive behaviour leads to exclusion from some classroom activities or from the school. For others, a learning difficulty may lead to or exacerbate behavioural and emotional difficulties, for example, a child who has difficulty in grasping the basics of literacy or numeracy may withdraw from lessons or try to divert attention away from the learning difficulty by disruptive behaviour. Difficulties in acquiring basic skills can also lead to low self-esteem and even depression.

There need not be a medical diagnosis for a child or young person to be identified as having BESD. However, children and young people with a medical diagnosis, including emotional disorders such as depression and eating disorders; conduct disorders such as oppositional defiance disorder (ODD); hyperkinetic disorders including attention deficit disorder or attention deficit hyperactivity disorder (ADD/ ADHD); and syndromes such as Tourette's, are all likely to have BESD, as defined in the SEN Code of Practice. Addressing BESD entails looking at what the child/young person, the school, parents or carers and other agencies might do differently together, in order to reduce the impact of difficulties (whatever their cause) on attainment, health and well-being. A diagnosis may provide pointers for the appropriate strategies to manage and minimise the impact of the condition. Equally, identified difficulties without a diagnosis must also be addressed.

The majority of children and young people with any form of BESD should be considered to have SEN if they require additional or different educational arrangements or interventions from those that are generally offered in a mainstream school. Although it is recognised that there are considerable challenges, children and young people with BESD should be supported in reaching expectations and participating fully in school. As a special educational need, BESD does not prevent children and young people achieving well.

Underlying reasons for BESD can encompass both 'within child' factors and external factors. There is a higher incidence of BESD identified in children with other special educational needs. It is sometimes difficult to discern the main cause of the behavioural or emotional difficulties or to decide whether BESD or another learning difficulty is the primary need. Understanding which is the primary need can help with identifying suitable interventions. The Department's guidance entitled *Promoting Children's Mental Health within Early Years and School Settings* provides advice and case studies on how such understanding can be reached and examples of interventions that can be successful in addressing these difficulties.

Early childhood experiences can have a major impact on later development, with the lack of a positive attachment to an adult being seen as particularly detrimental to some children. Parents are the biggest influence on a child's development. Social circumstances can also impact on development. Children who experience family difficulties, including parental conflict, separation, neglect, indifference or erratic discipline, are more likely to develop BESD.

Disability

Children and young people with SEN may also have a disability under the DDA. A report from the Prime Minister's Strategy Unit estimates that about 7 per cent of the child population may count as having a disability. The Disability Rights Commission Code of Practice for Schools explains that: *'It may not be immediately obvious that a child is disabled. Underachievement and difficult behaviour may, in some cases, indicate an underlying disability which has not yet been identified.'* Schools and early years settings need to be proactive in seeking out information about any underlying disability. This will mean working closely with parents and with children and young people themselves.

Local authorities, schools and early years settings must not discriminate against disabled children and young people. They must not treat disabled children 'less favourably' and they must make reasonable adjustments for them. The reasonable adjustment duty requires settings to think ahead and anticipate disabled children and young people. The Department's materials, *Implementing the DDA in schools and early years settings,* illustrate a wide range of reasonable adjustments for pupils whose disability has an impact on their behaviour.

Identification Rates

Research shows higher rates of BESD in socially deprived areas. Boys are four times more likely than girls to be identified as having BESD. After controlling for socio-economic disadvantage, gender and year group there is significant over-representation of Black Caribbean and Mixed White & Black Caribbean pupils who are around 1½ times more likely to be identified as having BESD than White British pupils. Travellers of Irish Heritage and Gypsy/Roma pupils are over-represented among many categories of SEN, including moderate learning difficulties, severe learning difficulties and BESD. Full details are in the Department's Research Report RR757, *Special Educational Needs and Ethnicity: Issues of Over and Under Representation.*

Some of the factors associated with the over-representation identified in this report included racism and bullying, negative teacher attitudes and, for some pupils, a curriculum perceived as lacking relevance.

Over 60 per cent of children and young people attending Pupil Referral Units (PRUs) have SEN. Many of these children and young people have BESD. Early intervention by early years settings, schools and local authorities should reduce the proportion being referred to PRUs over time. This guidance provides advice on developing a graduated approach to supporting children and young people with BESD, and on developing an appropriate range of provision.

Building Partnerships with Parents and Carers

The SEN Code of Practice (Chapter 2) stresses that partnership with parents plays a key role in identifying and addressing children and young people's SEN and in promoting a culture of cooperation between parents, schools (and other settings), local authorities and other organisations. Equally, for a disabled pupil, the DRC Code of Practice, paragraph 7.9, emphasises the importance of positive relationships with parents. Key to the sharing of information is 'an atmosphere and culture at the school which is open and welcoming, so that pupils and parents feel comfortable about disclosing information about a disability.'

Families are a key influence on a child's intellectual and social, emotional and behavioural development. Parents are usually the experts on their own child, and their knowledge about their child can provide a valuable insight about what works and what is needed. Parents can support the school's work in developing emotional, social and behavioural skills by reinforcing them at home and by helping their child develop insight into their difficulties. Schools should therefore work in partnership with parents, sharing respective insights and strategies.

It will sometimes appear that family dynamics are contributing to a child or young person's difficulties. In these circumstances, a parenting education programme may help parents to set clear and appropriate boundaries, provide social and emotional support and manage behaviour. Educational psychologists, behaviour support specialists, learning mentors, personal advisers or primary mental health workers from child and adolescent mental health service (CAMHS) teams may provide input into such programmes. Family SEAL workshops also help to create a positive family atmosphere by encouraging parents to use the SEAL approach to developing children's social and emotional skills.

Where parenting is identified as a factor contributing to a pupil's BESD, local authorities, school and early years settings may wish to suggest the development of voluntary parenting contracts. Where behaviour is a cause for concern, there is also scope for the local authority or school to apply to the local magistrates' court for a parenting order, if it is judged appropriate to require otherwise reluctant parents to cooperate or to undergo parenting classes. Further information is contained in the Department's *Guidance on Education-Related Parenting Contracts, Parenting Orders and Penalty Notices* (September 2007).

Child Protection

There will be circumstances where it is suspected that there is neglect or abuse at home. In such circumstances, it is essential that early years settings, schools and/or local authority officers bring their concerns to the attention of the local authority's social care services as quickly as possible. It is important for there to be regular training to ensure that all school staff are aware of child protection policies and procedures.

Schools and early years settings are reminded that paragraph 2.123 of the Government's guidance, *Working Together to Safeguard Children*, says that:

> *'Education staff have a crucial role to play in helping identify welfare concerns, and indicators of possible abuse or neglect, at an early stage. They should refer those concerns to the appropriate organisation, normally LA children's social care, contributing to the assessment of a child's needs and, where appropriate, to ongoing action to meet those needs. When a child has special educational needs or is disabled, the school will have important information about the child's level of understanding and the most effective means of communicating with the child. The school will also be well placed to give a view on the impact of treatment or intervention on the child's care or behaviour.'*

PREVENTION, IDENTIFICATION AND INTERVENTION

Whole School Approaches to Prevention and Early Identification

All schools and early years settings deal with children with a range of emotional and social difficulties and with difficult and sometimes disturbing behaviour. The Department's guidance entitled *Promoting Children's Mental Health within Early Years and School Settings* provides advice on whole school strategies for promoting mental health and for identifying difficulties that may arise.

The Social and Emotional Aspects of Learning (SEAL) programme in schools promotes the development of social and emotional skills. SEAL promotes positive behaviour, attendance, learning and the mental health of all children. It also provides for small group work for pupils who need more support, though the programme is not sufficient for children who have severe behavioural problems or mental health difficulties that require specialist help. Many schools that have implemented this programme have seen a marked improvement in the way pupils interact with each other both inside and outside the classroom. The SEAL programme also provides a helpful framework on which special schools can draw to meet the particular needs of their pupils. www.teachernet.gov.uk/seal

Whole-school approaches to managing pupil behaviour are described in DCSF guidance on *School Discipline and Pupil Behaviour Policies*—www.teachernet.gov.uk/wholeschool/behaviour/ (issued in April 2007) and also in earlier, independent advice from the Practitioners' Group on School Behaviour and Discipline chaired by Sir Alan Steer, *Learning Behaviour Principles and Practice—What Works in Schools* (2005).

Whole-school approaches can improve social and emotional well-being and reduce behaviour difficulties. The SEN Code of Practice explains (paragraphs 5.18 and 6.18), *'effective management, school ethos and the learning environment, curricular, pastoral and discipline arrangements can help prevent some special educational needs arising, and minimise others.'*

All children and young people with SEN or disabilities, including those with BESD, should be able to access and benefit from high quality early years and childcare provision. The Childcare Act 2006 provides a comprehensive statutory framework for improving outcomes for all young children, reducing inequalities between them, and supporting the delivery of the commitments in the Ten Year Childcare Strategy to give every child the best start in life and parents more choice about how to balance work and family life.

Prevention, early identification and intervention underpin the key duties set out in the Childcare Act on local authorities and their partners. High quality, integrated services that bring together health and early years professionals can support children's early learning and development, their successful transition to school and enhance their life chances. Early years settings should ensure they have a clear policy to support the early identification of needs. They should work with their local authority, in partnership with health services and voluntary sector partners, and most importantly with parents. Early years settings should have a clear inclusion policy and a named member of staff responsible for inclusion in the setting. They should also arrange staff training to enable them to work effectively and appropriately with children with BESD.

School admissions should be consistent with the Admissions Code of Practice. Schools, early years settings and local authorities must not discriminate in their admissions criteria or their admissions procedures. Children and young people with BESD (but who do not have a statement of special educational needs naming a particular school) have the same rights of admission to a school or early years setting as others. All schools and settings should admit pupils with identified special educational needs including those with BESD. They should also identify and provide for pupils whose SEN were not previously identified.

Extended schools and workforce reform are increasing schools' capacity to intervene early to address individual need. For example learning mentors and coaches facilitate children and young people's attendance, learning and personal development.

Personalised Learning

Personalised learning and teaching mean taking a highly structured and responsive approach to each child's and young person's learning, so that all are able to progress, achieve and participate. It means strengthening the engagement of pupils and their parents as partners in learning. Case studies covering personalised assessments and learning can be found at: www.standards.dfes.gov.uk/personalisedlearning.

Personalised learning has five key components:

- Assessment for learning—ascertaining where each pupil is in their learning, giving quality feedback to promote further learning and planning the next steps with shared objectives;
- Effective teaching and learning—building on the learner's experience, increasing and applying knowledge so that everybody can make maximum progress in their learning; expanding teaching repertoires and extending learning opportunities;
- A flexible curriculum—providing pupils with an enriched curriculum with a guaranteed core that is used as the basis for enquiry;
- Organising the school for personalised learning—enabling schools at local level to use workforce reforms and new technologies imaginatively, backed up by appropriate continuing professional development, school networks and collaboration;
- Partnerships beyond the classroom—addressing the needs of the whole child by offering a range of extended services that involve parents/carers and the community in children's education.

The 2005 Schools White Paper set out the Government's commitment to transform the support available for every child, including those who need support to help them catch up and those who have a particular gift or talent.

The National Strategies are working to strengthen schools' tracking of pupil progress and ensure effective use by teachers of Assessment for Learning and intervention strategies to improve and personalise teaching and learning. The National Strategies are providing schools with best practice materials, guidance and training on the most effective strategies to personalise learning to the needs of each pupil. It will be for each school to decide its own plans for delivering personalised learning and to determine how best to invest their new resources and deploy their staff to deliver them.

The introduction of the National Strategies' Three Waves model of intervention for behaviour and learning provides a rigorous, strategic approach to the early identification of need, targeted support and evaluation of outcomes as part of a whole school approach to personalisation. *Wave 1* support enables interventions through *Quality First* classroom teaching, *Wave 2* interventions entail targeted support which is designed to enable pupils to work at expected levels, and *Wave 3* support entails additional, personalised interventions designed to meet longer term and more complex needs.

Developing a Whole-School Approach to Behaviour Management which Takes Account of Children and Young People with SEN and Disabilities

The statutory SEN responsibilities of school governing bodies are summarised in the SEN Code of Practice, paragraph 1:21. They include:

- doing their best to ensure that the necessary provision is made for any pupil who has SEN;
- ensuring that pupils' SEN needs are made known to all who are likely to teach them;
- ensuring that teachers in the school are aware of the importance of identifying and providing for pupils who have SEN;
- having regard to the Code of Practice when carrying out their duties toward all pupils with SEN.

Schools, pupil referral units and early years settings in receipt of government funding for early education must have a written SEN policy. Schools' policies include a number of requirements that are particularly relevant to pupils with BESD:

- how pupils' SEN are identified, assessed and reviewed;
- arrangements for access to the curriculum for pupils with SEN;
- how resources are allocated to and amongst pupils with SEN;
- staff training on SEN;
- how the governing body evaluates the success of the education provided for pupils with SEN.

All policies, including those relating to behaviour management, should take account of the needs of children and young people with SEN and disabilities. The Department's guidance, *Promoting Children's Mental Health within Early Years and School*

Settings, provides advice and case studies which schools may find helpful when trying to determine which additional or alternative intervention might be effective.

The disability equality duty was brought in by the Disability Discrimination Act 2005. It requires schools and other 'public authorities' to promote equality of opportunity for disabled people. A specific duty, which applies to particular public authorities, including local authorities and publicly-funded schools (including city technology colleges, city colleges for technology of the arts and academies) includes a requirement to prepare and publish a disability equality scheme. The scheme must show how a public authority is meeting its general duty.

The Department's guidance, *Promoting Disability Equality in Schools*, sets out the specific requirements of a scheme, in full. Amongst these are requirements to:

- involve disabled people (pupils, staff, parents) in the preparation of the scheme;
- set out in their scheme the arrangements for gathering information on the effect of the school's policies on the educational opportunities available to and the achievements of disabled pupils;
- the school's methods for assessing the impact of its current or proposed policies and practices on disability equality.

Section 3.9 of the Department's guidance on *School Discipline and Pupil Behaviour Policies* provides practical advice on ways in which schools might need to take account of a child or young person's SEN and disability when applying the school behaviour policy. This may mean making reasonable adjustments or considering what additional or different action may need to be taken. Paragraph 3.6.3 of the same guidance explains:

> *'Any lawful use of sanctions must be reasonable and proportionate to the circumstances of the case [taking account of] the pupil's age, any special educational needs, any disability and any religious requirements affecting the pupil.'*

Paragraph 3.6.14 advises that schools should avoid sanctions becoming cumulative and automatic, as this is unlikely to enable their application in a way which always takes account of individual needs, age and understanding. Paragraph 3.6.17 adds that staff should also consider, when using sanctions, whether an apparent behaviour difficulty is in fact a manifestation of unidentified learning difficulties or other type of SEN.

Paragraph 3.6.8 says that consultation with parents, engagement with other agencies and the development of a pastoral support programme should feature in schools' systems for addressing issues around behaviour. Where a child or young person has (or is thought to have) special educational needs, the implementation of such systems should take account of, and be informed by, action being taken to address the child or young person's SEN.

The DRC Code of Practice for Schools explains, paragraph 6.13, that schools *'will need to review their policies, practices and procedures, as a matter of course, to ensure that they do not discriminate against disabled children.'* In addition disability equality schemes include the requirement to assess the impact of school policies on disability equality. This should include the impact of school behaviour policies. The DfES guidance, *Promoting Disability Equality in Schools* includes the following case study from a secondary school:

Case Study

The Head of Year 9 reviews referrals for behaviour and discipline following a discussion of the definition of disability on a staff training day. She thinks that more pupils are covered by the definition than the school had previously recognised and identifies a group of pupils with autistic spectrum disorders who are over-represented in the referrals. She meets with the pupils individually to discuss what steps the school might take to reduce the number of incidents. Following her discussions she meets with the pastoral deputy and the SENCO. They agree the following actions:

- the SENCO will contact the local authority for training on the communication needs of pupils with autism. The school wants to build this in on a regular basis, so that new staff can attend and existing staff can have refresher sessions;
- the deputy will circulate a note to ask other teachers with pastoral responsibilities to undertake similar reviews of referrals;
- the SENCO will involve the pupils and their parents in the development of a note to all staff to ensure that staff are aware of some key considerations in their interactions with the pupils;
- the deputy will bring forward the review of the school's behaviour policy to the next term; and
- the actions they agree will be incorporated into the school's disability equality scheme, but progress on reducing the number of incidents will be kept under review as part of the school's behaviour policy.

Exclusions

Exclusions data reveal a disproportionately high rate of exclusions of children and young people with SEN. Paragraph 46 of Part 2 of the Department's guidance, *Improving Behaviour and Attendance: Guidance on Exclusion from Schools and Pupil Referral Units,* is clear that, other than in the most exceptional circumstances, schools should avoid permanently excluding pupils with statements, and they should also make every effort to avoid excluding pupils who are being supported at *School Action* or *School Action Plus*. Paragraphs 45-50 of that guidance contain advice on the steps schools should take when considering whether to exclude a child or young person with SEN or with a disability. Those paragraphs are reproduced at Annex 1 to this guidance. Advice on monitoring of exclusions is provided at paragraphs 159 and 160 below.

Careful consideration should be given to whether there may be unidentified SEN when challenging behaviour is being addressed. If a child or young person has been identified as having SEN, consideration should be given to whether other interventions could provide an alternative to exclusion and would more effectively address the matters causing concern, see paragraphs 99 to 108 below. The Department's guidance, *Promoting Children's Mental Health within Early Years and School Settings*, provides advice that schools may find helpful when trying to determine which additional or alternative intervention might be effective.

Equally, schools need to be alert to the possibility that behavioural difficulties may mask an underlying disability. Schools should take care to make reasonable adjustments to policies that may discriminate against disabled pupils. A policy that provides an automatic sanction for a particular offence may need to be varied if its application to a disabled pupil might treat him less favourably than another pupil for a reason related to his disability. Schools also need to be alert to the range of ways in which incidents that might lead to an exclusion can be avoided, for example, whole school training on the communication needs of autistic pupils may help to avoid difficulties between staff and students and may be a reasonable adjustment that schools might be expected to make.

Further advice on matters to be considered before excluding a child or young person from a school (including a PRU) is provided in *School Discipline and Pupil Behaviour Policies* and in *Improving Behaviour and Attendance—Guidance on Exclusion from Schools and Pupil Referral Units*, 2007. These can be found at: http://www.teachernet.gov.uk/wholeschool/behaviour/exclusion/guidance2007/

A Graduated Approach to Addressing BESD as a Special Educational Need

The SEN Code of Practice explains there is a continuum of special educational needs and that, where necessary, increasingly specialist expertise should be brought to bear on a child/young person's difficulties. The Code describes this as a graduated approach to addressing special educational needs. The Code suggests that where persistent emotional or behavioural difficulties are not ameliorated through usual behaviour management, staff should decide on additional or different interventions at *Early Years Action* or *School Action*. Consideration should be given to whether a child or young person's behaviour or emotional/social needs arise from an underlying learning difficulty, for example dyslexia, that has not been identified or is not being appropriately addressed.

Paragraph 7:60 of the Code suggests that children and young people with BESD may require help with some or all of the following:

- flexible teaching arrangements;
- development of social competence and emotional maturity;
- adjusting to school expectations and routines;
- acquiring the skills of positive interaction with peers and adults;
- specialised behavioural and cognitive approaches;
- re-channelling or re-focusing to diminish repetitive and self-injurious behaviours;
- provision of class and school systems which control or censure negative or difficult behaviours and encourage positive behaviour;
- provision of a safe and supportive environment.

Provision may be made more effectively and efficiently for groups of pupils, for example, the development of social skills may be undertaken more effectively in groups. However the provision is made, *'The interventions are a means of matching special educational provision to the child's needs, and are therefore part of the continuous and systematic cycle of planning, action and review within the school to enable all children to learn and progress.'*

If, following assessment or evaluation, little or no progress continues to be made, staff should consider seeking external support through *Early Years Action Plus* or *School Action Plus* (see paragraphs 4.29, 5.55 and 6.63 of the *SEN Code of Practice*). At *Early Years Action Plus* or *School Action Plus*, external support services are engaged by schools to support them in developing interventions and removing barriers to achievement. The Code is clear that the involvement of such agencies need not be limited to this stage; outside specialists can play an important part in the very early identification of SEN and in advising schools on effective provision designed to prevent the development of more significant needs.

Where the child's difficulties *'have not responded to relevant and purposeful measures taken by the school or setting and external specialists'*, the school may wish to consider asking the local authority to undertake a statutory assessment of the child or young person's SEN, see Chapter 7 of the Code of Practice. A parent can request such an assessment at any time. The processes for undertaking statutory assessments and deciding on whether to issue a statement are described in Chapters 7 and 8 of the Code and are not repeated here.

A pastoral support programme is a school-based intervention to help individual pupils to manage their behaviour. Where a child or young person's BESD entails challenging behaviour, a pastoral support programme may be agreed between and supported by a range of agencies, see paragraphs 3.6.8 and 3.6.9 of *School Discipline and Pupil Behaviour Policies*. A pastoral support programme is particularly useful for those whose behaviour is deteriorating rapidly and who are in danger of permanent exclusion. The programme should identify precise and realistic targets for the pupils to work towards; it should be short, practical and agreed with parents. The local authority will be informed and other agencies involved.

This multi-agency approach may also be helpful in planning and providing support to a child or young person whose BESD entails being withdrawn, anxious or depressed, and/or engaging in self-harm. Other examples of such approaches are contained in the Department's guidance, *Promoting Children's Mental Health within Early Years and School Settings*.

Where the involvement of several agencies would help to address a child or young person's needs, it may be appropriate to assess those needs using the Common Assessment Framework (CAF). CAF provides a holistic assessment and enables practitioners and/or multi-agency teams to provide a co-ordinated response. One practitioner acts as the 'lead professional' for the particular child or young person, so that there is one point of contact for the family and one person to co-ordinate and review the action agreed. As CAF is implemented, schools should be aware of local arrangements for using the CAF and know who should undertake an assessment with the child and family and liaise with the multi-agency team. The outcomes would be reflected in the work of schools and other agencies with the child or young person at *Action Plus* (or in the statement of SEN) and in any pastoral support programme.

Schools and local authorities should remain awre that paragraph 7:30 of the Code of Practice says that in the great majority of cases the school will have assessed a child or young person's learning difficulties and made provision to address the identified needs, before any request is made to the local authority for a statutory assessment. In a very small minority of cases, children or young people may demonstrate such significant difficulties that the school may consider it impossible or inappropriate to go through their usual procedures, for example, a child with severe emotional or behavioural difficulties which require an urgent response from beyond the school. The Code says there is a need for a quick response from the local authority for such children.

Paragraph 8:23 of the Code of Practice explains that in exceptional circumstances it may be necessary to make an emergency placement for a child without a statutory assessment and a relevant statement. Examples include circumstances where: the parents, the school, relevant professionals and the local authority agree that a sudden and serious deterioration in a child's behavioural makes the current placement untenable or unsafe; and where a young person returns home from a secure unit or young offender institution. Paragraphs 8:24 et seq of the Code explain the further urgent steps that must be taken following a decision to make such an emergency placement.

CURRICULUM FOR CHILDREN AND YOUNG PEOPLE WITH BESD

All schools strive to develop and deliver their school curriculum in ways that match their aims, meet the varied needs of their pupils and fulfill statutory requirements. The curriculum in all schools should be balanced and broadly-based and provide opportunities for all pupils to learn and to achieve. It should promote pupils' spiritual, moral, social and cultural development and prepare all pupils for the opportunities, responsibilities and experiences of work and life.

The National Curriculum includes a statutory Inclusion Statement as part of the common requirements. The Statement sets out the requirement for teachers to adapt the curriculum as necessary by setting suitable learning challenges, responding to pupil's diverse learning needs and overcoming potential barriers to learning and assessment for individuals and groups of pupils. The Statement gives teachers greater flexibility to adapt the curriculum to an individual pupil's ability. It is designed to enable pupils with a wide range of special educational needs to progress and demonstrate achievement within the National Curriculum.

It should be noted that the National Curriculum does not apply to PRUs or education provided otherwise than in a school—although PRUs are required to ensure a balanced and broadly based curriculum is provided.

The flexibility offered by the Inclusion Statement is designed to reduce the need for formal disapplication or modification of the National Curriculum requirements. However, where that flexibility still does not meet an individual pupil's needs, it is possible, under Section 92 of the Education Act 2002 for the local authority to disapply the National Curriculum through a statement of special educational needs. Disapplication may be from all or part of the National Curriculum, including all or part of separate programmes of study and all or part of statutory assessment arrangements. Schools should, however, retain pupils' access to a broad and balanced curriculum or learning programme, including as much of the National Curriculum as possible.

In addition, under the terms of Section 93 of the Education Act 2002, head teachers have a power to disapply or modify the National Curriculum temporarily in order to help a child or young person during a temporary difficulty which is beyond the flexibility already in the National Curriculum (a month's illness, for example, does not usually require disapplication), or while s/he is being assessed with a view to making or amending a statement. Further information about disapplication is available online at: www.dcsf.gov.uk/disapply

Guidance to support the statutory Inclusion Statement can also be found within the National Curriculum handbook and on the National Curriculum website at www.nc.uk.net, under the heading 'Inclusion'.

Schools may also find it helpful to refer to guidance (being published early 2008) on curriculum delivery in PRUs and to take account of the national entitlement and timetable for the introduction of the fourteen new Diploma lines. In agreeing a local 14-19 prospectus, local authorities and partner organisations will wish to consider what each school and college in the area can offer young people with BESD.

Working within the statutory framework, each school should develop a curriculum which matches local and individual circumstances, building on pupils' strengths and needs. Under the Education (School Government) Terms of Reference (England) Regulations 2000, governing bodies and headteachers are required to produce a curriculum policy. This replaces the requirement under the School Standards and Framework Act 1998 for a curriculum plan. The approach taken should be broad brush. The policy should set out the principles underpinning the curriculum and reflect the school's commitment to developing all aspects of their pupils' lives. It allows schools to state values and aims as well as the general principles governing their approaches to issues such as inclusion and cross-curricular learning. Regulations make the head teacher responsible for preparing the policy and reviewing it annually. The governing body must consider and agree the policy and monitor and review its implementation.

Curriculum aims should be agreed with all members of the school staff, governors, parents, carers, visiting professionals (such as therapists and advisory teachers) and the pupils themselves. Once agreed, these aims will inform the development of local curriculum plans and establish an essential reference point for reviewing curriculum provision. There should be ongoing discussion and regular review to ensure that the school's curriculum aims respond to changing priorities.

Although the National Curriculum is specified in terms of individual subjects, schools are not required to teach these separately. They can organise their curriculum in ways which provide opportunities for appropriate and relevant learning; have meaning for pupils, parents, carers and staff; and use resources to maximum effect.

Curriculum content and experiences for pupils with BESD should be carefully sequenced to build on previous learning and ensure progression. They should emphasise personal development and essential life skills which will improve their achievement of the five Every Child Matters outcomes.

For children and young people with challenging behaviour, it is often helpful for teaching and learning to be well paced, tightly focused with specific learning objectives clearly expressed and broken down into small steps for each part of the lesson. Pupils with BESD are likely to require considerable support with personal and social development, including managing relationships with others in the classroom, or during wider activities in and around the school.

Lessons which are highly interactive with well-planned group work in a variety of groupings provide opportunities for speaking and listening and for children and young people to learn from one another. It can be beneficial for these children and young people to have the opportunity to experience the responsibilities of assuming a leadership role, given clear objectives and parameters.

Learning and development can also result from the ways in which pupils with BESD are helped to resolve conflicts and develop and maintain friendships. Approaches such as 'circles of friends' or peer mentoring can help to develop positive peer relationships. The DVD material in *Implementing the DDA in schools and early years settings* shows a number of useful strategies in action.

Children and young people with BESD may find it helpful to have one identified adult with whom they can discuss matters causing them concern. This may be a teacher or a learning mentor who has been clearly assigned this responsibility as part of the additional support provided for the pupil.

Schools will wish to be aware of pilot work developing work-focused learning for 14-16 year olds as an additional curriculum option. A wide range of good practice is being developed using a work-focus in ways which motivate young people by demonstrating the usefulness of learning for their future careers. Young people are also making progress in developing skills through practical learning outside classrooms fitting better with their preferred learning styles. The aim is that the good practice being developed will be adopted and adapted by schools throughout the country as they see fit. Further information is at www.qca.org.uk/14-19/11-16-schools/110_2474.htm On this website the guidance document entitled *Key Stage 4 Engagement Programme: Making the programme work for your students* contains many of the lessons learnt so far, and there is a growing body of case studies, written by practitioners, which may be transferable to other schools.

For young people aged 14-19, the Department is working with the QCA, schools and colleges to develop Diplomas, which will sit alongside A levels and GCSEs. Diplomas will combine theoretical and applied learning. By 2013 there will be national entitlement in fourteen lines of learning at levels 1, 2 and 3 covering all sectors of the economy. Level 1 will be broadly equivalent to 4-5 GCSEs, and level 3 will be broadly equivalent to 3 A levels.

The first five diploma lines will be available from September 2008. They will be in ICT, Society Health and Development, Engineering, Creative & Media, and Construction & the Built Environment. Pathfinder authorities are already testing elements of the Diplomas as they are developed. Further details can be obtained by e-mailing diploma@qca.org.uk

Workforce remodelling is a long-term change process focused on deploying staff in the most appropriate and efficient way, with teachers focused on teaching and learning, and other tasks being carried out by a wide range of support staff. An essential element of workforce reform is the building of a multi-skilled team to provide effective learning opportunities for all pupils. Schools that have remodelled effectively are well placed to respond to the many challenges they face, including how to support pupils with BESD.

TOWARDS DEVELOPING A RANGE OF PROVISION FOR CHILDREN AND YOUNG PEOPLE WITH BESD

The range of provision for children and young people with BESD will consist of:

(*a*) a range of settings able to work with certain levels of need, from early years settings and mainstream schools through to special schools, and

(*b*) a range of support enabling schools and early years settings to work in a multi-agency way with children and young people with BESD, including being able to work effectively with some who might otherwise need to be considered for transfer to another setting.

A Range of Settings

In the context of a local authority's statutory duty to promote high standards of education for all children, including those with SEN, paragraph 1:11 of the SEN Code of Practice says that local authorities should make effective arrangements for SEN by ensuring that:

- the needs of children and young people with SEN are identified and assessed quickly and matched by appropriate provision;
- high quality support is provided for schools and early education settings—including, through educational psychology and other support services, and arrangements for sharing good practice in provision for children and young people with SEN;
- children and young people can benefit from coordinated provision—by developing close partnerships with parents, schools, health and social services and the voluntary sector;
- strategic planning for SEN is carried out in consultation with schools and others to develop systems for monitoring and accountability for SEN;
- local authority arrangements for SEN provision are kept under review as required under Section 315 of the Education Act 1996.

When fulfilling their Section 315 responsibility to review their arrangements for SEN provision, local authorities and their partners (for example, the local Learning and Skills Council) should consider the effectiveness and scope of the range of settings they have in place for children and young people with BESD.

The DfES guidance *Planning and Developing Special Educational Provision* provides advice on planning and commissioning SEN services and settings. Paragraph 33 of that guidance summarises the types of provision that local authorities are putting in place for a range of SEN, including for children and young people with BESD. This explains that although terminology may vary from authority to authority, specialist provision may take a variety of forms:

- Mainstream schools—where children with SEN are supported at School Action and School Action Plus or through a statement;
- Specialist mainstream schools—which have a particular SEN specialism and provide outreach to other schools;
- Resourced Provision—where places are reserved at a mainstream school for pupils with a statement for a specific type of SEN. Pupils are taught mainly within mainstream classes but also use a base and some specialist facilities around the school;
- Designated Unit—where pupils with a statement of a specific type of SEN are taught wholly or mainly in separate classes specifically provided within a mainstream school;
- Special school—organised specifically to cater for children with statements who have particular types of SEN;
- Specialist special schools—which have a particular SEN or curricular specialism and provide outreach to other schools;
- Co-location—children with statements are educated in separate special school facilities with separate staff but on site with a mainstream school or vice versa. There should be some interchange of pupils, resources, staff and dual use of facilities.

Where appropriate, local authorities also commission specialist provision. Paragraph 36 of *Planning and Developing Special Educational Provision* says that local authorities should consider whether and how the particular expertise of non-maintained and independent schools (which often offer residential provision as well as specialist outreach advisory and support services) could contribute to local, regional, sub-regional and national provision.

This guidance does not provide detailed advice on the running of residential schools for children and young people with BESD. As suggested in paragraph 73 of Circular 9/94, for a small minority of pupils, boarding away from home may be wholly appropriate and beneficial and may indeed be the only way for them to make progress. Best practice entails these schools working with children and young people on addressing their needs during recreational activities in the evenings and at weekends, well beyond usual classroom hours.

Paragraphs 8:70 to 8:79 of the SEN Code of Practice, paragraphs 73-76 and 78-101 of Circular 9/94 and Chapter 3 of the Department's guidance entitled *The Management of SEN Expenditure* (read in the context of the current statutory framework) provide advice for local authorities when considering a placement in a residential school.

Pupil referral units (PRUs) are not planned or designed to be a long-term setting and should not be regarded as part of a local authority's range of planned SEN provision. In this context, local authorities will wish to consider whether data on the use of PRUs, the placement of children and young people from PRUs into other educational settings, managed moves, or data on exclusions suggest that changes need to be made to the range of settings and/or to the range of support that available to settings.

Local authorities should make clear to schools and PRUs the range of provision that is available, along with advice on criteria, access processes and referral routes. Local authorities should also be clear about whether such provision is available on a core (no cost) basis, or as a traded service.

Placement in and Moving on From Pupil Referral Units or Other Alternative Provision

As indicated in paragraph 8:92 of the SEN Code of Practice, local authorities are empowered by Section 319 of the Education Act 1996 to arrange for some or all of child's special educational provision to be made otherwise than at school. Sometimes, children and young people with BESD are placed in pupil referral units or other alternative provision. Such placements should not be viewed as part of the range of SEN provision. Rather they should be used for relatively short periods of time, while a more appropriate placement is arranged. As noted in paragraphs 4.28 and 4.29 of *Guidance for Local Authorities and Schools—Pupil Referral Units and Alternative Provision*:

> *'If a pupil's long-term needs cannot be met in a mainstream school, a special school rather than a PRU should be named on a statement of SEN. Where a pupil with a statement of SEN is placed in a PRU or other form of Alternative Provision because a place in a mainstream or special school appropriate to meet the needs specified in the statement is not yet available, regular planning and review of the placement is essential, alongside steps to provide the necessary support.'*

Guidance on monitoring placements of pupils in PRUs and other alternative provision is provided at paragraphs 159 and 160 below.

Managed Moves

Schools in many local authorities have agreed 'managed moves' protocols to enable pupils to move on to another school, to give them a fresh start and/or where other local schools have further behaviour management strategies available to benefit the pupil. It is important this only happens with the full knowledge and cooperation of all parties involved, including the parents, and in circumstances where this is in the best interests of the pupil. This is covered in paragraph 9(*d*) of the Department's guidance on exclusions: *Improving Behaviour and Attendance—Guidance on Exclusion from Schools and Pupil Referral Units*, published in September 2007. Some local authorities have similar protocols for moving pupils on a temporary basis to alternative provision, including PRUs, while remaining on their school roll.

Most of the principles applying to managed moves generally also apply to managed moves for pupils with SEN. The guidance stresses that a managed move should only take place with the agreement of the parents, head teachers, governors and the LA. Parents should never be pressured into removing their child from school under the threat of permanent exclusion. Managed moves are most successful when they are arranged prior to permanent exclusion. The process may take some time to arrange although protocols agreed between schools should set out a process which allows for a quick and seamless move from one school to another.

Best practice entails providing additional support for the pupil on transfer, perhaps from the local authority's behaviour support service, the receiving school's Learning Support Unit or from learning mentors as part of a well-planned induction programme. Many protocols provide for the pupil staying on the roll of their first school during a trial period, typically for half a term to allow the pupil time to settle in then review their progress. Any issues that might arise around school transport costs should be addressed and resolved early in the process of arranging a managed move.

Where a child or young person has a statement of SEN, discussions about the possibility of a managed move must include a review of the pupil's statement and the support appropriate to the pupil as set out in the statement. If it is decided that a child or young person should change schools, procedures summarised in the SEN Code of Practice for amending the statement and issuing a final statement naming a new school must be followed. Where the pupil has dedicated support or specialist resources specified in their statement, the same or similar provision will need to be arranged at the new school, and time will need to be allowed to put new arrangements in place. Careful consideration should be given to ensuring that the disruption of a transfer does not outweigh the benefits of a managed move.

A Range of Support

Local authorities should make sure that schools and early years settings have access to advice and support from educational psychologists, behaviour support services, whether provided centrally or as outreach from a special school, and child and adolescent mental health services (CAMHS). DCSF/DH's *National Service Framework for Children, Young People and Maternity Services* has established clear standards in promoting the health and well-being of children and young people and for providing high quality services.

Increasingly, schools as well as local authorities are developing provision for children and young people with BESD, not least because proportionately more resources and responsibilities are delegated to schools than was the case in the past.

It also follows from the delegation of resources to schools that many local authority services are provided to schools on a traded basis, that is schools are charged for using these services. This enables schools to decide to use their resources on those services which most appropriately address their pupils' needs.

Schools are increasingly working in partnerships to develop shared provision. Sometimes local authorities commission schools, or groups of schools, to provide services to other schools as part of developing provision across the local authority area. For example, all secondary schools are now expected to be in partnerships to improve behaviour and tackle absence, and primary schools, special schools and PRUs may also be involved.

Advice from special schools and PRUs can help mainstream schools prevent the escalation of behavioural difficulties. School partnership arrangements should help ensure that the needs of any excluded pupils with BESD are met in the most appropriate way, whether in a special school, temporarily in a PRU, another mainstream school, or other provision. School partnerships can also arrange reciprocal training, opportunities for secondment and consultation, and exchange of best practice in such areas as curriculum development.

Local authorities, schools or clusters of schools may also provide, or commission from the independent or voluntary sector providers, services such as nurture groups or similar arrangements for supporting children and their families where schools identify children with emotional or social difficulties and therefore need help to get the most out of school. Such arrangements could complement and augment the SEAL programme.

Children and young people with BESD and/or their families may require access to a range of services including CAMHS, educational psychology, behaviour support, social care services, speech and language therapy, physiotherapy and occupational therapy. Section 10 of the Children Act 2004 places a duty on local authorities to make arrangements to promote cooperation between the authority, specified organisations and other locally determined partners, to improve the well-being of children (well-being is defined as the five positive outcomes set out in Section 10(2)). Local authorities and other organisations should therefore be working together through Children's Trusts to improve outcomes for children and young people with BESD, as they would for other children and young people. This would include multi-agency review of provision, which would identify ways in which provision might be developed to address identified needs more effectively and improve outcomes. The DfES *Statutory Guidance on inter-agency cooperation to improve the well-being of children: children's trusts* explains the Section 10 duty.

The Department's guidance, *Planning and Developing Special Educational Provision,* sets out how local authorities and schools might review and develop the range of provision for children and young people with SEN. The principles in that guidance, including the summary of the range of settings in which educational provision might be made for children and young people with SEN, also apply to developing the range of provision for those with BESD.

MONITORING AND EVALUATION

Schools and local authorities should monitor and evaluate the impact of their provision on outcomes for children and young people with BESD, through the processes they have in place for monitoring and evaluating their overall strategies for improving outcomes for children with SEN and/or disabilities. This will include the careful review and use of data with particular focus on progress and outcomes.

Special Educational Needs

Section 315 of the Education Act 1996 requires local authorities to keep their SEN provision under review. When undertaking this review, it is important that local authorities consider the effectiveness of their arrangements for addressing the needs of children and young people with BESD. Local authorities may find the National Strategies' framework to support SEN self-evaluation helpful when undertaking such reviews—alongside evaluating the effectiveness of their school funding arrangements in supporting and raising the achievement of children and young people with SEN (paragraph 1:12 of the Code), and taking account of the local authority SEN policy framework summarised at paragraphs 1:13 to 1:15 of the Code.

Paragraph 1:21 of the Code reminds school governing bodies of their SEN statutory responsibilities. Paragraph 1:23 lists all the settings (including schools) that must have a written SEN policy. Amongst other things, paragraphs 1:23 to 1:25 summarise SEN responsibilities in early years settings and PRUs.

Paragraph 1:27 reminds schools that governing bodies must, on at least an annual basis, consider and report on the effectiveness of the school's work on behalf of children with SEN, and consider whether changes to their SEN policy are needed.

Disability Equality Schemes

Regulations under Part 5A of the DDA set out the requirements of a disability equality scheme and the Department's publication, *Promoting Disability Equality in Schools* provides guidance. Schools' duties include the requirement to assess the impact of school policies on disability equality. This should include an assessment of the impact of behaviour and discipline policies. Schools should consider whether disabled pupils are affected more than others by their behaviour policy or by the application of sanctions such as detentions or exclusions. The involvement of disabled pupils and information gathered by the school will form an important part of the school's assessment.

Priorities in the school's action plan should show how the school will promote equality of opportunity between disabled pupils and others on the policy and practice issues identified through the impact assessment. In addition, schools need to be able to evaluate the effectiveness of the actions identified in their scheme and reflect this evaluation in their discussions with:

- their School Improvement Partner; and
- Ofsted, when the school is inspected.

School Self-Evaluation

Schools' Self-Evaluation Forms (SEF) and SEN provision mapping should help to identify areas where there is a need to improve school performance and to ensure appropriate action is taken. These review processes will help to identify any action to build staff capacity and improve the confidence of staff in supporting children with a wide range of needs. The Audit Commission, working with the National Strategies, has produced an SEN/AEN Value for Money tool. This is an online resource pack which supports schools' own evaluation of their use of resources for special and additional educational needs. The tool provides helpful examples of provision mapping and helps schools to monitor and evaluate the impact their interventions are having on the progress of children and young people.

The focus of school self-evaluation on a continuing cycle of school improvement should ensure that the progress of all children is kept under review and that children receive appropriate support. The School Improvement Partner has an important role in: supporting and challenging a school's self-evaluation and the action it takes to address development needs; and in identifying and brokering sources of support to the school.

Data indicates that children and young people with SEN are more likely to be excluded from schools than others. This applies particularly to those with BESD. Local authorities and schools should consider the impact of their approach to working with children and young people with BESD on the exclusion trends. They will wish to consider what might be done differently to reduce the need for such exclusions. This might include reviewing the support available to schools that are working with children and young people with BESD. Similar lessons can be learned from analysing attendance data.

The placement of pupils in PRUs or other alternative education provision is discussed at paragraph 137 above. Local authorities should monitor the extent to which pupils with SEN and disabilities are being placed in PRUs or other alternative provision and the impact of measures being taken both to reduce the need for such placements and to reduce the length of time spent in them before pupils with SEN and disabilities transfer to more appropriate long-term placements. These measures are likely to entail reviewing and where appropriate making changes both to the range of settings and the range of support to schools. Schools will wish to monitor the impact of support they are receiving and the measures they are taking for themselves to increase their capacity to address the needs of children and young people with SEN and disabilities, including children and young people with BESD.

TRAINING AND DEVELOPMENT

The Professional Standards for Teachers (www.tda.gov.uk/standards) are statements of a teacher's professional attributes, professional knowledge and understanding, and professional skills. They provide clarity of the expectations at each career stage. The preamble to the Standards reminds teachers that their practice should be informed by an awareness, appropriate to their level of experience and responsibility, of legislation concerning the development and well-being of children and young people. Specific reference is made to the Disability Discrimination Acts 1995 and 2005 and relevant associated guidance, and; the special educational needs provisions in the Education Act 1996 and the associated *Special Educational Needs: Code of Practice* (DfES 2001).

Standard Q/C19 requires that teachers should *'know how to make effective personalised provision for those they teach including those with special educational needs or disabilities, and how to take practical account of diversity and promote equality and inclusion in their teaching'*. Furthermore Standard Q/C20 requires teachers to *'understand the roles of colleagues such as those having specific responsibilities for learners with special educational needs, disabilities and other individual learning needs, and the contributions they can make to the learning, development and well-being of children and young people.'* All providers of initial teacher education are required to ensure they prepare trainees to meet the professional standards.

The Professional Standards form a backdrop to performance management. One of the key underpinning principles of performance management is the need for an ongoing professional dialogue between teachers and their managers through the appraisal process. This dialogue forms a mechanism through which teachers' continuing professional development needs should be identified and met. The process of self-evaluation summarised at paragraph 157 of this guidance may also help to identify school level professional development needs including those that relate to working with children and young people with SEN, and/or BESD.

More information and advice on professional practice when working with children and young people with BESD can be obtained from:

- *Promoting Children's Mental Health within Early Years and School Settings:* http://www.teachernet.gov.uk/docbank/index.cfm?id=10867
- Ofsted's Healthy Minds Report (July 2005) http://www.ofsted.gov.uk/portal/site/Internet/menuitem.eace3f09a603f6d9c3172a8a08c08a0c/?vgnextoid=9edf2a5f74f3c010VgnVgnVCM1000003507640aRCRD
- the Learning Support Units website: http://www.teachernet.gov.uk/wholeschool/behaviour/learningsupportunits/casestudies/

The DfES and DRC materials *Implementing the DDA in schools and early years setting* are available from Prolog. The collection of film clips on DVD1 *Behaviour for learning* is particularly relevant to the education of children and young people with BESD, as is the 6th section of the guidance, *Promoting disability equality in schools*.

Schools and local authorities will also wish to be aware of the following national sources of material which can be used to support continuing professional development in working with children and young people with BESD, addressing challenging behaviour and addressing emotional and social development:

(*a*) the National Strategies run the National Programme for Specialist Leaders in Behaviour and Attendance, a specialist training programme for those working in these areas;

(*b*) To support teachers and other staff working with pupils with SEN, the Department for Children, School and Families, working through the National Strategies, has launched an Inclusion Development Programme (IDP). This is offering professional development in key areas of SEN starting, in 2008, with training on communication difficulties. As well as communication being fundamental to learning and progression, frustration born of inability to communicate can contribute to erratic or unpredictable behaviour in class. It is envisaged that a future round of IDP will specifically address behavioural, emotional and social difficulties;

(*c*) schools also have access to behaviour management training materials through the National Strategies;

(*d*) Staff CPD is fundamental to the effectiveness of the SEAL programme. Within the primary programme, CPD activities are suggested to help prepare staff to deliver each of the themes.
Within the secondary programme, guidance is provided in the section on professional development:
http://bandapilot.org.uk/secondary/pages/development.html

(*e*) The DCSF has also been provided with the following links to CPD resources available from professional associations:
http://www.teachers.org.uk/topichome.php?id=51
http://www.teachers.org.uk/resources/word/CPD–ScrollDownOview–Spring08_RS.doc
http://www.teachers.org.uk/resources/word CPD_tf32_tt58_ tt62INVITE_RS.doc
http://www.teachers.org.uk/resources/word/NUTCPDNEWSNo4.doc
http://www.teachers.org.uk/resources/pdf/CPDpages_i-ivNEW.pdf

(*f*) The DCSF is also aware of a professional development tool being developed published by Barnardo's, Inclusive education in primary schools: supporting children with social emotional and behavioural difficulties. The tool draws on the practice of many teachers who are working with children with BESD and offers practical advice on addressing these difficulties. Further details can be obtained by emailing: inclusive.ed@barnardos.org.uk (or call Mary Duffy on 0131-334 9893)

USE OF FORCE TO CONTROL OR RESTRAIN

Guidance published in November 2007 has replaced and supersedes DfES Circular 10/98. The Use of Force to Control or Restrain. The new guidance can be found at http://www.teachernet.gov.uk/docbank/index.cfm?id=12187—this sets out effective practice for schools in areas such as reducing the likelihood of incidents, carrying out a risk assessment, staff training and recording/reporting incidents, and covers matters to be considered when a child has special educational needs or a disability.

There is also *Guidance on the Use of Restrictive Physical Interventions for Staff Working with Children and Adults who Display Extreme Behaviour in Association with Learning Disability and/or Autistic Spectrum Disorders* (Circular 0204/2002) and *Guidance on the Use of Restrictive Physical Interventions for Pupils with Severe Behavioural Difficulties* (Circular 0264/2003).

GUIDANCE W.R.T. IMPROVING BEHAVIOUR AND ATTENDANCE, EXCLUSION FROM SCHOOLS, AND PUPIL REFERRAL UNITS

Statutory guidance on identifying, assessing and making provision for pupils with SEN, including those with behavioural, social and emotional needs, is given in the Special Educational Needs Code of Practice. Schools must have regard to this guidance.

School governing bodies have a statutory duty to do their best to ensure that the necessary provision is made for any pupil who has SEN. Early identification and intervention, accurate assessment and the arrangement of appropriate provision to meet pupils' SEN usually leads to better outcomes.

Other than in the most exceptional circumstances, schools should avoid permanently excluding pupils with statements. They should also make every effort to avoid excluding pupils who are being supported at *School Action or School Action Plus* under the Special Educational Needs Code of Practice, including those at *School Action Plus* who are being assessed for a statement. In most cases, the head teacher will be aware that the school is having difficulty managing a pupil's behaviour well before the situation has escalated. Schools should try every practicable means to maintain the pupil in school, including seeking LA and other professional advice and support at *School Action Plus* or, where appropriate, asking the LA to consider carrying out a statutory assessment. For a pupil with a statement, where this process has been exhausted, the school should liaise with their LA about initiating an interim annual review of the pupil's statement.

Where a child is permanently excluded, the head teacher should use the period between his or her initial decision and the meeting of the governing body to work with the LA to see whether more support can be made available or whether the statement can be changed to name a new school. If either of these options is possible, the head teacher should normally withdraw the exclusion.

It is extremely important that parents of children with SEN who are excluded from school receive advice on the options available for their child's future education. Schools might usefully advise parents that advice and information on SEN is available through their local SEN Parent Partnership. The Parent Partnership should also be able to provide details of voluntary agencies that offer support to parents, including those that can offer advice concerning exclusions.

Schools have a legal duty under the Disability Discrimination Act 1995 as amended not to discriminate against disabled pupils by excluding them from school because of behaviour related to their disability. This applies to both permanent and fixed period exclusions. The definition of disability under the Act covers pupils with physical, sensory or learning disabilities. Discrimination occurs where a person treats a disabled pupil less favourably than other pupils for a reason which relates to their disability, without justification. It also means failing to take reasonable steps to ensure that disabled pupils are not placed at a substantial disadvantage compared to their non-disabled peers. What constitutes a reasonable step will depend on the circumstances of each case. It must also be remembered that the reasonable adjustments duty requires schools to think ahead, anticipate the barriers that disabled pupils might face and remove or minimise them before a disabled pupil is placed at a substantial disadvantage. The Disability Rights Commission (DRC—now superseded by the Equality and Human Rights Commission) has published a Code of Practice which explains and illustrates schools' duties to disabled pupils, including in relation to exclusions. Schools, and those involved in exclusion decisions or appeals, should read the Code of Practice for Schools available from the DRC or on its website. The Department has published a training resource *Implementing the Disability Act in Schools and Early Years settings* for schools and local authorities. Section 1 of the resource provides a guide to the duties schools have under Part 4 of the DDA and provides more detail on the definition of disability in the DDA. Section 2 illustrates the process of making reasonable adjustments and includes 3 DVDs of reasonable adjustments filmed in schools in different parts of the country. DVD 1 includes a section on behaviour for learning. Schools can order a copy of the resource by phoning 0845 6022260 quoting reference 0160-2006DOC-EN.

It is unlawful to exclude a disabled pupil for a reason related to their disability without justification. When considering whether or not it is appropriate to exclude a pupil who may be disabled within the meaning of the Disability Discrimination Act 1995, head teachers should consider four questions:

(*a*) *Is the pupil disabled?*
The Act covers pupils with physical or mental impairment including sensory impairments and learning difficulties. The definition of disability is not the same as the definition of special education needs but there is likely to be a large overlap between those pupils who have SEN and those who are disabled. Further guidance on the definition of disability is included in *Guidance on matters to be taken into account in determining questions relating to the definition of disability*. Paragraphs D13 to D14 deal specifically with children and provide useful examples involving school pupils.

(*b*) *Is the exclusion for a reason related to the pupil's disability?*
The exclusion does not have to be because of the pupil's disability but 'for a reason related'. This means that if there is any connection between the behaviour resulting in the exclusion and the pupil's disability this is considered less favourable treatment for a reason related to the pupil's disability.

(*c*) *Would another pupil to whom the reason did not apply be treated in the same way?*
If the reason for the exclusion is the pupil's "behaviour" then it is necessary to consider whether or not another pupil who did not behave in that way would be excluded. It is not correct to compare the treatment of the disabled pupil with a non-disabled pupil. Instead the treatment of the disabled pupil should be compared with a pupil who did not behave in the same way.

(*d*) *Can the exclusion be justified?*
An exclusion of a disabled pupil for a reason related to their disability can only be justified if there is a "material" and "substantial" reason for it and the head teacher can show that there were no reasonable steps that could have been made to avoid the exclusion. Maintaining order and discipline in the school may well be a material and substantial reason if there was a specific incident that gave rise to the exclusion. The head teacher will also have to show that reasonable steps were made in response to the pupil's disability. This could include differentiating the school's general disciplinary or behavioural policy to take account of behaviour which is related to a pupil's disability; developing strategies to prevent the pupil's behaviour; requesting external help with a pupil (e.g. requesting a statutory assessment)

and staff training. Further guidance on reasonable steps that could be taken are provided in the DfES resource pack *"Implementing the Disability Discrimination Act in schools and early years settings"*.

Appeals against permanent exclusion, where discrimination is alleged to have taken place, or the disabled pupil has allegedly been placed at a substantial disadvantage by the exclusion procedures, will be heard by the Independent Appeal Panel. Claims alleging discrimination in respect of fixed period exclusions will be heard by the SEN and Disability Tribunal (SENDIST). Schools will be required, in disability discrimination claims, to demonstrate that their actions are justified and that there are no reasonable adjustments to their policies and practice they might have made to prevent the incident which led to the exclusion. Since many disabled pupils will also have special educational needs, schools may wish to consider the action they have take to address those needs in this context.

4

Developing Guidelines Towards Tackling Bullying of Children with SEN and Disabilities

INTRODUCTION

Bullying is one of the most damaging forms of discrimination. This guidance provides advice on dealing with bullying involving children with special educational needs (SEN) and disabilities. It is designed to help schools to:

- Support learners with SEN and disabilities.
- Understand, prevent and respond to bullying of children with SEN and disabilities.
- Eliminate disability based discrimination and harassment.
- Develop a non-bullying ethos.

And by doing so

- Raise achievement and participation in safe, positive environments.
- Meet legal safeguarding obligations and comply with the Disability Discrimination Acts and other legislation.
- Build on the requirements of the SEN Code of Practice.
- Uphold the fundamental human right of children to be free from abuse.

It is relevant to all types of school.

Safe to Learn defines bullying as: Behaviour by an individual or group usually repeated over time, that intentionally hurts another individual or group either physically or emotionally.

Bullying can involve verbal taunts, name calling, physical injury, damage to property, rumour spreading, shunning or ridicule. It can be manipulative, making the disabled pupil do something they should not, or deliberately engineering their discomfort or isolation. It can be done through mobile phones, websites and email (cyberbullying).

Some children with SEN and disabilities may not recognise that they are being bullied or that their own behaviour may be seen by someone else as bullying.

'In the classroom, if you ask for help it's like, they laugh at you. They scribble on your work 'n then you take it back to the teacher and you get blamed for scribbling over your work. (Boy with learning difficulties)

SEN and Disability; Who do We Mean?

Two main definitions are used to inform decisions about supporting children with SEN and disabilities. They are the Disability Discrimination Act 1995 definition of a disabled person as someone who has *'a physical or mental impairment which has a substantial and long-term adverse effect on his or her ability to carry out normal day-to-day activities,'* and the special educational needs definition of children who have learning difficulties or disabilities that make it harder for them to learn or access education than most children of the same age.

According to the social model of disability, *'disability is caused by the way society is organised, rather than by a person's impairment or difference. This approach looks at ways of removing barriers which restrict life choices for people with impairments or differences'* www.childreninthepicturc.org.uk/au_ socialmodel.htm

Why Issue Additional Guidance for Children with SEN and Disabilities?

Reports from the Children's Commissioner, the National Autistic Society and Mencap show that children with SEN and disabilities are more likely than their peers. A 2007 Mencap survey found that eight out of ten respondents had been bullied and six out of ten had been physically hurt.

Children with SEN and disabilities are a diverse population. They have many skills and talents. They also have a wide range of very different needs. This includes children with complex health needs, children with learning disabilities, children with sensory impairments and children with social and behavioural needs. Some of these children will require support in school, some will not. For all children with SEN and disabilities discrimination based on their needs can be a challenge. Children with SEN and disabilities may;

- be adversely affected by negative attitudes to disability and perceptions of difference;
- find it more difficult to resist bullies;
- be more isolated, not have many friends;
- not understand that what is happening is bullying;
- have difficulties telling people about bullying.

This needs to be addressed across the school and particularly in the school anti-bullying policy. Duties for schools and local authorities established through the Disability Discrimination Act 2005 have helped make tackling this a priority.

It is also important to recognise that all children are potentially vulnerable to bullying and that learners with SEN and disabilities may be bullied for a range of other reasons too. Many disabled people also experience bullying in adult life. This makes developing a positive culture and anti-bullying message in school even more important.

'Bullying's just... like I've only got 2 friends in this entire school...everyone else just like runs away from me or gives me abuse. Everything they do to me is abuse. Well, they sort of swear at me, hit me, throw stuff at me.'

Anti-Bullying Approaches

Anti-Bullying work takes two tracks. Preventative work is ongoing and sustained, providing a consistent ethos and framework, while responsive work comes into effect in dealing with bullying behaviour. Preventative work involves the whole school community in agreeing a set of standards on behaviour in school.

To achieve this, it is essential that all learners, parents and staff understand what is meant by bullying. Some learners with SEN and disabilities are less likely than others to recognise and report bullying behaviour. They may need help to do this. There are many effective approaches to address bullying behaviour, these should be used within a whole school approach to maximise their effectiveness. More information at: www.antibullyingalliance.org.uk

Because learners with SEN and disabilities will have varied needs, selecting the right approach needs sensitivity and awareness of the strengths of the children involved. For example;

- Learners with language difficulties are less likely to find verbal fogging techniques work for them.
- Some learners will struggle to remember details of an incident several days later. This means that in their case, action should be taken at once if it is to be meaningful.
- Some learners with SEN and disabilities cannot recognise bullying behaviour nor identify the child who is using bullying behaviour. In such circumstances, work with bystanders and ongoing proactive work will be most productive.

Moving Between Settings

For learners who use a mix of special and mainstream provision, bullying can be a particular concern as they are repeatedly moving in and out of different environments. This can either be between schools, between school sites, or from a specialist unit into mainstream classrooms. These moves can be one off or regular and often lead to children being exposed to new people and environments which can be daunting. Learners with autism often find change difficult and may be particularly anxious at these times.

All of these transfers require preparation and support. They may make learners vulnerable to bullying if not handled with care. Learners report that where they are seen as outsiders they are more at risk. Their safety can rely on bystander support and proactive strategies already in place. Some schools set up the following:

- Induction Groups for new learners.

- Opportunities to view the other site on a webcam or DVD.
- Prepare Welcome booklets.
- Provide support groups of peers in school.
- Have trained peer supporters visit primary or special schools before the proposed move.

'You can't do anything about it. You can't tell. 2 reasons – 1... you don't know their name [said due to size of the school] so they'll get away with it, 2... you'll get bullied even more cos they'll call you a grasser.'

Prevention: Actions

A whole school approach develops and reviews a strategy by regularly consulting the entire school community. Learners with a range of needs including learning disability, sensory impairment and behavioural, emotional and social difficulties, (BESD) may require specific communication support to state their views. Also in reporting bullying, staff will need to check their understanding. Many children with autism for example are assumed to understand much more than they do in social situations.

A range of tools can be developed with learners to counter prejudice and foster a positive ethos. These include;

- Posters.
- Films on DVD.
- anti-bullying songs.
- drama productions about bullying or difference.
- PowerPoint presentations.
- Online activities including researching topics and producing information for their school.
- Assemblies with a focus around different needs.

'They don't always believe you when you tell'

Where learners with SEN and disabilities are concerned, communication across the staff team is essential. All staff working with children need to know of their individual needs, although will not need to have detailed information on a particular child's SEN and disability unless there is a specific reason. This could be a reasonable adjustment to support their needs. They will need to know the extent to which a learners' SEN and disability may lead them to bully others or display disruptive behaviour.

Staff need to be alert to changes in learners' behaviour and make sure they understand the cause. Often it is due to factors not related to their SEN or disability. Some learners with SEN and disabilities may be unable to recognise that they are being bullied and may not be able to report it. They may have been threatened or feel that they will not be believed. A preventative programme challenges prejudice and works with the majority of learners to reinforce messages that bullying is not to be tolerated.

The list below highlights what to consider to make sure all learners feel confident they can report bullying and be heard.

- Is there a quiet place in school to go to and talk?
- Does the staff member understand the child's communication needs?
- Can the child understand the staff member?
- Are their personal communication tools available to them?
- Have they had time to calm down and fully tell what they want to?
- Does the child need a supporter?
- Are staff visible and available to all learners out of the classroom?

Responding: Actions

Bullying should not be tolerated and should always be followed by an immediate and appropriate response. This response should be selected from a menu of tools within consistently applied framework. A 'one size fits all' approach is unhelpful when supporting children with a range of SEN and disabilities who experience bullying.

When choosing an approach, knowledge of the learners particular needs and the impact on their social development is essential. For example for some children with learning difficulties who have been bullied, it may be necessary to act very quickly while the child can remember what took place. In other cases allowances may need to be made because a learner with BESD demonstrates anti-social behaviour but did not intend to bully.

'Listen to the child even if it takes them all day to tell you what the problem is.'

"I may not have speech, but I have a voice—I can give my opinions, I can even argue!!"

Action Summary

Celebrate the anti-bullying work of the school and all of its pupils.

Adopt a rights-based approach to bullying—children with SEN and disabilities have the same right to be safe as other children.

Have a robust and consistent whole-school approach to bullying, which makes it clear that bullying on the grounds of disability will not be tolerated.

Schools can also:

Embrace the Disability Equality Duty and proactively promote equality. Work to eliminate harassment and discrimination and produce a Disability Equality Scheme.

Ensure the school environment is welcoming, supportive and inclusive of children with SEN and disabilities.

Make disability equality training available to all staff.

Listen to the views of children with SEN and disabilities on bullying.

Promote their participation in developing and reviewing polices and practice using appropriate communication systems.

Establish appropriate, comfortable and safe support mechanisms to help Children with SEN and disabilities who are being bullied.

Use a variety of methods to explore the issues of disability, SEN and bullying in a supportive and non-threatening way within the curriculum to underpin an inclusive and positive school ethos involving all learners.

Ensure learners with SEN and disabilities have opportunities to participate in school clubs and groups, to develop friendships and take an active part in all aspects of school life.

Support learners with SEN and disabilities and prevent bullying, with schemes such as befriending and buddying schemes, peer mentoring and circle of friends.

Avoid making learners feel powerless, helpless or passive.

Legal Duties and Guidance—What do Schools Have to do?

The Disability Discrimination Act. The Disability Discrimination Act 1995 (as amended), Section 49A, requires schools to take a more proactive approach to promoting disability equality and eliminating discrimination. Among its provisions are requirements on schools to promote positive attitudes towards disabled people and to eliminate harassment. There are obligations for governors and head teachers.

The Act sets out two duties:

- a **general** duty to promote disability equality, which applies to all public authorities and schools.
- a **specific** duty on publicly-funded schools to prepare and publish a disability equality scheme showing how they are meeting the general duty.

The general duty requires schools, when carrying out their functions, to have due regard to the need to:

- Promote equality of opportunity between disabled people and others.
- Eliminate unlawful discrimination.
- Eliminate harassment of disabled people that is related to their disability.
- Take steps to take account of disabled people's disabilities, even where that involves treating them more favourably.
- Promote positive attitudes towards disabled people.
- Encourage participation by disabled people in public life.

Schools may need to:

- Raise awareness amongst staff and pupils of disability-related harassment.
- Understand the nature and prevalence of bullying and harassment.
- Recognise and address bullying and harassment.
- Involve pupils themselves in addressing bullying.

The specific duty requires schools to:

- Prepare and publish a disability equality scheme.
- Involve disabled people in its development.

- Implement the scheme.
- Report on it.

The need to eliminate harassment of disabled people should impact directly on disabled pupils' experience of bullying in schools. The resource pack *'Implementing the DDA in schools and Early Years Settings'* offers further information and can be found at: www.teachernet.gov.uk/wholeschool/sen/disabilityandthedda/ddapart0

Governors have a responsibility to:

- Lead on shaping the ethos of the school.
- Review the school's behaviour policies, set the agenda for making these effective; publish and review a disability equality scheme and ensure that staff and pupils are protected from discrimination on the grounds of disability.

Head teachers' legal responsibilities are to:

- Determine and publicise the more detailed measures (rules, sanctions, rewards and behaviour management strategies) on behaviour and discipline that form the school's behaviour policy, acting in accordance with the governing body's statement of principles. The measures must be determined with a view to encouraging good behaviour and respect for others by pupils and, preventing all forms of bullying among pupils.
- Consider whether any adjustments are needed to the policy to take account of the needs of children with SEN and disabilities.

As school policies are updated in line with disability equality duties, head teachers and the senior management team should ensure that they are understood and followed by the whole school community to enhance the experience of school life for learners with SEN and disabilities. It is a legal requirement to consult with the head, staff, parents and pupils when making or revising the statement of principles and to involve disabled people in developing the disability equality scheme.

The SENCO has a particular role to play in ensuring the well being of children with SEN and disabilities. As well as being champions of inclusion, SENCOs can:

Encourage staff training in disability equality and raise awareness of the disability equality duties.

Contribute to policy development and review and enable the participation of disabled children in consultations.

Ensure learners with SEN and disabilities who are bullied receive support and help in preventing and dealing with it.

Monitor the impact of anti-bullying interventions on individual learners with SEN and disabilities.

Ensure learners with social and behavioural needs receive appropriate support to prevent bullying behaviour where needed.

'Even if we look different, we've all got the same blood.' (Primary pupil)

Safe To Learn is a suite of guidance materials for mainstream and special schools.

It consists of an overarching document, *Safe to Learn: Embedding anti-bullying work in schools,* and supplementary guidance on the following specific forms of bullying:

- racism, religion and culture
- homophobic bullying
- cyberbullying
- special educational needs (SEN) and disability.

This document forms the supplementary guidance on identifying and dealing with bullying involving children and young people with SEN and disabilities (SEND). Practical guidance on dealing with allegations of bullying is provided in Section 4 of *Safe to Learn.* Teachers and others working in schools will find it helpful to use this Guidance as a supplement to *Safe to Learn* and to cross-reference back to it when necessary.

> For ease of reading, we have used 'children' to mean 'children and young people' throughout the text.
>
> To reflect legal terms, we have used Special Educational Needs and Disability (SEND) to describe the range of physical, learning, behavioural and sensory needs children and young people may have.

This guidance is designed to help schools support learners with SEN and disabilities to:

- understand, prevent and respond to bullying of children with SEN and disabilities
- increase the participation of all learners in the life of the school
- promote equality and diversity
- develop a non-bullying ethos.

And by doing so:

- raise achievement and participation in safe, positive environments
- take actions which meet their legal safeguarding obligations and comply with the Disability Discrimination Act 1995 (DDA) and other legislation
- build on the requirements of the SEN Code of Practice
- uphold the fundamental human right of children to be free from abuse.

What Do we Mean by Bullying?

'Bullying's just... like I've only got two friends in this entire school... everyone else just like runs away from me or gives me abuse. Everything they do to me is abuse. Well, they sort of swear at me, hit me, throw stuff at me.'

Definitions of Bullying

The publication *Safe To Learn: Embedding anti-bullying work in schools* describes bullying as: *'Behaviour by an individual or group usually repeated over time that intentionally hurts another individual or group either physically or emotionally.'* [para 1.6]

Bullying includes:

name calling; taunting; mocking; making offensive comments; kicking; hitting; pushing; taking belongings; inappropriate text messaging and emailing; sending offensive or degrading images by phone or via the internet; producing offensive graffiti; gossiping; excluding people from groups; and spreading hurtful and untruthful rumours. Although sometimes occurring between two individuals in isolation, it quite often takes place in the presence of others. [para 1.7]

The Anti-Bullying Alliance has produced this easy-to-read definition of bullying: *People doing nasty or unkind things to you on purpose, more than once, which it is difficult to stop.*

The DDA places additional duties on schools. The DDA requires schools to have due regard to a range of actions, which include:

- eliminating discrimination that is unlawful under the DDA
- eliminating harassment of disabled people that is related to their disability. More information on these duties can be found in Appendix 1.

For all children and young people, bullying can be a barrier to education and a fulfilled life. With this in mind, the government has made tackling bullying in schools a priority. This guidance addresses particular issues for learners with SEN and disabilities. Sections 2 and 3 examine prevention and responses in detail.

SEN and Disability, Who do we Mean?

'We all act strange at some time in our lives and we all need friends. Remember, you don't know if it could happen to yourself one day. I know I could never see it happening to me but it did.

Public bodies, local authorities and schools use two key definitions to inform their decisions about providing support to disabled children and those with SEN. One definition is from the DDA and the other is from the Education Act 1996. The extract below, from *Implementing the Disability Discrimination Act in schools and early years settings*, sets them out.

The DDA defines a disabled person as someone who has *'a physical or mental impairment which has a substantial and long-term adverse effect on his or her ability to carry out normal day-to-day activities.'*

The term 'physical or mental impairment' also includes sensory impairments and hidden impairments. In the DDA 'substantial' means 'more than minor or trivial'. 'Long-term' means that it has lasted or is likely to last more than 12 months or for the rest of the life of the person affected.

The definition is broad and includes children with a wide range of impairments, including learning disabilities, dyslexia, diabetes or epilepsy where the effect of the impairment on the learner's ability to carry out normal day-to-day activities is adverse, substantial and long-term. A significant number of learners are included in the definition.

'The term "special educational needs" (SEN) *has a legal definition, referring to children who have learning difficulties or disabilities that make it harder for them to learn or access education than most children of the same age.'*

Many children who have SEN will also be defined as having a disability under the DDA, particularly those at School Action Plus, Early Years Action Plus, or who have a statement of SEN. This should be considered for planning purposes and for the avoidance of discrimination.

For further information on these definitions see www.teachernet.gov.uk and www.equalityhumanrights.com

The social model of disability offers a different perspective on disability stating that:

> *'disability is caused by the way society is organised, rather than by a person's impairment or difference. The Social Model of Disability looks at ways of removing barriers which restrict life choices for people with impairments or differences. When barriers are removed, disabled people can be independent and equal in society, with choice and control over their own lives.'* (*www.childreninthepicture.org.uk/au_socialmodel.htm*)

The social model of disability definition was further set out in a policy context in the Cabinet Office report *Improving the Life Chances of Disabled People* (2005) as follows.

'Disability should be distinguished from impairment and ill health. For the purposes of this report, disability is defined as:

- *disadvantage experienced by an individual...*
- *... resulting from barriers to independent living or educational, employment or other opportunities ...*
- *... that impact on people with impairments and/or ill health.'*

In schools this ethos is a key element of developing a truly inclusive environment and an effective disability equality scheme and anti-bullying policy.

The Cabinet Office report goes on to outline a range of barriers that disabled people face, which is equally pertinent to schools.

'The types of barriers faced by disabled people include:

- ***attitudinal**, for example among disabled people themselves and among employers, health professionals and service providers*
- ***policy**, resulting from policy design and delivery which do not take disabled people into account*
- ***physical**, for example through the design of the built environment, transport systems, and*
- *those linked to **empowerment**, as a result of which disabled people are not listened to, consulted or involved.'*

Why Issue Additional Guidance for Children and Young People with SEN and Disabilities?

As the Cabinet Office report above shows, disabled children and those with SEN face a range of entrenched, institutional barriers, which schools are at the forefront of tackling.

In addition to these wide-reaching barriers, evidence shows that children with a range of needs are more likely to experience bullying than their peers. A report from the Children's Commissioner in 2006 and another by the National Autistic Society in 2007 demonstrate that children with SEN and disabilities are more likely than their peers to be bullied. In a 2007 survey of children with learning disabilities, Mencap found that eight out of 10 respondents had been bullied and six out of 10 had been physically hurt.

Like any group of children, those with an SEN or disability are a diverse population. They have many skills and talents. Between them, they also have a wide range of needs. The group includes children with complex health needs, children with learning disabilities, children with sensory impairments and children with behavioural needs. Some of these children will require a level of support in school, some will not. For all children with SEN or disability, bullying is a real issue. The common difficulties which some groups of children encounter need to be addressed in the school's anti-bullying policy. For example, they may find:

- negative attitudes to disability
- negative perceptions of difference
- it is more difficult to resist bullies due to their disability
- they are more isolated due to their disability
- they do not understand that what is happening is bullying
- they have difficulties telling people about bullying.

Bullying involving children with SEN and disabilities has—until recently—received limited attention at a national and local level. New duties for schools and local authorities established through the DDA 2005 have helped make tackling this a priority.

It is also important to recognise that all children are potentially vulnerable to bullying but that learners with SEN and disabilities may be bullied for a range of other reasons too. Furthermore, many disabled people experience bullying in adult life. This makes developing a positive culture and an anti-bullying message in school even more important.

Who is this Guidance Intended for?

This document is part of the Department for Children, Schools and Families (DCSF) *Safe to Learn* suite of anti-bullying guidance materials for schools. It is aimed at maintained schools (including maintained nursery schools), maintained special schools and Pupil Referral Units; although it is relevant to all types of school in England. Increasingly schools are required to work in partnership with a range of agencies, organisations and bodies, for example, in clusters, with local authorities, youth services and extended service providers. Increasingly, schools are expected to work in partnership with a range of other agencies. These agencies may also find this guidance useful. For example:

Children and Young People's Strategic Partnership Board
Children's Trusts/Services Authorities
Community safety teams
Educational psychology teams
Extended Schools remodelling advisors and
Extended Schools clusters
Local Children's Safeguarding Boards (LCSF)
Local multi-agency anti-bullying groups
The National Strategies
Residential and secure settings
Safer School partnerships
Voluntary and community sector groups
Youth Offending Services
Youth services.

The National Context: Every Child Matters

The Every Child Matters programme focuses the education sector and the wider children's sector on supporting children to achieve positive outcomes. Learners who may be experiencing impairment-related bullying are less likely to meet the outcomes of Every Child Matters.

- *Being healthy:* children with complex health needs may need extra support to access the curriculum and have a degree of independence from support staff to make friends.
- *Staying safe:* disabled children may experience physical or mental harm when bullied because of their impairment. They may also be more at risk of bullying because of their impairment (for example, they may be less able to move away or vary journeys to or around school because of mobility problems; have problems with communication or 'looking different'; have cognitive or other impairments which make anticipation and avoidance very difficult; and of course need, in some cases, personal support). They are also likely to have contact with far more people in their everyday lives, which may also increase the risk of bullying by staff as well as learners.
- *Enjoying and achieving*: children with SEN and disabilities may need extra support to access a full range of activities and the curriculum, and to achieve their full potential. Fear of bullying may prevent their full participation in school activities.
- *Achieving economic well-being:* children with SEN and disabilities often have fewer expectations placed upon them in accessing vocational qualifications and work. Being bullied could further contribute to their decision not to stay on in education.
- *Making a positive contribution:* children experiencing bullying related to their impairment will be discouraged from making a positive contribution to their school life and to their community.

Most recently, the government has published the *Children's Plan; Aiming High for Disabled Children; Aiming High for Young People:* A ten year strategy for *positive activities;* and *Aiming High for Children: Supporting families*. These documents set out government's intentions across a range of work areas on improvements for all children and young people. More information can be found at: www.dfes.gov.uk/publications/childrensplan and www.everychildmatters.gov.uk

Conclusion

Anti-bullying work is a key consideration in behaviour management and pastoral care. It has every child's right to be safe as a cornerstone and, additionally, offers unique opportunities to demonstrate an ethos of equality while developing social skills, responsibilities and relationships among all learners. It also encourages creativity and fosters a sense of belonging and citizenship.

In order to achieve this, learners with SEN and disabilities require particular attention. Schools and local authorities have specific duties under education- and rights-based legislation concerning disability. These duties are to ensure that learners' special educational needs are identified, assessed and provided for and that they are not discriminated against because they have an impairment. The Disability Equality Duty provides a clear legal framework for tackling bullying and harassment of children with SEN and disability.

LEGAL DUTIES AND GUIDANCE RELATING TO LEARNERS WITH SEN AND DISABILITIES

Beyond the general requirements set out in *Safe to Learn,* there is further legislation and guidance for supporting schools to embed effective practice when supporting learners with SEN and disabilities. The following pages give a summary of the key responsibilities of governors, headteachers and teachers.

These duties and policies are covered in detail in *Appendix 1* and in the resource: *Implementing the DDA in schools and early years settings—a training resource for schools and local authorities*. See www.teachernet.gov.uk/wholeschool/sen/disabilityandthedda/ddapart0 for further information.

Governors

Governing bodies have a responsibility to shape the ethos of a school. Creating an inclusive ethos so that all members of the school community feel safe and valued represents the most powerful intervention governors can make. While achieving an inclusive school requires a team effort, there are a number of ways governing bodies must take the lead: by developing policies and practice; and consulting the school community.

Develop Policies and Practice

Determine and keep under review the statement of principles that shapes the schools' behaviour policies.

- Set the agenda for effective behaviour and anti-bullying policies, which take account of all members of the school community.

- Publish and keep under review a disability equality scheme which sets out how the general disability equality duties will be implemented.
- Review all school policies in line with disability equality duties and remain aware that staff as well as pupils are protected in law from discrimination on the grounds of disability.
- Be proactive in eliminating harassment of disabled people that is related to their disability. As well as reacting to bullying and harassment of disabled pupils, governing bodies must act positively to prevent it. The disability equality duties provide a framework for this, requiring governing bodies to promote positive attitudes towards disabled pupils.
- Make reasonable adjustments to avoid placing disabled pupils at a substantial disadvantage in comparison with pupils who are not disabled. This is an anticipatory duty which means that governors and staff cannot wait until a pupil is attending the school before making adjustments. It may mean focusing resources on a particular aspect of school development such as staff training or changing a policy which impacts unfairly on particular groups of disabled pupils.
- Be proactive in improving access to teaching and learning for disabled pupils and increase their participation. Improve communication with them and make changes to the physical environment in ways which could prevent bullying.

Consulting the School Community

By consulting and involving all members of the school community, governors can ensure that policies are informed by and responsive to learners' experiences of bullying. It is a legal requirement to consult with the headteacher, staff, parents and learners when developing or revising the statement of principles; and to involve disabled people, who appear to have an interest in the way it carries out its functions, in the production of the disability equality scheme. See Section 3 for information on successful consultation and participation of learners with SEN and disabilities.

Headteachers

Headteachers have day-to-day responsibility for turning the governing body's vision for the school into reality. They should lead in building the school's ethos, making the school welcoming, supportive and inclusive of disabled pupils and staff to ensure they are at the core of planning and their needs are considered as a priority. This should be an expectation of the whole school community and of the services provided by and associated with the school.

Headteachers' Legal Responsibilities are as Follows

- To determine and publicise the more detailed measures (rules, sanctions, rewards and behaviour management strategies) on behaviour and discipline that form the school's behaviour policy, acting in accordance with the governing body's statement of principles. The measures must be determined with a view to encouraging good behaviour and respect for others on the part of the learners and, in particular, preventing all forms of bullying among learners.

- To consider whether any adjustments are needed to the policy to take account of disabled children.

As school policies are updated in line with disability equality duties, headteachers and the senior management team must ensure that they are understood and followed by the whole school community to enhance the experience of school life for disabled learners.

Action on Bullying

Initial steps schools should consider to tackle bullying and harassment of disabled pupils include:

- ensuring staff receive appropriate training in disability equality, and how to recognise and deal with bullying
- developing a system of recording incidents of bullying of learners with SEN and disabilities and ensuring staff know of and use it consistently (see *Safe to Learn,* para 5.7, for specific information)
- determining and ensuring the implementation of a policy for the pastoral care of learners that considers the particular needs of disabled learners
- celebrating the anti-bullying work of the school and its learners
- ensuring disabled learners have opportunities to participate in school clubs and groups, to develop friendships and take an active part in all aspects of school life
- involving disabled learners when reviewing policy documents, including the disability equality scheme and behaviour and anti-bullying policies, by ensuring that they are supported to participate
- ensuring 'pupil voice' policies enable the school to capture all aspects of their learners' communications, including behaviour-related information
- providing structures and systems that respond effectively to the 'pupil voice', so that the views of learners are known to be significant
- demonstrating and acknowledging a range of success measures, beyond those of the academic achievement traditionally valued by schools, so that all learners feel valued.

Teaching Staff

The National Curriculum Inclusion Statement sets out three principles of inclusion, which teachers are expected to consider at all levels of curriculum planning. These go beyond the boundaries of subject learning, looking at the wider context of learning. The three principles are:

1. Setting suitable learning challenges
2. Responding to pupils' diverse learning needs
3. Overcoming potential barriers to learning and assessment for individuals and groups of pupils.

Teachers should ensure that all learners feel secure and valued and consequently are able to learn and contribute to school life. Among the ways teachers can achieve this are by:

- promoting the well-being of individual learners and ensuring, as far as possible, that learners are free from bullying and harassment
- ensuring that learners who have experienced bullying are taken seriously
- helping learners to take responsibility for their actions
- helping learners to take a positive view of difference and challenging stereotypical views
- celebrating the successes of disabled learners
- helping learners to articulate their views and experiences
- modelling the behaviour and values they are trying to instil
- taking advantage of training opportunities to increase their understanding of disability and improve their ability to recognise bullying and manage behaviour
- providing well-differentiated accessible learning opportunities so that all learners experience the self-esteem and confidence that comes with success and achievement.

Special Educational Needs Coordinators (SENCOs)

Being responsible for coordinating provision for children with SEN and disabilities, the SENCO has an important and central role in ensuring their well-being. They are in close contact with learners with SEN and disabilities and the staff that teach them. They report regularly to parents on their children's progress. All school staff have a responsibility to support all learners who are bullied. SENCOs can contribute to this as they will often be aware of concerns in relation to bullying of children with SEN and disabilities.

As well as being champions of inclusion, SENCOs can:

- encourage staff training in disability equality and raise awareness of the disability equality duties
- contribute to policy development and review
- ensure that learners with SEN and disabilities who are vulnerable to bullying receive support and help in preventing and dealing with it
- monitor the impact of anti-bullying interventions on individual learners with SEN and disabilities
- ensure learners with particular social and behavioural needs receive appropriate support to prevent bullying behaviour.

The government has recently consulted on regulations designed to strengthen the role of SENCOs in schools. For more information see www.tda.gov.uk/teachers/sen/nationalstandards. aspx and www.teachernet.gov.uk

Support Staff

All school staff have a responsibility to support all learners. Learning support assistants are commonly working with one or a small group of learners with SEN and disabilities; and therefore have a key role in ensuring learners access the curriculum and in encouraging them to take part in wider school activities, like games at break times and making friends. Support staff who work closely with learners with SEN and disabilities may often have an important role in picking up signs that a child is being bullied, this is particularly important where a child may find it more difficult to report that they are being bullied.

Some schools are developing the role of Inclusion Mentor. More can be found on this at: www.teachernet.gov.uk

A Note on the Education and Inspections Act (2006)

This Act brings together existing and new provisions on school discipline into a single chapter of education law to make it easier for teachers and school staff to understand their powers. Amongst other things, the Act creates a clear, statutory power for members of school staff to impose disciplinary powers for inappropriate behaviours; enables headteachers to regulate the behaviour of learners when they are off the school site; and reiterates the power of school staff to use physical force in certain circumstances.

For more detailed information on duties please see Appendix 1 or *Implementing the DDA in schools and early years settings* at www.teachernet.gov.uk/wholeschool/sen/disabilityandthedda/ddapart0

Summary: Action on Bullying

Some steps to tackle bullying and harassment of disabled learners:

- Ensure staff receive appropriate training in disability equality and how to recognise and deal with bullying.
- Develop a system of recording incidents of bullying of learners with SEN and disabilities and ensure staff it is used consistently. Safe to Learn [para 5.7] has specific information.
- Determine and ensure the implementation of a policy for the pastoral care of pupils which considers the particular needs of disabled pupils.
- Celebrate the anti-bullying work of the school and its pupils.
- Ensure disabled learners have opportunities to participate in school clubs and groups, to develop friendships and take an active part in all aspects of school life.
- Ensure disabled learners are supported to participate when policy documents, including the disability equality scheme and behaviour and anti-bullying policies, are reviewed.

- Ensure 'pupil voice' policies enable the school to capture all aspects of their learners' communication, including behaviour-related information.
- Ensure structures and systems are in place to respond to 'pupil voice' so that the views of learners are known to be significant.
- Demonstrate and acknowledge a range of success measures, beyond those of academic achievement traditionally valued by schools, so that all learners feel valued.

PREVENTION

Anti-bullying work takes a two-track pathway. *Preventative* work is ongoing and sustained, providing a consistent ethos and framework, while responsive work comes into effect when bullying occurs. This section looks at preventative approaches as part of a comprehensive, wholeschool, anti-bullying strategy.

Responses to individual incidents work more effectively within a consistent whole-school approach. It is essential to develop a strong inclusive ethos where bullying and prejudice is not tolerated. This is the foundation upon which bullying of children with SEN and disabilities can be effectively addressed.

Headteachers must determine measures on behaviour and discipline that form the school's behaviour policy, acting in accordance with the governing body's statement of principles. The DCSF recommends that anti-bullying policies are developed as part of the school's wider behaviour policy. This policy should include references to learners with SEN and disabilities.

Developing a Whole–School Approach to Anti-Bullying

Safe to Learn sets out advice on developing a whole-school approach to preventing and dealing with bullying. The DCSF anti-bullying charter underpins this approach and can be found at: www.teachernet.gov.uk/wholeschool/behaviour/tacklingbullying/anitbullyingcharter.

An adapted version of the charter with a focus on disability and further tools can be found at: www.anti-bullyingalliance.org

Children who may not be able to report incidents themselves are particularly dependent on a whole-school proactive approach. Bullying usually requires an audience. The majority of learners are a powerful group who form bystanders, supporters and reinforcers, but they could become defenders. Without their tacit or active support, bullying diminishes. A strong anti-bullying programme is likely to provide other benefits, such as happier, more confident learners, a fall in truancy or school refusal and a rise in attainment.

Children with autism spectrum disorders (ASD) are particularly vulnerable as their difficulties with social interaction with peers may leave them isolated or unaware of the impact of their behaviour on others. Children with learning difficulties tend to have fewer friends than other children and a lack of friends puts children at a greater risk of being bullied. A whole-school approach should promote positive images of disability. Alongside this, practical steps should be taken, such as setting up lunchtime clubs that offer new friendship groups and quiet spaces, trained peer supporters and well-trained staff.

Children with learning difficulties are less likely to seek help than their peers. This may be due to difficulties they may have with reporting bullying, for example, learners with communication needs. Additionally, some children, particularly those with ASD and learning difficulties, may also find it hard to understand when they are being bullied. This could make them an easier target, as bullies may realise they can more easily avoid detection. A proactive prevention programme will consider these challenges and provide supportive and easy pathways to reporting and defending.

Clarifying What is Meant by 'Bullying'

In order to fully recognise the scale of the challenge faced by learners with SEN and disabilities, it is necessary to ensure that all children understand what bullying is. Children need help to distinguish between different behaviours. For some learners their impairment will mean that they will find it very difficult to identify bullying behaviour or may not be able to report it.

In Section 1, bullying is defined and a child-friendly version provided.

Accepted definitions include three elements. It is behaviour which:

1. intentionally hurts another person either physically or emotionally
2. is usually repeated over time
3. is an abuse of power leaving the victim defenceless.

Occasionally an incident is a one-off example of bullying and an intervention is required to avoid a repetition taking place. Some incidents require action from an outside agency such as police, fire service or community safety. Where a learner has retaliated after months of persistent bullying, we advise that this be considered differently from an unprovoked attack.

Group sessions, drama, posters and assemblies can be regularly used to explore how everyone would like to be treated and to define bullying, so that every member of the school community knows what it is and, equally, what would not be considered bullying (including, for example, a serious incident of another sort). Work to define bullying can be done in the classroom, Circle Time, PSHE and Citizenship lessons and by the school council. Learners can help make PowerPoint presentations or DVDs, perform in assemblies or design posters. Learners should be provided with safe and frequent opportunities to talk about what they think about bullying. Displays of work around the school will act to raise everyone's awareness.

A clear understanding prevents learners over-reporting any unpleasant remark or disagreement and also helps them to recognise and take action if they are being bullied. Through this activity, they may realise that their own behaviour is seen as bullying. Others may develop resilience when they realise that bullying is not tolerated.

Certain vulnerable young people may have difficulties judging what is socially acceptable behaviour and may be 'led' by other learners into behaviour which is unacceptable according to the school's behaviour policy. This manipulative behaviour may be viewed as a form of bullying.

The next step in a whole-school approach is to gather information. This should include all learners, staff, support staff and parents.

Participation of Learners with SEN and Disabilities

For a school anti-bullying policy to be meaningful and effective it needs to be developed in partnership with other groups and agencies who use the school building and with the full involvement of all learners, including those with SEN and disabilities.

To assess the effectiveness of any actions and strategies, schools need to consult children with a range of needs. Children with SEN and disabilities who participate in developing the school policy will be more likely to 'own' observe and implement the policy. They will feel listened to and valued; they will be aware of bullying and what to do about it. As a result they are likely to feel safer and more confident in the school's commitment to confront bullying.

To gather information regularly, school staff can use a range of methods including questionnaires, technology, drama, music sessions and circle time. More information on participation and consultation is available at

www.anti-bullyingalliance.org
www.participationworks.org.uk
http://sites.childrenssociety.org.uk/disabilitytoolkit/

> Simple adaptations to questionnaires can enable wider participation for some children. For example, a recorded questionnaire can be provided for learners with a sight impairment. Illustrations or smiley/sad faces, and graphics or simple scales from one to five, can assist learners with learning disabilities to give their views. Learning support assistants may be asked to help.
>
> New technology offers touch screens, voice-activated software and custom-designed equipment, all of which are valuable in offering opportunities for learners with physical disabilities to participate and give views in their own way.
>
> Further information can be found at: www.antibullyingalliance.org and www.ncb.org.uk/cdc

The involvement of all learners not only shows commitment to a whole-school approach to bullying and strengthens the inclusive ethos of the school, it also underpins the school's fulfilment of its duties under the DDA. In addition, school councils should be reviewed to ensure all children have a voice and are fully participating in the school council process (see www.schoolcouncils.org). There is a wealth of excellent resources available to support the participation of children and young people from:

www.participationworks.org.uk;
www.disabilitytoolkit.org.uk and www.nya.org.uk.

Disabled children and young people highlighted the following as key in developing effective participation practice.

Involve us from the start

- *'You can find out what's best for us by involving us'*
- *'Don't guess what we want'*

Respect us

- *'If you give us respect—we'll give you respect'*
- *'Trust us—we need to trust you'*

Listen to us

- *'Listen to me, no one else, listen to me. It's my body. Listen to me, its my life, listen to me'*
- *'If you don't listen to what we want—how can you give us what we want?'*

Be open and honest with us

- *'We ask questions to help us understand our world and to grow as people!'*
- *'Frustrating when you don't tell us stuff'*
- *'We all make mistakes'*

Make it fun!

- *'We're teenagers, we're young, we want to learn.'*

Prove you're listening to us

- *'Show us you want to listen'*
- *'My voice is my power'*
- *'Tell us what's changed'*

Involve all of us!

- *'Don't judge a book by its cover – we can all make choices'*
- *'I may not have speech, but I have a voice—I can give my opinions, I can even argue'*

Make sure we get something out of it

- *'Participation is a great way to help us learn how to make decisions and understand the choices we may face in the future!'*
- *'Empower us!'*
- *'Gives us new skills'*

Give us time

- *'Help us make decisions by giving your time—enough time'*
- *'I know what I want to say—give me time'*
- *'Give me time to get my message ready'*

Support us to make our own decisions

- *'I want more choice'*
- *'If you listen to us you can help us get a positive outcome'*

The poster, 'Top Tips for Participation: What disabled young people want' is available from www.ncb.org.uk/cdc_moh

Role of Parents

Schools are expected to engage parents as well as pupils and school staff in their delivery of the Disability Equality Duty and the development of their Disability Equality Scheme. Through this scheme, the school will be working to develop and maintain a whole school approach to effectively prevent and deal with discrimination and harassment of disabled pupils.

Parents are the experts on their children's behaviour and their physical and mental well-being. They have a key role to play in supporting their children if they bully others or experience bullying themselves. They can offer advice to school staff on extra support their child might need or any creative solutions that may help to resolve conflict. Parents have a wealth of knowledge schools will want to call upon when developing or reviewing their anti-bullying policy. It is important that schools listen to and respond to parents concerns and keep good communication going between them when dealing with bullying incidents relating to their children.

Parents may want to contact other organisations for support to discuss particular situations involving bullying and their child. Schools can pass on details of the local Parent Partnership Service, Contact a Family or other sources of local support. www.parentpartnership.org.uk and www.cafamily.org.uk.

Some schools will also have parent advisor roles as part of the delivery of the Children's Plan, which may be a further source of support: www.dfes.gov.uk/publications/childrensplan/

Where and When does Bullying Occur?

'They get you everywhere, even in class 'n' sometimes teachers laugh as well.'

Learners report that ongoing 'low level' harassment takes place in the classroom every day. This suggests that the presence of adults alone is not sufficient to stop bullying. While playtime activities are often supervised and some learners with complex needs may be accompanied by an assistant, for others the corridors, lunch queues, toilets and playgrounds represent areas and periods when bullying is most likely to occur.

Moving Between Settings

For learners who use a mix of special and mainstream provision, bullying can be a particular concern as they are repeatedly moving in and out of different environments. This can either be between schools or from a specialist unit into mainstream classrooms. These moves can be one-off or regular and often lead to children being exposed to new people and environments, which can be daunting. Learners on the autism spectrum often find change difficult and may be particularly anxious at these times. One of the most common fears learners report is that they will be bullied.

> The learner below attends a special school. He goes to college two days a week. While in school he feels safe, but at college he is vulnerable.
> *Learner: I get called nasty names. Two girls on a different course to me.*

> *Inquirer: When does this happen?*
> *In the canteen.*
> *Has it been going on long?*
> *He nods strongly.*
> *Have you told anyone?*
> *Member of staff.*
> *Did they do anything?*
> *Had words with them.*
> *Did it stop?*
> *No. It keeps carrying on. In my breaks and when I come to the canteen.*
> *I eat in the sandwich room now instead of the canteen. They call me gay at dinner.*

Strategies developed to support all learners in the move from primary school to secondary school can usefully be applied here. Programmes which address concerns and help to prepare and then integrate learners are being used successfully in many schools. This type of structured support may be particularly useful for those learners who depend on routine.

'We have an inclusion unit at the school so that students can be gradually integrated—this includes children with behavioural problems and SEN. They may start out being there 100 per cent of the time and be gradually integrated into school. This happened with one boy who had ADHD [attention-deficit hyperactivity disorder]. He enjoyed the activities in the inclusion unit—very hands-on activities, sport, less structure. He bonded well with two TAs who helped to gradually integrate him into school. He now spends very little time in the unit—he has completely turned around.'

Increasingly, schools are operating beyond the confines of one site. Schools can be creative and proactive in developing anti-bullying strategies that are effective across a range of sites and have sign-up from all partner agencies. Additionally, the Education and Inspections Act 2006 provides powers for a headteacher to take action on behaviour incidents out of school.

As the chart below illustrates there are a considerable number of potential moves which learners may experience.

Checklist

The checklist below illustrates some key areas of action for multi site operations.

- All site managers signed up to anti-bullying policy.
- Access and support for all learners in place for all sites.
- Transport included in sign-up to anti-bullying policy.
- Agreement reached on who deals with incidents of bullying on each site.
- Consistent use of sanctions across sites.
- Clarity achieved on who liaises with after-school clubs, extended activities, and homework clubs.
- Partner agencies using school premises to deliver services now all signed up to anti-bullying policy.

- Person identified at each site as responsible and key contact point for issues on bullying; everyone, children and staff, know who this is at each site.

Addressing a Culture of Discrimination

'I told my teachers at school and they said that I had special needs so I should get used to it as I would be bullied all my life. They also told me to stop playing out at break times then I would not get bullied.' (Mencap 2007)

A whole-school policy will directly address a culture of discrimination.

Research has found that children who believe that the bullying they experience is due to some internal unchangeable fact about themselves have been found to be the most vulnerable.

It is essential that they are led to understand that bullying behaviour is wrong, and that their impairment is not a valid cause.

The Social Model of Disability states that *'disability is caused by the way society is organised, rather than by a person's impairment or difference. This approach looks at ways of removing barriers which restrict life choices for people with impairments or differences. When barriers are removed, disabled people can be independent and equal in society, with choice and control over their own lives.* (Taken from www.childreninthepicture.org.uk/au_socialmodel.htm)

A culture of discrimination can be very subtle. In interviews to inform this guidance, parents stated that they often felt that their child was being unfairly blamed for being bullied due to their characteristic or difficult behaviour.

'The school had an irritated/impatient/cynical response and passed the blame on to the victim. [They said] 'If you had done this or that instead...' (Parent)

This was a particular concern for parents who had children with SEN and disabilities who had used bullying behaviour on other children. A child can acquire a reputation for being troublesome if they are acting out frequently—or presenting with difficult behaviour. They can be seen as the cause of all disruption.

'They used to blame my child for it. My child has now got a reputation so that sometimes he has been blamed for things when he wasn't even present.' (Parent of child with ASD)

Many learners with a range of emotional or behavioural impairments will know their own 'triggers' and will manage them well in a classroom environment with the support of staff. Others will not. Knowing the needs of each individual and how they may need to be supported can make a huge difference to their acceptance in the group and their confidence and feelings of safety as part of it. Furthermore, in research for this guide we found that generally, children respond well to having factual information about impairments and this can encourage them to respond positively to the needs of others. Use of the SEAL (Social and Emotional Aspects of Learning) materials, adapted to take account of impairments, could underpin this. For further information on SEAL, see www.standards.dfes.gov.uk/primary/features/primary/873235.

Meeting the requirements set out in the DDA to ensure the school environment is accessible—physically, intellectually and sensorily (for example, it has improved acoustics, hearing loops, and colour contrasts to support visual clarity)—will empower individuals and may reduce the risk of developing feelings of victimisation and occurrences of bullying. Confident and happy learners who feel part of their school are much less likely to experience or take part in bullying.

Informal or Inadvertent Exclusions

Learners with SEN and disabilities and their parents report experiencing informal exclusion from school activities. This is most common when learners with SEN and disabilities are not permitted to go on a school trip or event because reasonable adjustments are not made to support them. This limits opportunities for social development and the peer group will knit together even further without this excluded learner, further reinforcing their outsider status. The DDA requires schools not to treat disabled learners 'less favourably' and to increase access for disabled children and young people. They are to 'make reasonable adjustments to ensure that disabled learners are not at a substantial disadvantage.'

'Everyone should understand everyone's different, but they should all be included in everything. Like I haven't done P.E. for ages.' (Young person who uses a wheelchair)

Casual Exclusions

Casual exclusions are those, for example, where a peer group sits together to watch a performance or a film and a learner with SEN and disabilities is placed away from the others, next to a teacher or assistant, giving them no opportunity to socialise with their peers. Both learners with and without SEN and disabilities observe that this can hinder attempts by all parties to build friendships. This illustrates that there is a sensitive balance to be struck between keeping someone safe and undermining their own potential for social development with peers. Good practice consists of assisting integration and acceptance by peers, including widening participation with and access to them.

This practice of keeping learners with SEN and disabilities with staff means that many disabled children spend the vast majority of their time with adults rather than children. This means they often miss out on opportunities for age-appropriate behaviour and the exercise of autonomy. The most important protective factor in response to being bullied is that the student responds actively rather than passively. Children who can exercise some control over their own situation feel competent and effective. They experience significant psychological and social advantages.

Planning and Reviewing the Policy—Including Learners with SEN and Disabilities

'In class discussions ask everyone for their opinion and make sure everyone understands. Include the quiet ones as well. [My school] sometimes uses a 'no hands up' rule and the teachers pick people to answer. Another way of getting different people to answer is to use a 'Lucky Dip' if your name comes up—you have to answer.' (A 15-year-old)

Anti-bullying policies are most effective when they make reference to the needs of all groups of learners within the school. Below are ideas on how to ensure that the needs of learners with SEN and disabilities are considered in the policy document and its implementation.

Staff Actions

Governors should review the school's behaviour policies and disability equality scheme. It is a legal requirement to consult with the headteacher, staff, parents and learners when making or revising the statement of principles and to involve disabled people in the making of the disability equality scheme.

Senior Leadership teams and those with responsibility for pastoral care, inclusion and SEN should carry out all anti-bullying policy reviews and updates with the participation of all learners, staff and parents. Adjustments should be made to enable the participation of learners with SEN and disabilities and their parents. For example, by using parents' forums, Parent Partnership Services, questionnaires, school councils, facilitated groups.

Senior teams should work to change the school ethos and to move learners and staff away from any cultural perception that some children 'deserve' to be bullied or will 'inevitably' be bullied due to their impairment. The policy should include responses and sanctions. Training will be required for staff.

Staff should be informed about any learners' SEN and disabilities that might make them either vulnerable or likely to behave aggressively towards others. Any allowances or responses that are required for an individual should be known to all staff. Arrangements for transport and outings should ensure reasonable adjustments are made to ensure all children can participate.

Partner services (health and social workers) should work with schools to adapt and align their working practices. Any health professional should be encouraged to consider whether a learner presenting with any signs of injury or damage to personal belongings might be being bullied. Share any knowledge of particular conditions—such as those that make up the ASD spectrum, Behavioural, Emotional and Social Difficulties (BESD) or other SEN and disabilities—with schools in order to increase the understanding of the staff. Many local children's services will have a cross-agency information-sharing protocol that may be useful to include as part of the anti-bullying policy.

- All staff—including governors—have their training needs reviewed annually in relation to disability equality training; and more specific training is in place on how to support learners with SEN and disabilities in relation to bullying.
- Mainstream schools use the expertise of specialist and special school staff to support staff and learners in developing an inclusive environment.
- Staff are offered training and opportunities in which to gain experience and competence to prevent bullying of, and by, learners with SEN and disabilities.
- Ongoing training and development opportunities on disability and bullying are available to all staff with the full support of the school.

In interviews carried out to inform this work, parents said:

'(Staff need) more information, training and opportunity to put it into practice with mentoring from staff who work with pupils/students who have special needs.'
'There needs to be more training particularly for staff that work with the child—they could make arrangements with other schools and staff secondments.'

Further Support for Schools

When planning anti-bullying strategies, particular emphasis should be placed on the needs of learners with a range of SEN and disabilities; and a variety of methods should be developed to support them. Anti-Bullying Alliance regional advisors can help local authorities and schools to develop their policy and strategy, they offer training and updates on best practice. (See www.anti-bullyingalliance.org.uk.)

There is also a wealth of voluntary and private agencies who can provide further advice and support on the needs of learners with particular disabilities or SEN. (See the resources section for further details.)

There is a range of support networks through which schools can share effective practice on interventions and appropriate, consistent approaches such as those outlined in *Safe to Learn*. Support can be provided through: the National Strategies; educational psychology services; inclusion teams; local authority anti-bullying groups; Healthy Schools teams; and local children's safeguarding boards, which are responsible for children's safety, including victimisation and bullying, across all children's services.

Schools can also share expertise and network effectively, for example, through their local authority, school clusters, specialist teacher networks, special schools, and childminder networks. Also, the specific support outlined in Safe to Learn is available:

'The Department [DCSF] is working through the National Strategies Regional Advisers to spread good practice and work with identified schools to support and challenge them in improving their anti-bullying policies and strategies. As part of this, Regional Advisers and local authority Behaviour and Attendance Consultants will help these schools to identify any specific training needs.' [para 6.3]

Whole-school approach—summary of steps to reviewing the policy

- Define bullying.
- Gather accurate information on incidents, specifically those involving learners with SEN and disabilities. Examine how the policy is applied and the results of these incidents.
- Involve all learners, parents and staff, including support staff and governors, in the review.
- Provide a range of times and ways in which people can contribute, e.g. online, by post, talking in groups, film or drawing.
- Make sure governors and headteachers are committed to the process and let everyone know they think it's important.
- Promote positive images of disability and equality for all learners.
- Increase ways to report bullying for learners of all abilities and their parents.

- Evaluate and reflect on the effectiveness of interventions.
- Embed the work throughout the curriculum and school life.
- Plan collaboratively with any special school or unit and mainstream school that are sharing learners.
- Train staff and peer mentors or supporters.
- Focus on transitions through thorough preparation and integration.
- Adapt the strategy to the needs of all children.

'When everyone joins the school, they should agree to the rules about bullying that we've written as kids. They should be in reception, in classrooms, on walls.'

School Approaches and Activities—What Works?

The practical activities described here have been contributed by schools, children and young people with SEN and disabilities. Their active participation models the recommendation that they are fully involved in the development of an anti-bullying policy. They prioritise the question of seeking help and feeling helpless.

Seeking Help

'You can't do anything about it. You can't tell. 2 reasons – 1... you don't know their name [said due to size of the school] so they'll get away with it, 2... you'll get bullied even more cos they'll call you a grasser.'

'If you tell they'll beat you up more.'

'Grassing makes things worse—makes you scared to tell—like blackmail.'

Where learners with SEN and disabilities are concerned about bullying, communication across the staff team is essential. All staff working with children need to know of the risks, although they will not need to have detailed information on a particular child's impairment unless there is a specific reason, such as a reasonable adjustment to support their needs. They will need to know the extent to which learners' SEN and disabilities may lead them to bully others or display disruptive behaviour. Staff need to be observant to changes in learners' behaviour and make sure they understand the cause; often it is due to factors not related to their SEN or disability. Further, they will need to know the best way of communicating with each child, and the child's capacity to understand the nuances of behaviour and interaction.

'They don't always believe you when you tell'

Children with SEN and disabilities interviewed for this guidance maintain that they are often not believed or that they have been threatened and are too scared to tell a teacher what is happening to them. A recent report from Mencap found young people they interviewed had similar experiences.

Learners go though a complex decision-making process when deciding whether or not to report bullying. They will consider the risk, the extent to which they trust that effective action will be taken, and the procedures in place to enable them to do so. A number of learners with SEN or other SEN and disabilities may not recognise that they are being bullied, be unable to report that they are being bullied, or be fearful after receiving threats concerning reporting bullying. This makes preventative strategies and a strong anti-bullying ethos all the more important. *Safe to Learn* (para 5.1) illustrates a range of approaches that schools have taken to give learners a range of ways to report bulling, for example, by using questionnaires, bullying boxes and nominating particular staff to be available to help.

The following list highlights what to provide and to consider in order to ensure that learners feel confident they can report bullying and be heard.

- A quiet place to communicate
- What are the child's communication needs?
- Can they understand you?
- Are their communication tools available to them?
- Have they had time to calm down and fully tell what they want to?
- Allow plenty of time.
- Do they need a supporter?
- Are staff visible and available to all learners?
- Learners with a range of needs including learning disability, sensory impairment and Behavioural, Emotional and Social Difficulties (BESD) will require specific communication tools, and staff will need to check their understanding. Many children with autism, for example, are assumed to understand much more than they do.
- Do staff know about and understand how to use communication passports?

'Doesn't matter how many rules are in place. Teachers can't do owt about it, bullies are everywhere'

'They don't always believe you when you tell'

Pre-arranged Signals to Support Learners Who are Bullied

In this simple but personal approach, a teacher agrees that a check will be made several times a day or week. The teacher will simply give this signal to the learner who will signal back in return showing whether things are going well or not:

> *'Thumbs up, means things've been good, thumbs down mean it's been bad.'*
>
> *(If children report bullying, someone checks on the child each day by giving discreet thumbs up. If child gives a thumbs up it means it is a good day, if thumbs down, they go and talk to the child in private. Children who are bullying are also talked to.'*
>
> (Learner in Mainstream Primary)

Further examples of how staff can support learners is available from: www.anti-bullyingalliance.org.uk

Playground and Lunchtimes

If learners are consulted about bullying 'hot spots', and playtimes are identified as a particular problem, supervision can be increased at playtimes, or varied games offered. Some children may be particularly vulnerable to bullying at these times, especially if they do not have many friends or they find unstructured time difficult, as is the case with many learners on the autism spectrum. Clubs and quiet rooms or re-designed playgrounds are responses that have made substantial changes to the experience of learners at unsupervised times. Chess and computer clubs are popular alternatives to physical play. Certain learners who have particular sensory sensitivities may need to have a quiet retreat away from noise, close contact with others and even smells.

> *'We actually try not to call it a unit, more another resource base that children can use. We have an open-access policy. Able-bodied children can also choose to go in there. Any child is free to go into the unit—it can serve a purpose for them also—can be a safe place to play. There are lots of different things to do that children enjoy—such as a computer room. There are some parts that are only suitable for severely disabled children but if at all possible, all children are allowed in. Our work is inclusive high-level integration work.'*

Curriculum

Curriculum-based activities are successfully used in many settings to improve social relationships. PSHE and Citizenship offer explicit opportunities to explore bullying and discrimination. The Social and Emotional Aspects of Learning (SEAL) primary resources include a unit on bullying structured across key stages, 'Say No to Bullying', which is widely used. Some special schools are adapting the SEAL resources to meet some of the specific needs of their children. Secondary SEAL is also being used in secondary schools now, and bullying-related SEAL material will be available in June 2008. *Safe to Learn* (page 44) identifies a number of lessons that can be used to raise awareness of issues, explore difference, facilitate understanding of bullying and resolve issues. Further information on using the curriculum to support learners with SEN and disabilities can be found in *Implementing the DDA in schools and early years settings* available at www.teachernet.gov.uk/ wholeschool/sen/ disabilityandthedda/ddapart0

Music and drama workshops are popular with children and young people and offer group work opportunities to develop songs against violence and bullying.

Drama offers the tools to rehearse situations and ask the audience to help by telling the characters what to do next. 'Hot seating' can be used to enable learners to experience situations in turn. Learners can be helped by watching, then acting out, scenarios and rehearsing in advance what they could say or do if an incident occurs. This can also help some children with SEN and disabilities understand what bullying is and put their own experiences into context. This work is inclusive and many can join in. Successful work with learners who use bullying behaviour has involved specially written plays reflecting back at them how their own behaviour comes across (Durham Anti-Bullying Service); and deploying them to help other younger or vulnerable learners and, in some cases, other learners with SEN and disabilities (Marlborough School) in whole-class drama and music workshops. These workshops publicly examine how the whole class feels about bullying, without identifying individuals by name. Drama and music distance participants from the situation and allow them to talk about how they feel and what the reasons might be for the bullying actions.

For more information see: www.anti-bullyingalliance.org.uk

Rewarding Positive Behaviour

'Learners should be aware that there are consequences for their behaviour—with the focus on positive behaviour management and explaining to children and young people the impact of their behaviour.' (Secondary school)

Rather than a focus on the undesirable behaviour, this approach provides attention, praise and rewards for positive behaviour. It also uses group management techniques.

> *'For every negative comment that is made we make sure that there are at least three positive statements made about that child's behaviour.'* (Teacher)

Managing the way teams or partners are picked can change the dynamics of the group as the following learner explains.

> *'In my primary school, we did this sports day team thing, where they picked these teams so you could work together but loads of people didn't get picked cos they didn't have any friends, so like what I thought was everybody should just pick different people and give them a chance so they could show what they could do, not what they couldn't do, then they could all work together and help each other.'*

More influential than a focus on negative behaviour are simple activities that reinforce loyalty, trust or kindness, while offering rewards for positive behaviour.

> *Learner: 'We've got WOWs in class… miss can you explain?'*
> *Teacher: 'If the students behave well, they get a WOW sticker.'*
> *Learner: 'Makes us feel great [when we get one] like we've really achieved something. At the end of the week we count em all up and on Friday we get all our WOWs out and we get to choose something.'*
> *'...it's like you get stamps, and when you get a certain amount of stamps you get a merit and what you could do you could do is you could get a card if you'd been reported to bullying, and you could get a stamp if you didn't bully, you'd get a big reward.'*

Strategies to reinforce positive behaviour can exert pressure from the whole class on each member to achieve the promised reward. These may not be long lasting where children have Behavioural, Emotional and Social Difficulties (BESD), but are effective for the duration of the activity.

Step Aside: Exploring Consequences

Assisting young people to explore and identify the consequences of particular actions and behaviour may help some learners when tackling bullying. Below is a description of a technique for choosing an action and thinking through the consequences. Described here by a 10-year-old boy with autism, he clearly understood that he had to 'count to 10 and look at my options—if I don't step aside then I don't have time to think about what might happen next'.

'We do this book about someone who has a dog that gets lost. We draw these footsteps. Two going forward and two going to the side. You see what happens if you choose to go straight forward or if you step aside to have a think. If you don't choose to step aside a whole lot of other awful things happen. You need to take the time to think about what might happen before you decide what to do.'

RESPONDING TO BULLYING—ACTIONS AND AFTERWARDS

Bullying should not be tolerated and should always be followed by an immediate and appropriate response. But a 'one size fits all' approach is unhelpful when supporting children with a range of SEN and disabilities who experience bullying. By having a set of resources available, the appropriate method may be selected to deal with the specific case. When choosing an approach it is essential to know of the pupil's impairment and its impact on their social development. For example, in the case of some children with learning difficulties who have been bullied, it may be necessary to act very quickly while the child can remember what took place. In other cases, allowances may need to be made because a learner with Behavioural, Emotional and Social Difficulties (BESD) demonstrates anti-social behaviour but did not intend to bully.

Sanctions

'[Bullies should be given] a taste of their own medicine—see how it makes them feel. Show 'em like what's happening 'n' how it feels so they know.'

'They just play up again if they think you are just going to punish them.'

Safe to Learn says:

'The Department [DCSF] advises that sanctions are applied fairly, proportionately, consistently and reasonably, taking account of any special educational needs (SEN) or disabilities that pupils may have and taking into consideration the needs of vulnerable children. Bullying by children with disabilities or SEN is no more acceptable than bullying by other children and it should be made clear that their actions are wrong and appropriate sanctions imposed. However, for a sanction to be reasonable and lawful, schools must take account of the nature of the child's disability or SEN and the extent to which the child understands and is in control of what he/she is doing.' (Para 4.16)

More on the general principles of these approaches can be found in *Safe to Learn* at www.teachernet.gov.uk/wholeschool/behaviour/tacklingbullying/safetolearn. The duties under disability discrimination legislation are anticipatory, which means that reasonable adjustments and support should be put in place before issues arise to prevent learners with SEN and disabilities being disadvantaged as a result of their disability.

Responding to Common Types of Bullying

The following case studies and resources are designed to give ideas on how to effectively support learners with a range of needs. Many schools shared excellent practice and gave examples of how to deal effectively with bullying and create a culture of inclusion and participation. The examples below are based on practice from these settings.

Case Study 1—Long-term, 'Low Level' Bullying

'Low level' persistent bullying, name-calling, pushing, or spreading rumours can seem mild or even invisible to an outsider. In discussions with children with impairments, they described situations in which they have experienced persistent low-level bullying for long periods of time – eventually 'snapping' and in some cases responding with violence. This may be particularly likely where learners have impairments which affect their communication or their social or emotional skills so that they find it difficult to deal appropriately with the bullying when it first starts.

Simon

Simon is a bright 14-year-old student in a mainstream secondary school. He has Asperger's syndrome which means he sometimes finds it difficult to socialise with other students. Last year, Simon's form teacher had noticed he was becoming more withdrawn in his tutor group and was spending more time using his laptop at lunchtime club rather than taking part in games and activities which he previously enjoyed. His teacher had asked Simon a few times if everything was alright. Simon always replied that everything was fine with him.

A few weeks later, Simon physically attacked three other boys from his year. Simon was very upset and would not speak about the incident to staff. The school contacted his parents to tell them about the incident. Simon told his parents about the bullying he had experienced from the three boys. Over the year they had often asked him to join in discussions then made fun of his understanding of things, taken items from his bag and frequently jostled him as they passed in corridors. As a result of this constant, low-level bullying, Simon had become insecure, anxious and withdrawn. This eventually led to him feeling frustrated and led to his aggressive behaviour.

The school followed its policy and took the following action: immediately following the incident, Simon was taken from class and his teacher explained he would remove three stars from Simon's good behaviour book. The three boys were required to miss out on a class outing. Simon and the boys were also encouraged to take the opportunity to train as 'friends' for younger children, using the extended school activities.

The Bully Rep recognised that although the school had an active anti-bullying policy in place, Simon did not feel confident enough to tell someone directly about the bullying. To address this, the school asked the school council to consult all learners on changes to the anti-bullying strategy. The headteacher and Bully Rep (a teacher with specific responsibility for preventing and responding to bullying), made a commitment to work with the council and take their ideas seriously, and to contact parents and ask for their participation in this work. A range of multi-media projects were carried out, which produced an anti-bullying poster and a song, both of which were used in assemblies and around the school. The school also worked with parents to make sure they had access to information about bullying when they needed it and that they knew how the school dealt with bullying by following its published policy.

Case Study 2—Conditional Friendships

'People pretending to be your friends.'

'And also if you're out they try and make you steal from the shop.'

A confusing form of bullying is one which alternates phases of friendliness with phases of derision and ridicule. This on/off form of bullying can be used in a group context to manage and maintain social status within the group. Children are courted away from their friends; and membership of the group is made to appear desirable. When members become dependent on the group, the group turns against them and they are effectively isolated. This can be very difficult to understand for any child who finds themselves experiencing this behaviour. In turn, it may not be visible to an adult and is often underestimated because the apparent friendship is 'turned on' again under their gaze. A child, for example, with learning or social difficulties may be bewildered by this pattern and unable to counter it. Some learners report that they are coerced into stealing something from a shop or other unwanted activities by the perpetrators.

Zafirah

Zafirah is 10 years old and attends a mainstream primary school. She has Down's syndrome. She experienced bullying when a group of four girls in her class alternated phases of friendliness with making fun of her. The girls invited her to play at breaks then pretended not to know what Zafirah was talking about when she tried to join in. Zafirah was keen to make friends with the group and her impairment meant she found it difficult to make sense of their behaviour.

The girls eventually persuaded Zafirah to steal a CD from another learner's bag during the lunch break. Zafirah was seen by another girl who told a teacher. The teacher confronted Zafirah who became upset. The teacher took Zafirah away from the others and gave her plenty of time to calm down and explain what she thought had happened. The teacher knew about Zafirah's impairment and made sure she was very clear with her what would happen next. The teacher acted straight away as she understood it was important for Zafirah to remember that what was happening was a consequence of her recent actions. Zafirah was asked to immediately give the CD back and apologise. The teacher explained that she would also lose her merits for that week and a note would be made on her report book. The other girls were given a detention.

Zafirah and the girls took part in peer mediation to resolve the issues. Zafirah was offered her own peer mentor to support her. Parents were informed of the school's actions and asked to support them. The class teacher did some work on friendship in SEAL and PSHE lessons. The teacher also agreed with Zafirah's parents to set an Individual Education Plan target concerning better understanding of boundaries.

'I was called in to schoc' as a result of my child misbehaving, but actually it was other children telling her to do things. She hasn't got the ability to tell them this. They will ask her—did you do this? And she will say yes, but not that she was told to do this.' (Parent of child with Down's syndrome)

Case Study 3—Cyberbullying

'They text you... make you think they're gonna do something bad to you.'

As children turn increasingly to the internet and new technology for social networking, there is both an exciting opportunity for children with SEN and disabilities and a threat to their safety. Children need help to handle offensive messages, rumours or images that may be circulated about them. They also need to be shown how to act responsibly and safely in terms they can understand.

Shola

Shola is 15 and attends a unit attached to a mainstream school. She has cerebral palsy and limited use of her arms and legs. She uses assisted technology in class and to communicate. Shola really enjoys using IT equipment and is a keen member of a number of social networking sites. The school set up its own intranet for learners to use and Shola was on the school planning group who designed and built the site. To launch the site, the school used an assembly. When Shola approached the stage to do her bit of the presentation another student shouted out a derogatory remark. The remark was not challenged by staff. Soon after the intranet went live, pictures of Shola began to appear with cmments about her physical appearance and her personal life.

The school had a software programme enabling the IT department to identify the person who posted these pictures. They traced the student and promptly removed the pictures. The student's parents were immediately called in and the law of harassment explained to them; the school also reminded them of the school's code of conduct for anyone using the intranet signed by learners and parents. This had clearly been breached in this case so the school acted upon its written policy and excluded the boy for one day.

It was agreed through discussion with Shola, her parents, the student and his parents that he would prepare an assembly in which he would demonstrate the achievements of learners with disabilities and their use of technology to the whole school. Shola was consulted on this and was able to give her own views. The police community liaison officer was invited to the school to talk to learners about the seriousness of harassment.

The headteacher also began a review of staff training to make sure all staff felt confident in challenging discriminatory language and bullying in the school.

A Note on Exclusions

'They alienate your child rather than deal with the bully. They took my child out of the classroom because that's the only way they felt that she could stay safe.' (Parent of child with complex health needs).

'I got excluded because all the winding up, like, it happened so often that I just got really angry and couldn't control myself anymore, eventually I ended up taking my anger out on someone... and as a result I ended up getting excluded... because I was considered a health and safety matter by the school.' (Secondary school pupil with BESD)

In some schools where learners with SEN and disabilities have been bullied, the child experiencing bullying is instructed to stay at home for a fixed time or removed from their class. This is incorrectly perceived to be an acceptable way of keeping them safe from further bullying. However DCSF guidance is clear that this is not a solution.

Safe to Learn states:

'Pupils must not be excluded from school for being bullied, even if the school believes they are doing so for the child's benefit. The legislation on exclusion makes clear that "exclude...means exclude on disciplinary grounds". Exclusions guidance explicitly says that children should only be sent home for health and safety reasons where "because of a diagnosed illness such as a notifiable disease he or she poses an immediate and serious risk to the health and safety of other pupils and staff". Behavioural problems, even when related to a diagnosed condition such as ADHD or ASD, do not normally fall into this category.' (para 4.22)

The following case study looks at more creative approaches to ensuring all learners have access to every aspect of the school day.

Case Study 4—Joining in

'The reason [that we are getting bullied is] because you're in a wheelchair and they pick on you because you're not like them, do know what I mean?' (12-year-old-boy in mainstream secondary school)

Jay

Jay is an active young man who enjoys sport but was excluded by other learners in his mainstream school from participating at break times and activity times as he uses a wheelchair. Teachers noticed when, one lunchtime, other students started calling Jay names and telling him to go away when they were playing, then began jostling him when he didn't comply. Alternative activities were available inside the school but Jay made it clear to staff that he wanted to use the outside space like everyone else. Jay's teacher worked with him to look at options. The other boys were kept in for one break time and staff used that session to work with them on looking at the consequences of their actions. The teacher followed this up with the whole class in circle time (see box below).

The whole school, led by Jay's class and the school council, did a piece of work on looking at improvements to break time activities. The students were supported in looking at options by youth staff from the local authority. Their ideas were presented to the governors, who approved some work to improve the layout of the playground and the purchase of a range of sports equipment. The PE teacher with others then worked with learners to devise a range of group games which were accessible. For more information on making activities accessible see: http://www.efds.co.uk/

http://www.direct.gov.uk/en/DisabledPeople/Everydaylifeandaccess/

Circle Time

A useful way of asking questions is to use Circle Time and to ask learners to complete the following sentences:
'I don't like it when...'
'I wish I could help friends when...'
Bullying is a topic that inevitably comes up when these questions are raised.
'My child had severe eczema and the other kids were teasing her about it going "Uurrrgh don't touch her 'cos you'll catch it!" They used circle time to discuss what eczema is and how you can't catch it and explored how teasing made people feel. This helped a lot.'

Case Study 5—Provoked Behaviour

'My son's behaviour is very reactive, children target him and try to get him to blow. They try to get a response.' (Parent of boy with Behavioural, Emotional and Social Difficulties (BESD))

'I feel sad inside and I do cry when the tics get bad as they can hurt my body, it's like going to the gym 24/7. I don't go out except when I go to school as people treat me horribly and they copy my tics which I hate.' (11-year-old learner with Tourette's syndrome)

As with Case Study 1, the following scenario describes the reaction of a learner with particular communication needs reacting violently to sustained bullying. This kind of bullying and the reactions it can provoke are well documented; and the main *Safe to Learn* guidance gives the following advice.

'Some pupils who have been subjected to bullying are provoked into violent behaviour. A pupil can be excluded for violent behaviour; it is a matter for the headteacher's judgement, taking account of the evidence available, all the circumstances of the case and the need to balance the interests of the pupil concerned against those of the whole-school community. However, before deciding to exclude a pupil, the Department [DCSF] recommends that the headteacher always allow him or her to state their case, and check whether the incident may have been provoked by, for example, racial or sexual harassment or a child's SEN or disability. Where a pupil has retaliated after months of persistent bullying, we advise that this be considered differently from an unprovoked attack.' (para 4.23)

In addition, the DCSF Guidance on School Discipline and Pupil Behaviour Policies [s3.9] has practical advice on the ways schools might take account of a learner's impairment when applying the school behaviour policy. This may mean making reasonable adjustments or considering what additional or different action may need to be taken. The Guidance sets it out as follows.

'Any lawful use of sanctions must be reasonable and proportionate to the circumstances of the case [taking account of] the pupil's age, any special educational needs, any disability and any religious requirements affecting the pupil.' (para 3.6.3)

Paragraph 3.6.14 advises that schools should avoid sanctions becoming cumulative and automatic, as this is unlikely to enable their application in a way which always takes account of individual needs, age and understanding. Paragraph 3.6.17 adds that staff should also consider, when using sanctions, whether an apparent behaviour difficulty is in fact a manifestation of unidentified learning difficulties or other type of SEN.

In addition, where a child with SEN and disabilities has been bullied, they need to see what sanction has been applied and what the follow-up will be.

Tom

Tom reported to his teacher that he was being bullied by three others boys at a residential school for boys with emotional and behavioural difficulties. The bullying had been going on for some time and included repeated incidents of name-calling, shoving and intimidation, particularly between lessons; and culminated in a fight between the boys. Following the report, the teacher referred this straight to the year's Bully Rep (a teacher with specific responsibility for preventing and responding to bullying).

After spending time speaking with Tom, the Bully Rep liaised with the head of year and agreed that the three boys would receive a detention for their actions. To address bullying in the longer term, the Bully Rep used the detention to discuss the incident with the boys, both separately and as a group, to explore what had been happening, how this would make Tom feel and what they should do to resolve the issues. The boys each wrote letters of apology and it was agreed that they would meet with the Bully Rep for several sessions to explore bullying further and work on how to manage their behaviour and emotions. This included identifying a safe place to go, to calm down and 'let off steam' as they said they often felt angry and frustrated and needed to 'take this out on something'; this was communicated to all staff.

To effectively support Tom, following the initial time spent discussing the incident, how it made him feel and what would make him feel safe, it was agreed that at several times during the day, the Bully Rep would discreetly check he was OK by giving the thumbs-up sign. If Tom responded with his thumbs down, the Bully Rep would ensure time was set aside to speak to Tom. The rep was concerned about any form of retaliation that might follow.

In class groups, teachers facilitated discussion around dealing with feelings and emotions, bullying and what should be done to help stop it. Each class developed these into posters, which were then displayed in the classrooms and continued to be discussed regularly to keep the issue of bullying on the school's agenda.

The bullying described in these case studies may result from a combination of factors, such as other prejudice-based bullying, in addition to the learner's impairment. Where racist views are held, a disabled child from a minority group may be singled out for either or both of these differences or any other prejudice-based victimisation, simply because he or she may be an 'easy target'. There is some evidence from learners that homophobic insults and name-calling related to disability are used more frequently to members of ethnic minority populations, without using explicitly racist terms which learners know they should not employ. In this way, perpetrators believe they are less likely to be caught. *Safe to Learn* promotes a whole-school approach to bullying which aims to change the entire school environment and reduce all forms of bullying. All prejudice-driven bullying should be tackled with an effective approach that changes attitudes.

Different Methods Used in Schools as Sanctions—Suggestions from Children

'They could give them a detention or suspension or something... maybe they could give them some sort of rehabilitation class in the detention.' (Learner in mainstream secondary school)

'We get R cards as well which say what you've done right or wrong. Like you get one with an ear on it in red if you haven't been listening or one with legs on if you've been wandering around.' (Learner in special school)

'We have a Timeout card', counting to 10, Golden Time—a worry box and Bully Box.' (Learner in mainstream primary school with unit)

'Children get a red card if they break a rule, but they're given a warning first.' (Learner in mainstream primary school)

Actions after Bullying

Safe to Learn offers a range of general approaches schools can take to reinforce messages after bullying has taken place. Below are some approaches and resources that have proved successful in schools where bullying has involved learners with SEN and disabilities. These are used alongside sanctions and immediate actions a school might take.

Resource 1—Strengths Based Approaches

'If you see someone who has obvious differences, look past that and see what they CAN actually do. People see the wheelchair and don't actually see the person. Don't assume what they can do—actually talk to someone.'

Recognising and identifying individual strengths can be one of many tools to empower someone who has been bullied. This method can also help aggressive children and young people to avoid becoming labelled only by their behaviour or difficulties. Use of Strengths Cards or other activities to identify what everyone is good at offer positive opportunities.

Some schools are supporting learners with behavioural difficulties to work with learners with SEN and disabilities. This appears to be mutually beneficial—both for mentors, who are recognised and praised for their behaviour helping to raise their self-esteem, and for the mentored, who feel safer at school. This is closely supervised.

> *'We have started to try to recruit "characters" as peer mentors (those who might bully or who have behavioural difficulties, or who are not achieving well), these [young people] are heavily monitored by staff. Some of these young people have been turned around by the recognition that they are given for this—it has had a really positive effect on their behaviour and has improved the self-esteem of the peer mentor and the child that is mentored. They will help them with group work or help to teach them games such as chess.'* (Deputy headteacher)

Resource 2—Peer Mentoring

Peer mentoring schemes are used widely in schools, where a group of young volunteers are trained to provide a specific anti-bullying service such as support, listening or mediation. Learners with various SEN and disabilities volunteer for the training alongside their peers; and their involvement in the scheme not only indicates a strong commitment to inclusion in the school, but can also provide specialist knowledge to the peer support team. These schemes require good training followed by sustained support from adults.

> *'One boy with behavioural problems used to mentor a boy with SEN who was bullied—he used to walk him to lessons—this helped to protect the boy from being bullied. [The peer mentor] shone that day [when he first did this] he was took to the head of year to congratulate him on his behaviour and it made a huge difference to him and the other boy who felt safer and more protected—the other children were not likely to mess with [the peer mentor]. So he [the child with SEN] felt very safe.'* (Teacher)
>
> *'Peer mentors can play a part in welcoming new pupils to the school or unit. They are taken to visit Year 6 pupils in feeder primary schools to reassure them about secondary school. Disabled peer mentors are enabled to undertake this work.'*

For more information on peer support see www.ChildLine.org.uk

Resource 3—Activities that Help to Improve Children's Social and Emotional Skills

SEAL is a comprehensive approach to promoting the social and emotional skills that underpin effective learning, positive behaviour, regular attendance, staff effectiveness and the emotional health and well-being of all who learn and work in schools. For more information see: www.standards.dfes.gov.uk/primary/features/primary/873235/

Guidance booklets on Primary and Secondary SEAL are available from: www.bandapilot.org.uk/secondary/resources/welcome_page/sns_ssealguidance0004307.pdf (for Secondary SEAL); and www.bandapilot.org.uk/primary/seal/downloads/pns_seal137805_guidance.pdf (for Primary SEAL).

Activities that target attitude and behavioural change should be developmentally specific and take into account cognitive, emotional, behavioural and academic factors. Visual aides and concrete activities are helpful.

'We do work on social problem solving, anger management and activities to promote self-esteem and small group work.'

Activities to promote social skills such as empathy, anger management and social problem solving can be conducted in small group work sessions with targeted individuals or with the whole class during circle time activities. These may be particularly helpful for learners with social impairments such as autism. Learners are helped to consider the consequences and weigh up the different outcomes of certain actions. They are prepared and helped to know how to react to different challenges. An evaluation of multi-session social skills programmes, delivered by a regular teacher to children with Behavioural, Emotional and Social Difficulties (BESD), showed short-term positive effects, but that social skills were not maintained in the long-term. Nevertheless, for many learners this work presents opportunities to explore and agree both what constitutes the boundaries of acceptable behaviour and the importance of working within these boundaries if good outcomes are to be achieved in adult life.

For More Information, See http://www.nfer.ac.uk/research-areas/pims-data/summaries/coc-interventions-for-pupils-with-emotional-and–behavioural–difficulties.cfm

Resource 4—Solution Focused Brief Therapy

Solution focused brief therapy is an approach to counselling. It is brief, future-focused and works with the strengths of those who come by making the best use of their resources.

Young and Holdorf, who work within a Special Needs Support Service as the Anti-Bullying team, have shown that both the solution focused Support Group and SFBT for individuals can be 'effective strategies that work quickly when a learner needs help in a bullying situation...These strategies are useful because they do not "take sides", or presuppose any judgement about the cause of the difficulties, which so often takes place beyond the view of adults and is not open to "proof". Practitioners do not have to label learners "victims" or "bullies"—if a learner feels in need of help, that is enough.' This study is a useful, if small example of a local anti-bullying team evaluating their interventions. It also offers an assessment of the use of support groups, recommending them in a primary school setting.

The Anti-Bullying Service in the Special Needs Support Unit of Kingston Upon Hull has carried out useful evaluations of solution focused brief therapy and the Support Group Approach used in their service. Staff should be encouraged to 'embrace teachable moments' for bystanders when bullying incidents occur.

For more information on Young and Holdorf: http://www.blackwell-synergy.com/

More from Rebekah Hienrichs can be found at http://isc.sagepub.com/cgi/content/abstract/38/4/195

Resource 5—Peer Mediation

Peer mediation differs from other methods of peer support (such as mentoring, listening and befriending) in that mediators offer help and support the children involved in bullying after an incident has taken place. It can help everyone involved to resolve the issues; the mediators are there to help facilitate this but not to take over and sort it out themselves.

Peer mediation empowers trained learners to resolve low-level conflicts between the peers themselves. Peer mediators are trained to listen and respond to both sides as a neutral third party and to try to encourage the learners to come to a resolution themselves. A follow-up meeting is conducted with the mediators to see whether the conflict has been successfully resolved and to decide whether any further steps need to be taken. Mediators are supported and trained by adults and are advised to seek help from them if the dispute is of a more serious nature or if they have difficulties with resolving a conflict.

An evaluation of a scheme run in a special school for students with moderate learning difficulties has been carried out. The author concluded that learners with moderate learning difficulties could be taught to mediate successfully; and that they learnt valuable new social skills as a result of the training. One of the children interviewed for this guidance was very positive about his experience of peer mediation.

Child: What we did in my primary school about bullying, we did this peer mediation thing, where there were two people, the bully 'n' the one being picked on, 'n' if they had like a fight, we would sit 'em down 'n' let them decide what they thought they could do to sort it out.

Interviewer: Why do you think it worked so well?

Child: Because if you just tell 'em they often think that 'I don't wanna do that' 'n' its unfair, whereas if they decide together, they can like, form it as an agreement. I was a peer mediator 'n' it was really good 'n' if there was like a lot of 'em fighting I would take some 'n' my partner would take the other 'n' let them decide 'cos if you forced them to do something it might just aggravate 'em 'n' it'd carry things on.

Cartwright (2005) describes one peer scheme run in a special school. Learners had a range of SEN and disabilities. Teachers reported that the scheme was very successful and helped to empower the counsellors and support victimised children.

LEGAL DUTIES AND GUIDANCE FOR SCHOOLS

For a guide to general legislation regarding bullying, please see *Safe To Learn: Embedding Anti-Bullying work in schools.* Section 2.

For information on:

The Human Rights Act, please visit www.dca.gov.uk/peoples-rights/human-rights/publications.htm

The UNCRC, please visit www.everychildmatters.gov.uk/uncrc/

For legislation in relation to Cyberbullying, please visit http://publications.teachernet.gov.uk/default.aspx?PageFunction=productdetails&PageMode=publications&ProductId=DCSF–00685–2007

For legislation in relation to Homophobic bullying, please visit teachernet.gov.uk/wholeschool/behaviour/tacklingbullying/homophobicbullying

For legislation on bullying related to race, religion and culture, please visit www.teachernet.gov.uk/wholeschool/behaviour/tacklingbullying/racistbullying

Key Action Points for Schools from the Specific Legislation

Legal Duties

There are four main areas of law affecting disabled pupils in school, each of which can impact on the prevention or management of bullying:

- the disability equality duties (Sections 49A to 49D of the DDA, inserted by the Disability Discrimination Act 2005)
- the disability discrimination duties (Sections 28A to 28C of the DDA, inserted by the Special Educational Needs and Disability Act 2001 (SENDA)
- the planning duties (Sections 28D to 28E of the DDA, inserted by SENDA)
- the SEN legal framework (Part IV of the Education Act 1996)

The Disability Equality Duty and the Disability Discrimination Act 2005

The Disability Discrimination Act 2005 amended the DDA by inserting a new Section 49A which requires schools to take a more proactive approach to promoting disability equality and eliminating discrimination. Among its provisions are requirements on schools to promote positive attitudes towards disabled people and to eliminate harassment.

The Act sets out:

- a general duty to promote equality of opportunity between disabled persons and other persons, which applies to all public authorities
- a specific duty on publicly-funded schools to prepare and publish a disability equality scheme showing how they are meeting the general duty.

Responsibility for the general duty lies with:

- the governing body of a maintained primary or secondary school
- the proprietor of a city technology college, city college for technology of the arts, or an academy
- the governing body of a community special school or a foundation special school
- the local authority with respect to its pupil referral units.

The General Duty

The general duty requires schools, when carrying out their functions, to have due regard to the need to:

- promote equality of opportunity between disabled people and others
- eliminate unlawful discrimination
- eliminate harassment of disabled people that is related to their disability
- take steps to take account of disabled people's disabilities, even where that involves treating them more favourably
- promote positive attitudes towards disabled people
- encourage participation by disabled people in public life.

Each of the elements of the general duty could impact directly or indirectly on disabled pupils' experience of bullying at school. For example, in its statutory *Code of Practice on the Duty to Promote Disability Equality,* the Disability Rights Commission (DRC) stated that schools can promote positive attitudes towards disabled people in lessons such as citizenship and by ensuring that the views and contributions of disabled children are valued. These approaches help create a positive ethos about disabled people and a climate where bullying of disabled pupils becomes less likely as a result.

The need to eliminate harassment of disabled people should impact directly on disabled pupils' experience of bullying in schools. Section 6 of *Implementing the DDA in Schools and Early Years Settings, Promoting Disability Equality in Schools,* points out that such bullying is more prevalent than is often thought.

Schools may need to:

- raise awareness amongst staff and pupils of disability-related harassment
- understand the nature and prevalence of bullying and harassment
- recognise and address bullying and harassment
- involve pupils themselves in combating bullying
- ensure that disability–related harassment of disabled staff, parents, carers and other users of the school is identified and addressed.

The Specific Duty

Regulations made under Part 5A of the DDA set out a specific duty on publicly-funded schools, requiring them to prepare and publish a disability equality scheme, which sets out how the school is going to meet the disability equality duty and duties under the regulations themselves.

The main requirements of the specific duty are to

- prepare and publish a disability equality scheme
- involve disabled people who appear to the governing body to have an interest in the way it carries out its functions in its development
- implement the scheme
- report on it.

Disabled people with an interest in the way the governing body carries out its functions include disabled pupils, staff and parents. This provides a powerful mechanism for concerns about bullying linked to disability to be raised. The Code of Practice recognises that the views of disabled pupils will be crucial in identifying key issues and prioritising future action such as anti-bullying initiatives. Disability-related bullying and harassment is not restricted to pupils. Disabled staff, parents, carers and other users of the school may also experience it and under the disability equality duty schools need to consider what steps they may need to take to identify and address disability-related harassment for them too.

The need to involve disabled pupils, staff and parents does not stop there; the regulations also require schools to set out in their schemes how they will gather and use information to support the review of action plans and to inform subsequent schemes. For example, feedback from disabled pupils on anti-bullying initiatives or how the school's behaviour policy affects them might usefully inform future action.

Schools must look at a wide range of data when considering the impact of their policies and practices on disabled pupils. If they find there is low participation of disabled pupils in a particular school activity, they may need to look more deeply for causes, for example, whether disability-related bullying is a barrier to participation.

Schools also need to undertake a detailed analysis of outcome data for disabled pupils including broader outcomes such as those set out in *Every Child Matters* (see below).

Disability Discrimination Duties

Part 1 of the DDA defines disability. The definition is broad and includes more pupils than many people think. In effect it means that:

A disabled child has a physical or mental impairment which has a substantial, long-term, and adverse effect on their ability to carry out normal day-to-day activities.

SENDA, (the Special Educational Needs and Disability Act 2001) amended Part 4 of the DDA by extending anti-discrimination legislation on the grounds of disability to education. SENDA made it unlawful to discriminate, without justification, against disabled pupils and prospective pupils in all aspects of school life. The principle behind the legislation was that wherever possible disabled people should have the same opportunities as non-disabled people in their access to education.

Every aspect of school life is covered by the duties. Responsible bodies must not discriminate:

- in admissions
- in relation to education and associated services
- by excluding a learner.

There are two key duties for schools in relation to discrimination. These are:

1. Not to treat a disabled person, for a reason which relates to the person's disability, less favourably than it treats or would treat others to whom that reason does not or would not apply, without justification
2. To take such steps as it is reasonable for it to have to take to ensure that:
   (*a*) in relation to the arrangements it makes for determining the admission of pupils to the school, disabled persons are not placed at a substantial disadvantage in comparison with persons who are not disabled
   (*b*) in relation to education and associated services provided for, or offered to, pupils at the school by it, disabled pupils are not placed at a substantial disadvantage in comparison with pupils who are not disabled.

This is known as the reasonable adjustments duty. It means that schools must anticipate where barriers to learning lie and take action to remove them as far as they are able.

The DRC has produced a *Code of Practice for Schools* to explain and illustrate the disability discrimination duties. The Code explains terminology such as 'substantial' and 'reasonable' and gives further explanation of the definition of disability. Section 1 of DCSF guidance *Implementing the DDA in Schools and Early Years Settings* explains the definition in the context of schools.

Less Favourable Treatment

Less favourable treatment must be for a reason related to a child's disability if it is to constitute disability discrimination. For example, if a school provides less help to a bullied disabled learner, for the reason they believe that bullying of disabled pupils is inevitable and therefore too hard to combat, then this treatment would be for a reason related to the bullied learner's disability. The comparison would be with the support provided to other bullied pupils without that disability, to whom that reason did not apply. Schools need to consider whether reasonable adjustments could be made before attempting to justify less favourable treatment. For example, they could review their anti-bullying policies to check that they address bullying linked to disability; take whole-school action to raise the issue of bullying and disability; provide individual support for the bullied child and work with the bullies to improve their behaviour towards disabled pupils.

The Reasonable Adjustments Duty

If a school fails to make reasonable adjustments without lawful justification and this results in the disabled child being at a substantial disadvantage compared with other non-disabled pupils, then this would be disability discrimination. Failing to make reasonable adjustments can only be justified if there is a reason which is both material to the circumstances of a particular case and substantial. Treating a disabled learner less favourably may be justified on the same grounds. Factors which may be taken into account are described in chapter 6 of the *DRC Code of Practice for Schools.*

The duty to make reasonable adjustments does not include providing auxiliary aids and services (see SEN framework below) or making major alterations to the physical features of the school. Bullying is sometimes able to thrive because of the design of playgrounds and buildings and these may be addressed under the planning duties set out in the DDA.

The Planning Duties

Planning duties in the DDA were introduced by SENDA. They overlap with the reasonable adjustments duty and the disability equality duties described above. Section 28D of the DDA requires maintained schools, independent schools and non-maintained special schools to produce an accessibility plan.

Schools must have an accessibility plan which addresses:

- improving the physical environment of the school for the purpose of increasing the extent to which disabled pupils are able to take advantage of education and associated services provided or offered by the school (for example, increasing access to teaching and learning and also to wider participation in after-school clubs, sporting and cultural activities)
- improving communication of information to disabled pupils.

Disabled children who fear they may be bullied or isolated because of their disability may be put off taking advantage of facilities even if physical barriers are removed. *Promoting Disability Equality in Schools,* (Section 6 of DCSF guidance *Implementing the DDA in Schools and Early Years Settings*), recommends asking disabled pupils to identify such issues, which can be addressed in the school accessibility plan.

Accessible Schools: planning to increase access to schools for disabled pupils (LEA/0168/2002) suggests curriculum access should be considered at a 'whole school' level and gives the examples of schools using flexible grouping arrangements where disabled pupils can work with their peers, and encouraging peer support by setting up buddying or mentoring arrangements. These can act as powerful bulwarks against bullying.

Section 28E of the DDA requires schools to have regard to the need to allocate adequate resources to implementing the plan.

The SEN Legal Framework

The reasonable adjustments duty in the DDA does not require the responsible body to provide auxiliary aids and services. These should be provided under the special educational needs framework in Part IV of the Education Act 1996. Section 312 of that Act gives a definition of when a child has SEN. There is considerable overlap between children with a disability and those with SEN although not all disabled pupils have SEN, and not all pupils with SEN have a disability.

How help is provided under the SEN framework is described in the *SEN Code of Practice.* Extra help, such as pastoral support, to deal with or prevent bullying could be provided for a child receiving help at any level described by the Code. If disabled children themselves bully, perhaps because behaviour problems are linked to their disability, then it may be appropriate to provide help with social skills or mentoring, for example, as part of their package of support.

For further information about effective practice in implementing the DDA in schools and early years settings, see: *Implementing the DDA in schools and early years settings.* www.teachernet.gov.uk/wholeschool/sen/disabilityandthedda/ddapart0

Other Relevant Policies and Guidance

Staying Safe

Produced by DCSF, Staying Safe is a cross-government strategy for improving children and young people's safety, and covers the full span of the Every Child Matters staying safe outcome. Its main aims are to:

- raise awareness of the importance of safeguarding children and young people
- promote better understanding of safeguarding issues, encouraging a change in behaviour towards children and young people, and their safety and welfare
- ensure work in this area is coherent, and effectively coordinated across government
- reinforce existing activity by implementing a range of new commitments.

It includes a focus on children who are bullied and can be found at: www.everychildmatters.gov.uk/resources-andpractice/search/IG00312

The SEN Strategy

The government's policy for special educational needs was set out in *Removing Barriers to Achievement* (DfES/0117/2004). It included a commitment to develop practical ways of consulting and involving children both in terms of decisions about their own learning, including ways of removing barriers to learning and the development of school policies. *Working Together* (DfES/0134/2004) gives examples of how young people's involvement in policy and practice can have practical benefits in terms of reducing or preventing bullying. This guidance provides a basis for involving children and young people in decisions affecting all aspects of the life of the school. It includes examples of good practice for schools to use and adapt as they choose.

It supports learner involvement and personal development through opportunities that already exist in Citizenship Education, Personal, Social and Health Education and in other school activities, for example the National Healthy School Standard (NHSS) and the Connexions service. Ofsted also now gives pupils opportunities to give views about their education as part of the inspection process. It also supports Article 12 of the United Nations Convention on the Rights of the Child (UNCRC), gives children the right to put forward their views and ensures that those views are taken seriously.

The National Curriculum Inclusion Statement

Is part of the national curriculum and the requirements set out in it are equivalent of requirements in the rest of the curriculum and in the DDA. The inclusion statement sets teachers the task of overcoming potential barriers to learning including those, such as bullying, which are linked to pupils' special educational needs and disabilities. www.teachernet.gov.uk/management/atoz/n/nationalcurriculum

School Discipline and Behaviour Policies Guidance

Schools are advised to take account of a range of individual learner needs, particularly those of pupils with SEN and disabilities, when developing and implementing their behaviour policies.

The school's statement of principles, made by school governing bodies under Section 88 of the Education and Inspections Act 2006, should reflect a commitment to improving outcomes for all pupils and eliminating all forms of discrimination, harassment and bullying, as well as promoting equality of opportunity, the welfare of pupils and good relations across the whole school community.

The school discipline and behaviour policies guidance points out that the statement of principles should also ensure that vulnerable pupils—including those with special educational needs, physical or mental health needs—receive behavioural support according to their need.

The guidance recommends that communications about the behaviour policy should take appropriate account of individual learner's special educational needs and/or disability. Staff should also monitor any emerging patterns in relation to special educational needs and disability among other factors and take appropriate action to avoid bias. www.teachernet.gov.uk/wholeschool/behaviour/schooldisciplinepupil behaviourpolicies

Ofsted Self-Evaluation Forms

Schools are required to evaluate the extent to which pupils feel safe and adopt safe practices and as part of this are prompted to consider whether pupils feel safe from bullying and confident to talk to staff and others when they feel at risk. Bullying is one of the issues that inspectors will look for in a school and Ofsted inspectors will routinely seek views from pupils about their experience, including whether they feel free from bullying and harassment. https://forms.ofsted.gov.uk

5

Initiatives Towards Aiming High for Disabled Children: A Western Perspective

INTRODUCTION

Aiming High for Disabled Children (AHDC): Better support for families, launched in May 2007, is the transformation programme for disabled children's services. AHDC is jointly delivered by the DCSF and the Department of Health (DH). *AHDC—Best practice to common practice* provides an update on the key developments in the programme since the launch. The AHDC conference, *Transforming best practice to common practice* held on Wednesday 3 June 2009, highlighted the progress made as a result of the Aiming High for Disabled Children (AHDC) programme. The conference materials are now available and they include Ministers' speeches and presentations from the day.

The Government wants disabled children to be a priority, both nationally and locally: a commitment confirmed in the *NHS operating framework*, the Child Health Strategy, *Healthy lives, brighter futures* and in the Children's Plan.

Supported by substantial new funding and measures designed to make the system work better, the Government is assisting professionals, managers and children's services commissioners to deliver the programme. More information and resources are available for the following:

- short breaks
- childcare
- parent participation
- transition support
- palliative care
- core offer and national indicator.

AIMING HIGH FOR DISABLED CHILDREN

The Government's aim is to ensure that every child, irrespective of race, gender, background or circumstances gets the best start in life and the ongoing support that they and their families need to allow them to fulfil their potential. This Review has looked at what more can be done to improve the outcomes of disabled children and young people (0-19) and their families, examining the role that public services can play to make this aim a reality.

In line with the Government's report, *Improving the life chances of disabled people*, the Review has worked towards the best ways of creating equality for all disabled children. Improving their educational, social and emotional development, and their opportunities for independent living, choice and control, is a key part of this process. Government wants to ensure that disabled children and their families are enabled and empowered to make a full contribution to the society of which they are a part.

Disabled children and their families face a unique and often challenging set of circumstances that demand a unique and sometimes specialised response from both the universal and targeted services that support them. It is essential that they are able to influence the design and delivery of services which should be responsive to their needs.

To foster a responsive level of appropriate support for disabled children and their families, the Review has looked at the most effective means of providing disabled children and their families with greater transparency about their entitlements, both locally and nationally. The Review has also considered how evidence on effective practice and support for disabled children can be better evaluated and disseminated.

Underpinning better support and improved provision of specific services for disabled children and families is the need for:

- clear entitlements that are well understood, with minimum standards as part of a "core offer", which allow for local flexibility and innovation, but will ensure disabled children are not disadvantaged by how well local areas are accommodating both national standards and local priorities;
- disabled children, young people and their families to feel empowered and supported in the choices they make;
- coordinated planning and commissioning to ensure best use of finite resources across traditional health, social services and education boundaries; and
- focused, effective support early in life and at key transition points, with early support for disabled children and their families, which promotes emotional and social development for disabled children and their siblings, to help to improve outcomes for all.

Box 5.1 The Review of Children and Young People

In July 2005, the Government announced that a second Comprehensive Spending Review (CSR) would be undertaken, reporting in 2007. It will set the departmental spending plans and priorities for the years 2008-09, 2009-10 and 2010-11. Budget 2006 announced that the 2007 CSR would be informed by a series of policy reviews, one of which was a review of children and young people, building on the Government's strategy to improve their outcomes.

A discussion paper, setting out the evidence and analysis that has been gathered to inform the Review of Children and Young People was published in January 2007. It also provided a discussion of the issues and challenges raised by that evidence. The Review has drawn on a number of sources of evidence, including:

- research studies and evaluations of interventions to support children, young people and families;
- consultation with groups of young people, particularly those who have difficulty accessing services;
- consultation events with parents, practitioners, commissioners of services from public agencies or the third sector, academics and others with relevant expertise;
- smaller workshops, meetings and visits to experts or projects in relevant fields;
- a public Call for Evidence to support the Review's analysis—the Review's discussion paper provides details of those organisations and individuals that responded; and
- some new research commissioned to support the Review, which is also set out in more detail in the Review's discussion paper.

The Review of children and young people consists of four strands, including this strand on disabled children.

Engaging Children, Families and their Supporters

The Review has taken evidence that engaging disabled children and their families in the shaping of services, and in designing packages of care helps deliver improved outcomes that meet families needs. Therefore the Review has sought to engage closely with disabled children and young people, parents and their supporters, including professionals and the voluntary sector. The Review has consulted through responses to the Children and Young People Review Call for evidence last summer, joint HM Treasury and Department for Education and Skills seminars in July and October 2006, engagement with the disabled children pathfinder Children's Trusts, and visits to Local Authorities, Primary Care Trusts and voluntary sector organisations. A series of Parliamentary Hearings held in July 2006 have also supported the Review, with three hearings and hundreds of written submissions (see box 5.2 below). The Review would like to thank all of those who contributed and shared their expertise and experiences.

Box 5.2 Parliamentary Hearings and Report

A series of Parliamentary Hearings, supported by a consortium of charities working with disabled children and their families, were held to seek the views of disabled children, parents and professionals. The hearings followed the life cycle of a disabled child, covering the early years, family support and transition to adulthood.

MPs heard frank accounts from disabled young people, parents and professionals on areas of good practice, but also further challenges to the Government to improve services for disabled children and their families. Parliamentarians also contributed their constituency experiences. Hundreds of disabled children and young people, parents, professionals and organisations submitted written evidence, all of which informed the Parliamentary Hearings Report, published in October 2006.

Priority recommendations from the report included:

- significant additional resources targeted at disabled children and their families to be made available to planners and commissioners of universal and specialist services;
- additional funding linked to the development of minimum standards, or a 'core offer' for disabled children and families which would create a universal entitlement to a minimum level of service; and
- ministers should ensure that services for disabled children are part of every Local Area Agreement, and National Public Service Agreement targets should be developed for disabled children.

A link to the Parliamentary Hearings Report can be found on the Every Disabled Child Matters website, www.edcm.org.uk

These submissions and recommendations were helpful in informing the conclusions of the Review. This report sets out the Government's response.

Fulfilling the Potential of Every Disabled Child

Since 1997, Government has placed children at the centre of efforts to create a fairer and more just society. The *Every Child Matters* agenda has transformed the Government's approach to children and families. Public services are now focussed on ensuring that children are healthy, stay safe, enjoy and achieve, make a positive contribution, and achieve economic wellbeing.

To deliver these outcomes, the Government has put in place a package of reforms that promote better coordination of and integration of services for all children. Sure Start children's centres provide wrap around support for the youngest children, ensuring every child has the best start in life. Directors of Children's Services are now accountable for the wellbeing of every child in their area. Local Strategic Partnerships are also bringing together different parts of the public, private, community and voluntary sectors at a local level: allowing different initiatives and services to support one another so they can work more effectively together to meet the needs of their local communities. The 570,000 disabled children in England, around 100,000 of whom have complex care needs, need support from a wide range of services, and so should be benefiting even more than most from these reforms.

It has traditionally been the case that disabled children are likely to have poorer outcomes across a range of indicators compared to their non-disabled peers, including lower educational attainment, poorer access to health services and therefore poorer health outcomes, more difficult transitions to adulthood, and poorer employment outcomes. Families of disabled children are less likely to have one or both parents in work, and are more likely to suffer from family break up. Siblings of disabled children may also be more likely to suffer from emotional and behavioural problems, for example through sleep deprivation.

A lack of appropriate and timely support for disabled children to allow them to fulfil their potential not only affects disabled children and their families, it also prevents communities benefiting from the contribution that disabled children can make. Their talent will be wasted, and society will lack the tolerance and understanding of diversity that inclusion and support for disabled children and their families brings.

Progress to Date

There is a significant programme of work underway to improve outcomes for disabled children and their families, across all aspects of their lives. Government has instituted policy reform as part of the following strategies and frameworks:

- the Prime Minister's Strategy Unit report *Improving the life chances of disabled people,* set the Government the challenging goal of achieving substantial equality for disabled people by 2025. The report highlighted a number of changes that must be made in order to achieve this goal. In relation to disabled children and young people it focused on improved early support for families with young children and facilitating a smooth transition to adulthood. This Review builds on the work already underway to meet these recommendations;
- at school, children with Special Educational Needs (SEN) (including most disabled children) are benefiting from DfES' long-term strategy *Removing Barriers to Achievement.* This includes action to improve SEN provision in mainstream schools and to encourage joint working between mainstream and special schools. Ofsted has found that pupils with even the most severe and complex needs are able to make outstanding progress in all types of settings;
- the *National Service Framework for Children, Young People and Maternity Services* is benefiting disabled children and their families through setting standards for the first time in children's health and social care services health support. There are specific standards to address the requirements of children and young people who are disabled and/or have complex health needs and their families (standard 8), and to address the needs of children and young people who are ill (standard 6);
- the recent independent report on palliative care needs *Palliative Care Services for Children and Young People in England* which has highlighted the needs of children with life-limiting or life-threatening conditions. Most children with palliative care needs are disabled, and some children with a disability have palliative care needs. Improvements arising from this Review will benefit children with palliative care needs as they will benefit all other disabled children. The Government is currently considering the recommendations from the palliative care review; and
- strengthened local arrangements to safeguard children, including the establishment of Local Safeguarding Children Boards (LSCB) in 2006. LSCBs bring together a wide range of local partners across sectors, to consider how best to safeguard and promote the welfare of all children in the local area.

This work is supported and underpinned by legislative and policy actions taken by Government in recent years, including:

- the Children Act 1989, under which disabled children are defined as "Children in Need". Under the Act, Local Authorities have a general duty to "safeguard and promote the welfare of children in their area who are in need... To promote the upbringing of such children by their families, by providing a range and level of services appropriate to those children's needs";
- the Disability Equality Duty, introduced into legislation in 2005, which requires organisations across the public sector (including schools and hospitals, local and Central Government) to be proactive in ensuring that disabled people are treated fairly and are included in all aspects of policy development from the outset;
- the Childcare Act 2006 which requires Local Authorities to have particular regard to the needs of disabled children as part of their new duties to assess the childcare needs of families and to secure sufficient childcare to children up to and including age 14 (18 for disabled children); and
- a requirement on most public bodies to have a Disability Equality Scheme setting out how they will meet their responsibility to promote disability equality.

Disabled children and their families are also benefiting from more flexible support. Many local areas are encouraging parents and young people to be engaged in the design and delivery of services, or using direct payment to develop a package of social care support which fits around their needs, such as provision of short breaks services in a home setting for those who want them.

From birth to transition to adulthood, local areas are both establishing and developing new ways of encouraging coordinated provision designed around the child and family. This includes the Early Support Programme, which provides coordinated support for disabled children aged 0-5, and person centred planning at transition to adulthood.

Remaining Challenges

The Review has found many examples of good practice, where services for disabled children are fully meeting their needs, and those of their family. For example, in some areas, coordinated working, innovative practice in service delivery, and the involvement of disabled children, young people and their parents is fostering services that are more responsive and flexible to disabled children and their families needs, and families have told the Review that these are making a real difference to their lives.

However, as outlined in the interim discussion paper, good practice is not uniform across the country. Challenges remain:

- existing data does not present a full picture of the quality of provision in different areas. However, there is evidence that across local authorities, disabled children and families are offered different levels and standards of care, and that those most in need are not always the most likely to get support. Parents and young people in some areas feel that they are not sufficiently empowered, informed, or involved;

- research for the Review also showed that much provision is targeted on high need, high cost interventions, with a lack of focus on intervening early in a child's life, at a key transition point, or change in their condition. Local areas rightly prioritise those in greatest need, however a lack of early support is sometimes exacerbating the numbers of disabled children and families who reach crisis point and need more complex interventions; and
- despite strong examples of successful coordination in the planning and provision of innovative services, for example through the Early Support Programme which is encouraging multi-agency working, there is more that needs to be done to tackle remaining coordination problems. This includes differing eligibility criteria, differing referral systems and cultures, and differing and inconsistent data about the disabled children population across agencies.

This Review considers and sets out the further actions that will be taken to improve outcomes and equality of opportunity for disabled children and their families to address these issues. It aims to facilitate and better support improved outcomes for disabled children in the following areas:

- *empowerment*—offering parents and their disabled children choice and the power to take decisions about their own care and influence local priorities, to improve service quality and responsiveness;
- *responsiveness*—prioritising disabled children at a local and national level, with early interventions, coordinated and timely support, to bring up standards of provision across the country, make it easier for families to access holistic support, and prevent conditions deteriorating; and
- *service quality and capacity*—boosting provision of services which are vital for improving outcomes for disabled children and their families. The Review focuses mainly on specialist services such as short breaks, equipment and therapists, but also tackles barriers to accessing universal services such as childcare.

ACCESS AND EMPOWERMENT

Developing an approach that is more focused on service users leads to good service management and design and contributes to high-quality service provision. Involvement of children and their parents in planning services results in the provision of more appropriate services. Clarity over which services and support mechanisms are available, and consultation and involvement of service users to establish their views, preferences, and needs can help services work more efficiently and effectively, allowing for more flexible and tailored provision.

Local Authorities engage and respond to the views of disabled children and their families to differing degrees, and many young people and their families feel they are not sufficiently empowered. Survey data shows that disabled children and their parents are being involved in a range of decisions concerning their own care and in social service development. However, it also shows that participation varies considerably across areas with not all Local Authorities inviting participation. Disabled children and young people are also often excluded from wider consultations around local policy and planning within their neighbourhoods and communities.

Box 5.3 Empowerment

The concept of empowerment is intimately linked to the principle of rights and responsibilities for individuals. In this context, empowerment means:

- a *right* for citizens to 'opt-in' to networks of support to help influence and shape the services on offer. This creates a duty for service commissioners and providers to reach out to vulnerable groups and empower them in making their views known and heard; and
- recognition that with rights come *responsibilities* for citizens: to engage constructively with service providers in shaping service provision where possible, and understand competing priorities and local constraints.

Despite the principles of Every Child Matters, parents of disabled children feel there is a lack of information, too much duplication of assessments and services, and that access is difficult. Empowerment requires information: information for Local Authorities about their populations, and information for service users about the services available to them, and opportunities for consultation.

Empowering disabled young people and their families means:

- improved provision of information and greater transparency in decision making. Allowing more informed decisions, greater understanding of entitlements, and the process for accessing services;
- putting families in control of the design and delivery of their care package and services. Disabled young people and their parents are often experts on their impairment, and when packages of care are designed in partnership and aim to promote choice and control, they are more likely to be appropriate to their needs, and less likely to leave gaps in provision or to waste resources through inappropriate provision; and
- supporting disabled children and young people and their parents to shape services. This can also mean them playing a part in local mechanisms to facilitate citizen pressure to hold front-line services to account, linked to the new Local Government White Paper "Community Call for Action".

Information and Transparency

Increased transparency about individual entitlements, and increased availability of information at a local level should lead to greater equity in access to provision between families in the same area, through a clearer understanding of their entitlements and how they can access services. There is evidence that different areas make different levels of care available and that those most in need are not always most likely to get support. At a national level, increased transparency about eligibility criteria and levels of provision will give Government and parents a better picture of the levels of variation in provision across local areas. More easily comparable data will make it easier to benchmark local performance and consider what action needs to be taken to improve services. Within health services, the notion of entitlement to a particular service or intervention is less meaningful. Health services are determined by the individual health needs of the child or young person. However, these services still need clear standards about the process for assessing needs and its timeliness.

Empowering disabled children and their families through increased transparency and provision of information will reduce frustration at the uncertainty over the level and timing of support that will be provided, helping families plan and adapt to the level of support they can expect to receive. Directly involving disabled people in designing information can also improve the quality of information and satisfaction with services.

Further Action

Core Offer for Children

The Aiming High for Children report proposed a "Parents' Charter", setting out the minimum level of support parents should expect from local children's services. Given the importance of social care and health services for families with disabled children, the Government will establish a "core offer" for disabled children and their families. This core offer will help parents and young people better understand their entitlements within local areas, increase transparency about variation in provision across areas, and underpin and support standards such as the National Service Framework Standard 8 for disabled children.

The core offer for disabled children will encompass the following elements:

- **Information:** disabled children and their families able to access appropriate information at every stage of a.child's life;
- **Transparency:** levels of support for disabled children and their parents determined on a fair, understandable and transparent basis, with social care services eligibility criteria defined according to need and published by local authorities; clear information published and made available by Primary Care Trusts to families about how to access health care and support available for children with disabilities and complex health needs in the local area;
- **Participation:** disabled children and their families have the option to be fully involved in the way services are planned, commissioned and delivered in their area, increasing their choice and control, which may include access to a supported parents' forum. This participation will help to make sure that the *Community Call for Action* will deliver for all citizens, linked to the new duty on best value authorities to inform, consult and involve representatives of local people in their activities;

- **Assessment:** disabled children and their families to benefit from integration of assessment processes, with shared information, shared basic assessments including through the Common Assessment Framework, providing a gateway to more specialist assessments where necessary, and more high-level multi-agency assessments provided in the same place at the same time. As children and young people develop there will be a need for ongoing and differential assessment, but this should be provided in a coherent, coordinated way. Parents and young people will be told at assessment when they will get a response setting out what support they will be provided with; and
- **Feedback:** a clear and published complaints procedure for all families who are not happy with the services they are receiving (including through the *Community Call for Action* as set out in the Local Government White Paper).

Delivery against this commitment will be measured through the revised Local Government performance framework to be determined at the time of the Comprehensive Spending Review, and reinforced through Comprehensive Area Assessments, which will take an area based view on delivery of local priorities. Information on the offer should be distributed through local services, such as council offices, libraries and local voluntary sector groups, the Early Support Programme and the Transition Support Programme at a local level.

This core offer will take the form of a policy statement which will be developed by the Department for Education and Skills and Department of Health, with support from key stakeholders, and underpinned by guidance for each of the above elements in time for the Comprehensive Spending Review this Autumn. It is expected that Local Authorities and their partners consider the core offer policy statement in their local planning and provision of services, and ensure that it is published and accessible to the local community.

Putting Families in Control of Care Packages

Direct Payments

Direct payments are cash payments made in lieu of social service provision to individuals who have been assessed as needing services. They can be made to disabled people aged 16 or over, to people with parental responsibility for disabled children, and to carers aged 16 or over in respect of carer services. Since the Health and Social Care Act 2001, families assessed as eligible for social care services, including families with disabled children, must be offered the option of direct payments.

Direct payments create more flexibility and choice in the provision of social services, and allow people to make their own decisions about how care is delivered. If packages of care are designed by users, they are more likely to be responsive and appropriate, with resources less likely to be wasted on inappropriate provision. Some parents described direct payments as having positively "transformed their lives", however other service users in the review's consultation felt that the additional responsibility of managing a budget for services was too much of a burden, particularly given their existing care responsibilities. One survey of direct payments found that parents appreciated the flexibility, freedom, choice and control that direct payments offered, but found that managing the payments could be time consuming, and that there could be difficulties in finding suitable people to employ. Parents in the survey also felt that they could make sure that their child was happy with their carers if they chose them themselves with direct payments. Young people have also benefited from receiving direct payments, choosing who provides them with assistance and what activities they engage in.

Current Situation

Figures from the Commission for Social Care Inspection (CSCI) show that in 2005 there were over 2,700 families with disabled children and over 300 disabled young people aged 16-17 receiving direct payments, indicating low levels of take up. To promote further take-up of direct payments for families with disabled children, information for Local Authorities and parents has been placed on the Every Child Matters website and an updated version of *A Parent's Guide to Direct Payments* was published in summer 2006.

The Department of Health (DH) has developed a self-assessment tool for councils to review their direct payment systems in collaboration with partners. The focus is on identifying where local barriers exist to identify solutions to promote uptake of direct payments.

Benfits of Individual Budgets

Individual budgets build on some of the successful features of direct payments and apply the same principles of choice and control. There are, however, some key differences. Individual budgets include a number of income streams rather than simply social care services in order to give the individual a more joined-up package of support. Most importantly, individual budgets put people in the centre of the planning process, and recognise that they are best placed to understand their own needs and how to meet them.

Unlike direct payments, individual budgets can be held and managed by a broker (to help service users manage the budget and reduce the associated responsibility for arranging their own care). By facilitating the provision of a holistic package of support designed around the child and family, individual budgets can also help encourage coordinated provision of services, and avoid duplication in provision.

The *Improving life chances for disabled people* report recommended that the individual budgets approach should, in principle, be extended to families with disabled children. It states, "*The mechanisms, costs and benefits will need to be investigated through pilots coordinated with those for adults. The design and timing of these pilots will also need to be carefully coordinated with the roll-out of wider changes to the landscape of children's services*".

Current Situation

The Council for Disabled Children was recently commissioned by the Department for Education and Skills (DfES) to produce a scoping report covering the following issues relating to Individual Budgets:

- the implications of introducing individual budgets for Local Authorities and other stakeholders;

- the relevant evidence collated from various stakeholders;
- possible models to be used in the introduction of individual budgets; and
- the views of disabled children, young people and their families.

DfES is intending to carry out a scoping exercise taking account of the CDC report and the recommendations in this Review, with the aim of:

- looking at the financial level of these individual budgets and the different income streams that would need to come together;
- looking at what added value individual budgets bring to current practice; and
- demand for individual budgets and/or direct payments.

The scoping exercise will then be evaluated in order to inform the development of the concept of individual budgets for disabled children and their families more widely. It is envisaged that work will initially concentrate on older children and the preparation required to facilitate their successful transition to adult individual budgets.

One of the key elements of individual budgets is to bring together a variety of income streams in an integrated manner, to improve choice and control for the individual, and to facilitate coordinated provision of services. The majority of income streams being used by the individual budget pilot sites are only available to young people and adults over the age of 16. The largest potential source of income is the Social Care budget. Other budgets that could be included are the Integrated Community Equipment Services budget, and the Disabled Facilities Grant could be available for children under 16.

A number of Local Authorities and health providers are already creatively using aligned budgets or pooled budgets to transfer money to the local authority to part fund a package of care where the individual has specific health needs. However, more specific guidance would help enable this to become national practice rather than limited to those authorities where good joint working partnerships are in operation.

Further Action

To increase flexibility and choice in the provision of services, the Government will pilot Individual Budgets for disabled children and young people, building on the current scoping exercise, with full evaluation over the CSR period. This will involve as many funding streams as possible at a local level, and where there are legislative or systematic barriers, the pilot will consider how best to promote the principles behind individual budgets of greater choice and involvement in decision making by disabled young people and their families.

Government also recommends that some health funding streams, where there is already the potential and legal provision of pooled budgets, and where needs are predictable and specific to an individual, should be included in these pilots. On this basis, Government proposes including health funding streams for short breaks, equipment and wheelchairs. This will facilitate provision of a holistic package of support for the child and family, and help further coordinated provision from the family's perspective, complementing work at the local service provision level to improve joint commissioning.

Parents, Children and Young People Shaping Services

Despite policy and guidance which makes clear that service commissioners and providers should be fully involving parents in the design and delivery of services, and some areas with good practice in involving and consulting, participation for disabled children, young people and their families is variable across the country. One study found that where parents were 'active agents' rather than 'passive recipients', this can lead to lower levels of stress for families and better outcomes for both parents and children.

Local Empowerment Mechanisms

Strong and Prosperous Communities: The Local Government White Paper, sets out how the Government intends to strengthen the role of local government, and increase local flexibility, to deliver better outcomes across communities. The Government will create mechanisms for more citizen pressure and greater dynamism at a neighbourhood level, so that front-line services are more accountable to citizens.

The White Paper announced a new best value duty to involve local people in the design, delivery and assessment of local services and policies. Building on this commitment, a "*Community Call for Action*" will be extended across all public services to enable people to hold local bodies to account if services fail to meet their needs. Central Government will also work with local government and community organisations to identify and promote good practice in local charters, neighbourhood planning, citizenship learning and participatory budgeting.

To help achieve this aim Local Authorities need to consider how best to engage 'hard to reach' groups when deciding how to meet this duty. Any guidance that may be issued to support the implementation of the new best value duty will emphasise the need to take appropriate steps to engage these groups.

Parents' Formus

The Government recognises that given that some parents of disabled children may have substantial caring responsibilities, they may need additional support to express their views at a local level. Some areas already have well established arrangements in place for parents and carers of disabled children to participate and express their views, but others are still developing. A range of mechanisms need to be developed to support parents and carers, building on existing arrangements for parents of disabled children, linking where appropriate with other sources of support such as Parent Partnership Services and Local Involvement Networks, to avoid duplication.

Box 5.4 Exemplification Standards for Parent Partnership Services

The minimum standards for Parent Partnership Services (PPS) in the Special Educational Needs (SEN) Code of Practice include '...that parents' views are heard and understood, and inform and influence the development of local SEN policy and practice...'

In addition, the draft exemplification materials on the forthcoming guidance '*Informing and shaping local policy and practice*' expect parents and carers to be routinely consulted about SEN policy as a minimum, with PPS providing training and support to enable parents to subsequently participate in:

- discussions to inform policy development,
- review and evaluation of SEN;
- Parent Partnership Services; and
- children's services policy.

This will lead to full participation by parents in shaping policy development and practice.

All local services are now expected to consult with parents and involve them in the planning and development of services, however the concept of 'parent participation' means different things to different people. Having a facilitated forum, training in the most effective ways to voice views, or a parent support officer or disability champion can all help bring a representative group of parents together to participate in designing appropriate provision and communicate any local challenges.

There is no 'one size fits all' solution to parent's forums. They vary depending on many local factors. The structure that will work best in any area will depend on what parents want to achieve, the number of people involved and how they want to work. A forum can:

- be professionally led, an independent organisation, or a regular meeting run by parents;
- provide the opportunity for parents to raise individual issues regarding the provision of services for their children;
- allow parents to feed back views to service providers or commissioners, and develop partnerships with statutory and voluntary organisations;
- send newsletters to keep parents in touch; and
- deliver training workshops.

Evidence submitted to the Review and from fieldwork has found that the benefits of parents' forums include an increased feeling of control for parents over their child's wellbeing leading to lower levels of stress for families, better use of services and increased parental understanding of how services work, which often leads to better working relationships with professionals. Parents can also make an impact by asking the questions which no one else would think to ask, and benefit from making new contacts with other parents facing similar issues and supportive professionals. Professionals in turn will benefit from better relationships with parents, gaining a new perspective on the services that they are providing by finding out what parents and disabled children and young people really want.

Current Picture

There is currently support and guidance from the voluntary sector in meeting the information and support needs of both parents and professionals. For example, the charity Contact a Family offers:

- information about parent participation in a user friendly format aimed at both parents and professionals;
- key principles to ensure successful parent participation, drawn from their own parent participation work in different areas of the UK;
- examples of different models of participation, their strengths, weaknesses, in what circumstances they might work well and how they could be replicated;
- a range of printed resources on parent participation, some written for parents, some for parent groups and some for professionals;
- tailor made training for both parents and professionals designed to meet the different needs of each group we work with; and
- free e-newsletters for anyone interested in parent participation issues.

Box 5.5 *Cornwall Parent Carers Council*

Parents from the Parents Carer Council in Cornwall, in conjunction with the local voluntary befriending organisation, Face2Face, are in close consultation with the Local Family Services social services department. As a result, direct payments and other flexible solutions are being used to ensure that the most flexible, efficient packages of care are made available, and the best use is made of resources available to help families and children, helping to tackle their greatest challenges—be that inclusive childcare or flexible short break provision for families.

Parents are also helping shape services through designing and delivering training to childcare settings in providing for disabled children and their families. The dual benefits of transferring skills to the universal workforce, and allowing parents a platform to share their expertise and regain their confidence, was proving hugely beneficial to both promoting inclusive childcare settings, breaking down attitudinal barriers and improving the trust in universal settings for parents of disabled children.

A great deal of existing legislation and guidance on health, education, social care and early years mentions the need for user participation. The Disability Equality Duty promotes the participation of disabled people and this should include children and young people. However, evidence suggests that parents' forums are not yet established in every Local Authority, and in certain areas where the service provision is not very good, statutory bodies have few incentives to increase the voice of service users and the impact of parent forums.

A stronger local voice, which sets out Government policy on the future development of the user involvement system in health and social care, was published in July 2006. This included the replacement of Patients' Forums with Local Involvement Networks (LINks), as well as simplifying and strengthening Section 11 of the Health and Social Care Act 2001, which sets out NHS bodies' duties to involve and consult patients and the public.

Local Involvement Networks (LINKs)

LINks will strengthen the voice of local people in the health and social care system.

By providing flexible ways for a much larger number of people to engage with their local health as well as social care organisations, LINks will help shape services and priorities in ways that best suit communities and the people in them. They will promote public accountability in health and social care through open and transparent communication with commissioners and providers. This will include people who find it hard to be heard, such as disabled children and their families, and people with learning disabilities and mental health problems, including severely disabled people who wish to live independently.

Involving Children and Young People

Parent forums give an opportunity to parents of disabled children to express their views on the services they receive. However, the views of disabled children and young people should be taken into consideration as well, independent of the views of their parents. Consultation with disabled children and young people should generate useful advice on how to improve services, help to inform evaluation of specific services and lead to increased participation of disabled children and young people in society.

Research suggests that, while in general children are increasingly involved in decision-making, growth is slower for involving disabled children directly in decisions about their own care or in service planning more generally. One study found that when children did participate in consultation exercises, they viewed it as a very positive experience, and the case studies showed some examples of children influencing decisions made in their reviews and of changes to service provision as a direct result of the views children expressed.

Box 5.6 City Equals—Involving Disabled Children

Based in Sunderland, City Equals is run by nine young people aged between 13 and 25. They coordinate a group with varying disabilities working towards representing young people with disabilities across the City. The Group has been running since April 2003.

City Equals has been involved in a wide range of national and local consultations, including work on the *Youth Matters Green Paper*, the local Strategic Partnership review of transition services, Sunderland's anti-bullying charter and the State of the City Debate. The work with the Strategic Partnership on transition has been taken forward and is directly influencing transition reviews. Work by the group with local hospitals has convinced health professionals to change their practice by talking straight to disabled young people instead of consulting through parents and carers.

As part of National Youth Work Week, the group held an open day for parents and carers with the theme of 'Mental Health and Emotional Wellbeing'. The group did a display highlighting some of the issues faced by young people with disabilities. One young member said 'We decided to have a parents evening to show what we did and why we should be proud of holding our heads up.'

The group recently went to Birmingham and delivered a workshop at a national conference organised by *Young People Now* on how to involve disabled young people in shaping services.

City Equals is committed to involving the widest range of disabled young people. The group have been awarded funding to acquire Photo symbols; this enabled one young person to receive training needed to ensure his peers understand the concept of using pictures instead of words.

Equality 2025 is a new UK advisory network established by Government to advise on matters relating to disability. Equality 2025 members are all disabled people, and include two young people. As part of it's remit, Equality 2025 will be developing a strategy for engagement with disabled children and young people and those with parental responsibility. The aim is to engage and empower children and young people, and those with parental responsibilities, across the United Kingdom. This will be achieved by building on existing networks of disabled children and young people, working closely with the Council for Disabled Children.

Further Action

The Government expects all local areas to build on good practice in engaging parents of disabled children, such as parents' forums with the support of staff who have skills to support participation, to engage, support, and train parents to influence the design and delivery of services. Underpinned by £5 million of investment over the CSR period, this support should build on models from the voluntary sector and Parent Partnership Services, with organisations bidding for resources to support effective parent participation projects.

The Government also expects all Local Authorities, Primary Care Trusts, and schools to engage parents and disabled children and young people in the design and delivery of services appropriate to their needs, building on existing good practice. Most public bodies should be doing this as part of the responsibilities they now have to promote disability equality under the Disability Discrimination Act 1995, building on existing good practice. Actions being taken should be reflected in their Disability Equality Schemes and the actions of individual organisations should be coordinated in Children and Young People's Plans and Children's Trust arrangements as appropriate.

Providing a mechanism through which to engage disabled children and their parents will help ensure that the *Community Call for Action* will deliver for all citizens.

RESPONSIVE SERVICES AND TIMELY SUPPORT

Responsive services should be easily accessible for all disabled children and their families who need them, designed around the child and family, and delivered in a coordinated and timely manner. Where this is the case, disabled children, young people and their families will be supported to play a full role in the society of which they are part, and will benefit from equality of opportunity. Responsive services will facilitate improved educational, social and emotional development, improved independent living, choice and control.

Local flexibility in the design and provision of services is to be encouraged, allowing Local Authorities and Primary Care Trusts (PCTs) to focus resources where there is most need and to allow them to respond to the local priorities as voiced by their population.

As set out in the Children and Young People Review discussion paper, there is evidence that different Local Authorities and PCTs make different levels of care available, and that those most in need are not always most likely to get support.

Variation in how well local areas are accommodating both national standards and local priorities should not disadvantage disabled children in fulfilling their potential.

Minimum standards will mitigate against this, which is why this Review recommends a core offer for disabled children and their families. Building on this offer, this chapter sets out proposals to ensure greater responsiveness.

Local Authorities and PCTs rightly prioritise those in greatest need. However, a lack of early support and intervention may be exacerbating the numbers of disabled children who reach crisis point and need more complex interventions. This increases problems for the child and family and is more costly than early intervention.

Disabled young people may face additional challenges in the transition to adulthood. Support at transition to adulthood is vital to enable disabled young people to gain independence, choice and control over the assistance they need, and to achieve their aspirations. However, not all disabled young people are getting the coordinated, intensive support that they need.

There is much good practice in providing responsive services, for example:

- the *Every Child Matters: Change for Children* programme, with long-term investment by the Government, bringing together more opportunities and services into single settings like children's centres and schools;
- extended schools guidance, which makes it clear that children with special educational needs or disabilities must be able to access all services. It explains how special schools in particular often act as a hub for delivery of health, social care and respite services for children and parents. There is a range of specialist health and social care services that children, young people and adults need to access at different times in their lives which support both their general well being and their ability to learn; and
- the Early Support Programme which aims to achieve coordinated, family-focused services for young disabled children and their families across England. It focuses on better joint assessments, coordination of service provision, better information, the introduction of a lead professional or key worker, and the development of family-held, standard material to monitor children's development which can be shared across agencies.

Building on arrangements which are already working well in some local areas to promote responsive, high quality provision, this chapter examines:

- how to develop a better understanding of the disabled children population, to help with more efficient planning, commissioning and provision of services;
- the role of the new performance management framework being implemented as part of the Comprehensive Spending Review in prioritising disabled children, including national indicators in the Public Service Agreements and how these are implemented on the ground through Local Area Agreements;
- incentives to provide support and interventions early in a child's life, or at key transition stages, including better evidence on which early interventions are most effective;
- incentives to coordinate packages of care, with planning around the child and family and joined up assessments; and

- support to ensure a smooth transition to adulthood, reducing uncertainty, increasing awareness of options available, breaking down physical and attitudinal barriers to further education, employment and/or independent living.

Developing a Better Understanding of the Disabled Children Population

A clearer picture of the disabled children population and disabled children's needs at a local level is essential for effective planning, commissioning and provision of services.

The Review's fieldwork suggests that although some Local Authorities are developing a good understanding of their local population, and undertaking thorough needs assessments to help plan and predict the services and interventions disabled children and their families will need, others still do not have a proper understanding of the profile or even the size of their disabled children population.

Good quality, consistent, and up-to-date information is essential to the provision of services to all those in need, including disabled children. Collection and appropriate use of such information facilitates the operation of mutually aware, child-centred services working together to ensure the best possible outcomes for children, and especially for those with additional needs. Some Local Authorities (such as Halton—see box 5.7 below) demonstrate this very well, but where the range and quality of information is lacking disabled children and their families inevitably lose out.

Box 5.7 Good Quality Data to Promote Integrated, Timely Support

There are a number of Local Authorities who have developed methods of collecting data for disabled children and their families in a successful way. Halton, for example, use a single data set, which includes all health, social services and education data available on their vulnerable children population to improve communication, eligibility assessment and commissioning of services. The work of the Halton Children and Young People Strategic Partnership is firmly based on the operation of a Children and Young People Database, which is a key element of partnership working.

At its core, the Local Authority maintains pupil-centred data relating to pupil service, early years, grants and benefits (Free School Meals), e-Common Assessment Framework, Special Educational Needs and Admissions. However, beyond its core, it utilises information from a very wide range of organisations and information sources which affect the lives of children, including Youth Offending Teams, Colleges, Looked-After Children, the Traveller Service, exclusions, PCT 0-3 year olds, Connexions (including children not in education, employment or training), non-Halton schools, academic performance, and many more.

Current Situation

Statutory definitions relating to disability include "Children in Need", for social service purposes, Special Educational Needs (SEN) for education purposes, Hospital Episode Statistics for hospital admissions, and the Disability Discrimination Act definition.

Remaining Challenges

Volume 6 of the regulations and guidance on the Children's Act 1989 encourages Local Authorities to develop their own more positive working definitions of disability, and whilst some local areas are doing this and collecting data on their population in a proactive way, this hampers comparisons across the country on a like for like basis. There is no single definition of disability, as the current statistical definitions are rightly used to serve particular service needs, for example the clinical needs of the health definition. In addition, there are barriers to the Department of Health and PCTs using the Disability Discrimination Act definition of disability given that it may be too general a definition to help with planning and provision of medical services and interventions.

There is also a lack of longitudinal data at a national level, which exacerbates problems around planning for the population. There is ongoing work across government on improving the level and quality of data on the number and population of disabled children.

Further Action

There is an inconsistent picture of data collection on disabled children at the local level. Whilst some Local Authorities and PCTs are collecting good data, other areas lack the data they need to underpin their planning and equality duties and ensure that progress is being made by disabled children and their families.

To allow Local Authorities and PCTs to plan and provide for their population, Government will look to all Local Authorities and PCTs to collect data on:

- the number of disabled children in their area, where possible classified by type of disability; and
- the percentage of this disabled children population accessing both universal and specialist services, such as short breaks or therapy services.

Over time this data may be developed into a system of benchmarking which will allow Local Authorities and their partners to compare profiles and degrees of satisfaction with services, both overall and against Local Authorities in similar circumstances (i.e. "statistical neighbours").

This data collection should be based initially on the definition of disability in the Disability Discrimination Act, and all local areas should also use data on the number of disabled children taking up higher rate Disability Living Allowance as a proxy interim measure for the number of severely disabled children. This will be an important first step in helping Local Authorities and PCTs deliver for their populations, however to further help this planning and commissioning process, this process will be reviewed to help encourage more detailed needs assessment and to further support effective partnership working.

This work will be underpinned by guidance following the CSR on how Local Authorities should be collecting data on their disabled children population. Local Authorities should consider how to make this information available to citizens and across agencies, and it should be reflected in Children and Young People's plans by 2010-11.

The Government will also take forward further work to develop more consistent, compatible and comparable data on disability on which to base service planning, commissioning and provision at both a local and national level, to report in 2008-9. This work will be undertaken across different agencies and departments to reduce duplication and to join up national government and local agencies. The work will be coordinated by the ONS, with input from the Office for Disability Issues (ODI), the Department for Education and Skills (DfES), and the Department of Health (DH), and should be informed by:

- a DfES survey of Local Authorities to determine what data they currently collect on their disabled children population, what definitions they use, and how they use this data;
- a DfES Survey to investigate the reasons underlying the wide local variations in the proportions and classification of children with SEN and/or disabilities, to allow Local Authorities to reflect on their performance and learn from others;
- DfES research project on data collection in children's services including a schools pilot. This will look at the child or young person's own attribution of disability in a user-friendly manner, but based on the DDA definition. Different methods of data collection in schools will be evaluated and cost estimates made;
- DfES work on the refreshed Children in Need census for 2008-09;
- ODI work on a proposed longitudinal survey of disabled people;
- DH Child Health Mapping data work on developing a better understanding of disabled children in PCTs;
- DH work on Hospital Episode Statistics and identifying children in the set who have a disability; and
- development of a child health data set to support implementation of the *National Service Framework for Children, Young People and Maternity Services*, (DH, DfES, 2004), which will include developing data collected on disabled children to monitor the achievement and the delivery of NSF standards and quality requirements, to support the audit of service quality and coverage and to inform strategic planning processes and the prioritisation of service development and provision.

Performance Management

Current Situation

Nationally, there are a number of requirements that will influence local provision of responsive services for disabled children. These include:

- *legislation* such as the Children Act 1989, the Disability Discrimination Act (DDA) 1995, and the DDA 2005. Under the Children Act 1989, Local Authorities have a general duty to "safeguard and promote the welfare of children in their area who are in need... To promote the upbringing of such children by their families, by providing a range of services appropriate to those children's needs." The DDA 1995 makes it unlawful to discriminate against people in respect of their disabilities, and the DDA 2005 extends this to introduce a new duty on public bodies and authorities to have due regard to the need to promote equality of opportunity for all disabled people;

- *guidance,* such as the *National Service Framework for Children, Young People and Maternity Services,* which sets standards for the first time in children's health and social services. Standard 8 of the National Service Framework relates specifically to children and young people who are disabled and those with complex health needs; and
- *national level performance indicators and targets,* which encourage a focus on the disabled children's population. For example, the current child poverty PSA target encourages reducing poverty for disabled children and their families, while current targets on raising attainment require a focus on SEN as they are likely to have lower attainment.

Some local areas are already pioneering the use of local performance indicators to give clear signals to services about what they should achieve, responding to identified local priorities. Some of the indicators which the Review team have seen used at a local level to encourage improved outcomes for disabled children and their families include measuring the proportion of:

- parents/carers of children with severe and complex disabilities with access to information about services;
- children with complex needs receiving multi-agency assessments who access services to meet their identified needs;
- children with complex needs accessing mainstream education, inclusive play and leisure opportunities;
- disabled children participating in person centred transition reviews to enable them to influence their outcomes;
- disabled children accessing more flexible and individual services through direct payments;
- disabled children accessing short break services; and
- disabled children in inclusive settings.

Remaining Challenges

Many submissions to the Review have suggested enhancing these measures. There have also been suggestions to strengthen existing legislation to introduce legally enforceable duties on local bodies to assess and provide services. Introducing specific legislation cuts across existing general duties and local flexibility, and would be hard to put in place for all services which disabled children and their families need. Given the varied but often specific needs of disabled children and young people, it would not be possible to provide comprehensive entitlements which meet every individual's needs, for example, not all disabled children will need a wheelchair, or a certain number of hours of short break provision. While some submissions have suggested that service provision for disabled children should be determined and specified nationally, others have emphasised the importance of local areas having the autonomy to set local priorities to allow a continuation of the innovative, flexible provision which currently occurs in areas of good practice.

Stakeholders have also suggested using the performance management framework, which has played a fundamental role in driving up public service performance since 1998. The performance management framework is set to evolve in the 2007 Comprehensive Spending Review, with the introduction of a focussed set of Public Service Agreements (PSA) that articulate Government's highest-priority outcomes and typically span several departments, and a comprehensive set of Departmental Strategic Objectives for each department. Genuine focus and rationalisation in the PSA set, with a significant reduction in PSAs and a similar reduction in the number of underpinning indicators set from the centre will enable frontline delivery agents to balance national with local needs, without restricting options to deliver, and will allow greater space for innovative and responsive public services at a local level. In addition, the current Local Area Agreement outcomes framework will be replaced by a new framework for Local Authorities working alone or in partnership with quantitative areas for improvement in both national and local priorities articulated in the Local Area Agreements.

Box 5.8 The New Performance Management Framework

Public Service Agreements (PSAs) have played a vital role in galvanising public service delivery and achieving major improvements in outcomes since their introduction in the 1998 Comprehensive Spending Review (CSR). The 2007 CSR will build on the approach driving ambitious improvements in priority areas while developing the supporting performance management framework, to ensure a user-focused, devolved approach to public service delivery. The performance management framework in the CSR07 period will include:

- a comprehensive set of Strategic Objectives for each department;
- a focussed set of PSAs which articulate the Government's highest priority outcomes for the spending period and will typically span several departments;
- a single, cross-departmental Delivery Agreement for each PSA, developed in consultation with frontline workers and users, supported by a basket of national, outcome-focused indicators;
- an emphasis on central coordination working in synergy with greater bottom-up accountability, local flexibility and user responsiveness; and
- a premium on the use of high quality, timely data while freeing up the frontline by reducing low value data burdens.

Each department will agree and publish a new, comprehensive set of Strategic Objectives at the CSR. Departments will use these objectives to manage and report on performance and to inform resourcing decisions, ensuring a more holistic, coherent and better aligned framework for performance and financial management across the board.

Alongside Departmental Strategic Objectives, a new set of PSAs will set out the highest priority outcomes for the Government for the CSR07 period, with less than a third of the number of PSAs than in the current spending review period. Recognising that delivery of the Government's highest priority outcomes requires public services to adopt collaborative approaches across organisational boundaries, both at Whitehall and the frontline, these PSAs will not be constrained by departmental boundaries but will reflect a government wide set of priorities, articulating the most important areas for collective action.

> To ensure coherent cross-departmental working as well as buy-in throughout the delivery chain, each cross-cutting PSA will be underpinned by a single, published Delivery Agreement setting out plans for delivery, the role of each organisation in the delivery chain, and how progress towards the outcome will be measured and strengthening accountability at all levels. Departments are working together to draw up Delivery Agreements involving local authorities, frontline professionals, such as teachers and nurses, and service users so that frontline expertise informs the definition, measurement and delivery of priorities.
>
> Delivery Agreements will set out a small basket of national, outcome-focussed indicators that will be used to measure progress on each PSA. Indicators will be selected and developed in consultation with frontline professionals to ensure that they are appropriate and effective. Precise targets and minimum standards will continue to be key levers for improvement but will give more weight to the priorities of individual areas and communities—focusing action where there is most need for improvement.

Further Action

The Review has already highlighted the importance of empowering disabled children and young people and their families to help them influence services to make them responsive to their needs, through mechanisms for improving local accountability such as clear complaints procedures when services are not up to scratch. However, not all disabled young people and their families will want this responsibility, and this will be a more powerful tool if it is backed up by other ways of influencing services at the local level. It is important to maintain local flexibility in the design and provision of services, and Government wants to encourage even more responsive services, and greater coordination of provision, encouraging early intervention, supported by underpinning data to help planning and commissioning for the population.

The Review has considered the advantages and drawbacks of further legislation. In particular, it considered the challenges of ensuring that legislation is sensitive enough to be able to prescribe provision against a wide variation of need in the disabled children population. As innovation and flexibility are critical to improving the quality of services, and their impact on disabled children, young people and their families, the Government believes that the right approach is to strengthen and sharpen the performance management framework.

In order to focus service provision on improving outcomes, performance indicators need to be outcome-focused and meaningful. Difficulties arise when trying to design one performance indicator which would measure overall improvement in disabled children's outcomes. Having a performance indicator which is very specific and focused on one element of service provision can reduce flexibility in responding to the full range of needs for the population. For example, a performance indicator focused purely on short breaks may divert focus from other essential support services for disabled children and their families, such as equipment and inclusion in universal provision.

In addition, it is hard to design one indicator measuring improved outcomes for disabled children as a population, given that the population is so diverse. An indicator on improving educational attainment, for example, may not capture improvements in the degree of independent living made by disabled children and young people with learning difficulties, and may not fully capture improved life chances and conditions for children and young people with complex health needs. The Review has therefore explored an indicator using general satisfaction with both universal and specialist services for disabled children as a proxy for measuring improvements in outcomes, and an indicator around the 5 elements of the core offer, i.e. around information, assessment, transparency, feedback and participation.

Before reaching a final decision on an indicator as part of the CSR, DfES will carry out a feasibility study on how to measure whether families with disabled children and young people are benefiting from the core offer, including looking at the methodology for data collection from a suitable sample of families with disabled children and young people in all 150 Local Authorities and all PCTs on an annual basis, or a rolling programme of data collection from Local Authorities and PCT areas over a 3 year period. It is anticipated that a robust set of data collected in this way will encourage Local Authorities and PCTs to implement the core offer, address their responsibilities in this area, allow benchmarking across the country and inform parents and young people of the performance in the area in which they live. Over the longer term, the Government will continue to make sure that any indicator on disabled children is as focused on outcomes as possible.

Government will therefore ensure that high priority is given to improving outcomes for disabled children in the forthcoming CSR, with sharper incentives to embed a focus on disabled children at both a local and national level. In particular, Government will develop a national disabled children's indicator as part of the set of priority PSAs to be agreed across Government at the CSR.

To ensure that what we see in the best Local Authorities can be replicated across the country, this will be supported by better local level data on disabled children and regular monitoring of the progress made on improving outcomes for disabled children, with much greater use of comparisons across the country to judge how different local areas are performing.

Early Intervention

Current Situation

There is evidence that poor responsiveness sometimes manifests itself as late intervention. Local Authorities and PCTs currently rightly prioritise those in greatest need. However, a lack of early identification and intervention may be exacerbating the numbers of disabled children and families who reach crisis point and need more complex intervention, which increase problems for the child and family, and are more costly.

Early intervention is not just about providing support for disabled children and their families early in childhood. Disabled children and their families need properly coordinated support, delivered as soon as they need it, particularly at key transition points in their lives, and they need services and support to respond quickly when their circumstances or a child's condition changes.

Early support for disabled children and their families is essential to prevent problems such as deteriorating health, family stress and breakdown, children potentially being placed in care, and deteriorating emotional and social development for disabled children and their siblings.

Box 5.9 The Early Support Programme

The Early Support Programme, set up in 2002, is a partnership between the Government and the voluntary sector to improve the quality, consistency and coordination of services for disabled children and their families. Originally piloted from birth to three, it is being rolled out for disabled children in 2007-08 from birth to five across the country. Parents have been at the centre of the process since the beginning, helping to make multi-agency working and improved service provision a reality. The independent evaluation of the programme has found that the Early Support Programme has had positive effects on the quality of service provision, improvements in multi-agency working and a smooth process of referral, identification and initial assessment.

For parents whose experience of early support included multi-agency assessments and review or key working, there were clear advantages to inter-agency working, including a reduced sense of burden from otherwise having to coordinate services themselves, confidence engendered through the routine and predictable ways in which they knew professionals planned together, greater accountability, and increased opportunities for parents to become involved in decision making about their child's future.

Benefits of Early Intervention

Services can intervene earlier than they sometimes do, and make a difference to disabled children and their families' lives. For example:

- *short breaks*: families with disabled children often face particularly high stress and breakdown owing to the increased pressures of having a disabled child. A break from caring to be with their partner and/or other children can be the single most important factor in helping their relationship;
- *early provision of equipment or wheelchairs*: pressure relieving mattresses or special seating may prevent the development of pressure sores, contractures, or skeletal deformity. Once pressure sores develop, the patient can lose dignity, suffer considerable pain, and the NHS may have to pay for district nurses' time or expensive plastic surgery to solve the problem;
- *sleep programmes*: without early support to help parents manage their children's sleep patterns, parents and siblings may have to function on only a few hours of sleep, not to mention the detrimental effects on the disabled child themselves. Families testimonies include memory lapses, having to give up work, and siblings falling asleep at school or missing school having been awake all night; and
- *behavioural management*: this will prevent worsening educational outcomes, and reduce stress for parents and siblings.

> ***Box 5.10 A Parents Experience: The Consequences of a Lack of Early Intervention to Support Sleep Deprivation***
>
> "I get so tired I dream about sleep during the day. Not holidays or having fun, just sleep. Some nights I get around 5 hours, others as little as 3. I find it hard to get motivated because I often have aching sensation in arms and legs where so tired. When too tired get weepy. I forget things all the time, as you personally know, and am convinced that my lads probably do use this to their advantage, not that I blame them, I would if I could. Friendships are few and far between because I have become so lousy at calling people and keeping in touch. I used to be Mrs Efficient And Houseproud, not any more.... real life is here. I blunder through each day from one thing to the next. I get side-tracked, on route to doing one thing I find myself doing something completely different."

Remaining Challenges

There appear to be two underlying reasons why early intervention is not happening on a consistent basis. Firstly, in some circumstances there is a lack of knowledge and understanding of early interventions that can improve outcomes, for example behavioural management and sleep programmes. Comprehensive cost effectiveness studies covering the financial implication of the full range of potential benefits are scarce. Further research into the full economic and social benefits of these early interventions, and the potential to avoid problems later in a child's life or a worsening of their condition will help encourage a shift toward earlier support at key stages of a child and families' life.

Secondly, there is the challenge of shifting allocation from crisis provision to early intervention, given finite resources. Local Authorities and PCTs will always rightly prioritise those in greatest need. However, focusing more on early intervention may prevent some disabled children and their families reaching crisis point and developing such high support needs.

Further Action

To encourage early intervention to help prevent deteriorating outcomes for disabled children and their families and to promote development, the Government will provide additional resource over the CSR period to enable the new Centre for Excellence for Children and Family Services to evaluate and benchmark good practice on early intervention policies for disabled children, including interventions on behavioural management and parenting, sleep, communication and mobility. Priority must be given to ensuring that findings are disseminated to practitioners and parents in a way that impacts on practice.

Coordinating Care Across Services

Benefits of Coordinated Working and Provision

Good joint commissioning and delivery matters. Its absence puts an extra burden on parents in terms of extra stress and time demands. It can also raise waiting times (for example where children are waiting for separate assessments). Where families have coordinated support, through joint planning, commissioning, assessment and provision, or through a key worker or lead professional, disabled children and their families are more likely to benefit from better coordinated support from accessible, knowledgeabie professionals in both universal and specialist services.

Many local areas use key workers or teams working around the family and child, which may be part of the Early Support Programme. The philosophy of the Early Support Programme of joint working and shared understandings of goals and approaches across agencies has underpinned its success, reinforcing and enhancing existing good practice, and in other cases enabling previous ineffective structures of joint working to be left behind. Key working is a way of managing the package of support available and ensuring families access the services to which they are entitled, with workers being named individuals who act as a single point of contact for multiple services, empower families and help them navigate the system.

Available evidence on key workers suggests that they improve the overall quality of life of families with disabled children. Specifically, they can reduce parental stress and enable families to make better use of other services.

Box 5.11 Best Practice on Coordinated Provision

Wolverhampton is a pathfinder Early Support area, and through the Local Authority's Child Development Service (CDS) it coordinates the "Team Around the Child" programme. The programme involves a single assessment of need; a multi-agency referral panel; a well defined flexible model of early intervention and continuing support; an emphasis on empowering families by listening to their needs; and a training programme for key workers and professionals in the team.

Drawing on funding from the Department of Health as well as from the Early Support Programme, Wolverhampton has set up the Gem centre—a brand new building that co-locates education, care and health services for young children with complex needs. The CDS occupy one wing, while the others house audiology, physiotherapy and paediatrics departments, and Child and Adolescent Mental Health Services. The centre is equipped with state of the art facilities, including purpose built learning aids and computer software, and a "sensory room" with an array of light/sound equipment to explore the coordination of movement, cause and effect.

Staffing is planned around the needs of families, and services are integrated to provide a single experience for children and their parents—so for example, an audiologist might drop into a play session to take a mould of a child's ear, without breaking up the session. Key workers employed by the CDS use the centre as their base, but also work directly with families in their homes.

Current Situation

As set out in the Children and Young People Review discussion document, the Call for Evidence acknowledged that the Every Child Matters programme is making progress, with more joint working between different agencies, and some areas using pooled budgets and joint assessments. However, the Review has also found that this joint working is variable, with remaining challenges including differing eligibility criteria, incompatible computer systems, differing referral systems and cultures, and a lack of managerial commitment to joint working.

The Early Support Programme is facilitating the development of key worker schemes for disabled children and their families as part of a wider programme of support, including information materials, professional guidance and training. It has been well received as a successful programme and additional funding for 2007-08 will allow the programme to continue to embed it's approach across all local authority areas.

The *National Service Framework* Standard 8 on disabled children states that the Government expects all Local Authorities and Primary Care Trusts to ensure that "families caring for disabled children have a key worker/care manager to oversee the delivery of services from all agencies involved in the care and support of the family, and to ensure that the family has access to appropriate services".

DH Commissioning Framework

The Department of Health Commissioning Framework for Health and Wellbeing and performance frameworks for the CSR years provide a basis on which to further develop and improve joint commissioning and co-ordination of services. Part of the vision set out in *Our health, our care, our say* is to create services which are flexible, integrated, and responsive to people's needs and wishes. This includes the concept of PCTs as the local commissioner of health services on behalf of, and engaging with, their local population. To further facilitate cooperation at a local level, PCTs will be required jointly with Local Authorities to undertake a strategic needs assessment to identify local health priorities. PCTs will then be held to account using a new performance framework which DH is developing for the CSR years, which will link to the new PSA performance management framework.

Subject to consultation, there is an expectation that all PCTs will undertake a joint strategic needs assessment with local authorities, and publish a prospectus in 2008-09. It is envisaged that the joint strategic needs assessment will provide key analysis to feed into the development of local Sustainable Communities strategies and Local Area Agreements. This joint accountability and objectives identified in the joint strategic needs assessment and Local Area Agreements should encourage PCTs and Local Authorities to work more constructively together.

Remaining Challenges

An Audit Commission report from 2003 found that families with disabled children have to struggle through a maze of services to gain access to support. Where it is unclear which agency is responsible for delivering support for a disabled child, and there is a lack of joint responsibility, the disabled child's needs may be left unmet. Poor planning, data collection and commissioning also raise the risks that the population is not adequately supported.

The Review found particular problems in coordination around transition to adulthood for disabled young people. Case studies from a recent Audit Commission report found a confused picture about which services were leading on transition and the roles of the professionals involved, with one parent stating: "*The transition process can be quite confusing for parents and young people as a number of new professionals get involved. I have to explain the different workers' roles.*"

The report found that although there was good progress in some areas to improve coordination between social care, education, health, housing and other services, good practice is not happening everywhere, with inadequate provision, poor coordination of services and a failure to plan with young people and their families resulting in anxiety, delays, multiple assessments and confusion.

Further Action

In order to better coordinate service provision and encourage joint assessment and provision, the Government will take action to:

- include within the core offer for disabled children a focus on integrated assessment (see chapter 2); and
- continue to roll out the Early Support Programme to cover all disabled children aged 0-5 and to be embedded in programmes addressing the needs of this age group.

The Government also expects that all disabled children should benefit from coordinated service planning and delivery from Local Authorities and their partners, and support to help navigate the system. For example, a team around the child or family approach, building on the Early Support Model across the country and on the best practice of professionals in contact with the child taking a lead role in coordinating their package of care.

The Government will also develop a Transition Support Programme (see next section).

Support at Transition

Why Support at Transition Matters

It is accepted that for many disabled young people, having timely, comprehensive information and careers guidance is sufficient to ensure that they reach their goals when making the transition to adulthood.

However, for a smaller number of young people, more support is needed to help them to meet their goals and take their place in society. At the moment, the support that young disabled people receive is variable. Services may struggle to provide information at the right time, coordinate their responses with other agencies, and provide appropriate support to young people and their families.

Support at transition to adulthood is vital to enable disabled young people to gain independence, choice and control over the assistance they need, and achieve their aspirations. All disabled young people need access to sufficient information and support to ensure that they reach their goals when transferring from child to adult services, enabling them to remain safe, grow up and live the lives they want to live, and to play a full and active role in society.

Transition

Current Situation

The Education Act 1996, SEN regulations and the SEN code of practice set out a statutory transition planning process for young people with SEN statements from Year 9 onwards. The Connexions Service must arrange assessments of young people with learning difficulties and disabilities who are in the last year of compulsory schooling and are intending to go on to Further Education or training. Assessments must also be undertaken when these young people reach year 11 or at the point of leaving school and up to the age of 25. The Learning and Skills Council has to take account of these assessments.

Youth Matters: Next Steps has set out plans for comprehensive information, advice and guidance for all young people with targeted support for those with complex needs. It also sets out how Local Authorities, working through Children's Trusts, will work with all the relevant agencies to develop a more personalised, integrated and efficient support service for teenagers and ensure that those young people who need integrated support in a number of overlapping areas can have it effectively coordinated and delivered by a lead professional.

There is a core standard within the *National Service Framework for Children, Young People and Maternity Services* on 'Growing Up into Adulthood', and within the standard for Disabled Children and Young People and those with Complex Health Needs there is a marker of good practice on multi-agency transition planning. Work has also been carried out on transition under the *Valuing People/Learning Disability Strategy* and each Learning Disability Partnership Board should have a "transition champion".

The DfES has recognised the challenges that disabled young people at transition face, and has supported, through the Council for Disabled Children, the development of the Transition Information Network. The DfES has also commissioned the Council for Disabled Children to produce good practice guidance on transition which will be published in Summer 2007.

Extent of Provision

Children and young people with more complex needs require more carefully prepared and intricate packages of support as they transfer into adulthood. It is recognised that as there is an increasing population of young people who would not previously have survived into adulthood, the transition planning process and the services available beyond this have to develop in order to meet their needs.

Despite some good practice, many disabled young people do not end up in education, employment or training, or end up in the wrong provision for them. The Qualifications and Curriculum Authority is currently working to develop a coherent framework of provision for all levels of ability, including at pre-entry level, so that young people can find something suitable and demonstrate their skills to potential employers.

There is currently a lack of consistent multi-agency working to ensure that disabled young people are given a real choice about their futures. Parents have reported that if there are no arrangements in place when the young person leaves school, they can find themselves without provision. If arrangements are not made during the autumn term, young people can miss up to a year in education or training if the course or placement they are seeking is full.

A Commission for Social Care Inspection report last year stated that 'peoples' expectations of social care are changing. In future, people will expect social care that enable them to live independently, that give them choices, that are high quality and that leave them in control. For children, social care must support them and their families to make the most of their educational and life chances'.

Barriers to Enhanced Provision

Evidence submitted to the Review suggests the following barriers to smooth transition to adult services for children with disabilities:

- a lack of suitable provision for young people on transfer from school. Some disabled young people accept unsuitable and often part time courses in the absence of a full range of suitable options;
- lack of young person and family input into the transition planning process so that the aspirations and ambitions of the young person are often not know and realised, with transition planning meetings sometimes not involving the child and family;
- lack of multi-agency working to support transition and confusion over roles and responsibilities in transition planning;
- a gulf between child and adult services in health and social services;
- the timing of preparation for transition often does not always take into account the complexity of need; and
- the lack of recognition that transition occurs at the appropriate time for the individual rather than at a specific point in time for all young people.

Box 5.12 Examples of Best Practice for Support at Transition

Person Centred Planning

A joint initiative between the DfES and the Department of Health/Valuing People Support Team to improve the participation of young people and their families in transition review meetings has had a successful pilot across 70 Local Authorities. This is now a national programme involving almost all Local Authorities across England. The project aims to demonstrate how transition review meetings can be far more effective when using person centred planning strategies. With a small level of investment and innovative thinking about transforming processes, the programme has been successful in supporting young people to identify what is important to them and their aspirations for the future, supported by a transition plan.

Transition Teams

Greater collaboration across agencies is required in the field of transition. Transition teams are one way of achieving a change in culture, behaviour, attitudes and priorities towards this group of disabled young people in relation to transition planning.

> Examples of existing best practice include Suffolk, where a specific transition team comprising a range of specialists has been set up. In addition, Sandwell and Bolton have also developed specific transition teams. Leicester City have a jointly commissioned transitions development officer shared between the Learning Skills Council, the Learning Disabilities Partnership Board and the Disabled Children's Partnership Board.

Research into good practice suggests that:

- the process needs to be individual to the needs and aspirations of the young person;
- the process needs to be spread out over a number of years starting at the transition review following the young person's 14th birthday, with reviews held annually;
- statutory processes for transition need to be used consistently; and
- adults' and children's services need to work together to ensure that young people maximise their life chances as they enter young adulthood.

Transition planning and transition services need to be seen as a way to enable and support disabled young people to move towards and onto a new stage of life rather than from one service to another. Much good practice exists—but it needs to be pulled together and made consistent.

The Government will therefore initiate and develop a Transition Support Programme, underpinned by £19m of investment over the CSR, to be piloted initially and then rolled out across the country. This model should be based on the same principles as the early support programme, including transparency, coordination and support for parents, children and professionals. It should be based on the principle of enabling disabled young people to have choice and control over the support needed in their daily lives, and should be embedded as a new model of working for the years ahead.

This Transition Support Programme should include:

- a young person's information pack, including information on further education, training opportunities and work options;
- access to an advisor or key worker and advocacy and support;
- consolidation of the person centred planning process from age 14, with increased information for professionals, and coordinated and timely assessments based on the young person's aspirations, at key points to assist in the transition to adulthood, including signposting to future appropriate provision; and
- joint team working across agencies and with adult services to encourage a holistic approach, and choice and control for young people.

Improving Service Quality and Capacity

Respondents to the Review and wider research at a local and national level have highlighted a number of specific services that are particularly important to improving outcomes for disabled children, young people and their families. The specific services highlighted in the Review's Call for Evidence, the Parliamentary Hearings and report, seminars and visits in terms of both universal and specialist services were:

- *short breaks:* to support disabled children and families, giving families a break from care duties and allowing children to experience new relationships, environments and positive activities;
- *childcare provision:* which can facilitate parental employment, reduce family stress, and increase a child's social and educational development;
- *provision of appropriate equipment and wheelchairs:* to maximise mobility or communication, make it less physically tiring to care for a disabled child, and prevent deterioration of conditions;
- *therapists:* to manage posture, maximise mobility, provide support and advice on feeding, and improve and enable communication; and
- *training of staff in universal services:* to improve their knowledge and understanding to help make universal services more accessible for disabled children and their families.

Vital Services for Disabled Children

Short Breaks

Why Short Breaks Matter

Families with disabled children often face particularly high levels of stress which may result in family breakdown. For parents and siblings of disabled children, short breaks reduce stress, allow a rest from caring, provide time to carry out tasks and activities that other parents take for granted and allow more time with other children. Disabled children are disproportionately represented within the looked after population, making up 10 per cent of all children in care, and only around 5 per cent of the overall population.

The *National Service Framework for Children, Young People and Maternity Services* states that "Good short term break services are associated with reductions in maternal stress and a reduction in marital problems and breakdown". According to a survey of parents of disabled children, a break from caring to be with their partner and/or other children is the single most important factor in helping their relationship. The survey found that 76 per cent of families had experienced stress or depression and 72 per cent were suffering from lack of sleep. Similarly, the *Breaking Point* report from Mencap found that 80 per cent of families with children with severe or profound learning disabilities had reached breaking point due to lack of short breaks.

Furthermore, short breaks can also have a positive impact on disabled children, as they help to tackle social isolation, provide access to leisure activities, friendship networks, and promote development.

A recent report identified the following costs as being potentially preventable from increased short breaks provision:

- the cost to the family from parents not being in work;
- the cost to employers and the health service from parents' stress;
- the cost to schools from educating siblings with emotional and behavioural difficulties;
- the cost of foster care or a residential placement due to family breakdown;
- the cost to social and educational services of caring for a disabled child outside the family home; and
- the cost to the family of separation and marital breakdown.

In addition, there are other non-economic benefits, such as the happiness of the family and social inclusion of the child, which although not measurable in terms of costs are important to the child, family and society, and need to be taken into consideration.

Childcare

The Importance of Childcare

Provision of good quality childcare is an entitlement for disabled children, as it is for all children and families. Government wants to ensure that all families have the same access to appropriate childcare provision. The provision of good quality childcare will allow parents to return to work, reducing poverty and increasing employment opportunities if this is what parents choose. Good quality childcare can also improve children's outcomes and general wellbeing.

Work carried out on the costs and benefits of childcare for disabled children for the Review estimates that the annual monetary benefits of increased employment for both mothers of disabled children (who are more likely to be the main carers for children) and lone parents of disabled children are significant. As well as facilitating parental employment, childcare will benefit disabled children as it benefits non-disabled children, with the provision of high quality education and care at an early age reducing the risk of developing Special Education Needs at a later stage from 1 in 3 to 1 in 5. There may also be additional benefits to disabled children in terms of helping them feel included in mainstream provision, and facilitating their transition to inclusion in mainstream education provision when they reach school age.

Equipment and Wheelchairs

The Importance of Equipment

Equipment, from wheelchairs to communications aids, is essential to help disabled children and young people access school, leisure and other services, and to facilitate independent living. Good quality equipment services can also enable independent living in the community at low cost, compared to longer hospital stays. Provision of appropriate equipment maximises physical mobility and communication and makes it less physically and emotionally tiring caring for a disabled child.

Well-fitted wheelchairs can also prevent deterioration of conditions and other worsening health conditions, such as potentially expensive operations, or pressure sores, which make up 4.1 per cent of gross annual expenditure.

Box 5.13 The Benefits of Equipment—Case Study

Pressure-relieving mattresses or special seating may be particularly cost-effective by preventing the development of pressure sores, contractures, or skeletal deformity. Once pressure sores develop, the patient will lose dignity, suffer considerable pain, and the NHS will have to pay for district nurses' time and/or expensive plastic surgery to solve the problem. Apart from the fact that pressure sores cause considerable pain and can be life-threatening, the cost of prevention is small compared to the cost of community nursing time required once sores have developed, or to the £35,000 cost of the in-patient episode that would be needed to treat serious cases.

As well as creating problems for children and families, long waiting times also increase complaints and the time and energy which professionals have to spend responding and chasing progress, making the system less efficient. Waiting times can be a major factor in driving up staff costs and in disrupting the processing of applications, and indicates a lack of control in the application, ordering and delivery process.

The Workforce

Disabled children and young people and their families can expect to come into contact with the full range of the children's workforce, depending on the complexity of their needs. This continuum extends from universal services such as midwives, health visitors and Sure Start Children's Centre staff, through targeted provision such as Special Educational Needs Coordinators (SENCOs) and speech and language therapists.

Box 5.14 The Importance of the Workforce

Good quality staff can transform a child and family's experience of services. For many people, an outstanding member of staff can make an enormous impact on their lives by providing support, information, empathy and expertise.

One disabled child's parents described the positive impact of a member of staff who made a real difference to their family's life:

Father: "She was the one who got things moving, she'd come round and then she'd chat and we realised that we weren't getting the things we should have been getting. She did a lot of things".

Mother: "She did a lot of things that probably weren't in her job description as such...She helped with a lot of paperwork. A lot of what we've got now is down to her".

Benefits of Therapists

Therapy services for disabled children are key to improving their outcomes. Speech and language therapists, occupational therapists, and physiotherapists help to enable and promote communication, improve and manage posture, and maximise mobility. The ability to communicate is fundamental to children's learning and progression. As well as leading to lower attainment, an inability to communicate can find expression in erratic or challenging behaviour. Postural management and other occupational therapy and equipment services for disabled children can prevent deformities (which can start to develop at 3 months old), which may be more life limiting and painful than their original condition, and might impact on digestion and respiration which can lead to costly and painful surgery. In addition, a lack of appropriate equipment, seating, or advice on handling or facilitating communication may have a negative impact on carers, for example a bad back from continually lifting a disabled child in the wrong way.

Future Provision of Services

Short Breaks

Current Situation

Short break provision can encompass overnight short breaks, sitting schemes, befriending schemes and residential services. The Shared Care Network "Still Waiting" (2006) survey provides the most comprehensive picture of short break provision in the UK, however it is not complete as it does not have any information on disabled children receiving short breaks in residential settings. According to this survey there are 188 family based short break schemes in the UK providing services to an estimated 9,194 disabled children.

Following the principles of Every Child Matters, Local Authorities should be assessing local need in order to prioritise the way in which they meet the needs of children in their local area. Alongside this, the Government is increasing funding for short breaks through yearly increases in the Carer's Grant, leading to increases in services for parents of disabled children. The Carers Grant is worth £185m in both 2005-06 and 2006-07, with approximately 20 per cent allocated to children's services, including carers of disabled children. In addition, the Government has recently announced an increase of £25m for emergency respite care for 2007-08, some of which will be available for disabled children and their families.

Both existing and new resources need to be spent in the most cost effective manner, which combines service quality to both parents and children and measurable outcomes. Currently, there is variation in the ways short breaks are provided, with some Local Authorities demonstrating more flexibility than others in meeting the needs of families with disabled children, and providing more efficient services.

Box 5.15 Efficient and Effective Short Break Provision

Cheviots Children's Disability Service is part of Education Children's Services and Leisure within the London Borough of Enfield. Since the 1980s the Cheviots Management believed that many of the children in residential settings could live at home if there were more opportunities for parents/carers to access a short break. In line with current thinking and legislation they have realized that families with disabled children need more than just overnight breaks. They require services which reflect the changing nature of family life. With this in mind they began to develop a menu of options including holiday playschemes and home care support utilizing existing money that had previously been invested in long-term care.

In the 1990s Cheviots began to work more proactively with parent/carers and partner agencies to collectively develop and improve service delivery. Consulting with parents prompted the development of a home sitting service.

The service aims to provide families with the right level of support at the right time, through playschemes, after-school clubs, homecare, home sitting, weekend care, overnight breaks, direct payments and support for young carers. The array of available services provides a 24/7 delivery model. It is about 'making a difference' and ensuring families do not feel isolated. Sometimes that can be as little as 8 hours a month home sitting, particularly in the case of a young and newly diagnosed disabled child. Sometime it is a more substantial support package with three or more services. It offers families choice, supporting them in leading their lives.

Cheviots success culminated in the award of a Charter Mark in 1993 for excellence in the delivery of public services. Cheviots was one of the first social care agencies to be awarded Charter Mark and presented its model of service delivery at the launch of the following years awards.

Barriers to Enhanced Provision

There is a need for a better understanding of the current picture of short breaks provision and the need for such services. There is evidence, however, that there are lengthy waiting lists. The Shared Care Network survey shows that over 90 per cent of short break schemes reported having waiting lists, with families commonly waiting up to a year for services.

Evidence also suggests that there is a lack of staff in schemes to carry out proactive recruitment, training and support to carers and the necessary development and regulatory work in order to meet the needs of disabled children and their families. There are also capacity difficulties in some areas, with insufficient attention given to ensuring that there is a level playing field between public, private and voluntary sector provision.

Further Action

Recognising the critical importance and significant benefits of short breaks to disabled children and their families, Government will provide a specific grant of £280m over the CSR period to deliver a step change in the provision of short breaks. This grant makes provision for an additional 40,000 fortnightly short breaks for severely disabled children by 2010-11. Pathfinders involving local authorities and providers will develop best practice in building efficient, high quality short break provision based around the needs of disabled children and their families. Provision will then be rolled out across the country by 2010-11.

This funding will be underpinned with guidance from the DfES and DH (in partnership with the voluntary sector and the ODI), which will:

- assist local areas in planning more effectively for their population in need of short breaks, with a needs assessment of the local population;
- build and support a diverse and high quality market of public, private and voluntary sector providers;
- ensure provision is commissioned fairly and cost-effectively;
- present solutions to the particular problems faced by groups of children with autistic spectrum disorders, children with complex health needs and children from black and minority ethnic communities; and
- allow disabled children and their families to influence the range of provision, have real choice, and confidence that provision is safe.

The NHS CSR settlement will also provide additional funding to provide short breaks for disabled children with complex health care needs.

This should be accompanied by evaluation of the efficacy of different types of provision, which will continue to feed into best practice guidance, and data collected on the percentage of the population accessing short breaks at a local level to demonstrate that improvements are being made.

Childcare

Current Situation

Support for parents for childcare is provided through a number of sources, including the childcare element of the working tax credit. Families with disabled children receive an extra (means tested) £2,440 a year as a disability element of the child tax credit, and families with a severely disabled child receive an additional extra £980 a year.

In addition, the Sure Start grant includes resources to support the inclusion of all children in early years and childcare settings, including those with Special Educational Needs and disability. This funding can be used to support early intervention, provide training, and fund adaptations to equipment or facilities for childcare providers. In addition, funding from the Dedicated Schools Grant can be used to support the provision of area SEN Coordinators (SENCOs), to provide support to settings in delivering childcare for disabled children with SEN and disabilities.

Extent of Provision

Disabled children will also benefit from the free childcare available for all 3-4 year olds, however initial take-up statistics are lower for parents with disabled children or special education needs, with 82 per cent of children aged 3 and 4 with disabilities or SEN having used childcare in a sample week compared to 87 per cent of other children.

Survey evidence also suggests that families with disabled children are less likely to access childcare than other families. A Sure Start study found that children who had a statement of SEN were less likely than children with non-statemented needs or children without special needs to have received childcare (although part of this may be explained by the older age profile of statemented children).

These surveys aside, Government does not currently collect data on the numbers of disabled children accessing childcare. However, the Childcare Act 2006 places a duty on Local Authorities to assess the demand for and supply of childcare in their local area and identify gaps in provision. This is expected to improve the provision of data on the take-up of childcare by disabled children and their families. Under the Section 11 duty in the Childcare Act, Local Authorities will be required to assess the demand (by age and type of childcare) in each sub-local authority area for specialist childcare for disabled children and those with SEN, and the number and nature of places available for children who need special care due to a disability or SEN. Local Authorities will also be required to analyse the gap between demand and supply of childcare for disabled children who need special care, and reflect it at the level of the whole Local Authority area, in their published assessment documents. These documents will be finalised by the end of March 2008, and Local Authorities must keep them under review between assessments (which must take place at least every 3 years).

This is the first step towards fulfilling their duty to secure sufficient childcare to enable parents to work or to undertake education or training leading to work (which will come into force in April 2008). In order to meet this duty, Local Authorities must have particular regard to the provision of childcare which is suitable for disabled children. Childcare must be sufficient in terms of the number of places, affordability, and appropriateness, so far as is reasonably practicable.

Barriers to Enhanced Provision

Existing evidence and testimony from parents, the voluntary sector and professionals suggest that both affordability and accessibility can act as barriers to disabled children accessing childcare. Appropriate childcare places that meet the needs of disabled children may not be available, and where they are, survey evidence suggests that they tend to be more expensive. A recent survey found that 41 per cent of Children's Information Services in England reported insufficient provision of appropriate services for disabled children in their area for 0-13 year olds, and 32 per cent said they were unsure. For 14-18 year olds, 46 per cent reported insufficient provision of appropriate services, and 39 per cent were unsure.

The key barriers to disabled children accessing childcare, identified by surveys and qualitative feedback from parents and voluntary sector organisations, include:

- lack of awareness and information, perception and trust of services amongst parents of disabled children;
- attitudinal barriers on behalf of some providers;

- a lack of disability awareness training for the workforce, and specifically, issues with the level of specialist training and expertise in the workforce (for example for children with additional communication need or in behavioural management);
- the perceived and real cost to providers of securing the right capacity (such as facilities and equipment), and capability (such as staff with the right skills); and
- the cost of providing appropriate transport provision for disabled children and their families, to help them access services.

Further Action

High quality childcare for disabled children will improve disabled children's development, and will help their parents rejoin the workforce if they choose. Given that there is survey evidence that families with disabled children find it harder to find appropriate childcare for their disabled children, there is a case for further intervention to encourage better access to childcare for disabled children.

The Childcare Act 2006 placed an important new duty on LAs to secure sufficient childcare for working parents, and to pay particular regard to the needs of parents with disabled children. To help improve access to childcare and reduce attitudinal barriers, Government will set up a childcare accessibility project, initially piloted in 10 Local Authorities, with best practice rolled out to a larger number of Local Authorities. The project will test out ways of meeting provision for disabled children highlighted in the childcare sufficiency assessments which all Local Authorities will have undertaken by April 2008. New investment of £35m over the period will complement funding available through the General Sure Start Grant to assist with childcare providers' capital costs associated with the sufficiency duty.

This childcare accessibility project will be evaluated to collect better information on the degree of additional costs of childcare for disabled children, and it should be used to develop best practice on increasing accessibility of childcare which can be shared across the country. Data should also be collated as a result of local authorities' new duties under the Childcare Act to measure the number of disabled children accessing childcare.

The review found that the current backdating rules relating to the disabled and severely disabled child elements of Child Tax Credit mean that some families are missing out on the financial support that they are entitled to. Since May 2006, the Tax Credit Office has been using data from the Department for Work and Pensions on disability living allowance to award, and amend awards of the disabled element and the severe disability element of child tax credit, and the severe disability element of working tax credit, simplifying the process for claimants. The Government is now actively examining further options for streamlining the notification procedure between DWP and HMRC, and will also look for other ways in which to further improve the system in the future, in consultation with stakeholders, and will report on progress in this year's Pre-Budget Report.

Wheelchairs and Equipment

The last guidance on wheelchairs was issued in 1996, when electrically powered indoor outdoor wheelchairs (EPIOCs) became available for severely disabled people through the NHS. Additional ring fenced funding totalling £50m was available for EPIOCs and vouchers to offer financial aid to users who prefer to contribute to buying an alternative wheelchair of their choice privately, over the initial four year period. From April 2000 the funds were placed in health authority revenue allocations recurrently with annual increases.

Target times for the delivery of wheelchairs of 16 days for a powered wheelchair and 4 days for a non-powered wheelchair were introduced following a National Audit Office study which found that waiting times for powered wheelchairs ranged from 13-143 days and for non-powered wheelchairs from 3-28 days.

Effective joint working between the NHS and Local Authorities is essential to ensure the provision of high quality community equipment services, and parents and the sector have provided much anecdotal evidence that there is often a breakdown in joint working, with children falling between provision and waiting even longer for equipment.

The 1999 Health Act signals the Government's view that such joint arrangements should become the norm. The Act gives new powers to health authorities and councils to address these traditional problems by enabling:

- pooled budgets so that staff from either NHS or social services can commission or provide services from the same pool of money and integrated packages; and
- lead commissioners, where one Local Authority takes over entire responsibility for the service.

This approach is underpinned by the joint national priorities guidance and new performance frameworks for health and social services.

Extent of Provision and Barriers to Access

Many children and families currently face long waiting lists for both assessment and provision of equipment and wheelchairs. There is also variation in the overall time taken for social services to provide equipment, and for the NHS to provide wheelchairs. Provision may also focus too heavily on clinical need, and may fail to take into account the impact of independent mobility on social, development and educational attainment, or on family's preferences (for example, being able to get to school and sit up and learn in class).

Further Action

The DH *Community equipment and wheelchair review* is looking at a radical overhaul for assessment and provision of equipment and wheelchair services for all client groups, including disabled children, to improve the efficiency of provision, and reduce waiting times for assessment and provision of equipment. The review has taken a collaborative approach, involving all stakeholders, to designing a new model for service delivery of community equipment and wheelchairs.

The review found that there is a lack of informed and proactive commissioning, no evidence of cost modelling across health and social services, little emphasis on performance managing the service, little evidence of demand forecasting or planning, and some areas still operating legacy budgets. The programme has developed a new retail model for delivery of community equipment services. It puts users and carers at its heart and is supported by an outline business case. Over the next 10 months, the team will work with users and carers councils and their PCT partners, practitioners and other stakeholders to develop the outline model to operational status.

The Government will therefore continue to scope and ultimately deliver a radical reform of community equipment and wheelchair provision, with full consideration of and provision for the needs of children through the DH Community equipment and wheelchair review, including:

- DH working with DfES to ensure that the demand forecasting tool being developed by the Care Service Efficiency Delivery programme will reflect the differing requirements of children in the provision of community equipment and services, including an understanding of the disabled children population;
- assessment which considers the complete needs of the child, including social and educational needs as well as clinical needs, and the needs of the family and carers;
- the impact of equipment and wheelchairs on children's development, including the detrimental impacts of waiting considerable periods for equipment (such as growing out of equipment);
- the expectation that most parents young disabled people will not be in a position to self-fund; and
- dedicated staff in retail provision centres trained specifically in provision of fitting wheelchairs and equipment for children with complex needs, which takes account the specific safeguarding issues in relation to children.

Subject to CSR decisions, the NHS will provide additional resource for 2010-11, once the Community Equipment Review has bedded in, to update the stock of wheelchairs and improve provision of community equipment for disabled children.

The Workforce

Evidence provided to the Review shows that the experience of disabled children and their families varies greatly, with some recalling helpful and proactive support from professionals working with them, others reporting gaps, discontinuities and unmet needs in services, and some citing obstructive or insensitive responses from people and services.

Current Situation

Workforce issues need to be seen in the context of an increased emphasis on mainstreaming provision of services for disabled children. *Every Child Matters: Change for Children*, and the *National Service Framework for Children, Young People and Maternity Services* all anticipate significant increases in the numbers of children with disabilities and SEN in mainstream provision. The rapid development of the Children's Centre and Extended Schools programmes, together with the development of the Early Years Foundation Stage and the new role of the Early Years Professional, also imply a proactive approach to staff development around disability and Special Educational Needs.

In terms of specialist workforce issues, the number of therapists has been increasing since 1997. There are currently 6,623 Speech and Language Therapists working in the NHS, an increase of 36 per cent since 1997. These increases will support service improvements in the Government's core objectives including the National Service Frameworks (NSF). Through the NSF, PCTs and Local Authorities should ensure that the supply of timely therapy services is sufficient to meet the needs of children and young people who require it, based on assessed needs. As can be seen from box 5.16, many PCTs have developed more effective provision of therapy services through service redesign.

In addition, the DfES has decided to focus the opening round of its Inclusion Development Programme (continuing professional development for teachers and others) on speech, language and communication needs and dyslexia. This is in recognition of the fact that communication is essential to children's learning and development.

Box 5.16 Examples of Services Redesign: Increasing Efficiency of Therapy Services

In East Sussex, a drop-in monthly clinic was set up in 2002 to enable immediate access to children and parents without an appointment. The child either receives advice and a repeat check up at a later date or an appointment for a fuller assessment.

Waiting times have decreased from 8 months for assessment, and 12 months for treatment to commence to 1 month for assessment. The number of children taken on to the caseload has decreased by 50 per cent and therefore the overall wait for treatment has also decreased. The feedback from parents was such that drop-in clinics have been set up in all community clinics in this area.

Another innovative good practice initiative involved 4 geographical mini-teams which meet weekly to allocate work load—with some referrals requiring telephone reassurance only, others initial screening. Where 2 localities have high Do Not Attend rates, drop-in clinics have been developed (last 3 years) and the model will be developed in the Children's Centres.

There is a Specialist Support Service to parents/education where there have been detailed assessments and therapy in the past but it is no longer indicated and parents/teachers may need support and advice, supported by an educational psychologist.

At the end of an episode, clear and specific indicators for re-access are given and communicated to several professionals and parents. This prevents ongoing reviews but also prevents children slipping through the net.

Barriers to Accessing Services

Despite these improvements, parents identified problems in accessing universal services, hindering inclusion of their disabled child in society and placing unnecessary burdens on already stretched specialist services. A lack of skills and training make situations more difficult and upsetting for disabled children and their families, with problems ranging from poor practice in giving news on diagnosis exacerbating stress, to staff unable to offer the care they are engaged to provide for disabled children.

> ***Box 5.17 Problems in Accessing Universal Services***
>
> "you know perfectly well he's not going to be able to join in with a group because (*a*) they don't know how to deal with him and (*b*) they won't have the staff to deal with him... People are very keen to be seen to be doing inclusion but that doesn't just mean saying "Yes, come along". There's more to it than that."

Specific areas where training and preparation of staff appeared to be lacking across all services include communication and interpersonal skills, communicating directly, expertise in behavioural management (especially with Autistic Spectrum Disorder and challenging behaviour), moving and handling, and personal care. In addition, there is a perception that there is still some way to go in tackling attitudinal barriers (in terms of both leadership and the general children's workforce), which block inclusion in mainstream services such as childcare.

The Review also received evidence about long waiting lists and strict eligibility criteria for therapy services as a result of limited budgets and national shortages of trained professionals. For families, staff recruitment and retention problems have a major impact on the quality of the service that they receive. The Audit Commission found that many spoke of the loss of continuity of care resulting from high turnover, with new relationships having to be built from scratch each time a new worker was introduced. One family talked of seeing four speech and language therapists in the space of a year. Sometimes there would be a delay in the arrival of a new worker, setting back any advances that the child had achieved.

Further Action

There is currently a lack of a coherent approach to developing the skills and competencies required by those working with disabled children and young people with disabilities, underpinned by a lack of knowledge about current levels of expertise in the workforce. To help make services more accessible for disabled children, all those who work with children, young people and their parents and carers need appropriate training and development provision to ensure that they have an awareness of working with disability and the appropriate skills. This may involve disability awareness training, or may involve more intensive training, such as in communication or behavioural management.

As a step to meeting this goal, the Government will Commission the Children's Workforce Development Council (CWDC) working with Children's Workforce

Network (CWN), to research the skills and behaviours required by the workforce to service disabled children effectively and to identify gaps.

The Government recommends that PCTs and Strategic Health Authorities develop better data on the number of disabled children and young people in need of and receiving therapy services to allow them to better plan, commission, and recruit to provide for their population. This should be part of the wider data collection work recommended by the review in Chapter 3.

Next Steps and Future Prospects

This report is a further step along the way to meeting the Government's vision of equality of opportunity for all disabled children and their families. Building on the progress being made in implementing the *National Service Framework for Children, Young People and Maternity Services*, the Special Education Needs (SEN) framework *Removing Barriers to Achievement*, and the *Improving life chances for disabled people report*, it will further improve outcomes in terms of educational attainment, social and emotional development, and a degree of independent living, choice, and control.

As part of Budget 2007, the Government announced an early Comprehensive Spending Review (CSR) settlement for the Department for Education and Skills (DfES), informed by the findings of this Review. It will see education spending in England rise by 2.5 per cent a year in real terms on average between 2007-08 and 2010-11. This will allow the DfES to immediately start planning provision for disabled children for the CSR period, underpinned by £340 million of investment to:

- empower disabled children and their families, with a clear and transparent "core offer", piloting Individual Budgets, and £5 million to support best practice on engagement, such as parent forums;
- encourage more responsive services, with disabled children prioritised at both a local and national level, developing a national indicator on disabled children;
- provide better coordinated support, delivered as soon as disabled children and their families need it, with £19 million for a Transition Support Programme; and
- improve provision of key services, with a grant of £280 million over the CSR to boost provision of short breaks, and a childcare accessibility project underpinned by £35 million of additional resource.

HM Treasury and DfES will continue to work with other departments to ensure that the findings and recommendations of the Review are reflected in other departmental priorities, including the Department of Health who have a key role to play in improving disabled children and young people's lives.

Any additional costs to Local Authorities arising from new policy initiatives as a result of this review will be funded by the relevant Government Departments as required under the Government's new burden rules.

This vision cannot be achieved without the skills and expertise of local public services, voluntary groups, community groups, and the professionals working directly with disabled children and young people and their families. The Government will therefore continue to engage and collaborate with these groups to inform the way the recommendations in this review are implemented and built upon in the future.

This document represents the final report and recommendations from the third sub-review of the Policy Review of Children and Young People, to inform the CSR. Further details of the Comprehensive Spending Review can be accessed through the Treasury's website: www.hm-treasury.gov.uk.

Government would like to thank all of those who submitted evidence to this review, brought examples of the excellent work that they are doing across the country, and took the time to share their advice and expertise.

6

SEN Support, Outreach Services and Related Quality Standards: A UK Perspective

The standards which follow have been drawn up by the South East Regional Partnership (SCRIP/ SERSEN), in association with the South West Regional Partnership, through a DCSF-funded project. We are grateful to the Partnerships for their work on the standards and to all those who have contributed to their development, including local authority heads of service and SEN advisory staff, head teachers, voluntary organisations, representatives from the independent and non-maintained special school sectors, regional facilitators, National Strategies SEN Adviser Team, Ofsted and others.

SEN support and outreach services take a variety of forms and the generic standards set out here are intended to be broadly applicable irrespective of the particular configuration employed. The standards are not in any way mandatory, but are designed to be used as suggested markers against which services provided can be evaluated. It is hoped the standards will:

- Illustrate good practice in the provision of SEN support and outreach services
- Help guide the development of local provision and support
- Assist local authorities and others in determining appropriate resources and arrangements
- Assist in the monitoring and evaluation process.

Specifically, the standards are designed to lead to improved outcomes for children and young people (CYP) with SEN and disabilities. They contribute directly to the achievement of the five Every Child Matters (ECM) outcomes for CYP, namely:

- Being healthy
- Staying safe
- Enjoying and achieving
- Making a positive contribution
- Economic well-being.

The Government's aim is for all CYP, whatever their background or their circumstances, to have the support they need to meet these outcomes. Effective SEN support and outreach services have an important and central part to play in achieving this aim.

When developing services, providers should also have regard to the core offer standards, set out as part of the Government's 'Aiming High for Disabled Children' programme. The core offer sets out national expectations for how services are provided to disabled CYP under the five components of:

- Information
- Transparency
- Assessment
- Participation
- Feedback

Importantly, the standards can be used to contribute to an accurate area risk assessment for the Comprehensive Area Assessment (CAA) which will be introduced by Ofsted once the current Joint Area Review programme ends. A core function of the CAA will be to determine how well an area serves particular CYP and their families. The outcomes achieved by support services should feed into this process.

SEN SUPPORT AND OUTREACH SERVICES

SEN support and outreach services play a crucial role in helping to improve outcomes for CYP with SEN and disabilities. This guidance sets out quality standards for all SEN support and outreach services working in early years settings, mainstream and special schools, and other provision. The standards can be applied across the full range of services provided.

CYP with SEN and disabilities have the same entitlement as all CYP to participate equitably in education, to be included alongside their peers, and to achieve their full potential across the full range of the ECM outcomes.

Local authorities may develop SEN services themselves or commission them from other statutory, private or voluntary sector providers, including independent and non-maintained special schools.

Using the standards should improve:

(*i*) the offer made by these services
(*ii*) the outcomes for CYP with SEN and disabilities
(*iii*) the efficient and effective use of resources and should also:
(*iv*) assist in planning, developing, and commissioning services
(*v*) assist in developing effective partnership working
(*vi*) provide a framework for self-evaluation
(*vii*) build capacity within services and settings.

Planning, Developing and Commissioning Services

When devising or reviewing the Children and Young People's Plan, local authorities should carry out an audit and analysis of local needs, including the needs of CYP with SEN and disabilities and their families, informed by specialist expertise and appropriate consultation.

The analysis should lead to integrated commissioning arrangements for all support and outreach services within the local authority, through the mechanism of the local Children's Trust or other arrangements. These arrangements should always link to local Primary Care or NHS Trusts for health provision and services and, where appropriate, to local providers within the private and voluntary sector.

The standards will assist local authorities, integrated teams, school clusters and federations, early years settings and other provision, in commissioning SEN support and outreach services. They could also be used to inform service level agreements and other contractual arrangements. They provide a basis on which existing services can be monitored and developed to better meet the needs of the client group. Support and outreach services also play a role in school improvement. Where services are traded, commissioning arrangements should take into account the need for impartiality, and the ability to challenge schools, early years settings, and other provision about practice, without prejudicing any contractual arrangements.

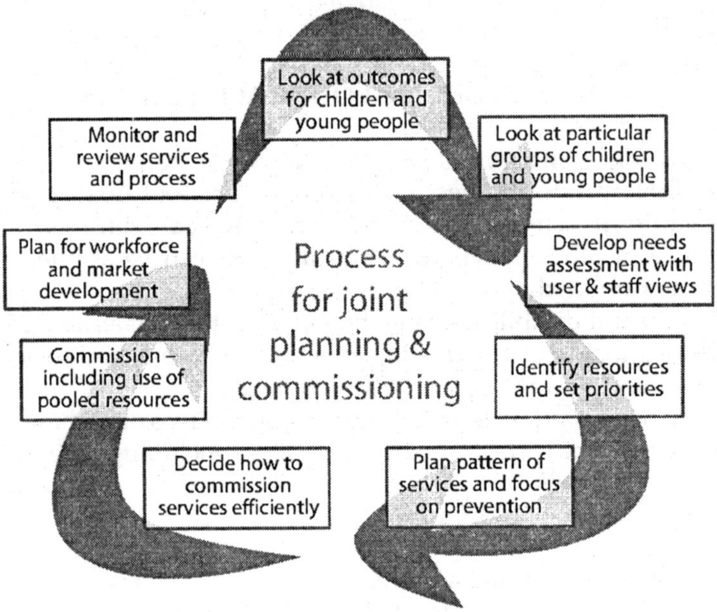

Self-Evaluation

Many SEN support services already have self-evaluation procedures in place, whilst outreach services will be contributing to the school self-evaluation framework. Rather than replacing these, services may choose to use the quality standards to provide a framework for comparison, which will enable gaps in the service to be identified. A comprehensive self-evaluation will cover all the areas set out in the standards, with appropriate supporting evidence being gathered on a regular basis.

Services will find it useful to benchmark their performance against similar services on a regional or national basis, although it is recognised that individual variation in local configuration of services may mean that direct comparisons cannot always be made.

Data from self-evaluation should be collected regularly, with annual data collated over a three year period, enabling trends to be identified towards targets which may be derived from benchmarking activity.

Many services collect data concerning activity levels and the perceptions of service users. To make use of the quality standards to promote service improvement, the information derived from collected data should be compared against these standards. Services can then rate themselves against the following criteria:

Outstanding—can consistently demonstrate high rates of progress in the majority of CYP, and provide evidence of continuous improvement in service management and delivery in most areas over a three year period.

Good—can demonstrate high rates of progress in the majority of CYP, and can provide evidence of improvement in service management and delivery in most areas.

Satisfactory—can provide consistent evidence of positive outcomes for CYP, and can show how data has been used to improve service management and delivery in some areas.

Inadequate—few examples of evidence showing positive outcomes for CYP can be provided.

Gathering Evidence

Evidence in support of the standards may fall into one of two broad categories:

(*i*) *Performance measures*—generally provided as numerical data which may reflect progress made by CYP in the form of targets achieved including those relating to: social, emotional, attitudinal or behavioural issues, attainment and achievement data, results of criterion and norm referenced testing, contextual value added, progress through the National Curriculum, or activity levels of the service.

(*ii*) *Perception measures*—generally of the recipients of the service including CYP, their parents and service staff, but also school improvement services, other partners, and local authority commissioners. This may take the form of evidence gathered from questionnaires, surveys and interviews. Anecdotal evidence may also be useful to support other evidence for illustrative purposes.

Identifying the Contribution of the Service

It is often difficult to separate the contribution made by a service to the progress of individual CYP from that made by the school, early years setting, or other provision, the contribution of parents, and the progress that may have been made anyway. These elements are central to any judgements about service effectiveness and include issues around value for money.

Whilst it is impossible to fully separate the impact of these different elements, where a support or outreach service has:

(*i*) intervened either directly (e.g. through regular individual 1:1 or small group contact) or indirectly (through consultation and advice to staff, or parents) and,

(*ii*) identified and set targets and,
(*iii*) implemented or advised on strategy to attain these targets,

evidence of progress towards these targets, which may be gathered jointly, can be attributed to the work of the service, whilst recognising that the outcome is the result of partnership working.

For example, a peripatetic teacher of the deaf may work directly with a young person on a regular basis on communication, or a pre-school home visitor may help parents set targets for their child and advise on home-based activities to achieve the targets. In both cases progress towards targets can be attributed to the work of the service, even though in the latter case the service may have not worked directly with the child to achieve them.

SEN SUPPORT AND QUALITY STANDARDS

These standards are presented in two sections, **outcomes** and **service management and delivery**. Whilst the effectiveness of a service will be judged by the quality of the outcomes it achieves, these will reflect how well the service is led and managed. External assessment of an SEN support or outreach service is likely to focus primarily on outcomes, but the delivery of excellence requires managers to ensure that they also focus on the means by which this can be achieved.

Section One: Outcomes

STANDARD 1. *Progress towards outcomes is systematically recorded and monitored.*

STANDARD 2. *The service promotes the use of interventions based on up-to-date specialist knowledge and expertise of suitably qualified professional staff.*

STANDARD 3. *Parents should always be consulted and, where appropriate, involved in supporting the learning and development of their child as part of any intervention.*

STANDARD 4. *Clear outcomes are agreed by the service and user, and steps taken to avoid the development of a culture of dependency.*

STANDARD 5. *Services have a clear purpose which takes into account local authority policies, the Children and Young People's Plan, the needs of particular schools, early years settings and other provision in the area, and the range of CYP needs.*

STANDARD 6. *The service regularly collects feedback about its interventions and uses it to improve the quality of service.*

Section Two: Service Management and Delivery

STANDARD 7. *Leaders have a clear vision, develop the aims and objectives of the service and embrace diversity.*

STANDARD 8. *Leaders motivate, support and recognise a culture of continuous improvement and excellence amongst all staff.*

STANDARD 9. *Leaders maintain positive relationships with CYP, parents, schools, early years settings and other provision.*

STANDARD 10. *CYP, parents, schools, early years settings, and other provision are fully involved in the development of services.*

STANDARD 11. *There is a service development plan which is developed, reviewed and updated regularly.*

STANDARD 12. *Key processes fully satisfy, and generate increasing value for, service users and other stakeholders.*

STANDARD 13. *Staff resources are planned, managed and improved.*

STANDARD 14. *Staff experience, knowledge and competencies are identified, developed, sustained, and recognised.*

STANDARD 15. *There is collaboration with other service providers to ensure that services are complementary, simple to use, effective and joined-up to deliver a better service to the user.*

STANDARD 16. *Finance and resources are managed effectively to support the performance and operational requirements of the service.*

Section One: Outcomes

Introduction to the Outcomes Standards 1-6

The primary purpose of SEN support and outreach services is to improve outcomes for CYP with SEN and disabilities. These may be relatively broad, such as ensuring that the current placement for an individual CYP can meet his/her needs, or quite specific as in achieving functional literacy.

Outcomes may be derived from objectives set out in a statement of special educational needs, individual or group targets or provision plans. They should be considered, where appropriate, in the context of the ECM outcomes and the National Curriculum Inclusion Statement.

With regard to the ECM outcomes, services should establish, where appropriate, links with health and other services and participate in Common Assessment Framework procedures, should ensure the safety of CYP, enable them to make a positive contribution in their setting, and support transition planning.

In addition to outcomes for CYP this section also addresses outcomes for parents, schools, early years settings, other partners, and staff.

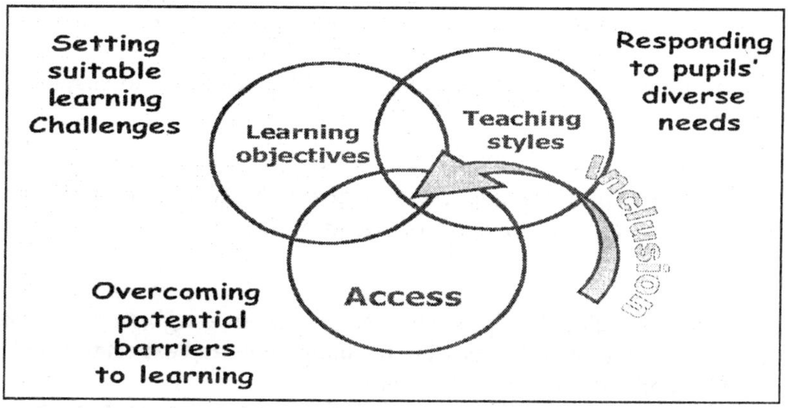

STANDARD 1. ***Progress towards outcomes is systematically recorded and monitored.***

Supporting evidence:

- Programmes and interventions are regularly monitored.
- Intervention strategies are modified to take account of the response of CYP, feedback is given to them and their own views are acted upon.
- Outcome data is systematically identified, collected and analysed over time to evaluate the effectiveness of intervention strategies.
- The progress of individuals or particular groups of CYP is monitored after intervention has finished, where appropriate, especially at important transition times between settings.

STANDARD 2. ***The service promotes the use of interventions based on up-to-date specialist knowledge and expertise of suitably qualified professional staff.***

Supporting evidence:

- Interventions are realistic within the setting's context and reinforce the three waves of intervention.
- Interventions and outcomes relate to one or more of the five ECM outcomes.
- Intended outcomes are agreed with CYP, their class or subject teacher and parents.
- Interventions are planned to enhance the development of self-confidence and self-esteem.
- Targets in intervention programmes are SMART.

STANDARD 3. ***Parents should always be consulted and, where appropriate, involved in supporting the learning and development of their child as part of any intervention.***

Supporting evidence:

- Interventions and intended outcomes are agreed with parents.
- Where appropriate, parents are involved in informing or supporting any intervention programme.
- Information is collected from parents/key workers/lead professionals concerning their views about the effectiveness of the service, and where appropriate, is acted upon.
- Parents are provided with information in an accessible and easy to understand manner.

STANDARD 4. ***Clear outcomes are agreed by the service and user, and steps taken to avoid the development of a culture of dependency.***

Supporting evidence:

- A contractual relationship, such as a service level agreement or partnership agreement, which clearly describes the obligations and expectations of all parties, is established with schools and other settings.

- Services are delivered in a manner designed to increase the capacity of schools, early years settings and other provision to meet user needs from within their own resources and expertise.
- Services are delivered in a manner that is consistent with target setting processes within the service.
- Planning for the use of additional adults ensures there is a balance between providing sufficient one-to-one attention to support the individual CYP's programme and ensuring that they are enabled to become more independent.

STANDARD 5. ***Services have a clear purpose which takes into account local authority policies, the Children and Young People's Plan, the needs of particular schools, early years settings and other provision in the area, and the range of CYP needs.***

Supporting evidence:

- Services are commissioned to undertake specific types of work reflecting local authority policies, the Children and Young People's Plan, and the achievement of the ECM outcomes.
- The service contributes to the achievement of local authority targets and capacity building as part of the overall range of provision.
- Written agreements are in place about the services provided to all those involved.
- There is collaboration with other services and statutory and voluntary agencies to ensure that the contribution of each is maximised for the benefit of CYP.
- Any significant proposed changes to the service comply with the SEN Improvement Test.

STANDARD 6. ***The service regularly collects feedback about its interventions and uses it to improve the quality of service.***

Supporting evidence:

- Views about the effectiveness of the service are collected from CYP.
- Feedback is gathered regularly in relation to the contribution of the service to the progress of individual and groups of CYP, to the continuing professional development of staff, and to the fulfilment of the school, early years setting or other provision's mission and objectives.
- There are audit trails of instances where feedback from service users has been used to change practice in service delivery.

Section Two: Service Management and Delivery

Introduction to the SMD Standards 7-16

The achievement of outcomes will depend on how well the service is led and managed. Where an outreach service is provided by a school, early years setting or other provision, the standards could be addressed through existing management processes.

However, there should be clarity about allocation of resources to the core business of the school, early years setting or other provision, and to the outreach service, and the impact of one upon the other.

Where services are traded, the principles of "full cost recovery" should be followed to ensure that these criteria can be adequately met.

This section addresses a range of service management areas including leadership (which can be exercised at more than one level in an organisation), policy, processes, staff, partnerships and resources.

STANDARD 7. *Leaders have a clear vision, develop the aims and objectives of the service and embrace diversity.*

Supporting evidence:

- The service has a clear purpose and values shared by all members of staff.
- The service development plan is reviewed regularly, in the context of local authorities' policies and strategy and the Children and Young People's Plan, and shared with staff.
- Managers demonstrate commitment and support for continual improvement.
- Managers articulate the values of the service and lead by example.
- The service has a process to review leadership effectiveness (e.g. 360° feedback).

STANDARD 8. *Leaders motivate, support and recognise a culture of continuous improvement and excellence amongst all staff.*

Supporting evidence:

- Managers engage with and listen to staff at all levels.
- All staff members are able to give examples of supportive, effective and motivational leadership and describe how their contribution to the service is recognised by managers.
- There is evidence to show that all staff are treated equally/fairly.
- Managers empower all staff to be involved in change.
- Managers ensure appropriate resources and support are provided for change initiatives.

STANDARD 9. *Leaders maintain positive relationships with CYP, parents, schools, early years settings and other provision.*

Supporting evidence:

- Fully accessible information is published about what users can expect from services, their costs and how well they perform in meeting the needs of CYP.
- Managers are involved in a range of external activities that develop and support the service, including sharing effective working practice with others.
- Managers can demonstrate how their involvement has delivered improvement and growth, and/or enhanced the reputation of the service.

- Complaints procedures are clear and accessible to service users and speedy and effective action is taken in response to complaints.
- Information from complaints is used to inform service development.

STANDARD 10. ***CYP, parents, schools, early years settings, and other provision are fully involved in the development of services.***

Supporting evidence:

- The views of CYP and parents, schools, early years settings, and other provision are sought in evaluating the service and when changes are proposed.
- Ideas and suggestions from service users and stakeholders are evaluated and, where appropriate, incorporated into plans.
- Policy and strategy are based on the present and future needs and expectations of all service users and stakeholders.
- Policies are designed to give service users choice about the services provided.
- Expectations are clearly stated and include arrangements for transparent communication, access to services, response times and accountability.

STANDARD 11. ***There is a service development plan which is developed, reviewed and updated regularly.***

Supporting evidence:

- The service development plan is based on information from performance measurement, research, learning and externally related activities such as benchmarking.
- The plan is aligned to the Children and Young People's Plan and local, regional and national policies.
- Managers and all staff understand the plan and recognise their role in fulfilling its objectives.
- The plan balances the long and short-term requirements of the service, addresses the needs of stakeholders, and takes account of contingency and risk.
- There is a robust process for communicating, reviewing and updating the service development plan.

STANDARD 12. ***Key processes fully satisfy, and generate increasing value for, service users and other stakeholders.***

Supporting evidence:

- Key processes uphold principles of inclusion in its widest sense and are clearly defined and communicated.
- All staff are clear about their own responsibilities.
- Performance measures, standards and improvement targets are in place for key processes, and planning for CYP takes account of recent research and published data.

- Resource allocation to CYP is regularly reviewed to ensure equitable access to services.
- Key processes are regularly reviewed, with employers and stakeholders having an opportunity to feed back on their effectiveness.

STANDARD 13. ***Staff resources are planned, managed and improved.***

Supporting evidence:

- Managers have the knowledge and skills they need to develop their staff effectively, and ensure that appropriate training and development opportunities are provided, and are accessible to all staff.
- All staff are consistently and effectively managed from recruitment through to exit, to the mutual benefit of the individual, the service and the organisation.
- Examples to demonstrate improvements in the efficiency and effectiveness of all staff, informed by the routine collection of information on staff satisfaction, turnover, sickness and absenteeism, can be identified at all levels.
- Managers ensure that appropriate professional guidance is accessible.
- Performance appraisal of all staff is effective, the achievement of staff performance targets is monitored, and the process leads to training and development aligned to the performance requirements of the service, and the defined needs of the individual.

STANDARD 14. ***Staff experience, knowledge and competencies are identified, developed, sustained, and recognised.***

Supporting evidence:

- All staff maintain high levels of specialist knowledge/appropriate qualifications, keep up-to-date with current research and methodologies, and have the necessary personal skills for partnership working with fellow professionals and others.
- All staff understand the nature of CYP needs and the range of provision that best promotes their achievements, and are able to provide new insights to overcome barriers.
- All staff are skilled in communicating with service users and stakeholders, and can disseminate and share information effectively and appropriately, including funding arrangements for additional or special educational needs within the local authority.
- The service recognises the contribution of all staff to its success, acknowledges individual achievements, and promotes policies designed to maintain a reasonable work/life balance.
- All staff have the opportunity to take part in service development activities and projects within the organisation. Data is gathered on the impact of training and development.

STANDARD 15. ***There is collaboration with other service providers to ensure that services are complementary, simple to use, effective and joined-up to deliver a better service to the user.***

Supporting evidence:

- There are clear links between key partnerships and the overall mission, vision and goals of the service.
- Services are commissioned to undertake specific types of work within their own local context, taking account of other local services.
- Management responsibilities and lines of accountability are clear in a multi-agency context.
- There is joint working with partners to encourage innovation and continuous improvement.
- Organisational and cultural differences with partners are recognised and addressed.

STANDARD 16. ***Finance and resources are managed effectively to support the performance and operational requirements of the service.***

Supporting evidence:

- A clear medium-term funding strategy is in place, linked to the service development plan and the Children and Young People's Plan.
- Financial resources are deployed to ensure equality of access for all service users.
- The service development plan includes strategies for maintaining and sustaining the quality of any premises and specialist resources to improve accessibility and standards of education.
- There is a policy for managing technology, including the maintenance of specialist equipment and the replacement of outdated equipment where it would otherwise impact on service provision.
- Review procedures are in place to identify and evaluate new and emerging technologies which may have an impact on service delivery.

7

SEN Related Laws in England, Scotland and Wales: Guidelines for Appeal Before the Tribunal

SEN RELATED LAWS IN ENGLAND AND WALES

The Special Educational Needs and Disability Tribunal (General Provisions and Disability Claims Procedure) Regulations 2002

Made	*24th July 2002*
Laid before Parliament	*5th August 2002*
Coming into force	*1st September 2002*

Arrangement of Regulations

Part I
General Provisions

1. Citation, commencement, application and extent
2. Interpretation
3. Members of lay panel
4. Establishment of tribunals
5. Membership of tribunal
6. Proof of documents and certification of decisions

Parts II to V
Disability Claims Procedure

Part II
Making a Claim and Statements of Case
(A) The Parent

7. Notice of claim
8. Reasons for making a claim
9. Statement of parent's case, and supplementary provisions
10. Withdrawal of a claim

11. Further action by the parent
12. Parent's representatives

(B) The Responsible Body

13. Statement of the responsible body's case, and supplementary provisions
14. Responsible body's representative
15. Failure to deliver a statement of case and absence of opposition
16. Representation at hearing and further action by the responsible body

Part III
Preparation for a Hearing

17. Acknowledgement of claim and service of documents by the Secretary of the Tribunal
18. Case statement period
19. Copy of documents for parties
20. Enquiries by the Secretary of the Tribunal
21. Directions and determination of preliminary issues
22. Varying or setting aside directions
23. Particulars, and supplementary statements
24. Disclosures of documents and other material
25. Failure to comply with directions
26. Summoning witnesses
27. Consolidating claims and hearing claims together with appeals under Part IV of the Education Act 1996
28. Notice of place and time of hearings and adjournments

Part IV
Determination of Claims

29. Power to determine a claim without a hearing
30. Hearings to be in private: arrangements and exceptions
31. Failure of parties to attend a hearing
32. Procedure at a hearing
33. Late written evidence
34. Evidence at a hearing
35. Adjournments and directions
36. Decision of the tribunal
37. Application or proposal for review of tribunal's decision
38. Review of tribunal's decision
39. Review of the President's decision
40. Orders for costs and expenses

Part V
Additional Powers of the Tribunal

41. Transfer of proceedings
42. Regulation of proceedings
43. Decisions agreed by the parties
44. Power to strike out
45. Power to exercise powers of President and chairman
46. Power to exercise the functions of a lay member
47. The Secretary of the Tribunal
48. Orders of the Court
49. Irregularities
50. Method of sending, delivering or serving notices and documents
51. Extensions of time

In exercise of the powers conferred by Sections 28J (1), (2), (3) and (8), 67 (1) and (3) and 68 (1) of the Disability Discrimination Act 1995, and Sections 333 (5), 334 (2), 336 (1), 569 (1) and 579 (1) of the Education Act 1996, the Secretary of State for Education and Skills, with the agreement of the National Assembly for Wales in accordance with Section 28J (4) of the Disability Discrimination Act 1995 and Article 5 of the National Assembly for Wales (Transfer of Functions) Order 1999, and after consultation with the Council on Tribunals in accordance with Section 8 of the Tribunals and Inquiries Act 1992, hereby makes the following Regulations:

Part I
General Provisions

Citation, Commencement, Application and Extent

1. (1) These Regulations may be cited as the Special Educational Needs and Disability Tribunal (General Provisions and Disability Claims Procedure) Regulations 2002 and shall come into force on 1st September 2002.

(2) Regulations 3 to 6 apply in relation to the jurisdiction of the Special Educational Needs and Disability Tribunal.

(3) Parts II to V of these Regulations apply in relation to the making of, and the proceedings of the Special Educational Needs and Disability Tribunal on, a claim of unlawful discrimination under the 1995 Act.

(4) These Regulations shall apply to England and Wales.

Interpretation

2. In these Regulations, unless the context otherwise requires—
"the 1995 Act" means the Disability Discrimination Act 1995;
"the 1996 Act" means the Education Act 1996;

"the case statement period" has the meaning assigned to it by regulation 18(1);

"child" means the person in relation to whom a parent makes, or may make, a claim;

"claim" refers to a claim of unlawful discrimination under Chapter 1 of Part IV of the 1995 Act;

"the clerk to the tribunal" means the person appointed by the Secretary of the Tribunal to act in that capacity at one or more hearings;

"hearing" means any sitting of the tribunal constituted for the purpose of receiving evidence, hearing addresses and witnesses or doing anything lawfully requisite to enable the tribunal to reach a decision on the claim or any question;

"parent" means a parent who has made, or may make, a claim to the tribunal under Section 28I(1) of the 1995 Act;

"the President" means the President from time to time of the tribunal;

"records" means the records of the tribunal;

"the Secretary of the Tribunal" means the person for the time being acting as the Secretary of the office of the tribunal;

"the tribunal" means the Special Educational Needs and Disability Tribunal but where the President has determined pursuant to regulation 4(1) that its jurisdiction is to be exercised by more than one tribunal, it means, in relation to any proceedings, the tribunal to which the proceedings have been referred by the President;

"working day" means any day other than a Saturday, a Sunday, any day from 25th December to 1st January inclusive, Good Friday, the first Monday in May, any day in August or a day which is a bank holiday in England and Wales within the meaning of the Banking and Financial Dealings Act 1971.

Members of Lay Panel

3. No person may be appointed to the lay panel unless the Secretary of State as respects England, or the National Assembly for Wales as respects Wales, is satisfied that the person—

(*a*) is not eligible for appointment to the chairmen's panel; and

(*b*) has knowledge and experience of children with—

(*i*) special educational needs; or

(*ii*) disabilities; or

(*iii*) if required, both.

Establishment of Tribunals

4. (1) The jurisdiction of the Special Educational Needs and Disability Tribunal shall be exercised by such number of tribunals as the President may from time to time determine.

(2) The tribunals exercising the jurisdiction conferred on them in accordance with paragraph (1) shall sit at such times and in such places as the President may from time to time determine.

Membership of Tribunal

5. (1) Subject to regulation 32(5) of these Regulations and to regulation 32(5) of the Special Educational Needs Tribunal Regulations 2001, the tribunal shall consist of a chairman and two other members.

(2) For each hearing–

(*a*) the chairman shall be the President or a person selected by him from the chairmen's panel; and

(*b*) the two other members shall be selected by the President from the lay panel, and shall have the knowledge and experience appropriate to the proceedings in question.

Proof of Documents and Certification of Decisions

6. (1) A document purporting to be a document issued by the Secretary of the Tribunal on behalf of the tribunal shall, unless the contrary is proved, be deemed to be a document so issued.

(2) A document purporting to be certified by the Secretary of the Tribunal to be a true copy of a document containing a decision of the tribunal shall, unless the contrary is proved, be sufficient evidence of its contents.

Parts II to V
Disability Claims Procedure

Part II
Making a Claim and Statements of Case
(A) The Parent

Notice of Claim

7. (1) A claim to the tribunal shall be made by notice which—

(*a*) shall state—

(*i*) the name and address of the parent making the claim and, if more than one address is given, the address to which the tribunal should send replies or notices concerning the claim;

(*ii*) the name and date of birth of the child;

(*iii*) that the notice is a notice of claim;

(*iv*) where it is alleged that a school has discriminated against the child, the name and address of the school;

(*v*) where it is alleged that a local education authority has discriminated against the child, or where a school named under sub-paragraph (*iv*) is maintained by a local education authority, the name of the local education authority;

(*b*) shall include, or be accompanied by, a statement of the parent's reasons for making the claim which must include information relating to the following matters—
   (*i*) the nature of the child's disability;
   (*ii*) the way in which it is alleged the child has been discriminated against;
   (*iii*) the date or dates on which the alleged discrimination took place.

(2) The parent shall sign the notice of claim.

(3) The parent must deliver the notice of claim to the Secretary of the Tribunal.

(4) Where the parent delivers a notice of claim, or otherwise seeks to institute proceedings, after the end of the period specified in paragraph 10(1) (and any extension under paragraph 10(2)) of Schedule 3 of the 1995 Act (Period within which proceedings must be brought), the President shall decide under paragraph 10(3) of that Schedule whether the tribunal will consider the claim out of time, and the President may seek further information from the parent before making the decision.

(5) The notice of claim may include a request that the claim be heard with an appeal against a local education authority under Part IV of the 1996 Act, in accordance with regulation 27(2).

Reasons for Making a Claim

8. (1) If the notice of claim does not include, or is not accompanied by, a statement of the parent's reasons for making the claim, including the information set out at regulation 7(1)(*b*), which the President considers sufficient to enable the responsible body to respond to the claim, he shall direct the parent to send particulars of the reasons for making the claim to the Secretary of the Tribunal within 10 working days of his direction.

(2) Regulations 21 and 25 shall apply in relation to a direction under paragraph (1).

(3) Particulars of reasons sent in response to a direction made in accordance with paragraph (1) shall be treated as part of the notice of claim.

Statement of Parent's Case, and Supplementary Provisions

9. (1) During the case statement period, the parent may deliver to the Secretary of the Tribunal a written statement of his case which may include the views of the child, and the parent must submit all written evidence on which he intends to rely and which he has not already submitted.

(2) The parent may amend the notice of claim or his statement of case, deliver a supplementary statement of reasons for making the claim,

deliver a supplementary statement of case, or make further amendments to any of these documents, if, in exceptional circumstances, permission is given by—

(*a*) the President; or

(*b*) at a hearing, the tribunal.

(3) The parent shall deliver to the Secretary of the Tribunal a copy of every amendment and supplementary statement for which permission was given.

(4) If permission is granted under paragraph (2)(*a*), the case statement period may, if necessary, be extended under regulation 51(1) or, if it has expired, a further period may be granted of no more than 15 working days.

(5) If, at the time permission is granted under paragraph (2), the responsible body has lost its entitlement to attend or be represented at the hearing in accordance with regulations 15 or 25, the giving of permission shall restore such entitlement and, if necessary, the hearing shall be rearranged or adjourned, as appropriate, so that the responsible body can attend or be represented.

Withdrawal of a Claim

10. The parent may withdraw his claim—

(*a*) at a hearing; or

(*b*) at any other time, by sending written notification to the Secretary of the Tribunal.

Further Action by the Parent

11. (1) The parent shall give the Secretary of the Tribunal the information requested in the enquiry made under regulation 20.

(2) If the parent does not intend to attend or be represented at the hearing, he may, not less than 5 working days before the hearing, send to the Secretary of the Tribunal additional written representations in support of his claim.

Parent's Representatives

12. (1) The parent may in the notice of claim or by giving written notice to the Secretary of the Tribunal at any later time—

(*a*) appoint a representative;

(*b*) appoint another representative to replace the representative previously appointed, whose appointment is cancelled by the later appointment;

(*c*) state that no person is acting as the parent's representative, which cancels any previous appointment.

(2) To appoint a representative, the parent must give the name, address and profession of the representative.

(3) If a person whom the parent has appointed as a representative notifies the Secretary of the Tribunal in writing that he is not prepared, or is no longer prepared, to act in that capacity–

(*a*) the Secretary of the Tribunal shall notify the parent;

(*b*) the appointment of that representative is cancelled.

(4) Subject to paragraph (5), at any time after the parent has appointed a representative, and until that appointment is cancelled—

(*a*) the Secretary of the Tribunal shall send all documents and notices concerning the claim to the representative instead of the parent;

(*b*) references in these Regulations (however expressed) to sending documents to, or giving notice to, the parent shall be construed as references to sending documents to, or giving notice to, the representative.

(5) Paragraph (4) applies—

(*a*) unless the parent notifies the Secretary of the Tribunal that he does not wish it to apply;

(*b*) subject to regulations 36(6) and 49(5).

(6) At a hearing, the parent may conduct his case himself (with assistance from one person if he wishes) or may appear and be represented by one person whether or not legally qualified:

Provided that, if permission is given by the President or, at a hearing, the tribunal, the parent may obtain assistance or be represented by more than one person.

(B) The Responsible Body

Statement of the Responsible Body's Case, and Supplementary Provisions

13. (1) During the case statement period, the responsible body shall deliver to the Secretary of the Tribunal a written statement of its case and all written evidence on which it intends to rely.

(2) The statement of the responsible body's case shall be signed by a person who is authorised to sign such documents on the responsible body's behalf and shall state whether or not the responsible body intends to oppose the claim, and if it does intend to oppose the claim it shall state—

(*a*) the grounds on which it relies;

(*b*) the name and profession of a representative authorised to deal with the claim on the responsible body's behalf, and an address for service.

(3) The responsible body may amend its statement of case, deliver a supplementary statement of case or amend a supplementary statement of case if, in exceptional circumstances, permission is given by—

(*a*) the President; or

(*b*) at a hearing, the tribunal.

(4) The responsible body shall deliver to the Secretary of the Tribunal a copy of every amendment and supplementary statement for which permission was given.

(5) If permission is granted under paragraph (3)(*a*), the case statement period may, if necessary, be extended under regulation 51(1) or, if it has expired, a further period may be granted of no more than 15 working days.

(6) If, at the time permission is granted under paragraph (3), the parent has lost his entitlement to attend or be represented at the hearing in accordance with regulation 25, the giving of permission shall restore such entitlement and, if necessary, the hearing shall be rearranged or adjourned, as appropriate, so that the parent can attend or be represented.

Responsible Body's Representative

14. (1) The responsible body may at any time change its representative for the purposes of the claim by notifying the Secretary of the Tribunal of the name and profession of its new representative.

(2) References in these Regulations (however expressed) to sending documents to, or giving notice to, the responsible body shall be construed as references to sending documents to, or giving notice to, the representative named in accordance with regulation 13(2)(*b*) or paragraph (1) above.

Failure to Deliver a Statement of Case and Absence of Opposition

15. If the Secretary of the Tribunal does not receive a statement of case from the responsible body within the case statement period or if the responsible body states in writing that it does not resist the claim, or withdraws its opposition to the claim, the tribunal shall—

(*a*) determine the claim on the basis of the notice of claim, and any other documentation already received or amended in accordance with regulation 9(1) and (2), without a hearing; or

(*b*) without notifying the responsible body hold a hearing at which the responsible body is not entitled to attend or be represented.

Representation at Hearing and Further Action by the Responsible Body

16. (1) At any hearing or part of a hearing the responsible body may—

(*a*) appear; and

(*b*) be represented by a legally qualified representative, in addition to any representative whose attendance is necessary in order for the responsible body to appear at the hearing under sub–paragraph (*a*).

(2) The President or, at a hearing, the tribunal may grant the responsible body permission to be represented by any further representatives to those permitted under paragraph (1).

(3) The responsible body shall give the Secretary of the Tribunal the information requested in the enquiry made under regulation 20.

(4) If the responsible body does not intend to be represented at the hearing it may, not less than 5 working days before the hearing, send to the Secretary of the Tribunal additional representations in support of its case.

Part III
Preparation for a Hearing

Acknowledgement of Claim and Service of Documents by the Secretary of the Tribunal

17. (1) Upon receiving a notice of claim the Secretary of the Tribunal shall—

(*a*) enter particulars of it in the records;

(*b*) send to the parent—

(*i*) an acknowledgement of its receipt and a note of the case number entered in the records;

(*ii*) a note of the address to which notices and communications to the tribunal or to the Secretary of the Tribunal should be sent;

(*iii*) notification that advice about the claims procedure may be obtained from the office of the tribunal; and

(*iv*) subject to regulation 18(2), a notice informing the parent of the requirements of regulation 9(1) and the case statement period;

(*c*) at the same time as sending to the parent the notice referred to in sub-paragraph (*b*)(*iv*), send to the responsible body—

(*i*) a copy of the notice of claim and any accompanying papers;

(*ii*) a note of the address to which notices and communications to the tribunal to the Secretary of the Tribunal should be sent; and

(*iii*) a notice informing the responsible body of the requirements of regulation 13(1) and of the case statement period, together with the consequences of failing to meet the requirements of that regulation within that period.

(2) Where it is necessary to determine the identity of the responsible body in relation to any claim, the President may make such enquiries as are necessary for this purpose.

(3) Where it appears to the President or the Secretary of the Tribunal that there may be more than one responsible body in relation to any claim, the President or the Secretary of the Tribunal may send the

documentation specified in paragraph (1)(*c*) to any or all such bodies as may be appropriate.

(4) Where the Secretary of the Tribunal is of the opinion that, on the basis of the notice of claim, the parent is asking the tribunal to consider a matter which is not within its jurisdiction, he may give notice to the parent—

(*a*) stating the reasons for his opinion; and

(*b*) informing the parent that the notice of claim will not be entered in the records unless, within a specified time (which shall not be less than 5 working days), the parent notifies the Secretary of the Tribunal that he wishes to proceed with it.

(5) Where the Secretary of the Tribunal is of the opinion that there is an obvious error in the notice of claim—

(*a*) he may correct that error and if he does so shall notify the parent accordingly and such notification shall state the effect of sub-paragraph (*b*); and

(*b*) unless within 5 working days the parent notifies the Secretary of the Tribunal that he objects to the correction, the notice of claim so corrected shall be treated as the notice of claim for the purposes of these Regulations.

(6) If the Secretary of the Tribunal has given a notice under paragraph (4), the notice of claim shall only be treated as having been received for the purposes of paragraph (1) when the parent notifies the Secretary of the Tribunal that he wishes to proceed with the claim.

Case Statement Period

18. (1) The case statement period shall—

(*a*) be a period of 30 working days commencing on the date on which notification issued further to regulation 17(1)(*b*)(*iv*) and 17(1)(*c*) (*iii*) is taken to have been delivered in accordance with regulation 50(6); and

(*b*) shall include any extension to that period ordered by the President under regulation 51(1).

(2) Where the President makes a direction in accordance with regulation 8 or makes enquiries under regulation 17(2), the Secretary of the Tribunal shall not send a notice to the parent as required by regulation 17(1)(*b*)(*iv*) or send any documents to the responsible body as required by regulation 17(1)(*c*) until particulars of reasons are received in response to the direction or the President has concluded his enquiries as the case may be.

Copy of Documents for Parties

19. (1) Subject to paragraph (2), the Secretary of the Tribunal shall—

(*a*) forthwith send to the responsible body a copy of any amendment to the notice of claim received during the case statement period;

(*b*) at the end of the case statement period send a copy of each party's statement of case and written evidence to the other party;

(*c*) forthwith send copies of any amendments or supplementary statements, written representations, written evidence (other than written evidence of which a copy is received in accordance with regulation 33(2)(*b*)) or other documents received from a party after the end of the case statement period to the other party to the proceedings.

(2) If a notice of claim, a statement of case, amendment, supplementary statement, written representation, written evidence or other document is delivered to the Secretary of the Tribunal after the time prescribed by these Regulations, the Secretary of the Tribunal shall not send a copy of it to the other party unless the President extends the time limit pursuant to regulation 51(1).

(3) Where the Secretary of the Tribunal sends any of the copies of documents referred to in paragraph (1) to a party who has already informed the Secretary of the Tribunal in response to the enquiries made under regulation 20(*a*)(*i*) and (*ii*) that the party does not wish to attend or be represented at the hearing, the Secretary of the Tribunal shall ask whether the party wishes to amend that response on the basis of the copies received.

Enquiries by the Secretary of the Tribunal

20. The Secretary of the Tribunal shall, at any time after having sent each party's statement of case and written evidence to the other party in accordance with regulation 19(1)(*b*)—

(*a*) ask each party—

(*i*) whether or not the party intends to attend the hearing;

(*ii*) whether the party wishes to be represented at the hearing in accordance with regulation 12(6) or 16(1) and if so the name of the representative;

(*iii*) whether the party wishes the hearing to be in public;

(*iv*) whether the party intends to call witnesses and if so the names of the proposed witnesses, their occupations, the likely subject matter of the evidence of each witness, and whether any of the witnesses is a medical or other expert;

(*v*) whether the party or a witness will require the assistance of an interpreter;

(*b*) enquire of the parent whether he wishes any persons (other than a person who will represent him or any witness whom he proposes to call) to attend the hearing if the hearing is in private and if so the name of such persons;

(*c*) inform each party of the effect of regulation 30(4)(*c*) and the provisions of regulation 34(1) and (2); and

(*d*) inform the parties that where an answer to the enquiries made under paragraphs (*a*) or (*b*) changes after the party has responded to the enquiries, the party concerned must inform the Secretary of the Tribunal in writing forthwith.

Directions and Determination of Preliminary Issues

21. (1) The President may, on the application of a party or on his own initiative, at any time before the hearing give such directions on any matter arising in connection with the proceedings as appear to him to be appropriate, including such directions as are provided in regulations 23 and 24, to enable the parties to prepare for the hearing or to assist the tribunal to determine the issues.

(2) An application by a party for directions shall be made in writing to the Secretary of the Tribunal and, unless it is accompanied by the written consent of the other party, shall be served by the Secretary of the Tribunal on that other party. If the other party objects to the directions sought, the President shall consider the objection and, if he considers it necessary for the determination of the application, shall give the parties an opportunity of appearing before him.

(3) If in the opinion of the President there would not be a reasonable time before a hearing of which notice has been given under regulation 28(1) to comply with a direction for which a party applies, he shall refuse the application.

(4) A direction shall—

(*a*) include a statement of the possible consequences for the claim, as provided by regulation 25, of a party's failure to comply with the requirement within the time allowed by the President;

(*b*) if made under regulation 24(2), contain a reference to the fact that, under Section 28J(9)(*a*) of the 1995 Act, any person who without reasonable excuse fails to comply with requirements regarding disclosure or inspection of documents shall be liable on summary conviction to a fine not exceeding level 3 on the standard scale; and

(*c*) unless the person to whom the direction is addressed had an opportunity to object to the direction, or he gave his written consent to the application for it, contain a statement to the effect that that person may apply to the President under regulation 22 to vary or set aside the direction.

(5) Where, in accordance with regulation 27(2), the President orders that a claim be heard together with an appeal under Part IV of the 1996 Act, the directions given under paragraph (1) shall relate to the claim only;

but in giving such directions the President may consider whether it is in the interests of the efficient disposal of the claim and the appeal, and in the interests of the parties, that the directions given with respect to the claim are the same as, or similar to, those given in the appeal.

(6) Where it appears to the President that there is an issue in any claim which must be determined prior to the substantive hearing of the claim and which cannot properly be determined by the giving of directions, he may summon the parties to appear before him for this purpose and may give any necessary directions relating to their appearance.

Varying or Setting Aside Directions

22. Where a party to whom a direction is addressed had no opportunity to object to the giving of such direction and he did not give his written consent to the application for it, he may apply to the President, by notice to the Secretary of the Tribunal, to vary it or set it aside, but the President shall not do so without first notifying the other party and considering any representations made by him.

Particulars, and Supplementary Statements

23. The President may give directions requiring any party to provide in or with that party's statement of case or otherwise, such particulars, supplementary statements or other evidence, in such form and at such times as may be necessary to enable the fair hearing of the claim.

Disclosures of Documents and Other Material

24. (1) The President—

(*a*) may give directions requiring a party to deliver to the tribunal any document or other material which the tribunal may require and which it is in the power of that party to deliver;

(*b*) shall impose a condition on the supply of a copy of any document or other material delivered in compliance with a direction given under this paragraph that the party receiving it shall use such document only for the purposes of the claim; and

(*c*) may require a written undertaking to observe that condition before supplying a copy.

(2) The President may grant to a party an order for such disclosure or inspection of documents (including the taking of copies) as might be granted under the Civil Procedure Rules 1998.

Failure to Comply with Directions

25. (1) If a party has not complied with a direction within the time specified in the direction the tribunal may—

(*a*) where the party in default is the parent, dismiss the claim without a hearing;

(*b*) where the party in default is the responsible body, determine the claim without a hearing;

(*c*) hold a hearing (without notifying the party in default) at which the party in default is not entitled to attend or be represented; or

(*d*) where the parties have been notified of the hearing in accordance with regulation 28(1), direct that neither the party in default nor any person whom he intends should represent him or give evidence on his behalf be entitled to attend the hearing.

(2) In this regulation "the party in default" means the party which has failed to comply with the direction.

Summoning Witnesses

26. (1) The President may by summons require any person in England and Wales to attend as a witness at a hearing of a claim at such time and place as may be specified in the summons, and at any adjournment of that hearing, and at the hearing to answer any questions or produce any documents or other material in his custody or under his control which relate to any matter in question in the claim:

Provided that—

(*a*) no person shall be compelled to give any evidence or produce any document or other material that he could not be compelled to give or produce at a trial of an action in a Court of law;

(*b*) in exercising the power conferred by this regulation, the President shall take into account the need to protect any matter that relates to intimate personal or financial circumstances or consists of information communicated or obtained in confidence;

(*c*) no person shall be required to attend in obedience to such a summons unless he has been given at least 5 working days' notice of the hearing or, if less than 5 working days, he has informed the President that he accepts such notice as he has been given;

(*d*) no person shall be required in obedience to such a summons to attend and give evidence or to produce any document unless the necessary expenses of his attendance are paid or tendered to him; and

(*e*) no summons shall require a child under the age of 12 to attend and give evidence at the hearing except where the President determines that the evidence of such a child is necessary to enable the fair hearing of the claim.

(2) A party seeking a witness summons shall apply in writing to the Secretary of the Tribunal at least 8 working days before the hearing, or later if the person to whom the summons is to be addressed consents in writing.

(3) A witness summons shall contain—
  (*a*) a reference to the fact that, under Section 28J(9)(*b*) of the 1995 Act, any person who without reasonable excuse fails to comply with any requirement to attend to give evidence and, if the summons so requires, to produce documents shall be liable on summary conviction to a fine not exceeding level 3 on the standard scale; and
  (*b*) a statement of the effect of paragraph (4).

(4) A person to whom a witness summons is addressed may apply to the President, by notice to the Secretary of the Tribunal, to vary it or set it aside, but the President shall not do so without first notifying the party who applied for the issue of the summons and considering any representations made by him.

Consolidating Claims and Hearing Claims Together with Appeals Under Part IV of the Education Act 1996

27. (1) Where more than one claim relates to the same child, or requires a decision on substantially the same issue, the President may order that they be heard together.

(2) Subject to paragraphs (3) and (4), where a claim relates to the same child and either arises from the same circumstances or requires a decision on substantially the same issue as an appeal against a local education authority under Part IV of the 1996 Act, the President may order that the claim be heard with the appeal.

(3) Nothing in paragraph (2) shall permit the President to make an order under that paragraph where a parent has failed to bring an appeal within the time limit for such appeals provided for by regulation 7(3) of the Special Educational Needs Tribunal Regulations 2001 or any extension granted under those Regulations.

(4) The President may only make an order under paragraph (2) if, in addition to complying with the requirements of paragraph (7), the making of an order would not cause undue delay to the determination of the appeal.

(5) The President may make an order varying or revoking an earlier order made under paragraphs (1) or (2).

(6) Subject to paragraph (7), the President may issue an order under this regulation on the written request of either party or on his own initiative.

(7) An order made under this regulation shall only be made if it appears to be just and convenient to do so, and before an order is made the parties to every claim or appeal affected shall be given an opportunity to be heard.

Notice of Place and Time of Hearings and Adjournments

28. (1) Subject to the provisions of regulation 29, the Secretary of the Tribunal shall, after consultation with the parties, fix the time and place of the hearing and send to each party a notice that the hearing is to be at such time and place.

(2) The notice of hearing referred to in paragraph (1) shall be sent—

(*a*) not less than 5 working days before the date fixed for a hearing under regulations 15, 37, 38 or 44;

(*b*) not less than 10 working days before the date fixed for the hearing in any other case; or

(*c*) in any case, within such shorter period before the date fixed for the hearing as the parties may agree.

(3) The Secretary of the Tribunal shall include in or with the notice of hearing—

(*a*) information and guidance, in a form approved by the President, as to attendance at the hearing of the parties and witnesses, the bringing of documents, and the right of representation or assistance as provided by regulation 12(6) or 16(1); and

(*b*) a statement explaining the possible consequences of non-attendance and the right to make representations in writing enjoyed by—

(*i*) the parent if he does not attend and is not represented; and

(*ii*) the responsible body if it does not attend and is not represented and if it has submitted a statement of its case, unless it stated in writing that it did not resist the claim or withdrew its opposition to the claim.

(4) The tribunal may alter the time and place of any hearing and the Secretary of the Tribunal shall give the parties not less than 5 working days (or such shorter time as the parties agree) notice of the altered hearing date:

Provided that any altered hearing date shall not (unless the parties agree) be before the date notified under paragraph (1).

(5) If the time and place of an adjourned hearing are announced at the hearing before the adjournment, no further notice shall be required.

(6) Nothing in paragraphs (1) or (4) shall oblige the Secretary of the Tribunal to consult, or send a notice to any party who is not entitled to attend or be represented at the hearing.

(7) In this regulation "working day" has the meaning ascribed to it in regulation 2 except that it shall include any day in August which is not a Saturday, Sunday, or bank holiday.

Part IV
Determination of Claims

Power to Determine a Claim Without a Hearing

29. (1) The tribunal may determine a claim or any particular issue without a hearing—

(*a*) if the parties so agree in writing; or
(*b*) in the circumstances described in regulations 15 or 25.

(2) The provisions of regulation 31(2) shall apply in respect of the determination of a claim, or any particular issue, under this regulation.

Hearings to be in Private: Arrangements and Exceptions

30. (1) A hearing shall not be in private if—
(*a*) both the parent and the responsible body request that the hearing be in public; or
(*b*) the President or, at a hearing, the tribunal orders that the hearing should be in public.

(2) The following persons (as well as the parties and their representatives and witnesses) shall be entitled to attend the hearing of a claim, even though it is in private—
(*a*) the child;
(*b*) subject to the provisions of paragraph (9) below, any person named by the parent in response to the enquiry under regulation 20(*b*) unless the President has determined that any such person should not attend the hearing and has notified the parent accordingly;
(*c*) a parent of the child who is not a party to the claim;
(*d*) the clerk to the tribunal and the Secretary of the Tribunal;
(*e*) the President and a member of the chairmen's or lay panel (when not sitting as a member of the tribunal);
(*f*) a member of the Council on Tribunals;
(*g*) a person undergoing training as a member of the chairmen's or lay panel or as a clerk to the tribunal;
(*h*) a person acting on behalf of the President in the training or supervision of clerks to tribunals;
(*i*) an interpreter;
(*j*) any person giving other necessary assistance to a person entitled to attend the hearing further to this regulation.

(3) The tribunal, with the consent of the parties or their representatives actually present, may permit any other person to attend the hearing of a claim which is held in private.

(4) Without prejudice to any other powers it may have, the tribunal may exclude from the hearing, or part of it—
(*a*) a person whose conduct has disrupted or is likely, in the opinion of the tribunal, to disrupt the hearing;
(*b*) a person, including the child, whose presence is likely, in the opinion of the tribunal, to make it difficult for any person to adduce the evidence or make the representations necessary for the proper conduct of the hearing;

(*c*) a representative or witness whom a party omitted to name, without reasonable cause, in response to the enquiry by the Secretary of the Tribunal under regulation 20.

(5) For the purposes of arriving at its decision a tribunal shall, and for the purposes of discussing a question of procedure may, notwithstanding anything contained in these Regulations, order all persons to withdraw from the sitting of the tribunal other than the members of the tribunal and any of the persons mentioned in sub-paragraphs (*d*) to (*g*), or, as their respective duties require, sub-paragraphs (*i*) and (*j*), of paragraph (2).

(6) Except as provided in paragraphs (7) and (8) none of the persons mentioned in sub-paragraphs (*a*) to (*j*) of paragraph (2) or paragraph (3) shall, save in the case of the persons specified in sub-paragraphs (*d*), (*i*) and (*j*) of paragraph (2) as their respective duties require, take any part in the hearing or (where entitled or permitted to remain) in the deliberations of the tribunal.

(7) The tribunal may permit the child to give evidence and to address the tribunal on the subject matter of the claim.

(8) The tribunal may permit a parent of the child who is not a party to the claim to address the tribunal on the subject matter of the claim.

(9) Where the parent has named more than two persons in response to the enquiry under regulation 20(*b*) only two persons shall be entitled to attend the hearing unless the President, or, at a hearing, the tribunal gives permission for a greater number to attend.

Failure of Parties to Attend a Hearing

31. (1) If a party fails to attend or be represented at a hearing of which he had been duly notified, the tribunal may—

(*a*) unless it is satisfied that there is sufficient reason for such absence, hear and determine the claim in the party's absence; or

(*b*) adjourn the hearing.

(2) Before disposing of a claim in the absence of a party, the tribunal shall consider any representations in writing submitted by that party in response to the notice of hearing and, for the purpose of this regulation the notice of claim and the parties' statements of their cases shall be treated as representations in writing.

Procedure at a Hearing

32. (1) At the beginning of the hearing the chairman shall explain the order of proceedings which the tribunal proposes to adopt.

(2) The tribunal shall conduct the hearing in such manner as it considers the most suitable to the clarification of the issues and generally to the

just handling of the proceedings; it shall, as far as appears to it appropriate, seek to avoid formality in its proceedings.

(3) The tribunal shall determine the order in which the parties are heard and the issues determined.

(4) The tribunal may, if it is satisfied that it is just and reasonable to do so, permit—

(*a*) the parent to rely on grounds not stated in his notice of claim or the statement of his case;

(*b*) the responsible body to rely on grounds not specified in its statement of its case.

(5) If at or after the beginning of a hearing a member of the tribunal other than the chairman is absent, the hearing may, with the consent of the parties, be conducted by the other two members and in that event the tribunal shall be deemed to be properly constituted and the decision of the tribunal shall be taken by those two members.

Late Written Evidence

33. (1) At the beginning of the hearing, a party may submit further written evidence which satisfies the conditions set out in paragraph (2) unless the tribunal, after considering any representations from the other party, is of the opinion that it would be contrary to the interests of justice.

(2) The conditions referred to in paragraph (1) are that—

(*a*) the evidence was not, and could not reasonably have been, available to that party before the end of the case statement period;

(*b*) a copy of the evidence was sent or delivered to the Secretary of the Tribunal and to the other party without undue delay and, in any event, at least 5 working days before the hearing; and

(*c*) the extent and form of the evidence is such that, in the opinion of the tribunal, it is not likely to impede the efficient conduct of the hearing.

(3) If paragraph (1) does not apply, the tribunal may give a party permission to submit further written evidence at the hearing if it is of the opinion that—

(*a*) the case is wholly exceptional; and

(*b*) unless the evidence is admitted, there is a serious risk of prejudice to the party seeking to rely on it.

(4) Before the hearing the tribunal may refer to copies of evidence sent to the Secretary of the Tribunal under paragraph (2)(*b*) above for the purpose of considering whether or not it satisfies the conditions in paragraph (2); but if the evidence is not admitted the tribunal shall disregard it in determining the claim.

Evidence at a Hearing

34. (1) In the course of the hearing the parties shall be entitled to give evidence, to call witnesses, to question any witness and to address the tribunal both on the evidence, including the written evidence submitted before the hearing, and generally on the subject matter of the claim:

Provided that neither party will be entitled to call more than five witnesses to give evidence orally (in addition to any witness whose attendance is required pursuant to paragraph (2)) unless the President or, at a hearing, the tribunal grants a party permission to call a greater number of witnesses.

(2) Evidence before the tribunal may be given orally or by written statement, but the tribunal may at any stage of the proceedings require the personal attendance of any maker of any written statement:

Provided that a party shall only be entitled to give evidence by written statement if such evidence is submitted with the notice of claim or the statement of his case or in accordance with regulation 33.

(3) The tribunal may receive evidence of any fact which appears to the tribunal to be relevant.

(4) The tribunal may require any witness to give evidence on oath or affirmation, and for that purpose there may be administered an oath or affirmation in due form, or may require any evidence given by written statement to be given by a statement of truth.

Adjournments and Directions

35. (1) The tribunal may from time to time adjourn the hearing.

(2) When a hearing is adjourned—

(*a*) the tribunal may give directions to be complied with before or at the resumed hearing;

(*b*) the chairman may announce provisional conclusions reached by the tribunal. The provisional conclusions are not a decision of the tribunal.

(3) A direction under paragraph (2)(*a*) may require a party to provide such particulars, evidence or statements as may reasonably be required for the determination of the claim.

(4) If a party fails to comply with such a direction, the tribunal shall take account of that fact when determining the claim or deciding whether to make an order for costs.

Decision of the Tribunal

36. (1) A decision of the tribunal may be taken by a majority and where the tribunal is constituted by two members under regulation 32(5) the chairman shall have a second or casting vote.

(2) The decision of the tribunal may be given orally at the end of the hearing or reserved and, in any event, whether there has been a hearing or not, shall be recorded forthwith in a document which, save in the case of a decision by consent, shall also contain, or have annexed to it, a statement of the reasons (in summary form) for the tribunal's decision, and each such document shall be signed and dated by the chairman.

(3) Neither a decision given orally nor the document referred to in paragraph (2) shall contain any reference to the decision being by majority (if that be the case) or to any opinion of a minority.

(4) Every decision of the tribunal shall be entered in the records.

(5) As soon as may be the Secretary of the Tribunal shall send a copy of the document referred to in paragraph (2) to each party, accompanied by guidance, in a form approved by the President, about the circumstances in which there is a right to appeal against a tribunal decision and the procedure to be followed.

(6) Where, under regulation 12 a parent has appointed a representative the Secretary of the Tribunal shall send a copy of the documents referred to in paragraph (5) to the parent as well as to the representative.

(7) Every decision shall be treated as having been made on the date on which a copy of the document recording it is sent to the parent (whether or not the decision has previously been announced at the end of the hearing).

Application or Proposal for Review of Tribunal's Decision

37. (1) A party may apply to the Secretary of the Tribunal for the decision of the tribunal to be reviewed on the grounds that—

(*a*) its decision was wrongly made as a result of an error on the part of the tribunal staff;

(*b*) a party, who was entitled to be heard at the hearing but failed to appear or to be represented, had good and sufficient reason for failing to appear;

(*c*) there was an obvious error in the decision; or

(*d*) the interests of justice require.

(2) An application that a decision of the tribunal be reviewed shall—

(*a*) be made not later than 10 working days after the date on which the decision was sent to the parties;

(*b*) be in writing stating the grounds in full.

(3) An application that a decision of the tribunal be reviewed may be refused by the President, or by the chairman of the tribunal which decided the case, if in his opinion it has no reasonable grounds of success.

(4) Unless an application that a decision of the tribunal be reviewed is refused in accordance with paragraph (3), it shall be determined, after the parties have had an opportunity to be heard, by the tribunal which

made the decision or, where that is not practicable, by a tribunal appointed by the President.

(5) The tribunal may on its own initiative propose to review its decision on any of the grounds referred to in paragraph (1), in which case—
   (*a*) the Secretary of the Tribunal shall serve notice on the parents not later than 10 working days after the date on which the decision was sent to them; and
   (*b*) the parties shall have an opportunity to be heard.

(6) If, on the application of a party or on its own initiative, the tribunal is satisfied as to any of the grounds referred to in paragraph (1)—
   (*a*) it shall order that the whole or a specified part of the decision be reviewed; and
   (*b*) it may give directions to be complied with before or at the hearing of the review.

(7) A direction under paragraph (6) may require a party to provide such particulars, evidence or statements as may reasonably be required for the determination of the review.

(8) If a party fails to comply with such a direction, the tribunal shall take account of that fact when determining the review or deciding whether to make an order for costs.

Review of Tribunal's Decision

38. (1) A tribunal which reviews all or part of a decision may—
   (*a*) by certificate under the chairman's hand set aside or vary that decision and substitute such other decision as it thinks fit; or
   (*b*) order a rehearing before the same or a differently constituted tribunal.

(2) If the decision is set aside or varied, the Secretary of the Tribunal shall alter the entry in the records to conform to the chairman's certificate and shall notify the parties accordingly.

Review of the President's Decision

39. (1) On the application of a party to the Secretary of the Tribunal or on his own initiative, the President may review and set aside or vary any decision of his if he is satisfied that—
   (*a*) the decision was wrongly made as a result of an error on the part of the tribunal staff;
   (*b*) there was an obvious error in the decision; or
   (*c*) the interests of justice so require.

(2) An application by a party for a review under paragraph (1) shall be made—
   (*a*) in writing stating the grounds in full;

(*b*) not later than 10 working days after the date on which he was notified of the decision.

(3) Where the President proposes to review his decision on his own initiative he shall serve notice of that proposal on the parties not later than 10 working days after they were notified of the decision.

(4) The parties shall have an opportunity to be heard on any application or proposal for review under this regulation and the review shall be determined by the President.

(5) If any decision is set aside or varied under this regulation the Secretary of the Tribunal shall alter the entry in the records and shall notify the parties accordingly.

(6) Where, in accordance with regulation 7(4), the President decides under paragraph 10(3) of Schedule 3 to the 1995 Act that a claim will not be considered out of time, the decision shall be capable of being reviewed under this regulation on the application of a parent as if he were party to a claim and in such a case the responsible body shall not be entitled to be heard or notified.

Orders for Costs and Expenses

40. (1) The tribunal shall not normally make an order in respect of costs and expenses but may, subject to paragraph (3), make such an order—

(*a*) against a party (including a parent who has withdrawn his claim or a responsible body which has withdrawn its opposition to the claim) if it is of the opinion that that party has acted frivolously or vexatiously or that his conduct in making, pursuing or resisting a claim was wholly unreasonable;

(*b*) against a party who has failed to attend or be represented at a hearing of which he has been duly notified; or

(*c*) against the responsible body where it has not delivered a statement of its case under regulation 13.

(2) Any order in respect of costs and expenses may be made—

(*a*) as respects any costs and expenses incurred, or any allowances paid; or

(*b*) as respects the whole, or any part, of any allowance (other than allowances paid to members of the tribunal) paid by the Secretary of State under Section 28J(5) of the 1995 Act to any person for the purposes of, or in connection with, his attendance at the tribunal.

(3) No order shall be made under paragraph (1) against a party without first giving that party an opportunity of making representations against the making of the order.

(4) An order under paragraph (1) may require the party against whom it is made to pay the other party either a specified sum in respect of the costs and expenses incurred by that other party in connection with the

proceedings or the whole or part of such costs as assessed if not otherwise agreed.

(5) An order under this regulation for costs to be assessed shall allow the County Court to make a detailed assessment of fast track trial costs either on the standard or indemnity basis as the order may specify in accordance with the Civil Procedure Rules 1998.

Part V
Additional Powers of the Tribunal

Transfer of Proceedings

41. Where it appears to the President that a claim pending before a tribunal could be determined more conveniently in another tribunal he may at any time, upon the application of a party or on his own initiative, direct that the proceedings be transferred so as to be determined in that other tribunal:

Provided that no such direction shall be given unless notice has been sent to both parties giving them an opportunity to make representations against the giving of the direction.

Regulation of Proceedings

42. Subject to the provisions of the 1995 Act and these Regulations, a tribunal may regulate its own procedure.

Decisions Agreed by the Parties

43. A tribunal may, if it thinks fit, make a decision in terms agreed in writing by the parties.

Power to Strike Out

44. (1) The Secretary of the Tribunal shall, at any stage of the proceedings, if the responsible body applies or the President so directs, serve a notice on the parent stating that it appears that the claim should be struck out on one or both of the grounds specified in paragraph (2) or for want of prosecution.

(2) The grounds referred to in paragraph (1) are that—

(*a*) the claim is not, or is no longer, within the jurisdiction of the tribunal;

(*b*) that notice of claim is, or the claim is or has become, scandalous, frivolous or vexatious.

(3) The notice under paragraph (1) shall invite the parent to make representations.

(4) The tribunal may, after considering any representations duly made by the parent, order that the claim should be struck out on one or both of the grounds specified in paragraph (2) or for want of prosecution.

(5) The tribunal may make an order under paragraph (4) without holding a hearing unless the parent requests the opportunity to make oral representations, and if the tribunal holds a hearing it may be held at the beginning of the hearing of the substantive claim.

(6) The President may, if he thinks fit, at any stage of the proceedings order that a statement of a party's case should be struck out or amended on the grounds that it is scandalous, frivolous or vexatious.

(7) Before making an order under paragraph (6), the President shall give to the party against whom he proposes to make the order a notice inviting representations and shall consider any representations duly made.

(8) For the purposes of this regulation—

(*a*) a notice inviting representations must inform the recipient that he may, within a period (not being less than 5 working days) specified in the notice, either make written representations or request an opportunity to make oral representations;

(*b*) representations are duly made if—

(*i*) in the case of written representations, they are made within the period so specified; and

(*ii*) in the case of oral representations, the party proposing to make them has requested an opportunity to do so within the period so specified.

Power to Exercise Powers of President and Chairman

45. (1) An act which these Regulations require or authorise the President to do may be done by a member of the chairmen's panel authorised by him.

(2) Where a member of the chairmen's panel authorised under paragraph (1)—

(*a*) selects the chairman of a tribunal, he may select himself;

(*b*) makes a decision, regulation 39 applies in relation to that decision as if it referred to the member of the chairmen's panel in place of the President.

(3) Subject to regulation 49(6), in the event of the death or incapacity of the chairman, or if he ceases to be a member of the chairmen's panel, following the decision of the tribunal, the functions of the chairman for the completion of the proceedings, including any review of the decision, may be exercised by the President or any member of the chairmen's panel.

Power to Exercise the Functions of a Lay Member

46. (1) In the event of the death or incapacity of a member of the tribunal other than the chairman, or if he ceases to be a member of the lay panel, following the decision of the tribunal, the functions of the tribunal in relation to any review of that decision may be undertaken by the other two members.

(2) This regulation shall not apply to a tribunal—

(*a*) which is constituted of two members in accordance with regulation 32(5);

(*b*) of which any person is authorised to act in place of the chairman in accordance with regulation 45(3).

The Secretary of the Tribunal

47. A function of the Secretary of the Tribunal may be performed by another member of the staff of the tribunal authorised by the President.

Orders of the Court

48. (1) If any decision of the tribunal is set aside, varied or altered in any way by order of the Court, the Secretary of the Tribunal shall alter the entry in the records to conform to that order and shall notify the parties accordingly.

(2) If a claim is remitted to the tribunal by order of the Court to be reheard, the Secretary of the Tribunal shall notify both parties that, during a period of 15 working days (or such shorter period as the parties may agree in writing), each may submit a supplementary statement of his case and further written evidence.

(3) If an order to strike out a claim is quashed or set aside by the Court, the Secretary of the Tribunal shall notify the parties—

(*a*) where the case statement period had not expired before the order to strike out took effect—

(*i*) in accordance with regulations 17(1)(*b*)(*iv*) and 17(1)(*c*)(*iii*), that a new case statement period shall be commenced; and

(*ii*) that, within the new case statement period, the parties may submit the documentation referred to in sub-paragraph (*b*) in respect of a statement of case or evidence submitted before the strike out took effect;

(*b*) where sub-paragraph (*a*) does not apply, that each party has a period of 15 working days to submit a supplementary statement of his case and further written evidence.

(4) The Secretary of the Tribunal shall forthwith send a copy of all statements and written evidence received from a party during the periods referred to in paragraphs (2) and (3)(*b*) to the other party.

Irregularities

49. (1) An irregularity resulting from failure to comply with any provision of these Regulations or of any direction of the tribunal before the tribunal has reached its decision shall not of itself render the proceedings void.

(2) Where any such irregularity comes to the attention of the tribunal, the tribunal may, and shall, if it considers that any person may have been prejudiced by the irregularity, give such directions as it thinks just before reaching its decision to cure or to waive the irregularity.

(3) Clerical mistakes in any document recording the decision of the tribunal or a direction or decision of the President produced by or on behalf of the tribunal or errors arising in such documents from accidental slips or omissions may at any time be corrected by the chairman or the President (as the case may be) by certificate under his hand.

(4) The Secretary of the Tribunal shall as soon as may be send a copy of any corrected document containing reasons for the tribunal's decision to each party.

(5) Where a parent has appointed a representative in accordance with regulation 12, the Secretary of the Tribunal shall (notwithstanding regulation 12(4)) send a copy of the document referred to in paragraph (4) above to the parent as well as the representative.

(6) Where these Regulations require the chairman to sign a document, but by reason of death or incapacity he is unable to do so, the other members of the tribunal shall sign it and certify that the chairman is unable to sign.

Method of Sending, Delivering or Serving Notices and Documents

50. (1) A notice given under these Regulations shall be in writing and a party whom the Regulations require to notify a matter to the Secretary of the Tribunal shall do so in writing.

(2) Notices and documents required by these Regulations to be sent or delivered to the Secretary of the Tribunal or to the Tribunal may be sent by post, by facsimile transmission or by electronic mail to or delivered at the office of the Tribunal or such other office as the Secretary of the Tribunal may notify to the parties.

(3) Notices and documents which these Regulations authorise or require the President or the Secretary of the Tribunal to send may (subject to paragraph (5)) either be sent by first class post or by facsimile transmission to or delivered at—

(*a*) in the case of a party—

(*i*) his address for service specified in the notice of claim or in a written reply or in a notice under paragraph (4), or

(*ii*) if no address for service has been so specified his last known address; and

(*b*) in the case of any other person, his place of residence or business or if such person is a corporation, the corporation's registered or principal office.

(4) A party may at any time by notice to the Secretary of the Tribunal change his address for service under these Regulations.

(5) The recorded delivery service shall be used instead of first class post for service of a summons issued under regulation 26 requiring the attendance of a witness.

(6) A notice or document sent by the Secretary of the Tribunal by post in accordance with these Regulations, and not returned, shall be taken to have been delivered to the addressee on the second day for normal postal deliveries after it was posted.

(7) A notice or document sent by facsimile transmission or electronic mail shall be taken to have been delivered when it is received in legible form.

(8) Where for any sufficient reason service of any document or notice cannot be effected in the manner prescribed under this regulation, the President may dispense with service or make an order for substituted service in such manner as he may deem fit and such service shall have the same effect as service in the manner prescribed under this regulation.

Extensions of Time

51. (1) Where these Regulations or a direction made under them requires or authorises a person to do something within a period of time, the President may, on the application of that person or on his own initiative, in exceptional circumstances extend that period of time.

(2) Where the President has extended a period of time reference in these Regulations to that period of time shall be construed as a reference to the period of time as so extended.

Catherine Ashton

Parliamentary Under Secretary of State Department for Education and Skills 24th July 2002

Explanatory Note

(*This note is not part of the Regulations*)

These Regulations contain general provisions relating to the Special Educational Needs and Disability Tribunal (the Tribunal) and also deal with the procedures of the Tribunal for claims of disability discrimination in schools.

The general provisions relate to the exercise of the Tribunal's jurisdiction under Chapter 1 of Part IV of the Disability Discrimination Act 1995 and Part IV of the Education Act 1996. The Regulations make provision for:

(*a*) the appointment of members of the lay panel by the Secretary of State (regulation 3);

(*b*) the establishment of individual tribunals to exercise the jurisdiction of the Tribunal (regulation 4);

(c) the selection of Tribunal members for hearings (regulation 5);
(d) proof of documents (regulation 6).

These Regulations also contain provisions in relation to the making of claims of disability discrimination in schools, under Chapter 1 of Part IV of the Disability Discrimination Act 1995, and with the procedures of the Tribunal for the purpose of determining those claims.

The procedures are set out in Parts II to V of the Regulations and broadly follow, with modification, the Tribunal's procedures for special educational needs appeals under Part IV of the Education Act 1996, which are contained in the Special Educational Needs Tribunal Regulations 2001 (S.I. 2001/600).

Regulation 27 prescribes the circumstances in which a disability discrimination claim may be heard with a special educational needs appeal.

EDUCATION (ADDITIONAL SUPPORT FOR LEARNING) (SCOTLAND) ACT

Contents

1. Main definitions
    1. Additional support needs
    2. Co-ordinated support plans
    3. Children and young persons who lack capacity
2. General powers and duties
    4. Duties of education authority in relation to children and young persons for whom they are responsible
    5. General functions of education authority in relation to additional support needs
3. Establishment of additional support needs and need for co-ordinated support plan
    6. Children and young persons for whom education authority are responsible
    7. Other children and young persons
    8. Assessments and examinations
4. Co-ordinated support plans
    9. Duty to prepare co-ordinated support plans
    10. Reviews of co-ordinated support plans
    11. Co-ordinated support plans: further provision
5. Exchange of information
    12. Duties to seek and take account of views, advice and information
    13. Provision of information etc. on occurrence of certain events
6. Supporters and advocacy
    14. Supporters and advocacy
7. Mediation and dispute resolution
    15. Mediation services
    16. Dispute resolution

8. Appeals
   17. Additional Support Needs Tribunals for Scotland
   18. References to Tribunal in relation to co-ordinated support plan
   19. Powers of Tribunal in relation to reference
   20. References to Tribunal and powers of Tribunal: further provision
   21. Appeal to Court of Session against Tribunal decision
9. Placing requests
   22. Placing requests
10. Miscellaneous
   23. Other agencies etc. to help in exercise of functions under this Act
   24. Power to prescribe standards etc. for special schools
   25. Attendance at establishments outwith the United Kingdom
   26. Publication of information by education authority
   27. Code of practice and directions
11. General
   28. Requests under this Act: further provision
   29. Interpretation
   30. Transitional provision: recorded children and young persons
   31. Duty to inform in writing or alternative permanent form
   32. Ancillary provision
   33. Modification of enactments
   34. Orders, regulations and rules
   35. Commencement and short title
12. 1. Schedule 1
   Additional Support Needs Tribunals for Scotland
   2. Schedule 2
   Children and young persons with additional support needs: placing requests
   3. Schedule 3
   Modification of enactments

The Bill for this Act of the Scottish Parliament was passed by the Parliament on 1st April 2004 and received Royal Assent on 7th May 2004.

An Act of the Scottish Parliament to make provision for additional support in connection with the school education of children and young persons having additional support needs; and for connected purposes.

Main Definitions

1. Additional Support Needs

(1) A child or young person has additional support needs for the purposes of this Act where, for whatever reason, the child or young person is, or is likely to be, unable without the provision of additional support to benefit from school education provided or to be provided for the child or young person.

(2) In sub-section (1), the reference to school education includes, in particular, such education directed to the development of the personality, talents and mental and physical abilities of the child or young person to their fullest potential.

(3) In this Act, "additional support" means—

(*a*) in relation to a prescribed pre-school child, a child of school age or a young person receiving school education, provision which is additional to, or otherwise different from, the educational provision made generally for children or, as the case may be, young persons of the same age in schools (other than special schools) under the management of the education authority for the area to which the child or young person belongs,

(*b*) in relation to a child under school age other than a prescribed pre-school child, such educational provision as is appropriate in the circumstances.

2. *Co-ordinated Support Plans*

(1) For the purposes of this Act, a child or young person requires a plan (referred to in this Act as a "co-ordinated support plan") for the provision of additional support if—

(*a*) an education authority are responsible for the school education of the child or young person,

(*b*) the child or young person has additional support needs arising from—

(*i*) one or more complex factors, or

(*ii*) multiple factors,

(*c*) those needs are likely to continue for more than a year, and

(*d*) those needs require significant additional support to be provided—

(*i*) by the education authority in the exercise of any of their other functions as well as in the exercise of their functions relating to education, or

(*ii*) by one or more appropriate agencies (within the meaning of Section 23(2)) as well as by the education authority themselves.

(2) For the purposes of sub-section (1)—

(*a*) a factor is a complex factor if it has or is likely to have a significant adverse effect on the school education of the child or young person,

(*b*) multiple factors are factors which—

(*i*) are not by themselves complex factors, but

(*ii*) taken together, have or are likely to have a significant adverse effect on the school education of the child or young person.

3. *Children and Young Persons who Lack Capacity*

(1) For the purposes of this Act, a child or young person lacks capacity to do something if the child or young person is incapable of doing it by reason of

mental illness, developmental disorder or learning disability or of inability to communicate because of a physical disability.

(2) However, a child or young person is not to be treated as lacking capacity by reason only of a lack or deficiency in a faculty of communication if that lack or deficiency can be made good by human or mechanical aid (whether of an interpretative nature or otherwise).

General Powers and Duties

4. Duties of Education Authority in Relation to Children and Young Persons for Whom they are Responsible

(1) Every education authority must—
  (*a*) in relation to each child and young person having additional support needs for whose school education the authority are responsible, make adequate and efficient provision for such additional support as is required by that child or young person, and
  (*b*) make appropriate arrangements for keeping under consideration—
    (*i*) the additional support needs of, and
    (*ii*) the adequacy of the additional support provided for, each such child and young person.

(2) Sub-section (1)(*a*) does not require an education authority to do anything which—
  (*a*) they do not otherwise have power to do, or
  (*b*) would result in unreasonable public expenditure being incurred.

5. General Functions of Education Authority in Relation to Additional Support Needs

(1) Every education authority must in exercising any of their functions in connection with the provision of school education, take account of the additional support needs of children and young persons having such needs.

(2) Every education authority must, subject to sub-section (3), provide such additional support as is appropriate for each child—
  (*a*) under school age (other than a prescribed pre-school child),
  (*b*) belonging to the authority's area, and
  (*c*) who has additional support needs arising from a disability (within the meaning of the Disability Discrimination Act 1995 (c. 50)) which the child has.

(3) The duty in sub-section (2) applies only where the authority has established, in pursuance of Section 7(5) of this Act, that the child has the additional support needs referred to in sub-section (2)(*c*) following the child having been brought to the authority's attention as having or appearing to have such needs by a Health Board.

(4) An education authority may provide such additional support as is appropriate for children (other than children to whom the education authority

have a duty under sub-section (2)) and young persons belonging to the area of the authority—

(*a*) having additional support needs, but

(*b*) for whose school education the authority are not responsible.

Establishment of Additional Support Needs and Need for Co-ordinated Support Plan

6. Children and Young Persons for Whom Education Authority are Responsible

(1) Every education authority must make such arrangements as they consider appropriate for identifying—

(*a*) from among the children and young persons for whose school education they are responsible—

(*i*) those who have additional support needs, and

(*ii*) those having additional support needs who require a co-ordinated support plan, and

(*b*) the particular additional support needs of the children and young persons so identified.

(2) Where an education authority receive from a person specified in sub-section (3) a request to establish whether any child or young person for whose school education the authority are responsible—

(*a*) has additional support needs, or

(*b*) requires a co-ordinated support plan,

the authority must, in accordance with the arrangements made by them under sub-section (1), comply with the request unless the request is unreasonable.

(3) The persons referred to in sub-section (2) are—

(*a*) in the case of a child, the child's parent,

(*b*) in the case of a young person—

(*i*) the young person, or

(*ii*) if the authority are satisfied that the young person lacks capacity to make the request, the young person's parent.

(4) Where, in pursuance of a request referred to in sub-section (2), an education authority establish that a child or young person has additional support needs, the authority must inform the person who made the request of that fact.

(5) Sub-section (6) applies where a child or young person for whose school education an education authority are responsible comes to the attention of the authority as—

(*a*) having, or appearing to have, additional support needs, or

(*b*) having such needs and requiring, or appearing to require, a co-ordinated support plan.

(6) Where this sub-section applies, the education authority must, in accordance with the arrangements made by them under sub-section (1), establish whether the child or young person does have additional support needs or, as the case

may be, require a co-ordinated support plan, unless the authority consider it unreasonable to do so.

(7) Sub-sections (2) and (6) are without prejudice to sub-section (1).

7. Other Children and Young Persons

(1) Where an education authority receive a request of a type specified in sub-section (2) relating to any child or young person—
   (*a*) belonging to the area of the authority, but
   (*b*) for whose school education the authority are not responsible,
the authority may, in accordance with the arrangements made by them under Section 6(1), comply with the request.

(2) The types of request referred to in sub-section (1) are—
   (*a*) a request from a person specified in sub-section (3) to establish whether the child or young person in relation to whom the request is made—
      (*i*) has additional support needs, or
      (*ii*) would, if the education authority were responsible for the school education of the child or young person, require a co-ordinated support plan,
   (*b*) in the case of a child or young person being provided with school education at an independent school or a grant-aided school, a request from the managers of the school to establish whether the child or young person would, if the education authority were responsible for the school education of the child or young person, require such a plan.

(3) The persons referred to in sub-section (2)(*a*) are—
   (*a*) in the case of a child, the child's parent,
   (*b*) in the case of a young person—
      (*i*) the young person, or
      (*ii*) if the authority are satisfied that the young person lacks capacity to make the request, the young person's parent.

(4) Sub-section (5) applies where a child or young person—
   (*a*) belonging to the area of an education authority, but
   (*b*) for whose school education an education authority are not responsible,
comes to the attention of the authority (otherwise than as a result of a request referred to in sub-section (1)) as having, or appearing to have, additional support needs.

(5) Where this sub-section applies, the education authority may, in accordance with the arrangements made by them under Section 6(1), establish whether the child or young person does have additional support needs.

(6) Sub-section (7) applies where, in pursuance of this section, an education authority establish that a child or young person—
   (*a*) has additional support needs or
   (*b*) would, if the education authority were responsible for the schoo

education of the child or young person, require a co-ordinated support plan.

(7) Where this sub-section applies, the education authority must provide the persons mentioned in sub-section (8) with such information and advice as to the additional support required by the child or young person as they consider appropriate.

(8) The persons referred to in sub-section (7) are—

(*a*) in the case of a child, the child's parent,

(*b*) in the case of a young person—

(*i*) the young person, or

(*ii*) if the authority are satisfied that the young person lacks capacity to understand the information or advice, the young person's parent,

(*c*) where the authority establish the matter referred to in sub-section (6) pursuant to a request made by the managers of an independent school or a grant-aided school, those managers.

8. *Assessments and Examinations*

(1) Where—

(*a*) an education authority propose—

(*i*) in pursuance of any provision of this Act, to establish whether a child or young person has additional support needs or requires, or would require, a co-ordinated support plan, or

(*ii*) to review under Section 10 any such plan prepared for any child or young person, and

(*b*) the appropriate person makes a request that the education authority arrange for the child or young person to whom the proposal referred to in paragraph (*a*) relates to undergo, for the purposes of the proposal, a process of assessment or examination (such a request being referred to in this section as an "assessment request"),

the education authority must comply with the assessment request unless the request is unreasonable.

(2) In sub-section (1)(*b*), "the appropriate person" means—

(*a*) where the proposal referred to in sub-section (1)(*a*) arises from a request referred to in Sections 6(2), 7(1) or 10(4), the person making the request,

(*b*) in any other case—

(*i*) where the proposal relates to a child, the child's parent,

(*ii*) where the proposal relates to a young person, the young person or, where the authority are satisfied that the young person lacks capacity to make the request, the young person's parent.

(3) Where a child or young person is to undergo a process of assessment or examination in pursuance of an assessment request, the process is to be carried out by such person as the education authority consider appropriate.

(4) In sub-section (1)(*b*), the reference to assessment or examination includes educational, psychological or medical assessment or examination.

Co-ordinated Support Plans

9. Duty to Prepare Co-ordinated Support Plans

(1) Where an education authority establish in pursuance of any provision of this Act that a child or young person for whose school education they are responsible requires a co-ordinated support plan, they must prepare such a plan for the child or young person.

(2) A co-ordinated support plan prepared under sub-section (1) must contain—

(*a*) a statement of the education authority's conclusions as to—

(*i*) the factor or factors from which the additional support needs of the child or young person arise,

(*ii*) the educational objectives sought to be achieved taking account of that factor or those factors,

(*iii*) the additional support required by the child or young person to achieve those objectives, and

(*iv*) the persons by whom the support should be provided,

(*b*) a nomination of a school to be attended by the child or young person,

(*c*) the name and other appropriate contact details of—

(*i*) the officer of the authority responsible for the discharge of the authority's duty under sub-section (5)(*d*) of Section 11, or

(*ii*) if the authority arrange under sub-section (6) of that section for that duty to be discharged by another person, that other person, and

(*d*) the name and other appropriate contact details of an officer of the authority from whom—

(*i*) in the case of a plan prepared for a child, the child's parent, Modification of enactments

(*ii*) in the case of a plan prepared for a young person, the young person or, where the authority are satisfied that the young person lacks capacity to seek advice or information, the young person's parent, can obtain advice and further information.

(3) The references in sub-section (2)(*a*) to educational objectives are to objectives set to secure that the child or young person benefits from school education (within the meaning of Section 1(1)) provided or to be provided for the child or young person.

10. Reviews of Co-ordinated Support Plans

(1) Every education authority must keep under consideration the adequacy of any co-ordinated support plans prepared (and not discontinued) for any children or young persons belonging to their area.

(2) The education authority must carry out a review of each such co-ordinated support plan—

(*a*) on the expiry of the period of 12 months beginning with the date on which the plan was prepared, and

(b) thereafter, on the expiry of each successive period of 12 months beginning with the date on which the previous review (whether carried out under this sub-section or sub-section (3) or (4)) of the plan was completed.

(3) An education authority may carry out a review of such a co-ordinated support plan before the expiry of a period referred to in sub-section (2) only—

(a) pursuant to a request referred to in sub-section (4), or

(b) if the authority consider it necessary or expedient to do so because of a significant change in the circumstances of the child or young person for whom the plan was prepared since the plan was prepared or, as the case may be, last reviewed.

(4) Where the education authority receive from a person specified in sub-section (5) a request to carry out a review of any such co-ordinated support plan as is mentioned in sub-section (1) before the expiry of a period referred to in sub-section (2), the authority must carry out a review of the plan unless the request is unreasonable.

(5) The persons referred to in sub-section (4) are—

(a) in the case of a co-ordinated support plan prepared for a child, the child's parent,

(b) in the case of a co-ordinated support plan prepared for a young person—

(i) the young person, or

(ii) where the education authority are satisfied that the young person lacks capacity to make the request, the young person's parent.

(6) In reviewing any co-ordinated support plan under this section, the education authority must, in accordance with the arrangements made by them under Section 6(1), establish whether the child or young person for whom the plan was prepared still requires such a plan and—

(a) if so, continue the plan for the child or young person and make such amendments of it as the authority consider necessary or appropriate, or

(b) if not, discontinue the plan.

11. Co-ordinated Support Plans: Further Provision

(1) Sub-section (2) applies where an education authority propose—

(a) in pursuance of any provision of this Act, to establish whether any child or young person requires, or would require, a co-ordinated support plan,

(b) to review under Section 10 any such plan prepared for any child or young person.

(2) Where this sub-section applies, the education authority must—

(a) before proceeding, inform the persons mentioned in sub-section (3) of their proposal, and

(b) on establishing the matter referred to in sub-section (1)(a) or, as the case may be, completing the review referred to in sub-section (1)(*b*), inform those persons of—

(*i*) the outcome, and

(*ii*) the rights (if any) which they have under Section 18(1) to make a reference to a Tribunal in connection with the outcome.

(3) The persons referred to in sub-section (2)(*a*) are—

(*a*) in the case of a child, the child's parent,

(*b*) in the case of a young person—

(*i*) the young person, or

(*ii*) if the authority are satisfied that the young person lacks capacity to understand the information, the young person's parent,

(*c*) where the proposal arises as a result of a request referred to in Section 7(1) made by the managers of an independent school or a grant-aided school, those managers.

(4) Sub-section (5) applies where an education authority—

(*a*) prepare a co-ordinated support plan for any child or young person under this Act, or

(*b*) amend any such plan—

(*i*) following a review carried out under Section 10, or

(*ii*) pursuant to a requirement made by a Tribunal under sub-section (4)(*b*) or (5)(*b*)(*ii*) of Section 19.

(5) Where this sub-section applies, the education authority must—

(*a*) give a copy of the plan or amended plan—

(*i*) in the case of a child, to the child's parent,

(*ii*) in the case of a young person, to that young person or, if the authority are satisfied that the young person lacks capacity to understand the plan, to the young person's parent,

(*b*) ensure that additional support is provided by them for the child or young person in accordance with the plan or amended plan so far as they have power to do so,

(*c*) seek to ensure that additional support is provided for the child or young person in accordance with the plan or amended plan by any person (other than the education authority) identified in the plan as a person by whom such support should be provided,

(*d*) co-ordinate, so far as possible, the provision of additional support for the child or young person as mentioned in paragraphs (*b*) and (*c*) by the authority and any other persons by whom such support is to be provided, and

(*e*) inform such persons as they consider appropriate, being persons who will be involved in the provision of additional support for the child or young person, of such matters contained in the plan or amended plan as they consider appropriate.

(6) The education authority may arrange for the discharge of their duty under sub-section (5)(*d*) by another person.

(7) Sub-section (6)—

(*a*) does not affect the responsibility of the education authority for the discharge of their duty under sub-section (5)(*d*), and

(*b*) is without prejudice to any other power of the education authority to arrange for the discharge of any of their functions under this Act by another person.

(8) The Scottish Ministers may by regulations make further provision as to co-ordinated support plans including, in particular, provision as to—

(*a*) the form of such plans,

(*b*) the information (in addition to that required by Section 9(2)) to be contained in them,

(*c*) the preparation, keeping, disclosure, discontinuance and destruction of such plans,

(*d*) the procedures to be followed in carrying out reviews of such plans under Section 10,

(*e*) the transfer of such plans when the children and young persons for whom they are prepared move from the area of one education authority to that of another,

(*f*) without prejudice to the generality of the other paragraphs in this sub-section, the times by which—

(*i*) such plans are to be prepared, and

(*ii*) reviews of them under Section 10 are to be completed, and

(*g*) such other matters in relation to co-ordinated support plans as the Scottish Ministers think necessary or expedient.

RELATED TO SEN ORIENTED TRIBUNALS AND INQUIRIES IN ENGLAND AND WALES

The Tribunal Procedure (First-tier Tribunal) (Health, Education and Social Care Chamber) Rules 2008 (No. 2699 (L. 16))

Contents

Go to Preamble

1. PART 1

Introduction

1. Citation, commencement, application and interpretation
2. Overriding objective and parties' obligation to co-operate with the Tribunal
3. Alternative dispute resolution and arbitration

2. PART 2

General Powers and Provisions

4. Delegation to staff
5. Case management powers
6. Procedure for applying for and giving directions

7. Failure to comply with rules etc.
8. Striking out a party's case
9. Substitution and addition of parties
10. Orders for costs
11. Representatives
12. Calculating time
13. Sending and delivery of documents
14. Use of documents and information
15. Evidence and submissions
16. Summoning of witnesses and orders to answer questions or produce documents
17. Withdrawal

3. PART 3

Proceedings Before the Tribunal other than in Mental Health Cases

1. CHAPTER 1

Before the Hearing

18. Application of Part 3
19. Application for leave
20. The application notice
21. The response
22. Order that a school be regarded as not registered pending determination of an appeal

2. CHAPTER 2

Hearings

23. Decision with or without a hearing
24. Entitlement to attend a hearing
25. Notice of hearings
26. Public and private hearings
27. Hearings in a party's absence
28. Power to pay allowances

3. CHAPTER 3

Decisions

29. Consent orders
30. Decisions

4. PART 4

Proceedings Before the Tribunal in Mental Health Cases

1. CHAPTER 1

Before the Hearing

31. Application of Part 4
32. Procedure in mental health cases
33. Notice of proceedings to interested persons
34. Medical examination of the patient

2. CHAPTER 2

Hearings

35. No disposal of proceedings without a hearing
36. Entitlement to attend a hearing
37. Time and place of hearings
38. Public and private hearings
39. Hearings in a party's absence
40. Power to pay allowances

3. CHAPTER 3

Decisions

41. Decisions
42. Provisional decisions

5. PART 5

Correcting, Setting Aside, Reviewing and Appealing Tribunal Decisions

43. Interpretation
44. Clerical mistakes and accidental slips or omissions
45. Setting aside a decision which disposes of proceedings
46. Application for permission to appeal
47. Tribunal's consideration of application for permission to appeal
48. Application for review in special educational needs cases
49. Review of a decision
50. Power to treat an application as a different type of application

6. SCHEDULE

Time Limits for Providing Application Notices and Responses—

Go to Explanatory Note

After consulting in accordance with paragraph 28(1) of Schedule 5 to the Tribunals, Courts and Enforcement Act 2007, the Tribunal Procedure Committee has made the following Rules in exercise of the power conferred by Sections 9(3), 22 and 29(3) and (4) of, and Schedule 5 to, that Act.

The Lord Chancellor has allowed the Rules in accordance with paragraph 28(3) of Schedule 5 to the Tribunals, Courts and Enforcement Act 2007.

Supplementary Menus and Contents

Legislation Views

- Plain Version
- Single Page Version
- Print Version (PDF 130 kb)
- Why keep printing? Go green. Buy your official copy...

Related Pages

- Explanatory Memorandum (PDF 104 kb)
- Correction Slip (PDF 8 kb)
- Copyright Guidance Note on the Re-Use of Legislation

Feeds

- Feed icon The Tribunal Procedure (First-tier Tribunal) (Health, Education and Social Care Chamber) Rules 2008
- Feed icon Tribunals and Inquiries, England and Wales
- Feed icon UK Statutory Instruments

PART 1: Introduction

Citation, Commencement, Application and Interpretation

1. (1) These Rules may be cited as the Tribunal Procedure (First-tier Tribunal) (Health, Education and Social Care Chamber) Rules 2008 and come into force on 3rd November 2008.

(2) These Rules apply to proceedings before the Tribunal which have been assigned to the Health, Education and Social Care Chamber by the First-tier Tribunal and Upper Tribunal (Chambers) Order 2008.

(3) In these Rules—

"the 2007 Act" means the Tribunals, Courts and Enforcement Act 2007;

"applicant" means a person who—

(*a*) starts Tribunal proceedings, whether by making an application, an appeal, a claim or a reference;

(*b*) makes an application to the Tribunal for leave to start such proceedings; or

(*c*) is substituted as an applicant under rule 9(1) (substitution and addition of parties);

"childcare provider" means a person who is a childminder or provides day care as defined in Section 79A of the Children Act 1989, or a person who provides childcare as defined in Section 18 of the Childcare Act 2006;

"disability discrimination in schools case" means proceedings concerning disability discrimination in the education of a child or related matters;

"dispose of proceedings" includes, unless indicated otherwise, disposing of a part of the proceedings;

"document" means anything in which information is recorded in any form, and an obligation under these Rules or any practice direction or direction to provide or allow access to a document or a copy of a document for any purpose means, unless the Tribunal directs otherwise, an obligation to provide or allow access to such document or copy in a legible form or in a form which can be readily made into a legible form;

"Health, Education and Social Care Chamber" means the Health, Education and Social Care Chamber of the First-tier Tribunal established by the First-tier Tribunal and Upper Tribunal (Chambers) Order 2008;

"hearing" means an oral hearing and includes a hearing conducted in whole or in part by video link, telephone or other means of instantaneous two-way electronic communication;

"legal representative" means an authorised advocate or authorised litigator as defined by Section 119(1) of the Courts and Legal Services Act 1990;

"mental health case" means proceedings brought under the Mental Health Act 1983 or paragraph 5(2) of the Schedule to the Repatriation of Prisoners Act 1984;

"nearest relative" has the meaning set out in Section 26 of the Mental Health Act 1983;

"party" means—

(*a*) in a mental health case, the patient, the responsible authority, the Secretary of State (if the patient is a restricted patient or in a reference under rule 32(8) (seeking approval under Section 86 of the Mental Health Act 1983)), and any other person who starts a mental health case by making an application;

(*b*) in any other case, a person who is an applicant or respondent in proceedings before the Tribunal or, if the proceedings have been concluded, a person who was an applicant or respondent when the Tribunal finally disposed of all issues in the proceedings;

"patient" means the person who is the subject of a mental health case;
"practice direction" means a direction given under Section 23 of the 2007 Act;
"respondent" means—

(*a*) in an appeal against an order made by a justice of the peace under Section 79K of the Children Act 1989, Section 20 of the Care Standards Act 2000 or Section 72 of the Childcare Act 2006, the person who applied to the justice of the peace for the order;
(*b*) in an appeal against any other decision, the person who made the decision;
(*c*) in proceedings on a claim under Section 28I of the Disability Discrimination Act 1995, the body responsible for the school as determined in accordance with paragraph 1 of Schedule 4A to that Act or, if the claim concerns the residual duties of a local education authority under Section 28F of that Act, that local education authority;
(*d*) in proceedings on an application under Section 4(2) of the Protection of Children Act 1999 or Section 86(2) of the Care Standards Act 2000, the Secretary of State; or
(*e*) a person substituted or added as a respondent under rule 9 (substitution and addition of parties);

"responsible authority" means—

(*a*) in relation to a patient detained under the Mental Health Act 1983 in a hospital within the meaning of Part 2 of that Act, the managers (as defined in Section 145 of that Act);
(*b*) in relation to a patient subject to guardianship, the responsible local social services authority (as defined in Section 34(3) of the Mental Health Act 1983);
(*c*) in relation to a community patient, the managers of the responsible hospital (as defined in Section 145 of the Mental Health Act 1983);
(*d*) in relation to a patient subject to after-care under supervision, the Primary Care Trust or Local Health Board which has the duty to provide after-care for the patient.

"restricted patient" has the meaning set out in Section 79(1) of the Mental Health Act 1983;

"special educational needs case" means proceedings concerning the education of a child who has or may have special educational needs;

"Suspension Regulations" means regulations which provide for a right of appeal against a decision to suspend, or not to lift the suspension of, a person's registration as a childcare provider;

"Tribunal" means the First-tier Tribunal;

"working day" means any day except a Saturday or Sunday, Christmas Day, Good Friday or a bank holiday under section 1 of the Banking and Financial Dealings Act 1971.

Overriding Objective and Parties' Obligation to Co-operate with the Tribunal

2. (1) The overriding objective of these Rules is to enable the Tribunal to deal with cases fairly and justly.
   (2) Dealing with a case fairly and justly includes—
      (*a*) dealing with the case in ways which are proportionate to the importance of the case, the complexity of the issues, the anticipated costs and the resources of the parties;
      (*b*) avoiding unnecessary formality and seeking flexibility in the proceedings;
      (*c*) ensuring, so far as practicable, that the parties are able to participate fully in the proceedings;
      (*d*) using any special expertise of the Tribunal effectively; and
      (*e*) avoiding delay, so far as compatible with proper consideration of the issues.
   (3) The Tribunal must seek to give effect to the overriding objective when it—
      (*a*) exercises any power under these Rules; or
      (*b*) interprets any rule or practice direction.
   (4) Parties must—
      (*a*) help the Tribunal to further the overriding objective; and
      (*b*) co-operate with the Tribunal generally.

Alternative Dispute Resolution and Arbitration

3. (1) The Tribunal should seek, where appropriate—
      (*a*) to bring to the attention of the parties the availability of any appropriate alternative procedure for the resolution of the dispute; and
      (*b*) if the parties wish and provided that it is compatible with the overriding objective, to facilitate the use of the procedure.
   (2) Part 1 of the Arbitration Act 1996 does not apply to proceedings before the Tribunal.

PART 2: General Powers and Provisions

Delegation to Staff

4. (1) Staff appointed under Section 40(1) of the 2007 Act (tribunal staff and services) may, with the approval of the Senior President of Tribunals, carry out functions of a judicial nature permitted or required to be done by the Tribunal.
   (2) The approval referred to at paragraph (1) may apply generally to the carrying out of specified functions by members of staff of a specified description in specified circumstances.

(3) Within 14 days after the date on which the Tribunal sends notice of a decision made by a member of staff under paragraph (1) to a party, that party may apply in writing to the Tribunal for that decision to be considered afresh by a judge.

Case Management Powers

5. (1) Subject to the provisions of the 2007 Act and any other enactment, the Tribunal may regulate its own procedure.

(2) The Tribunal may give a direction in relation to the conduct or disposal of proceedings at any time, including a direction amending, suspending or setting aside an earlier direction.

(3) In particular, and without restricting the general powers in paragraphs (1) and (2), the Tribunal may—

(*a*) extend or shorten the time for complying with any rule, practice direction or direction, unless such extension or shortening would conflict with a provision of another enactment containing a time limit;

(*b*) consolidate or hear together two or more sets of proceedings or parts of proceedings raising common issues, or treat a case as a lead case;

(*c*) permit or require a party to amend a document;

(*d*) permit or require a party or another person to provide documents, information or submissions to the Tribunal or a party;

(*e*) deal with an issue in the proceedings as a preliminary issue;

(*f*) hold a hearing to consider any matter, including a case management issue;

(*g*) decide the form of any hearing;

(*h*) adjourn or postpone a hearing;

(*i*) require a party to produce a bundle for a hearing;

(*j*) stay proceedings;

(*k*) transfer proceedings to another court or tribunal if that other court or tribunal has jurisdiction in relation to the proceedings and—

(*i*) because of a change of circumstances since the proceedings were started, the Tribunal no longer has jurisdiction in relation to the proceedings; or

(*ii*) the Tribunal considers that the other court or tribunal is a more appropriate forum for the determination of the case; or

(*l*) suspend the effect of its own decision pending the determination by the Tribunal or the Upper Tribunal of an application for permission to appeal against, and any appeal or review of, that decision.

Procedure for Applying for and Giving Directions

6. (1) The Tribunal may give a direction on the application of one or more of the parties or on its own initiative.

(2) An application for a direction may be made—
(*a*) by sending or delivering a written application to the Tribunal; or
(*b*) orally during the course of a hearing.

(3) An application for a direction must include the reason for making that application.

(4) Unless the Tribunal considers that there is good reason not to do so, the Tribunal must send written notice of any direction to every party and to any other person affected by the direction.

(5) If a party, or any other person given notice of the direction under paragraph (4), wishes to challenge a direction which the Tribunal has given, they may do so by applying for another direction which amends, suspends or sets aside the first direction.

Failure to Comply with Rules etc.

7. (1) An irregularity resulting from a failure to comply with any requirement in these Rules, a practice direction or a direction, does not of itself render void the proceedings or any step taken in the proceedings.

(2) If a party has failed to comply with a requirement in these Rules, a practice direction or a direction, the Tribunal may take such action as it considers just, which may include—
(*a*) waiving the requirement;
(*b*) requiring the failure to be remedied;
(*c*) exercising its power under rule 8 (striking out a party's case);
(*d*) exercising its power under paragraph (3); or
(*e*) except in mental health cases, restricting a party's participation in the proceedings.

(3) The Tribunal may refer to the Upper Tribunal, and ask the Upper Tribunal to exercise its power under Section 25 of the 2007 Act in relation to, any failure by a person to comply with a requirement imposed by the Tribunal—
(*a*) to attend at any place for the purpose of giving evidence;
(*b*) otherwise to make themselves available to give evidence;
(*c*) to swear an oath in connection with the giving of evidence;
(*d*) to give evidence as a witness;
(*e*) to produce a document; or
(*f*) to facilitate the inspection of a document or any other thing (including any premises).

Striking Out a Party's Case

8. (1) With the exception of paragraph (3), this rule does not apply to mental health cases.

(2) The proceedings, or the appropriate part of them, will automatically be

struck out if the applicant has failed to comply with a direction that stated that failure by the applicant to comply with the direction would lead to the striking out of the proceedings or that part of them.

(3) The Tribunal must strike out the whole or a part of the proceedings if the Tribunal—

(*a*) does not have jurisdiction in relation to the proceedings or that part of them; and

(*b*) does not exercise its power under rule 5(3)(*k*)(*i*) (transfer to another court or tribunal) in relation to the proceedings or that part of them.

(4) The Tribunal may strike out the whole or a part of the proceedings if—

(*a*) the applicant has failed to comply with a direction which stated that failure by the applicant to comply with the direction could lead to the striking out of the proceedings or part of them;

(*b*) the applicant has failed to co-operate with the Tribunal to such an extent that the Tribunal cannot deal with the proceedings fairly and justly; or

(*c*) the Tribunal considers there is no reasonable prospect of the applicant's case, or part of it, succeeding.

(5) The Tribunal may not strike out the whole or a part of the proceedings under paragraph (3) or (4)(*b*) or (*c*) without first giving the applicant an opportunity to make representations in relation to the proposed striking out.

(6) If the proceedings, or part of them, have been struck out under paragraph (2) or (4)(*a*), the applicant may apply for the proceedings, or part of them, to be reinstated.

(7) An application under paragraph (6) must be made in writing and received by the Tribunal within 28 days after the date on which the Tribunal sent notification of the striking out to that party.

(8) This rule applies to a respondent as it applies to an applicant except that—

(*a*) a reference to the striking out of the proceedings is to be read as a reference to the barring of the respondent from taking further part in the proceedings; and

(*b*) a reference to an application for the reinstatement of proceedings which have been struck out is to be read as a reference to an application for the lifting of the bar on the respondent from taking further part in the proceedings.

(9) If a respondent has been barred from taking further part in proceedings under this rule and that bar has not been lifted, the Tribunal need not consider any response or other submission made by that respondent.

Substitution and Addition of Parties

9. (1) The Tribunal may give a direction substituting a party if—

(*a*) the wrong person has been named as a party; or
(*b*) the substitution has become necessary because of a change in circumstances since the start of proceedings.

(2) The Tribunal may give a direction adding a person to the proceedings as a respondent.

(3) If the Tribunal gives a direction under paragraph (1) or (2) it may give such consequential directions as it considers appropriate.

Orders for Costs

10. (1) Subject to paragraph (2), the Tribunal may make an order in respect of costs only—
(*a*) under Section 29(4) of the 2007 Act (wasted costs); or
(*b*) if the Tribunal considers that a party or its representative has acted unreasonably in bringing, defending or conducting the proceedings.

(2) The Tribunal may not make an order under paragraph (1)(*b*) in mental health cases.

(3) The Tribunal may make an order in respect of costs on an application or on its own initiative.

(4) A person making an application for an order under this rule must—
(*a*) send or deliver a written application to the Tribunal and to the person against whom it is proposed that the order be made; and
(*b*) send or deliver a schedule of the costs claimed with the application.

(5) An application for an order under paragraph (1) may be made at any time during the proceedings but may not be made later than 14 days after the date on which the Tribunal sends the decision notice recording the decision which finally disposes of all issues in the proceedings.

(6) The Tribunal may not make an order under paragraph (1) against a person (the "paying person") without first—
(*a*) giving that person an opportunity to make representations; and
(*b*) if the paying person is an individual, considering that person's financial means.

(7) The amount of costs to be paid under an order under paragraph (1) may be ascertained by—
(*a*) summary assessment by the Tribunal;
(*b*) agreement of a specified sum by the paying person and the person entitled to receive the costs ("the receiving person"); or
(*c*) assessment of the whole or a specified part of the costs incurred by the receiving person, if not agreed.

(8) Following an order for assessment under paragraph (7)(*c*), the paying person or the receiving person may apply to a county court for a detailed assessment of costs in accordance with the Civil Procedure Rules 1998

on the standard basis or, if specified in the order, on the indemnity basis.

Representatives

11. (1) A party may appoint a representative (whether a legal representative or not) to represent that party in the proceedings.

(2) If a party appoints a representative, that party (or the representative if the representative is a legal representative) must send or deliver to the Tribunal and to each other party written notice of the representative's name and address.

(3) Anything permitted or required to be done by a party under these Rules, a practice direction or a direction may be done by the representative of that party, except—

(*a*) signing a witness statement; or

(*b*) signing an application notice under rule 20 (the application notice) if the representative is not a legal representative.

(4) A person who receives due notice of the appointment of a representative—

(*a*) must provide to the representative any document which is required to be provided to the represented party, and need not provide that document to the represented party; and

(*b*) may assume that the representative is and remains authorised as such until they receive written notification that this is not so from the representative or the represented party.

(5) At a hearing a party may be accompanied by another person whose name and address has not been notified under paragraph (2) but who, subject to paragraph (8) and with the permission of the Tribunal, may act as a representative or otherwise assist in presenting the party's case at the hearing.

(6) Paragraphs (2) to (4) do not apply to a person who accompanies a party under paragraph (5).

(7) In a mental health case, if the patient has not appointed a representative, the Tribunal may appoint a legal representative for the patient where—

(*a*) the patient has stated that they do not wish to conduct their own case or that they wish to be represented; or

(*b*) the patient lacks the capacity to appoint a representative but the Tribunal believes that it is in the patient's best interests for the patient to be represented.

(8) In a mental health case a party may not appoint as a representative, or be represented or assisted at a hearing by—

(*a*) a person liable to be detained or subject to guardianship or after-care under supervision, or who is a community patient, under the Mental Health Act 1983; or (*b*) a person receiving treatment for mental disorder at the same hospital as the patient.

Calculating Time

12. (1) An act required by these Rules, a practice direction or a direction to be done on or by a particular day must be done by 5 pm on that day.

(2) If the time specified by these Rules, a practice direction or a direction for doing any act ends on a day other than a working day, the act is done in time if it is done on the next working day.

(3) In a special educational needs case or a disability discrimination in schools case—

(*a*) if the time for starting proceedings by providing the application notice to the Tribunal under rule 20 (the application notice) ends on a day from 25th December to 1st January inclusive, or on any day in August, the application notice is provided in time if it is provided to the Tribunal on the first working day after 1st January or 31st August, as appropriate; and

(*b*) the days from 25th December to 1st January inclusive and any day in August must not be counted when calculating the time by which any other act must be done.

(4) Paragraph (3)(*b*) does not apply where the Tribunal directs that an act must be done by or on a specified date.

Sending and Delivery of Documents

13. (1) Any document to be provided to the Tribunal under these Rules, a practice direction or a direction must be—

(*a*) sent by pre-paid post or delivered by hand to the address specified for the proceedings;

(*b*) sent by fax to the number specified for the proceedings; or

(*c*) sent or delivered by such other method as the Tribunal may permit or direct.

(2) Subject to paragraph (3), if a party provides a fax number, email address or other details for the electronic transmission of documents to them, that party must accept delivery of documents by that method.

(3) If a party informs the Tribunal and all other parties that a particular form of communication, other than pre-paid post or delivery by hand, should not be used to provide documents to that party, that form of communication must not be so used.

(4) If the Tribunal or a party sends a document to a party or the Tribunal by email or any other electronic means of communication, the recipient may request that the sender provide a hard copy of the document to the recipient. The recipient must make such a request as soon as reasonably practicable after receiving the document electronically.

(5) The Tribunal and each party may assume that the address provided by a party or its representative is and remains the address to which documents should be sent or delivered until receiving written notification to the contrary.

Use of Documents and Information

14. (1) The Tribunal may make an order prohibiting the disclosure or publication of—
   (*a*) specified documents or information relating to the proceedings; or
   (*b*) any matter likely to lead members of the public to identify any person whom the Tribunal considers should not be identified.

(2) The Tribunal may give a direction prohibiting the disclosure of a document or information to a person if—
   (*a*) the Tribunal is satisfied that such disclosure would be likely to cause that person or some other person serious harm; and
   (*b*) the Tribunal is satisfied, having regard to the interests of justice, that it is proportionate to give such a direction.

(3) If a party ("the first party") considers that the Tribunal should give a direction under paragraph (2) prohibiting the disclosure of a document or information to another party ("the second party"), the first party must—
   (*a*) exclude the relevant document or information from any documents that will be provided to the second party; and
   (*b*) provide to the Tribunal the excluded document or information, and the reason for its exclusion, so that the Tribunal may decide whether the document or information should be disclosed to the second party or should be the subject of a direction under paragraph (2).

(4) The Tribunal must conduct proceedings as appropriate in order to give effect to a direction given under paragraph (2).

(5) If the Tribunal gives a direction under paragraph (2) which prevents disclosure to a party who has appointed a representative, the Tribunal may give a direction that the documents or information be disclosed to that representative if the Tribunal is satisfied that—
   (*a*) disclosure to the representative would be in the interests of the party; and
   (*b*) the representative will act in accordance with paragraph (6).

(6) Documents or information disclosed to a representative in accordance with a direction under paragraph (5) must not be disclosed either directly or indirectly to any other person without the Tribunal's consent.

(7) Unless the Tribunal gives a direction to the contrary, information about mental health cases and the names of any persons concerned in such cases must not be made public.

Evidence and Submissions

15. (1) Without restriction on the general powers in rule 5(1) and (2) (case management powers), the Tribunal may give directions as to—
   (*a*) issues on which it requires evidence or submissions;
   (*b*) the nature of the evidence or submissions it requires;
   (*c*) whether the parties are permitted or required to provide expert evidence, and if so whether the parties must jointly appoint a single expert to provide such evidence;
   (*d*) any limit on the number of witnesses whose evidence a party may put forward, whether in relation to a particular issue or generally;
   (*e*) the manner in which any evidence or submissions are to be provided, which may include a direction for them to be given—
      (*i*) orally at a hearing; or
      (*ii*) by written submissions or witness statement; and
   (*f*) the time at which any evidence or submissions are to be provided.

(2) The Tribunal may—
   (*a*) admit evidence whether or not—
      (*i*) the evidence would be admissible in a civil trial in England and Wales; or
      (*ii*) the evidence was available to a previous decision maker; or
   (*b*) exclude evidence that would otherwise be admissible where—
      (*i*) the evidence was not provided within the time allowed by a direction or a practice direction;
      (*ii*) the evidence was otherwise provided in a manner that did not comply with a direction or a practice direction; or
      (*iii*) it would otherwise be unfair to admit the evidence.

(3) The Tribunal may consent to a witness giving, or require any witness to give, evidence on oath, and may administer an oath for that purpose.

(4) In a special educational needs case the Tribunal may require—
   (*a*) the parents of the child, or any other person with care of the child or parental responsibility for the child (as defined in Section 3 of the Children Act 1989), to make the child available for examination or assessment by a suitably qualified professional person; or
   (*b*) the person responsible for a school or educational setting to allow a suitably qualified professional person to have access to the school or educational setting for the purpose of assessing the child or the provision made, or to be made, for the child.

(5) The Tribunal may consider a failure by a party to comply with a requirement made under paragraph (4), in the absence of any good reason for such failure, as a failure to co-operate with the Tribunal, which could lead to a result which is adverse to that party's case.

Summoning of Witnesses and Orders to Answer Questions or Produce Documents

16. (1) On the application of a party or on its own initiative, the Tribunal may—

(*a*) by summons require any person to attend as a witness at a hearing at the time and place specified in the summons; or
(*b*) order any person to answer any questions or produce any documents in that person's possession or control which relate to any issue in the proceedings.

(2) A summons under paragraph (1)(*a*) must—
(*a*) give the person required to attend 14 days' notice of the hearing, or such shorter period as the Tribunal may direct; and
(*b*) where the person is not a party, make provision for the person's necessary expenses of attendance to be paid, and state who is to pay them.

(3) No person may be compelled to give any evidence or produce any document that the person could not be compelled to give or produce on a trial of an action in a court of law.

(4) A summons or order under this rule must—
(*a*) state that the person on whom the requirement is imposed may apply to the Tribunal to vary or set aside the summons or order, if they have not had an opportunity to object to it; and
(*b*) state the consequences of failure to comply with the summons or order.

Withdrawal

17\. (1) Subject to paragraphs (2) and (3), a party may give notice of the withdrawal of its case, or any part of it—
(*a*) at any time before a hearing to consider the disposal of the proceedings (or, if the Tribunal disposes of the proceedings without a hearing, before that disposal), by sending or delivering to the Tribunal a written notice of withdrawal; or
(*b*) orally at a hearing.

(2) Notice of withdrawal will not take effect unless the Tribunal consents to the withdrawal except—
(*a*) in proceedings concerning the suitability of a person to work with children or vulnerable adults; or
(*b*) in proceedings started by a reference under Section 67 or 71(1) of the Mental Health Act 1983.

(3) A party which started a mental health case by making a reference to the Tribunal under Section 68, 71(2) or 75(1) of the Mental Health Act 1983 may not withdraw its case.

(4) A party which has withdrawn its case may apply to the Tribunal for the case to be reinstated.

(5) An application under paragraph (4) must be made in writing and be received by the Tribunal within 28 days after—

(*a*) the date on which the Tribunal received the notice under paragraph (1)(*a*); or

(*b*) the date of the hearing at which the case was withdrawn orally under paragraph (1)(*b*).

(6) The Tribunal must notify each party in writing of a withdrawal under this rule.

PART 3: Proceedings Before the tribunal other than in Mental Health Cases

Chapter 1: Before the Hearing

Application of Part 3

18. This Part does not apply to mental health cases.

Application for Leave

19. (1) This rule applies to applications for leave to bring proceedings under—

(*a*) Section 4(1)(*b*) of the Protection of Children Act 1999 (appeal against a decision not to remove the applicant from the list kept under Section 1 of that Act);

(*b*) Section 4(2) of the Protection of Children Act 1999 (application to have the issue of the applicant's inclusion in the list kept under Section 1 of that Act determined by the Tribunal);

(*c*) Section 86(1)(*b*) of the Care Standards Act 2000 (appeal against a decision not to remove the applicant from the list kept under Section 81 of that Act);

(*d*) Section 86(2) of the Care Standards Act 2000 (application to have the issue of the applicant's inclusion in the list kept under Section 81 of that Act determined by the Tribunal); and

(*e*) Section 32 of the Criminal Justice and Court Services Act 2000 (application to have the issue of the continuation of a disqualification order determined by the Tribunal).

(2) An application to the Tribunal for leave must—

(*a*) give full reasons why the applicant considers that the Tribunal should give leave; and

(*b*) comply with paragraphs (1) to (4) of rule 20 (the application notice) as if the application for leave were an application notice.

(3) The Tribunal may make any directions it considers appropriate before determining the application for leave.

(4) The Tribunal must—

(*a*) notify the applicant of its decision in relation to the application for leave; and

(*b*) if it gives leave, give directions as to the future conduct of the proceedings.

The Application Notice

20. (1) If rule 19 (application for leave) does not apply, an applicant must start proceedings before the Tribunal by sending or delivering an application notice to the Tribunal so that it is received—
   (*a*) if a time for providing the application notice is specified in the Schedule to these Rules (time limits for providing application notices and responses), within that time; or
   (*b*) otherwise, within 28 days after notice of the act or decision to which the proceedings relate was sent to the applicant.

(2) The application notice must be signed by the applicant and must include—
   (*a*) the name and address of the applicant;
   (*b*) the name and address of the applicant's representative (if any);
   (*c*) an address where documents for the applicant may be sent or delivered;
   (*d*) the name and address of any respondent;
   (*e*) details of the decision or act, or failure to decide or act, to which the proceedings relate;
   (*f*) the result the applicant is seeking;
   (*g*) the grounds on which the applicant relies; and
   (*h*) any further information or documents required by an applicable practice direction.

(3) The applicant must send with the application notice a copy of any written record of any decision under challenge, and any statement of reasons for that decision that the applicant has or can reasonably obtain.

(4) If the applicant provides the application notice to the Tribunal later than the time required by paragraph (1) or by any extension of time under rule 5(3)(*a*) (power to extend time)—
   (*a*) the application notice must include a request for an extension of time and the reason why the application notice was not provided in time; and
   (*b*) unless the Tribunal extends time for the application notice under rule 5(3)(*a*) (power to extend time) the Tribunal must not admit the application notice.

(5) In proceedings under Suspension Regulations, the applicant must send or deliver a copy of the application notice and any accompanying documents to the respondent at the same time as it provides the application notice to the Tribunal.

(6) In proceedings other than proceedings under paragraph (5), when the Tribunal receives the application notice it must send a copy of the application notice and any accompanying documents to each other party.

The Response

21. (1) When a respondent receives a copy of the application notice, the respondent must send or deliver to the Tribunal a response so that it is received—
   (*a*) if a time for providing the response is specified in the Schedule to these Rules (time limits for providing application notices and responses), within that time;
   (*b*) otherwise, within 21 days after the date on which the respondent received the application notice.

(2) The response must include—
   (*a*) the name and address of the respondent;
   (*b*) the name and address of the respondent's representative (if any);
   (*c*) an address where documents for the respondent may be sent or delivered;
   (*d*) a statement as to whether the respondent opposes the applicant's case and, if so, any grounds for such opposition which are not contained in another document provided with the response;
   (*e*) in a special educational needs case, the views of the child about the issues raised by the proceedings, or the reason why the respondent has not ascertained those views; and
   (*f*) any further information or documents required by an applicable practice direction or direction.

(3) The response may include a statement as to whether the respondent would be content for the case to be dealt with without a hearing if the Tribunal considers it appropriate.

(4) If the respondent provides the response to the Tribunal later than the time required by paragraph (1) or by any extension of time under rule 5(3)(*a*) (power to extend time), the response must include a request for an extension of time and the reason why the response was not provided in time.

(5) The respondent must send or deliver a copy of the response and any accompanying documents to each other party at the same time as it provides the response to the Tribunal.

Order that a School be Regarded as not Registered Pending Determination of an Appeal

22. (1) This rule sets out the procedure for the making of an order under Section 166(5) of the Education Act 2002 that a school is to be regarded as not registered for the purposes of Section 159 of that Act until the Tribunal determines an appeal under Section 165(2) of that Act (decision to remove an independent school from the register).

(2) In this rule—
   (*a*) "the applicant" means the applicant bringing the appeal under Section 165(2) of the Education Act 2002; and

(*b*) "the respondent" means the respondent to that appeal.

(3) The respondent must make any application for an order under this rule in writing and must send or deliver it to the Tribunal and the applicant so that it is received within 28 days after the date on which the respondent received a copy of the application notice starting the appeal.

(4) An application under paragraph (3) must—

(*a*) be signed by the respondent and dated;

(*b*) state the grounds for the application;

(*c*) state the nature of the evidence that will be provided in support of the application and the names of the witnesses who will give that evidence;

(*d*) specify any working days in the following 30 days when the respondent or a witness named under sub-paragraph (*c*) would not be available to attend a hearing, and provide reasons why they would not be available; and

(*e*) include, so far as practicable, any documentary evidence (including witness statements) that the respondent intends to rely on.

(5) The applicant must send or deliver a written response to the application under paragraph (3) to the Tribunal and the respondent so that it is received within 16 days after the date on which the respondent sent that application to the applicant under paragraph (3).

(6) The response must—

(*a*) acknowledge receipt of the application and any documentary evidence included with it;

(*b*) state whether the applicant requests that the application be decided at a hearing, and if so—

(*i*) state the nature of the evidence that will be provided in support of the applicant's case and the names of the witnesses who will give that evidence; and

(*ii*) specify any working days in the following 16 days when the applicant or a witness named under sub-paragraph (*b*)(*i*) would not be available to attend a hearing, and provide reasons why they would not be available; and

(*c*) include, so far as practicable, any documentary evidence (including witness statements) that the applicant intends to rely on.

(7) If the applicant fails to comply with paragraph (5) the applicant will not be entitled to take any further part in the proceedings in relation to the application.

(8) If the applicant complies with paragraph (5) and requests that the application be decided at a hearing, the Tribunal must hold a hearing to consider the application.

(9) Any hearing to consider the making of an order must be held as soon as reasonably practicable, and if the respondent has applied for such an order any such hearing must be held no later than the earlier of—

(*a*) 14 days after the date on which the Tribunal received the applicant's response to the application; or

(*b*) 30 days after the date on which the respondent sent the application to the applicant.

(10) If the Tribunal is considering whether to make an order on its own initiative, the Tribunal—

(*a*) may not do so without giving the applicant an opportunity to make representations at a hearing in relation to the making of the order;

(*b*) must give directions as to the provision to the Tribunal by the parties of documents or evidence that the parties wish to be taken into account.

Chapter 2: Hearings

Decision With or Without a Hearing

23. (1) Subject to paragraphs (2) and (3), the Tribunal must hold a hearing before making a decision which disposes of proceedings unless—

(*a*) each party has consented to the matter being decided without a hearing; and

(*b*) the Tribunal considers that it is able to decide the matter without the hearing.

(2) This rule does not apply to a decision under Part 5.

(3) The Tribunal may dispose of proceedings without a hearing under rule 8 (striking out a party's case).

Entitlement to Attend a Hearing

24. Subject to rules 22(7) (exclusion of applicant from proceedings to consider an order under Section 166(5) of the Education Act 2002) and 26(5) (exclusion of a person from a hearing)—

(*a*) each party is entitled to attend a hearing; and

(*b*) in a special educational needs case, or a disability discrimination in schools case, the child is entitled to attend a hearing, and the Tribunal may permit the child to give evidence and to address the Tribunal.

Notice of Hearings

25. (1) The Tribunal must give each party entitled to attend a hearing reasonable notice of the time and place of the hearing (including any adjourned or postponed hearing) and any changes to the time and place of the hearing.

(2) The period of notice under paragraph (1) must be at least 14 days, except that—

(*a*) in proceedings under Suspension Regulations the period of notice must be at least 3 working days;

(*b*) the period of notice in respect of a hearing to consider the making of an order under Section 166(5) of the Education Act 2002 must be at least 7 days; and

(*c*) the Tribunal may give shorter notice—
(*i*) with the parties' consent; or
(*ii*) in urgent or exceptional circumstances.

Public and Private Hearings

26. (1) Subject to the following paragraphs, all hearings must be held in public.
(2) Hearings in special educational needs cases and disability discrimination in schools cases must be held in private unless the Tribunal considers that it is in the interests of justice for a hearing to be held in public.
(3) Subject to paragraph (2), the Tribunal may give a direction that a hearing, or part of it, is to be held in private.
(4) Where a hearing, or part of it, is to be held in private, the Tribunal may determine who is permitted to attend the hearing or part of it.
(5) The Tribunal may give a direction excluding from any hearing, or part of it—
(*a*) any person whose conduct the Tribunal considers is disrupting or is likely to disrupt the hearing;
(*b*) any person whose presence the Tribunal considers is likely to prevent another person from giving evidence or making submissions freely;
(*c*) any person who the Tribunal considers should be excluded in order to give effect to a direction under rule 14(2) (withholding information likely to cause harm);
(*d*) any person where the purpose of the hearing would be defeated by the attendance of that person; or
(*e*) in a special educational needs case or a disability discrimination in schools case, the child, if the Tribunal considers that the child's presence at the hearing would be adverse to the child's interests.
(6) The Tribunal may give a direction excluding a witness from a hearing until that witness gives evidence.

Hearings in a Party's Absence

27. If a party fails to attend a hearing the Tribunal may proceed with the hearing if the Tribunal—
(*a*) is satisfied that the party has been notified of the hearing or that reasonable steps have been taken to notify the party of the hearing; and
(*b*) considers that it is in the interests of justice to proceed with the hearing.

Power to Pay Allowances

28. The Secretary of State may pay such allowances for the purpose of or in connection with the attendance of persons at hearings as the Secretary of State may determine.

Chapter 3: Decisions

Consent Orders

29. (1) The Tribunal may, at the request of the parties but only if it considers it appropriate, make a consent order disposing of the proceedings and making such other appropriate provision as the parties have agreed.

(2) Notwithstanding any other provision of these Rules, the Tribunal need not hold a hearing before making an order under paragraph (1), or provide reasons for the order.

Decisions

30. (1) The Tribunal may give a decision orally at a hearing.

(2) Subject to rule 14(2) (withholding information likely to cause harm), the Tribunal must provide to each party as soon as reasonably practicable after making a decision which finally disposes of all issues in the proceedings (except a decision under Part 5)—

(*a*) a decision notice stating the Tribunal's decision;

(*b*) written reasons for the decision; and

(*c*) notification of any rights of review or appeal against the decision and the time within which, and the manner in which, such rights of review or appeal may be exercised.

(3) Ins proceedings under Suspension Regulations, the documents and information referred to in paragraph (2) must be provided at the hearing or sent within 3 working days after the hearing.

(4) The Tribunal may provide written reasons for any decision to which paragraph (2) does not apply.

PART 4: Proceedings Before the Tribunal in Mental Health Cases

Chapter 1: Before the Hearing

Application of Part 4

31. This Part applies only to mental health cases.

Procedure in Mental Health Cases

32. (1) An application or reference must be—

(*a*) made in writing;

(*b*) signed (in the case of an application, by the applicant or any person authorised by the applicant to do so); and

(*c*) sent or delivered to the Tribunal so that it is received within the time specified in the Mental Health Act 1983 or the Repatriation of Prisoners Act 1984.

(2) An application must, if possible, include—
- (*a*) the name and address of the patient;
- (*b*) if the application is made by the patient's nearest relative, the name, address and relationship to the patient of the patient's nearest relative;
- (*c*) the provision under which the patient is detained, liable to be detained, subject to guardianship, a community patient or subject to after-care under supervision;
- (*d*) whether the person making the application has appointed a representative or intends to do so, and the name and address of any representative appointed;
- (*e*) the name and address of the responsible authority in relation to the patient.

(3) Subject to rule 14(2) (withholding evidence likely to cause harm), when the Tribunal receives a document from any party it must send a copy of that document to each other party.

(4) If the patient is a conditionally discharged patient (as defined in the Mental Health Act 1983) the Secretary of State must send or deliver a statement containing the information and documents required by the relevant practice direction to the Tribunal so that it is received by the Tribunal as soon as practicable and in any event within 6 weeks after the Secretary of State received a copy of the application or a request from the Tribunal.

(5) In proceedings under Section 66(1)(*a*) of the Mental Health Act 1983 (application for admission for assessment), on the earlier of receipt of the copy of the application or a request from the Tribunal, the responsible authority must send or deliver to the Tribunal—
- (*a*) the application for admission;
- (*b*) the medical recommendations on which the application is founded;
- (*c*) such of the information specified in the relevant practice direction as is within the knowledge of the responsible authority and can reasonably be provided in the time available; and
- (*d*) such of the documents specified in the relevant practice direction as can reasonably be provided in the time available.

(6) If paragraph (4) or (5) does not apply, the responsible authority must send or deliver a statement containing the information and documents required by the relevant practice direction to the Tribunal so that it is received by the Tribunal as soon as practicable and in any event within 3 weeks after the responsible authority received a copy of the application or reference.

(7) If the patient is a restricted patient the responsible authority must also send the statement under paragraph (6) to the Secretary of State, and the Secretary of State must send a statement of any further relevant information to the Tribunal as soon as practicable and in any event—
- (*a*) in proceedings under Section 75(1) of the Mental Health Act 1983,

within 2 weeks after the Secretary of State received the relevant authority's statement; or

(*b*) otherwise, within 3 weeks after the Secretary of State received the relevant authority's statement.

(8) If the Secretary of State wishes to seek the approval of the Tribunal under Section 86(3) of the Mental Health Act 1983, the Secretary of State must refer the patient's case to the Tribunal and the provisions of these Rules applicable to references under that Act apply to the proceedings.

Notice of Proceedings to Interested Persons

33. When the Tribunal receives the information required by rule 32(4), (5) or (6) (procedure in mental health cases) the Tribunal must give notice of the proceedings—

(*a*) where the patient is subject to the guardianship of a private guardian, to the guardian;

(*b*) where there is an extant order of the Court of Protection, to that court;

(*c*) subject to a patient with capacity to do so requesting otherwise, where any person other than the applicant is named by the authority as exercising the functions of the nearest relative, to that person;

(*d*) where a health authority, Primary Care Trust, National Health Service trust or NHS foundation trust has a right to discharge the patient under the provisions of Section 23(3) of the Mental Health Act 1983, to that authority or trust; and

(*e*) to any other person who, in the opinion of the Tribunal, should have an opportunity of being heard.

Medical Examination of the Patient

34. (1) Before a hearing to consider the disposal of a mental health case, an appropriate member of the Tribunal must, so far as practicable—

(*a*) examine the patient; and

(*b*) take such other steps as that member considers necessary to form an opinion of the patient's mental condition.

(2) For the purposes of paragraph (1) that member may—

(*a*) examine the patient in private;

(*b*) examine records relating to the detention or treatment of the patient and any after-care services;

(*c*) take notes and copies of records for use in connection with the proceedings.

Chapter 2: Hearings

No Disposal of Proceedings Without a Hearing

35. (1) The Tribunal must not dispose of proceedings without a hearing.

(2) This rule does not apply to a decision under Part 5.

Entitlement to Attend a Hearing

36. (1) Subject to rule 38(4) (exclusion of a person from a hearing), each party to proceedings is entitled to attend a hearing.

(2) Any person notified of the proceedings under rule 33 (notice of proceedings to interested persons) may—

(*a*) attend and take part in a hearing to such extent as the Tribunal considers proper; or

(*b*) provide written submissions to the Tribunal.

Time and Place of Hearings

37. (1) In proceedings under Section 66(1)(*a*) of the Mental Health Act 1983 the hearing of the case must start within 7 days after the date on which the Tribunal received the application notice.

(2) In proceedings under Section 75(1) of that Act, the hearing of the case must start at least 5 weeks but no more than 8 weeks after the date on which the Tribunal received the reference.

(3) The Tribunal must give reasonable notice of the time and place of the hearing (including any adjourned or postponed hearing), and any changes to the time and place of the hearing, to—

(*a*) each party entitled to attend a hearing; and

(*b*) any person who has been notified of the proceedings under rule 33 (notice of proceedings to interested persons).

(4) The period of notice under paragraph (3) must be at least 14 days, except that—

(*a*) in proceedings under Section 66(1)(*a*) of the Mental Health Act 1983 the period must be at least 3 working days; and

(*b*) the Tribunal may give shorter notice—

(*i*) with the parties' consent; or

(*ii*) in urgent or exceptional circumstances.

Public and Private Hearings

38. (1) All hearings must be held in private unless the Tribunal considers that it is in the interests of justice for the hearing to be held in public.

(2) If a hearing is held in public, the Tribunal may give a direction that part of the hearing is to be held in private.

(3) Where a hearing, or part of it, is to be held in private, the Tribunal may determine who is permitted to attend the hearing or part of it.

(4) The Tribunal may give a direction excluding from any hearing, or part of it—

(*a*) any person whose conduct the Tribunal considers is disrupting or is likely to disrupt the hearing;

(*b*) any person whose presence the Tribunal considers is likely to prevent another person from giving evidence or making

(c) any person who the Tribunal considers should be excluded in order to give effect to a direction under rule 14(2) (withholding information likely to cause harm); or

(d) any person where the purpose of the hearing would be defeated by the attendance of that person.

(5) The Tribunal may give a direction excluding a witness from a hearing until that witness gives evidence.

Hearings in a Party's Absence

39. (1) Subject to paragraph (2), if a party fails to attend a hearing the Tribunal may proceed with the hearing if the Tribunal—

(a) is satisfied that the party has been notified of the hearing or that reasonable steps have been taken to notify the party of the hearing; and

(b) considers that it is in the interests of justice to proceed with the hearing.

(2) The Tribunal may not proceed with a hearing in the absence of the patient unless—

(a) the requirements of rule 34 (medical examination of the patient) have been satisfied; and

(b) the Tribunal is satisfied that—

(i) the patient has decided not to attend the hearing; or

(ii) the patient is unable to attend the hearing for reasons of ill health.

Power to Pay Allowances

40. The Tribunal may pay allowances in respect of travelling expenses, subsistence and loss of earnings to—

(a) any person who attends a hearing as an applicant or a witness;

(b) a patient who attends a hearing otherwise than as the applicant or a witness; and

(c) any person (other than a legal representative) who attends as the representative of an applicant.

Chapter 3: Decisions

Decisions

41. (1) The Tribunal may give a decision orally at a hearing.

(2) Subject to rule 14(2) (withholding information likely to cause harm), the Tribunal must provide to each party as soon as reasonably practicable after making a decision which finally disposes of all issues in the proceedings (except a decision under Part 5)—

(a) a decision notice stating the Tribunal's decision;

(b) written reasons for the decision; and

(c) notification of any right of appeal against the decision and the time within which, and the manner in which, such right of appeal may be exercised.

(3) The documents and information referred to in paragraph (2) must—
(*a*) in proceedings under Section 66(1)(*a*) of the Mental Health Act 1983, be provided at the hearing or sent within 3 working days after the hearing; and
(*b*) in other cases, be provided at the hearing or sent within 7 days after the hearing.

(4) The Tribunal may provide written reasons for any decision to which paragraph (2) does not apply.

Provisional Decisions

42. For the purposes of this Part and Parts 1, 2 and 5, a decision with recommendations under Section 72(3)(*a*) or (3A)(*a*) of the Mental Health Act 1983 or a deferred direction for conditional discharge under Section 73(7) of that Act is a decision which disposes of the proceedings.

PART 5: Correcting, Setting Aside, Reviewing and Appealing Tribunal Decisions

Interpretation

43. In this Part—

"appeal" means the exercise of a right of appeal on a point of law under Section 11 of the 2007 Act; and

"review" means the review of a decision by the Tribunal under Section 9 of the 2007 Act.

Clerical Mistakes and Accidental Slips or Omissions

44. The Tribunal may at any time correct any clerical mistake or other accidental slip or omission in a decision, direction or any document produced by it, by—
(*a*) sending notification of the amended decision or direction, or a copy of the amended document, to all parties; and
(*b*) making any necessary amendment to any information published in relation to the decision, direction or document.

Setting Aside a Decision which Disposes of Proceedings

45. (1) The Tribunal may set aside a decision which disposes of proceedings, or part of such a decision, and re-make the decision or the relevant part of it, if—
(*a*) the Tribunal considers that it is in the interests of justice to do so; and
(*b*) one or more of the conditions in paragraph (2) are satisfied.

(2) The conditions are—
(*a*) a document relating to the proceedings was not sent to, or was not received at an appropriate time by, a party or a party's representative;

(*b*) a document relating to the proceedings was not sent to the Tribunal at an appropriate time;

(*c*) a party, or a party's representative, was not present at a hearing related to the proceedings; or

(*d*) there has been some other procedural irregularity in the proceedings.

(3) A party applying for a decision, or part of a decision, to be set aside under paragraph (1) must make a written application to the Tribunal so that it is received no later than 28 days after the date on which the Tribunal sent notice of the decision to the party.

Application for Permission to Appeal

46. (1) A person seeking permission to appeal must make a written application to the Tribunal for permission to appeal.

(2) An application under paragraph (1) must be sent or delivered to the Tribunal so that it is received no later than 28 days after the latest of the dates that the Tribunal sends to the person making the application—

(*a*) written reasons for the decision;

(*b*) notification of amended reasons for, or correction of, the decision following a review; or

(*c*) notification that an application for the decision to be set aside has been unsuccessful.

(3) The date in paragraph (2)(*c*) applies only if the application for the decision to be set aside was made within the time stipulated in rule 45 (setting aside a decision which disposes of proceedings) or any extension of that time granted by the Tribunal.

(4) If the person seeking permission to appeal sends or delivers the application to the Tribunal later than the time required by paragraph (2) or by any extension of time under rule 5(3)(*a*) (power to extend time)—

(*a*) the application must include a request for an extension of time and the reason why the application was not provided in time; and

(*b*) unless the Tribunal extends time for the application under rule 5(3)(*a*) (power to extend time) the Tribunal must not admit the application.

(5) An application under paragraph (1) must—

(*a*) identify the decision of the Tribunal to which it relates;

(*b*) identify the alleged error or errors of law in the decision; and

(*c*) state the result the party making the application is seeking.

Tribunal's Consideration of Application for Permission to Appeal

47. (1) On receiving an application for permission to appeal the Tribunal must first consider, taking into account the overriding objective in rule 2, whether to review the decision in accordance with rule 49 (review of a decision).

(2) If the Tribunal decides not to review the decision, or reviews the decision and decides to take no action in relation to the decision, or part of it, the Tribunal must consider whether to give permission to appeal in relation to the decision or that part of it.

(3) The Tribunal must send a record of its decision to the parties as soon as practicable.

(4) If the Tribunal refuses permission to appeal it must send with the record of its decision—

(*a*) a statement of its reasons for such refusal; and

(*b*) notification of the right to make an application to the Upper Tribunal for permission to appeal and the time within which, and the method by which, such application must be made.

(5) The Tribunal may give permission to appeal on limited grounds, but must comply with paragraph (4) in relation to any grounds on which it has refused permission.

Application for Review in Special Educational Needs Cases

48. (1) This rule applies to decisions which dispose of proceedings in special educational needs cases, but not to decisions under this Part.

(2) A party may make a written application to the Tribunal for a review of a decision if circumstances relevant to the decision have changed since the decision was made.

(3) An application under paragraph (2) must be sent or delivered to the Tribunal so that it is received within 28 days after the date on which the Tribunal sent the decision notice recording the Tribunal's decision to the party making the application.

(4) If a party sends or delivers an application to the Tribunal later than the time required by paragraph (3) or by any extension of time under rule 5(3)(*a*) (power to extend time)—

(*a*) the application must include a request for an extension of time and the reason why the application was not provided in time; and

(*b*) unless the Tribunal extends time for the application under rule 5(3)(*a*) (power to extend time) the Tribunal must not admit the application.

Review of a Decision

49. (1) The Tribunal may only undertake a review of a decision—
   (*a*) pursuant to rule 47(1) (review on an application for permission to appeal) if it is satisfied that there was an error of law in the decision; or
   (*b*) pursuant to rule 48 (application for review in special educational needs cases).
(2) The Tribunal must notify the parties in writing of the outcome of any review, and of any right of appeal in relation to the outcome.
(3) If the Tribunal takes any action in relation to a decision following a review without first giving every party an opportunity to make representations, the notice under paragraph (2) must state that any party that did not have an opportunity to make representations may apply for such action to be set aside and for the decision to be reviewed again.

Power to Treat an Application as a Different Type of Application

50. The Tribunal may treat an application for a decision to be corrected, set aside or reviewed, or for permission to appeal against a decision, as an application for any other one of those things.

Schedule Time Limits for Providing Application Notices and Responses

Type of Proceedings	*Time for Application Notice*	*Time for Response*
Under Suspension Regulations (suspension of registration as a childcare provider)	10 working days after written notice of the decision was sent to the applicant	3 working days after the respondent received the application notice
Under section 79M of the Children Act 1989, except against a notice under section 79L(1)(a) of that Act (notice of intention to refuse an application for registration for childminding or providing day care) Under paragraph 10 of Schedule 26 to the School Standards and Framework Act 1998 (appeal against a decision of the Chief Inspector for Wales) Under section 68 of the Care Standards Act 2000 (appeal against a decision of the Council) except an appeal against a refusal under section 58 of that Act (refusal of an application to be included on a register of social workers) Under section 74(1)(b) to (e) and (2) of the Childcare Act 2006 (appeal against steps taken by the Chief Inspector except refusal of application for registration or against a prescribed determination)	28 days after written notice of the decision was sent to the applicant	20 working days after the respondent received the application notice

(*Contd.*)

Type of Proceedings	Time for Application Notice	Time for Response
Under section 21 of the Care Standards Act 2000 (refusal or cancellation of registration, or variation of conditions of registration, by registration authority or by order of a justice of the peace) Under section 32 of the Health and Social Care Act 2008 (appeal against a decision of the Care Quality Commission or an order of a justice of the peace cancelling registration) Health and Social Care Act 2008 Under section 166 of the Education Act 2002 (appeal against steps taken by the registration authority)	28 day time limits are set out in section 21(2) of the Care Standards Act 2000, section 166(2) of the Education Act 2002 and section 32(2) of the Health and Social Care Act 2008	20 working days after the respondent received the application notice
Under section 65A of the Children Act 1989 (refusal to give consent for a person who is disqualified from fostering a child privately to carry on, be otherwise concerned in the management of, have any financial interest in, or be employed in, a children's home) Under section 79M of the Children Act 1989 against a notice under 79L(1)(a) of that Act (notice of intention to refuse an application for registration for childminding or for providing day care) Under section 4 of the Protection of Children Act 1999 (inclusion of a person on a list of individuals who are considered unsuitable to work with children, a refusal to remove a person from such list, or determination of inclusion on the list where a person has been provisionally included on the list for more than 9 months) Under section 68 of the Care Standards Act 2000 where the appeal is against a refusal under section 58 of that Act (refusal of an application to be included on a register of social workers) Under section 86 of the Care Standards Act 2000 (inclusion of a person on a list of individuals who are considered unsuitable to work with vulnerable adults, a refusal to remove a person from such list, or determination of inclusion on the list where a person has been provisionally included on the list for more than 9 months) Under the Education (Prohibition from Teaching or Working with Children) Regulations 2003 (decision to give a direction, or a refusal to revoke a direction, prohibiting or restricting a person from working in education or in a job which brings them regularly into contact with children) Under section 74(1)(a) of the Childcare Act 2006 (refusal of registration as a childcare provider)	3 months after written notice of the decision was sent to the applicant	20 days after the respondent received the application notice
Under regulations made under section 28X of the National Health Service Act 1977 (decision contingently to remove a person from a list maintained by a Primary Care Trust or Local Health Board of persons authorised to perform primary medical, dental or ophthalmic services, or local pharmaceutical services)	(a) for the first application in relation to a decision, 3 months after the decision was made; (b) for any further application in respect of the same decision, 6 months after the Tribunal made its last determination in relation to that decision;	21 days after the respondent received the application notice

(Contd.)

Type of Proceedings	Time for Application Notice	Time for Response
	(c) for any further application in respect of the same decision where the parties apply jointly to the Tribunal with a view to seeking— (i) the same variation of conditions, (ii) the same imposition of different conditions, or (iii) for the contingent removal to be revoked, 1 month after the Tribunal made its last determination in relation to that decision.	
Under Part 4 of and Schedule 27 to the Education Act 1996 (provision of education to a child with special educational needs)	2 months after written notice of the decision was sent to the applicant	30 working days after the respondent received the application notice
Under section 28I of the Disability Discrimination Act 1995 (disability discrimination in the education of a child)	6 months after the decision or act complained of	30 working days after the respondent received the application notice

Explanatory Note

(This Note is not Part of the Rules)

Part 1 of the Tribunals, Courts and Enforcement Act 2007 (c.15) establishes a new tribunal structure comprising a First-tier Tribunal and an Upper Tribunal. Appeal functions of existing tribunals are being transferred to this structure and assigned to chambers within the new tribunals. These Rules govern the practice and procedure to be followed in the First-tier Tribunal in proceedings which have been allocated to the Health, Education and Social Care Chamber by the First-tier Tribunal and Upper Tribunal (Chambers) Order 2008.

Part 1 contains provisions for interpreting and applying the Rules and sets out the overriding objective of the Rules.

Part 2 contains general powers and provisions including the Tribunal's general case management powers, the giving of directions, the power to strike out a party's case, the service of documents and rules about evidence, submissions and witnesses.

Part 3 contains provisions on starting proceedings and on responses and replies in cases other than mental health cases. It also makes provision for hearings and for decisions made by the Tribunal in those cases.

Part 4 contains provisions on starting proceedings and on statements by authorities in mental health cases. It also makes provision for hearings and for decisions made by the Tribunal in those cases.

Part 5 deals with correcting, setting aside, reviewing and appealing against Tribunal decisions.

SEN: A SCOTTISH LEGAL PERSPECTIVE

The Education (Additional Support for Learning) (Scotland) Act 2004 is an Act of the

Scottish Parliament that received Royal Assent in 2004. It seeks to redefine the law in Scotland relating to the provision of special education to children with additional needs by establishing a framework for the policies of inclusion and generally practicing the "presumption of mainstreaming" in Scottish education. The Act is an attempt to broaden the narrow definition of Special Educational Needs (SEN) which has typically been used to define children with special needs.

Special Educational Needs (SEN)

Under the SEN model, certain children were classified as having special needs, and a formal "Record of Needs" (RoN) was opened and maintained. The opening of an RoN placed a legal obligation on the local authority to meet the needs of the child or young person as defined in the record. Additional support, staffing, resources and places at special schools were largely dependent on the needs and targets set out in the student's RoN.

Principles

The new Act defines a system of Additional Support Needs (ASN). The Act states that, at some point in their education, all children may require some form of additional support. The Act says: "A child may require additional support for a variety of reasons. These may include those who are being bullied, are particularly gifted, have experienced a bereavement, or are not attending school regularly, as well as those who have behavioural or learning difficulties, mental health problems, or specific disabilities such as deafness or blindness."

Implementation

The Act places a duty on education authorities to establish procedures for identifying and meeting the additional support needs of children and young people. The identified needs must be kept under review and it will be the responsibility of all agencies to help education authorities meet their duties. The Act defines such agencies as "including the local authority's social work services, any health board, any other local authority or other agency specified by Scottish Ministers, such as Careers Scotland or further education colleges."

The new structure is intended to make accessing support easier for parents and carers. Where parents believe that their child has additional support needs they are able to request assessments which they believe are necessary; education authorities also have this ability. In situations where there is disagreement, education authorities will be under a duty to provide mediation services and they will be required to have arrangements in place for resolving disputes.

The Act is intended to provide support for children with long or short term barriers to learning, including children with severe and complex needs. Where more than one support service is involved in the provision of support for a child, a Co-ordinated Support Plan (CSP) will be drawn up by the relevant agencies, (e.g., school and grief counsellor).

SEN RELATED ASPECTS OF DISABILITY DISCRIMINATION ACT

The SEN and Disability Act 2001 and the Disability Discrimination Act 2005 amended the Disability Discrimination Act 1995. The Disability Discrimination Act (DDA) requires schools:

- not to treat disabled pupils 'less favourably'
- to make reasonable adjustments to ensure that disabled pupils are not at a substantial disadvantage
- to draw up plans to show how, over time, they will increase access to education for disabled pupils (school accessibility plans)
- to comply with the Disability Equality Duty
- to prepare, publish, implement and report on a Disability Equality Scheme.

The Disability Equality Duty includes an important duty to eliminate harassment of disabled people that is related to their disability. Schools therefore need to tackle the bullying of children with SEN and disabilities as part of complying with this part of the Disability Equality Duty. Guidance on tackling the bullying of children with SEN and disabilities can be found in this Act.

A short summary of schools' duties under disability discrimination law can be found in this Act. Similar duties apply to local authorities.

Guidance entitled *Implementing the Disability Discrimination Act in schools and early-years settings* contains many examples of how schools have successfully included disabled pupils. The first link below (the DDA resource) contains details of how this guidance can be obtained by schools and voluntary organisations. The links below take you to various pages and downloads which include copies of some parts of the guidance.

Letter from Sarah McCarthy-Fry to all Schools about Tackling Bullying and Exclusions, and on Implementing, Monitoring and Evaluating Disability Equality Schemes

Sarah McCarthy-Fry, the minister with responsibility for SEN and disabilities, has written to all headteachers and chairs of governing bodies. She stresses the importance of continuing to tackle bullying in schools, especially as research indicates that children with SEN and disabilities can be particularly vulnerable to bullying. The letter also asks schools to look carefully at how exclusions of children with SEN and disabilities can be reduced, and ensure there is monitoring and evaluation of the progress being made by children with SEN and disabilities. Schools should also ensure they have consulted on and published a disability equality scheme. The scheme must be actively implemented, monitored and evaluated, to drive the improvement of outcomes for disabled children.

GUIDELINES FOR PARENTS FOR APPEALING A SEN DECISION: A CASE STUDY

Introduction

First Tier Tribunal (Special Education Needs and Disability Discrimination)

On the 3rd November 2008 SENDIST became part of the First-tier Tribunal. It is in the Health, Education and Social Care Chamber (HESC). The tribunal is independent. The Government cannot influence the tribunal's decision, and the Panel has no connection with any Local Authority (LA).

The Tribunal considers parents appeals against decisions of LA' s about children's special educational needs when parents cannot reach agreement with the LA.

Individual appeals are heard by a panel of three appointed people. The panel is chaired by a tribunal judge (who is a lawyer), and the other two members are non-legal (specialist) members who have knowledge and experience of special educational needs and disability.

The Tribunal also considers parents claims of disability discrimination in schools. For more information about how to make a claim about disability discrimination, please contact our helpline on 0870 241 2555, or refer to our booklet How to Make a Disability Discrimination Claim.

We have to operate according to Rules and Practice Directions. These are available on our website www.sendist.gov.uk.

We use the word 'tribunal' throughout this booklet although it can have different meanings. A Hearing which decides the case is held by a tribunal panel of three but there are times when a tribunal judge is able to make a decision alone. In both cases we are a 'tribunal'.

Also, although the Rules talk about an "application" that includes an appeal. In this booklet we will continue to use the word appeal (and claim for disability discrimination cases).

We use the term LA to cover a local council's local education authority and the newly created children's services in the area where you live. As different local authorities have different titles, we thought it best to be consistent throughout this booklet.

You must appeal within 2 months of the LA' s final written decision being sent to you.

If you have not received an acknowledgment within two weeks of sending in your appeal, please call us on 0870 2412555.

Making an Appeal

When You Can Appeal?

If you have not been able to reach agreement with your Local Authority (LA) about your child's special educational needs, you may be able to appeal to us.
There is a two month time limit for appealing to us which starts from the date on the LA's letter giving their final written decision. Even after making an Appeal to us, you should continue to try to resolve the matter with the LA.

What You Can Appeal About?

You can appeal if the LA:

- Will not carry out a statutory assessment of your child's special educational needs, following a request by you or by your child's school.
- Refuses to make a statement of your child's special educational needs, after a statutory assessment.
- Refuses to reassess your child's special educational needs if the LA has not made a new assessment for at least six months, following a request by you or by your child's school.
- Decides not to maintain (decides to cancel) your child's statement.
- Decides not to change the statement after reassessing your child.
- Refuses to change the school named in your child's statement, if the statement is at least one year old (but you can only ask for a school that is funded by an LA). This is limited to the same type of school as the school named in the statement and it is not possible to ask us to alter Parts 2 or 3 (described below in more detail).

If the LA has made a statement, or has changed a previous statement, you can appeal against any or all of:

- The part which describes your child's special educational needs (part 2).
- The part which sets out the special educational provision (help) (part 3) that the LA thinks your child should receive.
- The school or type of school named in part 4 of the statement.
- The LA not naming a school in part 4.

Important—please note that if you disagree with parts 2 or 3 of the statement, you will need to give reasons why and explain what changes you would like made.

If you disagree with either the school named or the type of school described in part 4, then you will need to ensure that you tell us the name or the type of school you want your child to attend. We will also need you to give reasons why you think the school you have asked for is suitable for your child.

If you cannot name a particular school, we can take account of your wishes, if you describe the type of school you want naming in part 4.

The LA does not have to name a school in part 4 of the statement if it is satisfied that you are making suitable alternative arrangements for your child's special education as set out in the statement. If, in that event, you are unhappy that the LA has not named a school in part 4 then you will have to explain why.

Are there Any Issues the Tribunal Cannot Deal With?

Yes, you cannot appeal to us if:

- You are unhappy about the way the LA carried out the assessment, or the length of time that it took.

- You are unhappy about how the LA or the school is arranging to provide the help set out in your child's statement.
- You are unhappy about the way the school is meeting your child's needs at School Action or School Action Plus.
- You are unhappy about the description in parts 5 and 6 of the statement of your child's non-educational needs or how the LA plans to meet those needs.
- The LA will not amend the statement following an annual review.
- The LA refused to name an independent school (which normally charges fees for a child's education), a non-maintained school (a special school that normally charges fees) or a different type of school (e.g. a special school when your child currently attends a mainstream school or the other way around) where you asked for a change to part 4 in a statement that was at least a year old.

With regard to the last two bullet points, you would need to ask your LA to reassess your child and appeal to us if they refused that reassessment or if you remained dissatisfied at some later point in the process of amending your child's statement.

Because there may be some legal difficulties, we may not be able to consider an Appeal if your child is over 16 and not on the roll of a school, or is going to a further or higher education college. It will depend on each individual case.

Who do I Appeal to About the Issues the Tribunal Cannot Deal With?

Firstly you should discuss your concerns with your child's school or the LA. If you are still not happy then you can complain to the Secretary of State for Children, Schools and Families. If he agrees with your complaint he may ask the school or the LA to take action to put things right. You can get a guidance booklet from:

DCSF Publications Centre,

PO Box 5050,
Sherwood Park,
Annesley,
Nottingham,
NG15 0DG
0845 60 222 60

You may also be able to complain to the Local Government Ombudsman. You can get a booklet giving you guidance on this either from the LA or by contacting:

Local Government Ombudsman,

10th Floor,
Millbank Tower,
Millbank,
London SW1P 4QP
020 7217 4620

How to Appeal

You can appeal to us by filling in the Appeal form at the back of this booklet, ensuring that all the documents that we need are provided.

The Appeal Process

1. **When to appeal**—You have two months from the date on the LA's decision letter.
2. **Making an Appeal**—You appeal by filling in an Appeal form and returning it to us.
3. **Registration**—We will register your Appeal within 10 working days of receiving it. We will tell you that we have registered your Appeal and inform you of the date your Appeal will be heard.
   Depending on the type of Appeal, we will also send you either some automatic directions setting out a time table to provide information and documents (if we decide that the case is straightforward) OR a Further Information form (with explanatory notes) for you to complete and return to us. We will also send a copy of your appeal to the LA.
4. **Response from the LA**—The LA has to respond within 30 working days of us sending them a copy of your Appeal notice. They will send a copy of their response and any accompanying documents to both us and you. ***Please let us know (in writing or by e-mail) if you do not receive the response within 8 weeks of us registering your Appeal.***
5. **Case Management Process**—Each appeal will be 'case managed' following registration. This process is to ensure that you, the LA and the tribunal have all the information necessary for us to reach a decision on the day of the Hearing. If your application is quite straightforward we will send automatic directions to you and to the LA. For some appeals it may be necessary to hold a face-to-face meeting or telephone conference before the hearing. In such a case, when your Appeal is registered you will be sent a 'further information' form, explaining what type of case management your appeal will require.
6. **Informing you of the Place for your Hearing**— At least 10 working days before the Hearing we will inform you of the venue and the time of your Hearing.
7. **The Hearing**—The Hearing will take as long as necessary to enable the Tribunal to hear all the evidence relating to the appeal. For example, an appeal against a refusal to assess may take no more than half a day, but an appeal about the contents of Parts 2, 3 and 4 of a statement may take a full day, depending on the complexity of the case.
8. **Decision**—You should receive the Tribunals decision in writing within 10 working days of the Hearing.

Note—You and the LA can ask us to increase any of the time limits mentioned in the above process, including the two month time limit in which to appeal. To do this you have to write to us giving reasons on a Request form. We will send you this form when we register your appeal. It is also available on our website **www.sendist.gov.uk**. A Tribunal judge will decide whether an extension is given or not.

Is there a Code of Practice?

Yes, the government has made an SEN Code of Practice which both the LA and SEND "must have regard to". This Code of Practice was issued in 2001 and is available from the Department for Children, Schools and Families (DCSF). DCSF Publications Centre (address is on page 4). The reference code is DfES/581/2001. It is also available from the teachernet website at www.teachernet.gov.uk/docbank/index.cfm?id=3724

Can I Get Advice About Whether I Can Appeal?

The LA should have told you about the following groups that you may be able to get advice from

- A voluntary organisation which helps people with special needs
- A parents' group
- An independent parental supporter
- A parent partnership adviser

The LA should also have told you about its named officer who you can work with to try and resolve the issues you are appealing against.

Can I Get Help if I Decide to Make an Appeal?

The groups above and your LA officer may be able to put you in touch with an independent supporter or a representative.

You may be entitled to get Legal Aid (or public) Funding. A solicitor will be able to advise you on whether you are entitled to this. The Law Society or your Local Citizens Advice Bureau will be able to give you the names of solicitors who participate in the Legal Aid scheme and are experienced in these matters.

The Appeal Form

This section gives you details of what is required on the Appeal form

Section 1—Your child. This section is asking for details of your child.

Section 2—Your contact details. This section is asking for your details and the contact details of any representative that you may have.

Section 3—Special requirements. This is asking if you have any special requirements with regards to the appeal documents and the Hearing. For example whether you need the documents translated into Braille or another language or will require wheelchair access or need an interpreter or signer.

Section 4—Your Appeal. This section asks for information about the Local Authority and also asks about what you are appealing against.

Section 5—Your reasons for Appeal. This section is important, as this is where you need to state your reasons for appeal. There are some guidance notes later in this booklet to assist you.

Section 6—Claims about Disability Discrimination. This section asks whether you have an existing Disability Discrimination Claim or if you would like more information about how to make a Disability Discrimination Claim.

Section 7—Lodging the Appeal. This section explains where your completed appeal form must be sent.

Frequently Asked Questions—The Appeal Form

What if I Don't Send all the Right Information or Documents?

We may have to contact you about getting the information or documents to us. If we do not have enough papers to register your appeal we will return the appeal form to you with a list of what we require. You will then have 10 working days to send them to us. If this means that the appeal form will arrive after the two month time limit, you will have to ask for an extension of the time in which to appeal.

We can register a case even if we do not have all of the documents. If this happens we will write to you asking you to provide the missing documents within 10 working days. If we do not receive them in that time, the tribunal can strike out your appeal (This means that your appeal will not happen).

Do I Have to Send Original Documents?

No. Please only send us photocopies of the original documents.

Do I Have to Send the Appeal Myself?

No, but you must sign the appeal form yourself, unless your legal representative signs it for you (see below). If you are appealing jointly with another person, both of you must sign the form. Please be aware that we will only send any information about the Appeal to one person named on the Appeal form, the choice is yours (see the form, below). If you do not indicate a person we will send the information to the first named person.

If you have a representative and you wish them to receive all the letters and papers for the Appeal on your behalf, you should give their name and address on the form. A legally qualified representative may sign the form on your behalf if you have given them permission to do so. If you state on the form that your representative is going to receive all the papers, then you will not receive any correspondence in connection with your Appeal before the Hearing; it will all be sent to your representative. You will be sent the final decision, however, when it is issued. You must let us know in writing if you decide to stop using your representative or if the details of your representative change.

Do I Have to Complete My Appeal Form in English?

No, if English is not your first language, you may appeal in your own language and we will arrange to have it translated.

What if I Have Any Other Needs?

Please ensure that these requests are stated on your Appeal form.

For example if you need a signer or an interpreter at the Hearing, or need any special arrangements to be made so you can attend the Hearing.

How Long Will My Appeal Take to be Heard?

If there is a Hearing, you should have a final decision within four to five months of making your Appeal. If you reach an agreement with the LA it may take less time. If August is included then it will be five to six months as August is not classed as a working month by the rules that govern SEND.

What Happens Next

What Should I Include in My Case Management Form?

Unless the case is straightforward (and we send you automatic directions) once we have registered your Appeal, we will send you a form asking for Further Information. This form will have some explanatory notes on what to do next to help you prepare for your Hearing. The Case Management process will set out a timetable for when you should send any up-to-date information and any other written reports you have. You can also let us know your child's views. A few parents may wish to submit a short CD or DVD. In this case you will need to send us five copies and keep a copy for yourself. Please note that we do not have the facilities to watch videos or DVD's at the Hearing.

What Will the LA do About My Appeal?

The LA will have the same timetable as you to send us further information and evidence. The LA's response must say whether or not they oppose your Appeal and, if they do, then they need to give reasons as to why. They should provide a summary of the facts and let us know what your child thinks about the issues. Generally LAs must find out children's views wherever possible. They may also contact you about the Appeal, as they may have looked at the evidence again and feel that they can provide some or all of what you want.

The LA may also apply to strike out (bring to an end) your Appeal if they believe it is a case that we are not able to hear. If this happens we will send you a copy of the LA's application so you can comment on it, and we will give you the opportunity to explain to the Tribunal why you think your appeal should continue.

What Happens if the LA Does not Oppose the Appeal?

If the LA does not oppose your Appeal, we will write and ask if you wish to withdraw your Appeal (we will send you a withdrawal form to sign and return to us). Before you withdraw your Appeal you will need to decide if you are happy with what the LA has said it will do. If you are appealing about the contents of your child's statement, the LA must give us full details of the changes it has agreed to make.

If the LA tells us that it does not oppose the Appeal, but you do not withdraw your appeal, we will treat the Appeal as decided in your favour. The LA will then have a fixed period in which to provide what you have asked for.

What if the LA Does not Send Us or You a Response?

If the LA does not send a response by the end of the time in which they have to reply, it may not be able to take any further part in the appeal.

If you wish to continue with the Appeal it will be passed to a tribunal judge who will either

- deal with your appeal by reading the papers which have been submitted, or
- decide that there should be a Hearing which the LA would not attend.

Can I Comment on the LA's Response?

The Case Management process allows you to make comments.

Can I Send in Any More Documents?

You should try to send in all your documents with your Appeal. The Case Management timetable will set out if and when other documents can be sent.

Can I Bring New Evidence to the Hearing?

Not normally. If you want to rely on evidence outside the timetable, you will have to apply to us on the Request form. Permission may or may not be given, depending on the reasons you give.

What if the LA has More Evidence?

The same rules apply to the LA as to you.

What if I Find it Difficult to Get Hold of a Document that is Important to My Case?

If you apply to us well before the Hearing on the Request form, we may be able to make an order to get the LA or anyone else who may have relevant information to release it. We do not need to ask the LA if it has any objections in providing the document before ordering it to be released. However, if the LA does object to releasing the information a tribunal judge will consider the objections and then decide whether or not to order the LA to release the document. You will be able to comment on the LA's objections before a decision is made.

You may also be able to ask the tribunal to require someone who is not a party to the Appeal to release a document in their possession. That person or body is not the LA but could be another body such as the NHS or Social Care.

Can I Change My Appeal?

Any changes to the Appeal must be made in writing and on our Request form. We will send you this form when we acknowledge your Appeal and it is also available on our website.

As required by the form, you must also set out the amendments sought and the reasons for the amendment. You must also send the form to the other party.

Can I Withdraw My Appeal?

Yes, but this can only be done with our consent. If done at least 10 working days before the hearing, consent will usually be given. The application to withdraw needs to be made on our Request form.

If you wish to withdraw less than 10 days working days before the hearing the application needs to be made in writing on our Request form setting out the reason why the withdrawal is late. Your request will be considered by a Tribunal Judge who will decide what further action, if any should be taken.

What Will Happen to My Appeal if I Move to Live in Another LA Area?

You should write to us and inform us if you move to another area. We will then contact the new LA to tell them about the Appeal, as the new LA will be treated as having made the decision that you are appealing about. There will then have to be a new Case Management process and timetable for supplying evidence. The old LA will take no further part in the Appeal.

The Hearing

Please Note: A DVD is available to give you some idea before the day what happens at a hearing. This DVD is available upon request. You can call 0870 241 2555 to request your copy.

Where Will My Hearing be Held?

We hold hearings throughout the country at various Tribunal Service buildings, and we will try and hold your hearing as close to where you live as possible. In special circumstances we may hold your hearing in a local hotel. We aim to limit travel to no more than one-and-a half hours in each direction by public transport.

What Time Will My Hearing Start and How Long Will it Last?

Your hearing will be fixed for a certain time which is usually 10 am or 2 pm. Please arrive 30 minutes before the hearing time so that you can meet the clerk, familiarise yourself with the arrangements and ask any questions you may have. The length of your hearing will depend on what you are appealing about and the number of witnesses attending.

Who Will Hear My Appeal?

Your Claim will be heard by a panel of three Tribunal members. There will be a legally qualified tribunal Judge and two specialist members.

Do I Have to Come to the Hearing?

You do not have to come to the hearing but it is helpful if you do. The panel will want to hear anything you have to say and you may want to ask questions of the LA and any witnesses they may bring. If you do not come, the questions will not be asked on your behalf.

Can I Have a Representative at the Hearing?

You can send someone to the hearing to represent you whether or not you come yourself. If you do have a representative, you must inform us on the Further Information Form who will be attending. The form will be sent to you when we register your appeal.

You may ask a solicitor or a barrister to represent you but you will not get public (or Legal Aid) funding for this and you will need to tell us on the Further Information Form about this representation.

Can Both Parents Come to the Hearing?

Yes, anyone who is a parent of the child, even if not a party to the appeal, may attend the hearing.

If, for some reason, you do not want the other parent to come to the hearing you will need to let us know why. We may agree to limit that person's involvement in the case.

Can My Child Attend the Hearing?

Yes, they can come and give evidence. However, you should remember that it is unlikely that they will stay for the full hearing and you must arrange for someone to look after your child whilst they are not in the hearing. The clerk will not be able to look after your child and it is unlikely that there will be a child friendly place for them and their carer to use in the Hearing building.

Do I Need to Say if I am Bringing Witnesses?

Yes, you will need to inform us on the Further Information Form who you will be bringing with you. If you do not give us this information they may be prevented from participating in the hearing or even being in the room where the hearing is held. If you change your witnesses you should inform us immediately.

Please note: It is often not necessary to bring any witnesses at all. If you do want to bring a witness, you are normally allowed to bring no more than 3 to the hearing. This is because we want to ensure that hearings are over within a day and that we focus on only the relevant issues.

If you wish to bring any more than three witnesses (in addition to yourself) you will need to request permission in writing on the Further Information Form. We do have power to limit the number of witnesses.

What if a Witness Refuses to Come to the Hearing?

If you have asked someone and they are unhappy about attending, you can write to us explaining why you feel it is important they attend. We will need to receive your request at least 10 working days before the hearing.

If the Tribunal agree, we will issue a witness summons that you should give to the person. That person would then have to attend the hearing unless there are very good reasons why they cannot.

Can I Bring Anyone Else to Support Me During My Hearing?

Yes, you can bring another person with you for support but they will not be able to take part in the hearing, and you must tell us on the Further Information Form who they will be. If you think that you want more than one supporter, please ask us on our Request Form. We have power to exclude any person from the hearing. As it is a private hearing we will not agree to people other than supporters attending. If your representative is training someone on our Tribunal process, we will normally allow them to attend provided that they make a request in writing at least 10 working days before the hearing. They will not be allowed to take part in the hearing.

Will I be Able to Ask My Own Questions?

Yes, you will have the chance to ask questions of the LA witnesses and also add anything you feel is important but has not been mentioned.

What Expenses Can be Claimed?

You and your witnesses can claim travel expenses to come to the hearing. If you bring a friend or a relative to look after your child, you will be able to Claim their travel expenses as well.

You should use public transport where possible (bus, tram, standard class rail travel). If you travel by car you can claim a fixed amount for mileage. We will only pay for taxi fares if public transport is not available, or if you have particular needs (you must tell us about these before making your claim for expenses). Any taxi fare should be authorised in advance. We cannot pay for car parking and tolls.

Your witnesses can also claim a fixed amount for loss of earnings. We will send you details about claiming expenses when we write to you to tell you about the arrangements for your hearing. At the hearing the clerk will give you the relevant forms to fill in and return to us. We will then either send the expenses by post or put them straight into your account. If waiting for the expenses would cause you financial difficulty please let us known advance of the hearing, as we may be able to arrange to give you a cheque on the day, but this is not always possible. If you do not tell us in advance, we cannot give you a cheque on the day of the hearing.

The Decision

When Will I Know the Tribunal's Decision?

You should receive the decision and reasons by post within 10 working days of the

Hearing. The decision will be posted to you and to the LA. Although some decisions may take longer due to their complexity.

Does the Decision Have to be in English?

No, you can request for the decision to be translated into another language or Braille. However, if you request this it will delay you receiving your decision.

How Long Does the LA Have to Put in Place the Tribunal's Decision?

When your Appeal has been decided the LA must comply with our decision within a fixed period, beginning with the date the decision was issued.

- To start the assessment or reassessment process—**4 weeks**
- To make a statement—**5 weeks**
- To change a statement—**5 weeks**
- To change the school named in line with parents wishes—**2 weeks**
- To continue a statement—**immediately**
- To cancel (cease to maintain) a statement—**immediately**

These timescales also apply when the LA tells us it doesn't oppose the appeal. If the LA does not comply with the order in the time required, you may have to apply to the High Court to enforce.

What Can I Do if I Am not Happy about the Tribunal's Decision?

We will send you a leaflet setting out in detail your options when we send you the decision. However, the following is a brief outline of your options.

When you have received a decision from the Tribunal you may consider that the decision is wrong in law or that there is another reason why the Tribunal should look again at its decision. If you think it is wrong in law you can appeal to the Administrative Appeals Chamber of the Upper Tribunal but you must first apply to us for permission to appeal.

Applications for permission to appeal against our decision and other applications that you can make following a Tribunal decision are explained in detail in the Guidance that will be sent to you with your decision.

Who Can Make an Application?

You can make an Application if you have been a party to an appeal or claim before the First-tier Tribunal in a special educational needs or disability discrimination case. This includes a parent, or person having parental responsibility, a local authority or a responsible body for a school.

What Applications Can I Make?

Following a decision of the First-tier Tribunal it is possible to make the following Applications:

A. You can apply for permission to appeal if you think that the Tribunal's decision was wrong in law.

B. You can ask the Tribunal to review its decision because there has been a change in relevant circumstances since the decision was made.

C. You can ask the Tribunal to set aside its decision in certain circumstances.

These three Applications are explained in detail in the Guidance we will send you with your decision.

When Can I Make an Application?

An Application must be made so that it is received by the Tribunal no more than 28 days from the date on the letter by which the Tribunal sent you the decision.

If you are applying more than 28 days after the decision was sent, you will need to apply for an extension of time, giving the reasons why you are applying late. If the Tribunal does not agree to extend the time, your application will not be considered.

Notice of Appeal Form Checklist—What to Send Us with this Form

If you want to appeal against your Local Authority's refusal to assess or reassess your child's special educational needs or if the Local Authority has assessed but does not make a statement of special educational needs, we will require:

- A copy of the letter from the Local Authority notifying you of its decision and of your right to appeal.
- Your reasons for making the appeal—this can be found on Section 5 of the appeal form.

If you are appealing against any or all of parts 2, 3 and 4 of the statement of special educational needs or against the school named in a statement that is over a year old, we will require:

- A copy of the letter from the Local Authority notifying you of its decision and of your right to appeal.
- Your reasons for making the appeal—this can be found on Section 5 of the appeal form.
- A copy of your child's current statement that came with the letter mentioned above (usually called a final statement or final revised statement).
- The appendices that accompanied the statement. These are a set of documents that are attached to the statement. Please note: If you are appealing against an amended statement the LA may not have attached all of the appendices. You will need to take these from the original statement.
- Written confirmation that you have informed the school that you want it to be named in part 4.

If you wish to appeal against the Local Authority's decision to cancel (or no longer maintain) your child's statement, we will require:

- A copy of the letter from the Local Authority notifying you of its decision and of your right to appeal.
- Your reasons for making the appeal—This can be found on Section 5 of the appeal form.
- A copy of your child's current statement (the one the LA says it is going to cancel).

To make an appeal to the First Tier Special Educational Needs and Disability you will need to fill in this form and return it to us no later than 2 months after the Local Authority sent you its decision.

FIRST-TIER TRIBUNAL (SPECIAL EDUCATIONAL NEEDS AND DISABILITY) IN ENGLAND AND WALES

From 3rd November 2008 the Special Educational Needs and Disability Tribunal ceased to exist as a stand-alone body and became part of a new two-tier Tribunal structure; the First-tier Tribunal and the Upper Tribunal. The two new Tribunals consist of chambers that group together jurisdictions dealing with similar work or requiring similar skills.

The existing judges and non-legal members of the Special Educational Needs and Disability Tribunal all transferred into the new two-tier system and continue their vital work in much the same way as they did before. Special Educational Needs and Disability now sits in the Health, Education and Social Care (HESC) Chamber of the First-Tier Tribunal. Appeals against the panel's decisions now go to the Upper Tribunal instead of to the High Court.

Parents whose children have special educational needs can appeal to the First-tier Tribunal (Special Educational Needs and Disability) against decisions made by Local Education Authorities in England about their children's education.

The applications forms and guidance can be found by visiting the Parents area.

Appeals registered under the old Rules.

Any case that was registered before the 3rd November will proceed through the First-tier Tribunal process under the Regulations that applied to the Special Educational Needs and Disability Tribunal (SEND). These appeals can be easily identified as they will have been given an Appeal Reference Number lower than 08-03261.

The only exception will be for a small number of cases that were pre-registered before the 3rd November with a letter requesting further information being issued to the applicant. In these cases, if all of the required information was received on or after 3rd November, the appeal will proceed under the relevant First-tier Tribunal Rules.

The Rules for the First-tier Tribunal (Special Educational Needs and Disability) will apply to any application to review or appeal decisions after a final tribunal decision has been made if the decision was issued after 3rd November irrespective of when the hearing took place. This means that these provisions will apply to any case that is proceeding under the old regulations.

Anyone wishing to make an appeal against a decision made by the Tribunal (either SEND or First-Tier) on or after November 3rd will need to follow the relevant First-tier Tribunal Rules and appeal to the Upper Tribunal.

TRIBUNAL HEARING

Your parents and the Children's Service cannot agree about some part of your education. They might not agree about the help you need in school. They might not agree which school you should go to.

Your parents and the children's Service have agreed to come to the Tribunal hearing to talk about what is best for you and your education.

All the people at the hearing will be friendly and polite with each other.

Everyone has agreed that the Tribunal should make the final decision.

Where Will the Hearing Be?

The Tribunal will happen in a town or city closer to the area in which you live.
It can be held in Tribunal Service buildings or hotels.
There will be somewhere for you to sit and wait and talk to each other.
You will be able to go to the toilet when you need to.

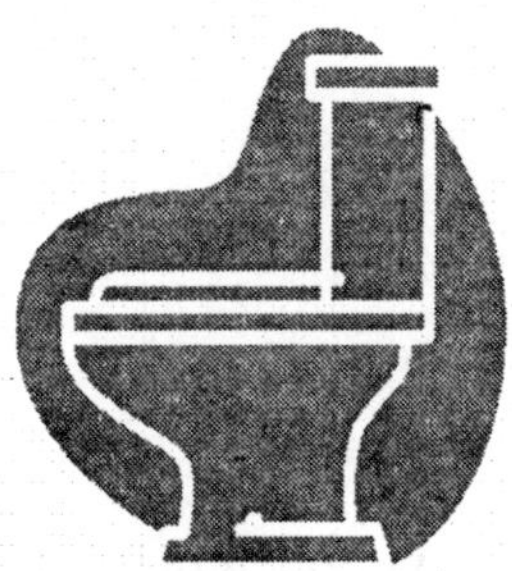

What Do I Have to Do?

Before the hearing we would like to find out how you feel about the things you do in school. You could write about the activities that you and your friends enjoy, or you could draw a picture, or even take photographs. Your parents can send these to us.

Who Will Be at the Tribunal?

- The Clerk
- You and your parents will be met by the clerk, who can be a man or a woman. The clerk will show you where to wait and will answer any questions you have. The clerk will lead the way into the room when it is time for the hearing.

The Tribunal Panel

There are three people on a Tribunal panel. One person knows about the law and is in charge of the hearing. The other two people have worked with children with special education needs and know what is important for them in schools. These three people will have read a lot of papers about you and will be very interested to meet you and talk to you. Everyone wears ordinary clothes, not uniforms, robes or wigs.

Your Parents and their Representative

Parents can ask someone to help them at the hearing.

This person is their representative. Your parents can also bring witnesses to tell the panel about how you are doing in school.

Someone from your school, such as a teacher or support assistant might be there.

Sometimes, it might be someone from your family or who knows your family well.

The Children's Service

The Children's Service (sometimes called the Local Authority) may also have a representative and a witness. A teacher or someone else from your school might also be there with them.

Will I Stay in the Hearing Room All the Time?

Most children stay for the start of the hearing and then are taken back to school by a family friend or a relative. You will be asked to tell the panel how you feel about school at the moment, what you like to do in school, and what you think needs to happen to help you learn. Your parents representative and the Children's Service representative might also ask you some questions about school. You will sit with your parents and can leave the hearing room at any time.

What Will Happen at the Tribunal?

Your parents and the other visitors will sit at a long table. The tribunal panel will sit at the other side of the table. Your parents will be invited to tell the panel about your work in school. People from the Children's Service will then tell the panel what they do to help you to learn. The panel will ask your parents and the Children's Service some questions. Most hearings last for either a morning or an afternoon but some hearings can last all day.

What Happens After the Hearing?

When the hearing is finished your parents will go home. The panel will stay behind and talk about all they have heard. They will stay until they decide what should happen. The tribunal will send your parents a letter after about three weeks.

Glossary of SEN Related Terms

Algorithm: Procedures or steps in a systematic process, (e.g.: steps in computer programming). The Flow Chart for Diagnostic Approach to Scholastic Backwardness follows an Algorithm.

Assessment: Estimate of the intensity of disability or disorder. For an LD child a detailed assessment of academic skills, language and motor skills is done to find out the levels of functioning.

Behaviour Modification: Modifying or changing undesirable behaviour to desirable or more acceptable ones. It involves systematic application of the principles of the Learning Theory.

Co-morbid Disorders: Presence of another disorder along with an already existing disorder.

Comprehension: Refers to the ability to understand, and is the objective in reading.

Counsellor: A professional (usually with a masters degree in Psychology or Social Work) who is trained to analyse a social or psychological problem and help the client find an alternate solution.

Decoding: A process in reading. It involves understanding the phoneme-grapheme relationships and translating printed words into spoken language. These skills enable to pronounce words correctly.

Diagnostic Approach: An approach in which the diagnosis or identification of a disease or disorder is made by means of symptoms.

Diagnostic Manuals: Books of instruction that contain the symptoms of diseases or disorders that aid in the diagnosis. Diagnostic and Statistical Manual (DSM) Ed. IV, and International Classification of Diseases (ICD) Revision X are examples.

Diagnostic Test: A test that provides an in-depth assessment of a skill area, including strengths and weaknesses and error patterns.

Discrepancy: Inconsistency, or failure to correspond. There is an inconsistency or difference between a child's innate ability or potential and his performance (performance on paper does not correspond to actual potential).

Disorder: A disturbance which upsets physical or psychological functions. A Learning Disorder is caused because of defective brain areas responsible for academic skills like reading, writing etc.

Dyscalculia: Difficulty to calçulatè, manipulate number or do simple sums, caused due to impairment in related areas in the brain.

Dysfunction: Malfunction or impairment of function. LD is referred to as a Central Nervous System (CNS) dysfunction because the brain areas responsible for academic skills are affected.

Dyslexia: Difficulty to read (Greek word: dys-difficulty, lexis-words), Children with Dyslexia find it difficult to read or to understand what is read.

Flow Chart: Graphic representation of the successive steps in a procedure or system. A flow chart indicating the possible causes of poor school performance is used to diagnose the causes for scholastic backwardness in a given child.

Grapheme: The written symbols. A child is able to write words or spell only if he possesses good Phoneme-Grapheme correspondence (sound-letter associations). LD children may have difficulty with phoneme-grapheme correspondence.

Grapho Motor skills: Ability to draw diagrams or to sketch using motor co-ordination skills.

Handicap: A disadvantage or impediment. Children with LD are handicapped because their academic skills do not function optimally.

I.E.P.: Individualized Education Programme. It is an educational programme formulated for each child with Special Needs, in accordance with the child's deficits (Needs) and skills.

Impulsivity: A sudden inclination to act without thinking of consequences. Many children with Attention Deficit Disorders are found to be impulsive.

Inclusive Education: The system of education where children with special needs are integrated in regular mainstream schools, thus minimizing segregation from peers.

IQ Tests: Tests for measuring Intelligence Quotient. Provide a global estimate of scholastic potential. IQ tests are generally done to rule out poor intelligence.

Mental Retardation: Sub-average general intellectual functioning. The impairment may be reflected in a slow rate of maturation, reduced learning capacity and/or inadequate social adjustment, present singly or in combinations. Children with Borderline Intelligence are also called Slow Learners.

Milestones of development: Specific stages of development in the life cycle of a child. A child is expected to attain certain stages of development at specific period of time. Example—holding head erect at three months, talking monosyllables by eight months to fifteen months etc.

Mnemonic: A short form or symbol or code intended to aid memory. It is a clue for retrieving learned information. Mnemonic devices help students to remember content.

Morbidity: A state of illness, disease or disorder.

Motor Co-ordination Skills: The ability of the brain to co-ordinate gross and fine motor movements. Fine-Motor Co-ordination is the ability to use the small muscles to accomplish tasks requiring precision such as writing, buttoning, lacing, cutting etc. Gross-Motor Co-ordination is the ability to use the large muscles in a co-ordinated, purposeful manner to engage in activities like running, throwing and kicking. In LD children, the activities affected are self-help skills like buttoning, lacing and academic tasks like handwriting, drawing diagrams, copying shapes etc.

Multidisciplinary Approach: An Approach using combination of various Disciplines to tackle a problem/situation. The LD child requires a combination of services of professionals from various disciplines like Psychiatry, Psychology, Social Work, Speech Pathology, Special Education etc. due to the multiple problems in his growth and development.

Multisensory approach: An instructional approach in which the teacher uses more than one of the child's senses. It involves the use of all sensory modalities including Visual, Auditory, Kinesthetic and Tactile.

Obsessions: These are repetitive images or thoughts that intrude repetitively into a person's mind, which the person tries to resist, and on resisting develops anxiety. Example—after washing the hand, a repetitive thought occurs that the hand is still unclean. (If it is not washed again, the person becomes anxious).

Phoneme: A unit of sound that combines with other sounds to form words. It is the smallest unit of language. A phoneme alone does not convey meaning.

Phonetics: The study of speech sounds and their production, classification and transcription.

Phonics: A method of teaching reading based upon sounds.

Pointers: It refers to a clue or indication. There are certain pointers for LD which a classroom teacher can pick up and thus aid in the process of diagnosis.

Pre-academic skills: Basic skills that a preschool child has to be equipped with, before starting formal school instruction. These skills are also called 'Readiness skills' for learning.

Referral: A formal request for evaluation. For a child experiencing learning or behavioural problems, referral to a professional may be required.

Remediation: The process of correcting or strengthening areas of skill deficits. In LD children, it refers to special instruction to help overcome difficulties in learning.

Resource Room: A Special Education placement in which children receive intensive individual or small group instruction for less than half the day. The children are usually instructed for the remainder of the day in a regular classroom.

Scanning: To examine details. It is a reading strategy which involves careful reading of key sentences, phrases and words to locate specific information rapidly.

Scholastic Backwardness: Not being able to perform academically in accordance to age, grade and potential. LD is one of the major reasons for scholastic backwardness.

Self-esteem: A concept or opinion one has about oneself. Children with LD generally have poor self-esteem as they are not able to perform well in school.

Sensory deficits: Difficulty caused due to malfunctioning of sense organs particularly the ears and eyes. Poor school performance can be caused due to deficits like visual or hearing impairment.

Sight Vocabulary: Words the reader recognizes without applying phonetic analysis and are learned as whole words. They include frequently used words, words the reader recognizes instantly from repeated exposure and words that have irregular spellings (of, an, the etc.).

Skimming: Reading to gather salient facts. It is a reading strategy where students isolate and rapidly read key sentences, phrases and words to identify the main ideas.

Social skills: Children have to posses these skills to learn socially appropriate behaviour. Those who lack these skills are unable to pick up social cues like other children, or predict social consequences of their actions.

Soft Neurological signs: Subtle evidence of difficulties, on neurological examination, in processing sensations and controlling movements. These signs are more common in children with Specific Learning Disorders.

Special Educational Needs (SEN): Children with Skill Deficits requiring Special Educational Instructions. Children with Learning Disorders require special educational inputs as they may be unable to profit from instruction in the regular classroom.

Strategies: Planning methods for achieving goals. Learning strategies are techniques, principles or rules that enable a student to learn independently. Support strategies are techniques for help and remediation.

Syllabication: It is the process of dividing a word into its component parts. Each syllable contains a vowel sound. There are one syllable, two syllable and multisyllable words.

Therapist: A practitioner who resorts to any particular kind of treatment. Eg: Psychotherapist, Psychologist. A teacher is considered a therapist for children with LD for she is the best person to cater to the special educational needs of the LD child.

Tics: Tics are involuntary, sudden, rapid, recurrent, non-rhythmic, stereotyped motor movements or vocalizations. This is a Neurological Disorder and is amenable to treatment.

Transpose: Change of position in a series. One of the frequently committed errors in maths is transposing the answer when copying it from the working column. Eg: 23156 is copied as 21356.

Under achievers: Students whose academic achievement is below that of the expected standard.

Visuo Spatial Deficit: Deficits in Visuo spatial skills. It is a Neuropsychological function, where a person is able to understand a figure or drawing on any particular background. This skill is required to understand the layout of a figure or written matter.

Bibliography

Advani, L. (2002). "Education: A Fundamental Right of Every Child Regardless of His/Her Special Needs." *Journal of Indian Education; Special Issue on Education of Learners with Special Needs.* New Delhi: NCERT.

Alur, M. (2002). "Special Needs Policy in India", in S. Hegarty and M. Alue (eds.), *Education and Children with Special Needs: From Segregation to Inclusion.* New Delhi: Sage.

Anita, B.K. (2000). *Village Caste and Education.* Jaipur: Rawat Publications.

Applebee, A. (1998). *Curriculum and Conversation: Transforming Traditions of Teaching and Learning.* Reviewed by B. Day and T. Yarbrough, *Journal of Curriculum Studies,* 30 (3): 357-74.

Balasubramanian, K. (2004). *The Helping Hand (A Short Story about a Disabled Child).* Hyderabad: Spark-India.

Baquer, A. and A. Sharma (1997). *Disability: Challenges vs. Responses.* New Delhi: CAN.

Bhattacharya, B. (2001). Multi-coloured Wings. Kolkata: Indian Institute of Cerebral Palsy.

Booth, T. (1996). "Stories of Exclusion: Natural and Unnatural Selection", in E. Blyth and J. Milner (eds.), *Exclusion from School: Inter Professional Issues from Policy and Practice.* London: Routledge.

UNESCO (2000). *Inclusion in Education: The Participation of Disabled Learners. World Education Forum: Education for All 2000 Assessment.* Paris: UNESCO.

Borah, J.R. (2003). An In-depth Study into the Problems of Education of the Mentally Retarded Children in Assam. Ph.D Thesis, Guwahati University.

Bose, K. (1996). Studying the Effectiveness of Computer Programmes as Remedial Strategies for Overcoming Specific Learning Disabilities. Ph.D Thesis, Jamia Millia Islamia.

Chadha, A. (2002). "Inclusive Education in DPEP." *Journal of Indian Education. Special Issue on Education of Learners with Special Needs.*

Chib, M. (2000). *Citizenship and Barriers.* Mumbai: The Spastic Society of India.

Chopra, G. (1998). Module for Training Anganwadi Workers for Early Detection of Childhood Disabilities. Ph.D Dissertation, University of Delhi.

Connell, R. (2002). *Gender,* Cambridge, Polity.

Corker, M. and S. French, Eds. (1999). *Disability Discourse.* Buckingham, Open University Press.

Cronbach, L.J. and R.E. Snow (1977). *Abilities and Instructional Methods.* New York: Irvington.

Dash, A. (1997). Impact of Adapted Physical Education on the Physical Fitness of Mentally Retarded Children. *Disabilities and Disabilities,* 11(1): 9-15.

Department of Education (1986): *National Policy on Education,* 1986. New Delhi: MHRD, GOI.

Department of Education (2000). *Sarva Shiksha Abhiyan: A Programme for Universal Elementary Education.* New Delhi: MHRD, GOI.

Department of Education (2003). *Inclusive Education Scheme (Draft).* New Delhi: MHRD, GOI.

DPEP (2000). *Empowerment through Education: Identification and Enrolment of Children with Special Needs in DPEP.* New Delhi: Education Consultant of India Limited.

DPEP (2001). Towards Inclusive School in DPEP. NOIDA; Ed.CIL.

DPEP (2003). *In India,* 2005, Publication Division, Ministry of Information and Broadcasting, Government of India.

Evans, P. (1997). *Inclusive Education, A Global Agenda* (Eds.) S.J. Pijl, J.W. Meijer & S. Hegarty: Routledge, London, 1997.

Farrell, P. and M. Ainscow (2002). "Making Special Education Inclusive: Mapping the Issues", in P. Farrell and M. Aincow (eds.), *Making Special Education Inclusive.* London: Fulton.

Five Year Plans: *http: www.planning commission.hic.in /plans/ planrel/five Yr/ 7th/ vol 2 / 7v2ch10.html.* Accessed on May 21, 2004.

Government of India (2001). *The Provisional Population Census Report (2001).* New Delhi: GOI.

Govinda, R. (2002). *India Education Report.* New Delhi: National Institute of Educational Planning and Administration (NIEPA).

Gupta, H.O. and A. Singh (1994) "Status of Science Teaching in Indian Schools for the Visually Impaired Children", *School Science 32: 21-23(2).*

Hegarty, S. and M. Alur (eds.) (2002). *Education and Children with Special Needs.* New Delhi: Sage.

Iyanar, J. (2001). "Listening to Different Voices—Inclusion and Exclusion of People with Disabilities in Education", *Asia Pacific Disability Rehabilitation Journal,* 12 (2): 155-59.

Jain, M. (2004). "Civics, Citizens, and Human Rights: Civics Discourse in India." *Contemporary Education Dialogue* 1(2): 165-98, Ministry of Human Resource Development (2002). *Janshala.* Janshala National Office, Department of Elementary Education and Literacy, MHRD, GOI.

Jayaram, M. (ed.) (2004). Proceedings of the Seminar on Issues Related to Disability in the Community. Mysore, All India Institute of Speech and Hearing.

Jha, M.M. (2002). *School Without Walls: Inclusive Education for All.* Oxford: Heinemann.

Jose, S.J. and G. Kareparampil (1995). *Persons with Disabilities in Society—A Handout.*

Julka, A. (2004). Strengthening Teacher Education Curriculum from the Perspective of Children with Special Educational Needs. Unpublished Report. New Delhi: NCERT.

Karanth, P., and J. Rozario (2003). *Learning Disabilities in India.* New Delhi: Sage.

Krejci, M. (1998). "A Study of the Use of Yoga with Mentally Retarded Children." *Disabilities and Disabilities, 12*(2): 75-80.

Krishna Swamy and Shankar (2003). *Integration & Inclusion—How are they Different?* Paper presented in the National Seminar on Inclusive Education Practices in Schools, NCERT, 2003.

Lele, V. and A. Khaledkar (1994). A Study to Identify the Learning Problems of Hearing Impaired Children in Language Textbook (Marathi) of Primary Level and Development of Supplementary Explanatory (Instructional) Material to Improve their Uses of Language. Independent study. Nasik: Shrimathi Mai Lele Shravan Vikas Vidyalaya.

Lewis, A. (1991). Primary Special Needs and the National Curriculum, Routledge, London.

Loreman, T. and Deppeler, J.M. (2001). "Inclusive Education in Victoria", *Interaction, 14*, 13-17.

Luthra, P.N. (1974). "Role of the Department of Social Welfare in the Rehabilitation of the Handicapped", *Journal of Rehabilitation in Asia, 15*: 9-19.

Malhotra, S. (2003) *Management of Attitudinal Barriers at Different Levels of Inclusive Education Implementation.* Paper presented in the National Seminar on Innovative Approaches to Education and Empowerment of the Disabled. NCERT, 2003.

Mani, M.N.G. (2000). *Inclusive Education in Indian Context.* Coimbatore: Ramakrishna Mission Vidyalaya.

Mani, M.N.G. and Mulhariah, N. (2003) *Creating Effective Classroom through Cooperative Learning.* Paper presented in the National Seminar on Innovative Approaches to Education and Empowerment of the Disabled. NCERT, 2003.

Project Integrated Education for the Disabled. (1993). New Delhi: NCERT.

Meekosha, H. (2004) Gender and Disability. (Draft entry for the forthcoming Sage Encyclopaedia of Disability written in 2004), http://socialwork.arts.unsw.edu.au/April, 2004.

Mehta, V. (1982). *Vedi.* New York: Oxford University Press.

Ministry of Human Resources Development (MHRD) (1990). *Towards an Enlightened and Humane Society: NPE 1986—A Review.* New Delhi: GOI.

Ministry of Human Resource Development (1992). *Revised Programme of Action, 1992.* New Delhi: GOI.

Ministry of Human Resources Development (MHRD). *Annual Report 2002-03.* New Delhi: GOI.

Ministry of Human Resources Development (2000). Sarva Shiksha Abhiyan: Framework for Implementation, Department of Elementary Education & Literacy, New Delhi; GOI.

Ministry of Social Justice and Empowerment of India. *Annual Report (2000-01),* New Delhi: GOI.

MHRD *Annual Report (2001-02).* New Delhi: GOI.

Ministry of Welfare (1995). *Handbook on Disability Rehabilitation.* New Delhi: GOI.

Mishra, A. (2000). "India: Special Education", in C.R. Reynolds, and F.E. Janzen **(eds.)**, *Encyclopaedia of Special Education: A Reference for the Education of the Handicapped and other Exceptional Children and Adults*, 2e. USA: John Wiley and Sons.

Mishra, V.K. (2004). *Eminent Disabled People of the World*. New Delhi.

Mohapatra, C.S. (2004). *Disability Management in India: Challenges and Commitments*. New Delhi: National Institute for the Mentally Handicapped (NIMH) and the Indian Institute of Public Administration.

Mohit, A. (2003). "Human Rights Model and Access", *International Journal of Human Rights*.

Mohite, P. (1994). *Working with Disabled Children: Curriculum and Assessment*. Independent Study. Baroda: The Maharaja Sayaji Rao University of Baroda.

National Council of Educational Research and Training (NCERT) (1998). *Sixth All-India Educational Survey*. New Delhi: NCERT.

NCERT (2000). *Assessment of Needs for Inclusive Education: Report of the First Regional Workshop for SAARC Countries*. New Delhi: NCERT.

NCERT (2000). *National Curriculum Framework for School Education* (NCFSE). New Delhi: NCERT.

NCERT (2001). *Indian Educational Abstracts*. New Delhi: NCERT.

National Institute for the Mentally Handicapped (NIMH) (2005). *Status of Education of Children with Disabilities*. Hyderabad: United Nations Development Programme (UNDP) and NIMH.

National Sample Survey Organisation (NSSO) (1991), *A Report on Disabled Persons*. New Delhi: NSSO.

National Sample Survey 58th round July to December 2002 (2003). National Sample Survey Organisation, Ministry of Statistics and Programme Implementation, Government of India.

Nosek, M.A. and R.B. Hughes (2003). "Psychological issues of women with physical disabilities; the continuing gender debate." *Rehabilitation Counselling Bulletin 46* (4); 224.

NSSO (2002). "Disabled Persons in India". Website of the Office of Chief Commissioner of Persons with Disabilities in India, http://www.ccdisabilities.nic, in/disability%20india.htm. Accessed on October 1, 2003.

Paranjpe, S. (1996). "Achievement of Normal and Hearing Handicapped Pupils at the End of the Primary Cycle", *Disabilities and Impairments—*, *19*(2): 73-86.

Pijl, S.J. and Meijer, C.J.W. (1991). "Does Integration Count for Much? An Analysis of the Practices of Integration in Eight Countries", *European Journal of Special Needs Education*, 2: 63-73.

Puri, M. and Abraham, G. (eds.) (2004). *Handbook of Inclusive Education for Educators, Administrators and Planners*. New Delhi: Sage.

Quinn, S. and K. Ryba (2000). "Linking Inclusive Policies with Best Teaching Practices", in D. Fraser, R. Moltzen, and K. Ryba (eds.), *Learners with Special Needs in Aotearoa*, New Zealand. Dunmore Press.

Rehabilitation Council of India (2000). *Status of Disability in India (2000).* New Delhi: Rehabilitation Council of India.

Rehabilitation Council of India (2001). *Status of Disability in India (2001).* New Delhi: Rehabilitation Council of India.

Renaissance Group (1999). http:/www.uni.edu/coe/inclusion and http://www.rushservices.com/inclusion.

Rioux, M.H. and Mohit, A. (2005). *Human Rights Disability and Law: National Human Rights Commission.* New Delhi.

Rohindekar, S.R. and Usha, M.N. (1988). *Educational and Vocational Needs of Physically Handicapped Children.* Bangalore: Institute for Social and Economic Change.

Rutter, M. and W. Yule (1975). "The Concept of Specific Reading Retardation", *Journal of Child Psychology and Psychiatry,* 16: 181-97.

Ryndak, D.L. and S.K. Alper (1996). *Curriculum Content for Students with Moderate and Severe Disabilities in Inclusive Settings.* Boston: Allyn and Bacon, pp. 5-6.

Sharma K. (2002). "Altitudinal Changes—Breaking the Psycho-social Barriers", *Journal of Indian Education,* 27(4): 85-89.

Sharma, P.L. (1997). "Education of Children with Hearing Impairment", *The Primary Teacher,* 12 (1): 26-29.

Sharmista, P.S. (2003). *Linguistic Concept Attainment as One of the Indicators for Successful Inclusion of the Hearing Impaired. Indicators of Quality Education,* New Delhi: NCERT, pp. 181-192.

Singh, S. (2001). "Educational Needs, Relevant Curriculum and Rehabilitation Expectations of Handicapped Children." *Indian Educational Review, 37*(1): 84-96.

Singhal, N. and Rouse, M. (2003). "We Do Inclusion: Practitioner Perspectives in some Inclusive Schools in India", *Perspectives in Education, 21*(3): 85-98.

Singhal, N. (2004), Education in 21st Century, Conflict, Reconciliation and Reconstruction. Paper presented at the British Association for International and Comparative Education (BAICE) Conference, University of Sussex, September 3-5, 2004.

Subrahmanian, R. (2003). "Right to Education: Opportunities and Challenges", *Education Dialogue, 1*(1): 76-96.

Taneja, N. (2001). "The 93rd Amendment Bill: A Fraud in the Name of Rights to Education", *Communist People's Democracy, 15*(47 and 25)-16.

Thakur Hari Prasad Institute of Research and Rehabilitation of Mentally Retarded (2001) *Therapeutic Effect of Dance, Music and Yogasana on Mental Retardation.* An internal study, Hyderabad, India.

Tomlinson, S. (1982). A Sociology of Special Education, London: Routledge and Kegan Paul.

Tyler, S. (1990). "Subtypes of Specific Learning Difficulty: A Review" in P.D. Pumfrey and C.D. Elliott (eds.), *Children's Difficulties in Reading, Spelling and Writing,* Lewes: Falmer, pp. 29-39.

Umadevi, M.R. (1997). Effectiveness of a Remedial Programme on Improving Reading Comprehension Skills among Dyslexic Children. Ph.D Thesis. Kuvempu University.

UNESCO (1994). *The Salamanca Statement and Framework for Action on Special Needs Education.* Paris: UNESCO.

UNESCO (1997). *International Standard Classification of Education.* Paris: UNESCO.

UNESCO (2001). *Open File on Inclusive Education: Support Materials for Managers and Administrators.* Paris: UNESCO.

Valmiki, A. (2003). Towards Culturally Inclusive Education: Preparing Culturally Responsible Teachers to Engage in Culturally Specific Pedagogy. Paper presented in the National Seminar on Inclusive Education Practices in School—, Bangalore, India, February 26-27, 2003.

Werner, D. *Disabled Village Children.* Berkeley, CA: The Hesperian Foundation.

Wolf, G. (1995). *Landscapes: Children's Voices.* Madras: Tara Publishing Group.

Web Links

Every Child Matters

http://www.everychildmatters.gov.uk

Social Emotional Aspects of Learning

http://www.teachernet.gov.uk/seal
http://bandapilot.org.uk/primary/seal/downloads/books/pns_seal132705_newbeg_pur.pdf
http://bandapilot.org.uk/secondary/pages/development.html

Promoting Children's Mental Health within Early Years and School Settings

http://www.teachernet.gov.uk/docbank/index.cfm?id=10867

Guidance on School Discipline and Pupil Behaviour Policies

http://www.teachernet.gov.uk/wholeschool/behaviour/schooldisciplinepupil behaviourpolicies/

Personalised Assessment and Provision

http://standards.dfes.gov.uk/personalisedlearning

School Standards and Progress

http://www.teachernet.gov.uk/teachingandlearning/schoolstandards/

National Strategies' Three Waves Model

http://www.standards.dfes.gov.uk/secondary/keystage3/all/respub/ns_ws_ped_pers

Guidance on Exclusion from Schools and Pupil Referral Units

http://www.teachernet.gov.uk/wholeschool/behaviour/exclusion/guidance2007/

Guidance on Education-Related Parenting Contracts, Parenting Orders and Penalty Notices

http://www.dcsf.gov.uk/schoolattendance/uploads/Parenting%20Contract-Guidance%20PNsPCsPOs%20FINAL2007.pdf

Guidance for Local Authorities and Schools—Pupil Referral Units and Alternative Provision

http://publications.teachernet.gov.uk/default.aspx? PageFunction=productdetails&Page Mode=publications&ProductId =LEA%2f0024%2f 2005&

National Service Framework for Children, Young People and Maternity Services Standard 9: The Mental Health and Psychological Well-being of Children and Young People

http://www.dh.gov.uk/en/Publicationsandstatistics/Publications/PublicationsPolicyAndGuidance/Browsable/DH_4094607

Guidance on School Partnership to Improve Behaviour and Tackle Persistent Absence

http://www.teachernet.gov.uk/wholeschool/behaviour/collaboration

Intervening Early and Current Interventions Used by Primary Schools

http://publications.teachernet.gov.uk/default.aspx? PageFunction=productdetails&PageMode=publications&ProductId=DfES+0131+2002&

Guidance on Planning and Developing Special Educational Provision

http://www.dfes.gov.uk/schoolorg/guidance.cfm?id=24

National Curriculum

http://www.nc.uk.net

Disapplication of the National Curriculum

http://www.dcsf.gov.uk/disapply

Re-motivating Young People

www.qca.org.uk/14-19/11-16-schools/110_2474.htm

Diplomas

diploma@qca.org.uk

Professional Standards for Teachers

www.tda.gov.uk/standards

Ofsted's Healthy Minds Report (July 2005)

http://www.ofsted.gov.uk/portal/site/Internet/menuitem.eace3f09a603f6d9c3172a8a08c08a0c?vgnextoid=9edf2a5f74f3c010VgnVCM1000003507640aRCRD

The Learning Support Units Website

http://www.teachernet.gov.uk/wholeschool/behaviour/learningsupportunits/casestudies/

National Programme for Specialist Leaders Training Materials

http://www.teachernet.gov.uk/wholeschool/behaviour/npsl_ba/resources/studymaterials/besd/

National Healthy Schools Programme

http://www.healthyschools.gov.uk/Theme-EHW.aspx?ThemeID=4&CriteriaID=41

Behaviour Improvement Programme

http://www.dfes.gov.uk/behaviourimprovement

Sure Start

http://www.surestart.gov.uk

School Behaviour Partnerships

http://www.teachernet.gov.uk/wholeschool/behaviour/collaboration/

Healthy Minds (Ofsted July 2005) Case Studies

http://www.ofsted.gov.uk/portal/site/Internet/menuitem.eace3f09a603f6d9c3172a8a08c08a0c/?vgnextoid=9edf2a5f74f3c010VgnVCM1000003507640aRCRD

14-19 Pathways

http://www.dfes.gov.uk/14-19/index.cfm?sid=1

14-19 Good Practice

http://www.dfes.gov.uk/14-19/index.cfm?sid=9

Use of Force

http://www.teachernet.gov.uk/docbank/index.cfm?id=12187

Physical Interventions

http://www.teachernet.gov.uk/wholeschool/sen/schools/piguide/

Index

Able-bodied children, 122
Absenteeism, 198
Abuse, 16-17, 21, 70, 93, 95, 100, 111
  child, 15
  civil, 17
  emotional, 16
  financial, 17
  peer, 17
  physical, 16
  sexual, 16
  systemic, 17
  types of, 16
  verbal, 16
Academic achievement, 25, 107, 110
Academic skills, 27, 41, 43-45, 53-54, 56-57, 60
  assessment, 43
  tests of, 44
Academic success, 28, 62
Access services, 149, 162, 181
Achievement tests, 26
Additional Support Needs (ASN), 229-36, 272
Administrative Appeals Chamber, 285
Alcohol misuse, 16
American Psychological Association, 8
Anomalies, 6, 28
Anti-bullying policies, 102, 105, 107, 109-10, 114-15, 118-20, 125, 138
Anti-bullying services, 131, 133
Anti-social behaviour, 97, 124
Anxiety, 41, 46-49, 51-52, 58, 60, 67, 170
  disorders, 48-49
  psychological symptoms of, 49
  school manifest, 51
  severe, 49
Aphasia, 24
Arbitration Act, 245
Aristotle, 35
Aromatherapy, 21
Ashton, Catherine, 228
Asperger's syndrome, 125
Assessment kits, 45
Assessment
  childcare sufficiency, 181
  differential, 150
  eligibility, 159
  holistic, 77
  medical, 236
  personalised, 72
  specialist, 150
Assistive Technology, 13-14
Aston Index and Mann Suiter Test, 45
Attendance Consultants, 119
Attention Deficit Disorders, 42, 59-60
Attention Enhancement, 60
Attention-deficit hyperactivity disorder, 32, 41, 44-48, 51-52, 58-60, 67-68, 115, 128
Auditory memory, 28
Auditory processing disorders, 24
Autism, 2, 75, 95-96, 114, 121-22, 124, 132
Autism spectrum disorders, 14-15, 110
Autistic spectrum disorders, 4, 75, 89, 110-11, 116, 128, 179, 185

Banking and Financial Dealings Act, 203, 244
Behaviour
  difficulties, 68, 71, 74, 129
  disorders, 43, 50, 57-58
  therapy, 49-50
Behavioural
  impairments, 116
  skills, 70
  emotional and social difficulties, 4-5, 65-69, 71-73, 75-89, 91, 96-97, 118, 121, 123-24, 128-29, 132

Benchmarking activities, 191
Benefit and Disability Living Allowance, 10
Biological factors, 16
Birmingham, 156
BlazeSports America, 13
Bowe, Frank, 7, 10
Braille, 13, 278, 285
Brain
  cells, 46
  damage, 48
  -developmental disorders, 47
  disturbances, 50
  injuries, 15-16
Break time activities, 128
Breathlessness, 49
Brief Therapy, 133
Brigance Diagnostic Inventory of Basic Skills, 45

Cancer, 39
Care Trust, 244
Careers guidance, 170
Casual Exclusions, 117
Central Nervous System Dysfunction, 22
Cheviots Children's Disability Service, 178
Child-centred services, 159
Child Development Service (CDS), 168
Child labour, 1
Child misbehaving, 127
Child Protection, 70
Childcare
  disabled children accessing, 180-81
  free, 179
  inclusive, 155
  specialist, 180
Children Act, 65, 85, 146, 161, 243-44, 253
Children's Workforce Development Council (CWDC), 185
Christmas day, 244
Chromosomal disorders, 14
Citizenship Education, 140
Civil Rights of Institutionalized Persons Act, 19
Classroom adjustments, 27
Clerical Mistakes, 227, 241, 266
Clinical Psychologist, 25, 43
Code of practice, 230
Code of Practice, 65-66, 73, 77-78, 87, 89-90, 136, 154, 278
Cognitive
  ability, 25
  disability, 14
  factors, 28
  impairments, 31
Coles, Gerald, 32
Collins, Marva, 32
Commission for Social Care Inspection (CSCI), 151
Common Assessment Framework, 77, 150
Communication Disorder (CD), 46, 126
Co-Morbid Childhood Disorders, 44, 46
Comorbid disorders, 26
Comprehensive Area Assessment (CAA), 150, 189
Comprehensive Test of Phonological Processing (CTOPP), 26
Computer software, 168
Computer-based assistive technology, 14
Consumer movement, 6
Continuing professional development (CPD), 4, 72, 88, 184, 195
Co-ordinated Support Plan (CSP), 229-31, 233-39, 272
Co-ordination disorders, 44
Cornwall Parent Carers Council, 155
Correction Slip, 242
Council for Disabled Children, 151, 157, 171
Courts and Enforcement Act, 242, 271
Courts and Legal Services Act, 243
Criminal Justice and Court Services Act, 255
Curricular specialism, 82
Curriculum-based activities, 122
Curriculum-based Remediation, 55

Davila, Robert, 10
Defiant Disorder, 48
Department for Children, Schools and Families, 4-5, 84, 89, 103, 110, 119, 124, 129, 141, 278
DePoy, Elizabeth, 8
Depressed children, 49
Developmental Disabilities Services and Facilities Construction Act, 14
Developmental Disorders, 46, 58, 62-63, 232
Diabetic child, 51
Direct Support Professional (DSP), 20
Disability
  Act, 5, 11, 134, 137
  awareness training, 181, 185

benefit, 12
bullied learner's, 137
Claims Procedure, 200, 202, 204
definition of, 3, 67, 75, 90-91, 102, 137, 160
discrimination, 33, 137-38, 243-44, 251, 259-60, 274, 278
discrimination, 94
Education Act, 11, 26, 33
equality duty, 74, 97, 99, 105-8, 114, 134-36, 138, 146, 155, 273
equality scheme, 74, 86, 97-99, 106-7, 109, 114, 118, 135-36, 146, 157, 273
gendered, 2
insurance, 12
living allowance, 10
locomotor, 2
math, 24
multiple, 2
particular, 119
pensions, 12-13
psychosocial, 5
-related bullying, 136
rights movement, 5
social model of, 7, 18, 94, 102
standard, 10-11
tribunal, 38, 200, 202-3, 228, 287
visual, 2
Discrimination Act, 3, 10, 65, 67, 69, 74, 90-92, 94, 98-103, 116-17, 134-35, 137-40, 160-62, 202, 228-29, 273
Disabled Peoples' International (DPI), 8
Discrimination Acts, 93
Discrimination, visual, 45
Disorders, behavioural, 57
Display Extreme Behaviour in Association, 89
Disruptive Behaviour Disorders, 46, 59
District Primary Education Programme (DPEP), 1
Dizziness, 49
Double handicap, 9
Down's syndrome, 15, 126-27
DRC (Disability Rights Commission), 67, 90, 135, 137
DRC Code of Practice for Schools, 74, 138
Drop-in clinics, 184
Drug misuse, 15
DSM-IV, 24-25
Duffy, Mary, 89
Dybwad, Rosemary, 19
Dyscalculia, 24, 33
Dysgraphia, 24
Dyslexia, 3-4, 24, 31, 33, 41-42, 76, 101, 184
Dysphasia, 24
Dyspraxia, 24, 33

Early Intervention, Benefits of, 166
Early Support Programme, 146-47, 150, 158, 166, 168-70, 173
Eating disorders, 68
Education Act, 45, 65-67, 79, 81, 83, 85, 87, 101, 134, 139, 171, 201-2, 215, 228-29, 257, 259
Education and Inspections Act, 109, 115, 140
Educational attainment, 182, 186
Educational psychologists, 37-38, 41, 67, 70, 84, 184
Education-related parenting contracts, 70
Electronic spellers, 27
Emotional
difficulties, 68
disorders, 22, 41, 44, 46, 48, 51, 57-58, 60, 67
maturity, 76
skills, 70-71, 125, 132
Employers' Forum on Disability (EFD), 10-11
Epilepsy, 3, 15-16, 18, 101
Error analysis, 45
Every Child Matters (ECM), 4, 65, 80, 104, 136, 139, 144, 148, 151, 158, 168, 177, 184, 188
Explosive situation, 59
Eye-contact, 60

Family stress, 165, 174
Fetal Alcohol Spectrum Disorder, 14
Fidgettiness, 48
Fine motor difficulties, 23
Flashcards, 56
Flow Chart for Poor School Performance, 42
Freeman-Sheldon syndrome, 15
Functional skills, 33
Fundamental skills, 27

General Intelligence Test, 44
Gilson, Stephen, 8
Gray Oral Reading Test IV, 26
Gray's Diagnostic Reading Tests, 26
Gross Domestic Product (GDP), 13
Gross Motor Development, 31

Gross motor difficulties, 23
Guidance on Education-Related Parenting Contracts, 70

Halton Children and Young People Strategic Partnership, 159
Handicapped Children Act, 33
Handicapping conditions, 22
Hard-to-manage child, 61
Head injuries, 28
Health Act, 182
Health and Social Care Act, 150, 155
Health, Education and Social Care (HESC), 239, 242-43, 271, 274, 287
Hearing
  adjourned, 216
  fair, 213-14
  full, 283
  loops, 117
  oral, 243
  private, 240-41, 260, 264, 284
  resumed, 220
  room, 292
Human Rights Act, 134
Human Rights Commission, 90
Hyperactivity, 46-47
Hyperkinetic disorders, 67-68

Inclusion Development Programme, 4, 88, 184
Inclusive Education, 1, 34, 89
Inclusive environments, 102, 118
Inclusive schools, 55, 105
Inclusive society, 36
Individual education plan, 28, 45, 56, 126
Individualised Education Programme, 45, 56
Individualism, 18
Inquiries Act, 202
Inspections Act, 109, 115, 140
Institutionalized Persons Act, 19
Integrated Education Programme, 56
Intellectual impairments, 5
Intelligence Deficits, 40
Intelligent child, 41
Internal Organ Dysfunction, 49
Internalizing Disorders, 60
International Dyslexia Association, 24
International Year of Disabled Persons, 10
Interpersonal skills, 185
IQ tests, 44
IQ-Achievement Discrepancy, 25

Language disorders, 24, 43-44
Language therapy, 85
Learning disabilities, 2, 12, 22-26, 28-33, 89-90, 94, 103, 112, 156, 174, 232
  and US Law, 33
  government programmes diagnose, 25
  including, 3, 96, 101, 121
  programmes, 30
  strategy, 171
Learning disorder, 22, 25, 31, 33, 41-48, 50-52, 56-57, 59-60, 62, 64
Learning skills, 28
Life skills, 21
Living allowance, 181
Local Authorities and Primary Care Trusts, 157, 169
Local Safeguarding Children Boards (LSCBs), 145
López, Oscar, 10

Mathematical ability, 22
Maths Skills, 44
Mc Evan, Elaine K., 51
McCarthy-Fry, Sarah, 273
Memory lapses, 166
Mental disorders, 5, 251
Mental Health Act, 243-44, 250, 254, 261-64, 266
Mental health difficulties, 71
Mental illness, 34, 232
Mental impairment, 3, 5, 11, 91, 94, 101, 137
Ministry of Human Resources Development (MHRD), 2
Motor
  ability, 23
  clumsiness, 24
  co-ordination, 46
  skills, 24
Mountain biking, 13
Movement Assessment Battery Test, 31
Multi-agency assessments, 162, 166
Multisensory Teaching methods, 60
Multi-skilled teams, 81
Muscle activities, 23
Music therapy, 21

National Healthy School Standard (NHSS), 140
National Programme for Specialist Leaders in Behaviour, 88
National Service Framework for Children, 84, 145, 161-62, 171, 174, 184, 186
National Service Frameworks (NSF), 184
Neuro-developmental disorders, 2
Neurological
  disorder, 51
  examinations, 43
  handicaps, 39
  impairments, 28
  wiring, 33
Neuromusculoskeltal, 2
Neuropsychological differences, 29
Neuropsychological Disorders, 51
Neuropsychologists, 25
NHS Trusts, 190, 263
Non-special education, 30-31

Obsessive Disorders, 50, 52
Occupational therapy, 21, 85, 177
Organizational skills, 24, 60

Paralympic sports, 13
Parent Partnership Services (PPS), 118, 154, 157
Park, Sherwood, 276
Perfectionism, 50
Phobia, 49, 52
Phobic situations, 49
Phonemic awareness, 24
Phonological awareness, 26
Physical impairments, 14, 67
Physiotherapy, 85, 168
Playtime activities, 114
Pleasurable activities, 49
Pneumonia, 39
Poor academic achievement, 27
Poor literacy skills, 29
Poor School Performance (PSP), 39-43, 51-52, 62
Poor visual-spatial skills, 24
Pre-Academic Skills, 45
Primary Care Trusts, 143, 149, 157-61, 165, 167, 169, 184, 263
Protection of Children Act, 244, 255
Provocative behaviour, 48
Psychiatric illnesses, 16
Psychogenic factors, 22

Racism, 69, 100
Reading
  comprehension test, 26
  disability, 23-24
  disorders, 44
  fluency test, 26
  skills, 44
Reckless behaviour, 47
Recreational activities, 82
Rehabilitation Act, 33
Remedial programmes, 55
Remedial Teaching, 52
Repatriation of Prisoners Act, 243, 261
Resource Room (RR), 55-56
Restlessness, 47-48
Rief, Sandra F., 51
Risk assessment, 89
Risk factors, 28
Rote-memory, 24

Scholastic Backwardness, 39
School phobia, 46, 67
School Standards and Framework Act, 79
SEAL (Social and Emotional Aspects of Learning), 71, 85, 89, 116, 122, 132
Seizure Disorder, 51
Self-advocacy skills, 17
Self-Evaluation Forms (SEF), 86, 140
Self-injurious behaviour, 17, 76
SEN and Disability Tribunal (SENDIST), 92, 274
Sensory impairments, 3, 22, 91, 94, 96, 101, 103, 121
Sex education services, 22
Sexual harassment, 129
Sexualised behaviour, 17
Short-term memory, 23
Sight impairments, 112
Skill areas, 60
Skill deficits, 54, 56
Skills Council, 81, 171
Social Care Act, 150, 155
Social difficulties, 5, 65-67, 71, 75, 79, 83, 85, 88, 91, 118, 123, 126, 132
Social impairments, 132
Social interaction, 17, 25, 110
Social Model of Disability, 102, 116
Social phobia, 49
Social Skill Deficits, 53

Social skills, 24, 57, 66, 77, 132, 139
Socio-economic factors, 29
Special abilities Test, 44
Special education, 1, 12, 25, 28, 30-33, 91, 180, 186, 272, 274-75, 291
Special Educational Needs and Disability Act, 134, 137
Special Educational Needs and Disability Tribunal, 38, 200, 202-3, 228, 287
Special Educator, 26, 43, 51, 55
Specialist reacher, 55-56, 119
Specialist training programme, 88
Specialized tests, 26
Speech and Language
  and co-ordination disorders, 43-44
  pathologist, 43-44
  tests, 44
  therapists, 184
Speech clarity, 44
Speech recognition software, 13
Speech therapy, 21
Spell words, 44
Spelling
  assessment, 44
  difficulties, 44
  skills, 24
Spinal cord injuries, 8
Standardized tests, 44
Stanford Achievement Test, 26
Stanford Diagnostic Reading Assessment, 26
Strategic Partnership Board Children's Trusts, 104
Stress
  chronic, 48
  diagnosis exacerbating, 185
  lower levels of, 153-54
  maternal, 174
  parental, 168
Substantial gainful activity (SGA), 11

Teachers
  general education, 30
  punitive, 41
  sensitised, 52
  special education, 18, 30
  trained, 55
  unbiased, 50
Teaching Aids, 56
Test of Word Reading Efficiency (TOWRE), 26
Tests of Oral Reading and Comprehension Skills (TORCS), 26
Tic Disorders, 50-52, 58, 129
Tingling, 49
Tourette's syndrome, 13, 129
Transition Support Programme, 150, 170, 173, 186
Tribunals and Inquiries Act, 202
Triple jeopardy syndromes, 11

UK's Disability Discrimination Act, 19
Underachievement, 69
Underachieving child, 39
United Nations Convention on the Rights of the Child (UNCRC), 134, 140
United Nations Economic and Special Commission for Asia and the Pacific (UNESCAP), 36
US Education Act, 2
US Rehabilitation Act, 11

Vision blurring, 49
Visual aids, 60
Visual impairments, 3
Visual memory, 23, 28
Visual perception, 23, 28
Voice-activated software, 112

Weschler Individual Achievement Test II, 26
Weschler Intelligence Scale for Children (WISC), 44
Wide Range Achievement Test III, 26
Wilson, Daniel J., 9
Word
  blindness, 24
  decoding, 24
  processors, 27
  recognition, 18, 24, 26
World Programme of Action Concerning Disabled Persons, 10

Zafirah's impairment, 126